ACCA

PRACTICE & REVISION KIT

Paper 2.2

Corporate and Business Law

(English and Scottish)

BPP Professional Education
January 2005

First edition 2001
Fifth edition January 2005

ISBN 0 7517 2174 3 (Previous edition 0 7517 1556 5)

British Library Cataloguing-in-Publication Data
A catalogue record for this book
is available from the British Library

Published by

BPP Professional Education
Aldine House, Aldine Place
London W12 8AW

www.bpp.com

Printed in Great Britain by W M Print
45-47 Frederick Street
Walsall, West Midlands
WS2 9NE

We are grateful to the Association of Chartered Certified Accountants for permission to reproduce past examination questions. The answers to past examination questions have been prepared by BPP Professional Education.

CONTENTS

The headings in this checklist/index indicate the main topics of questions, but questions often cover several different topics.

Preparation questions, listed in italics, provide you with a firm foundation for attempts at exam – standard questions.

Some questions set under the old syllabus *Legal Framework* paper are included because their style and content are similar to those which appear in the Paper 2.2 exam. Where appropriate the questions have been amended to reflect the new syllabus exam format.

Candidates for the Scottish variant should see the index on page 267.

BPP
PROFESSIONAL EDUCATION

BPP PROFESSIONAL EDUCATION

Question and answer checklist/index

Download from the ACCA's website: www.accaglobal.com/students

Download from the ACCA's website: www.accaglobal.com/students

TOPIC INDEX

Listed below are the key Paper 2.2 syllabus topics and the numbers of the questions in this Kit covering those topics.

If you need to concentrate your practice and revision on certain topics, or if you want to attempt all available questions that refer to a particular subject (be they preparation or exam standard), you will find this index useful.

EFFECTIVE REVISION

What you must remember

Effective use of time as you approach the exam is very important. You must remember:

> **Believe in yourself**
> **Use time sensibly**

Believe in yourself

Are you cultivating the right attitude of mind? There is absolutely no reason why you should not pass this exam if you adopt the correct approach.

- **Be confident** – you've passed exams before, you can pass them again
- **Be calm** – plenty of adrenaline but no panicking
- **Be focused** – commit yourself to passing the exam

Use time sensibly

1   **How much study time do you have**? Remember that you must **eat, sleep,** and of course, **relax**.

2   **How will you split that available time between each subject?** A **revision timetable,** covering **what** and **how** you will revise, will help you organise your revision effectively.

3   **What is your learning style?** AM/PM? Little and often/long sessions? Evenings/weekends?

4   **Do you have quality study time?** Unplug the phone. Let everybody know that you're studying and shouldn't be disturbed.

5   **Are you taking regular breaks?** Most people absorb more if they do not attempt to study for long uninterrupted periods of time. A five minute break every hour (to make coffee, watch the news headlines) can make all the difference.

6   Are you **rewarding yourself** for your hard work? Are you leading a **healthy lifestyle**?

What to revise

Key topics

You need to spend most time on, and practise full questions on, **key topics**.

> Key topics
> - Recur regularly
> - Underpin whole paper
> - Appear often in compulsory questions
> - Discussed currently in press
> - Covered in recent articles by examiner
> - Shown as high priority in study material
> - Tipped by lecturer

Difficult areas

You may also still find certain areas of the syllabus difficult.

Difficult areas

- Areas you find dull or pointless
- Subjects you highlighted as difficult when taking notes
- Topics that gave you problems when you answered questions or reviewed the material
---

DON'T become depressed about these areas; instead do something about them.

- Build up your knowledge by **quick tests** such as the quick quizzes in your BPP Study Text.

- Work carefully through **numerical examples** and **questions** in the Text, and refer back to the Text if you struggle with computations in the Kit.

- **Note down weaknesses** that your answers to questions contained; you are less likely to make the same mistakes if you highlight where you went wrong.

Breadth of revision

Make sure your revision has sufficient **breadth**. You need to be able to answer all the compulsory questions and enough optional questions on the paper. On certain papers all major topics in the syllabus will be tested, through objective test questions or longer questions. On other papers it will be impossible to predict which topics will be examined in compulsory questions, which topics in optional questions.

Paper 2.2

In this paper do not spend all your revision reading your Study Text and passcards and the answers in this Kit. You should be able to explain and apply the law and practising questions, especially twenty mark questions, will help you to do that.

How to revise

There are four main ways that you can revise a topic area.

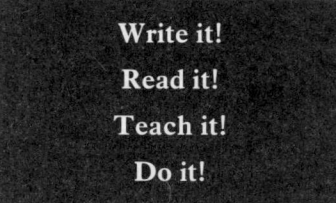

Write it!

The Course Notes and the Study Text are too bulky for revision. You need a slimmed down set of notes that summarise the key points. Writing important points down will help you recall them, particularly if your notes are presented in a way that makes it easy for you to remember them.

Read it!

You should read your notes or BPP Passcards actively, testing yourself by doing quick quizzes or writing summaries of what you have just read.

Teach it!

Exams require you to show your understanding. Teaching what you are revising to another person helps you practise explaining topics. Teaching someone who will challenge your understanding, someone for example who will be taking the same exam as you, can help both of you.

Do it!

Remember that you are revising in order to be able to answer questions in the exam. Answering questions will help you practise **technique** and **discipline**, which examiners emphasise over and over again can be crucial in passing or failing exams.

1   First do the **preparation questions** included for the syllabus area. These provide you with a firm foundation from which to attempt exam-standard questions.

2   The more exam-standard questions you do, the more likely you are to pass the exam. At the very least, you should attempt the **key questions** that are highlighted.

3   You should produce **full answers** under **timed conditions,** and don't cheat by looking at the answer! Look back at your notes or at your BPP Study Text instead if you are really struggling. Produce answer plans if you are running short of time.

4   Always read **Tutor's hints** in the answers. They are there to help you, and will show you which points in the answer are the most important.

5   **Don't get despondent** if you didn't do very well. Refer to the **topic index** and try another question that covers the same subject.

6   When you think you can successfully answer questions on the whole syllabus, attempt the **two mock exams** at the end of the Kit. You will get the most benefit by sitting them under strict exam conditions, so that you gain experience of the four vital exam processes.

- Selecting questions
- Deciding on the order in which to attempt them
- Managing your time
- Producing answers

BPP's *Learning to Learn Accountancy* book gives further invaluable advice on how to approach revision.

BPP has also produced other vital revision aids.

- **Passcards** – Provide you with clear topic summaries and exam tips
- **Success tapes** – Help you revise on the move
- **Videos** – Show you an overview of key topics and how they are related
- **i-Pass CDs** – Offer you tests of knowledge to be completed against the clock

You can purchase these products by completing the order form at the back of this Kit or by visiting www.bpp.com/acca

REVISION PROGRAMME

Below is a suggested **step-by-step revision programme**. Please note that this is not the only approach – you may prefer to do your revision in a different order, and your college may suggest a different approach. However, **as a minimum you must do the key questions if you want to pass the exam.**

The BPP programme requires you to devote a **minimum of 25 hours** to revision of Paper 2.2. Any time you can spend over and above this should only increase your chances of success. Prepare full answers instead of answer plans to some of the questions if you have any extra revision time.

Suggested approach

1   For the topics covered in each revision period, **review** your notes and the relevant summaries in the **Paper 2.2 Passcards**.

2   Then do the **key questions** for that section. These are **shaded** in the table below, and, as we indicated earlier, are the questions you must attempt, even if you are short of time. Try to complete your answers without referring to our solutions.

3   Because your available study time may be limited, for some questions we have suggested that you prepare **answer plans** rather than full solutions. This means that you should spend about 30% of the full time allowance for that question on brainstorming the question and drawing up a list of points to be included in an answer.

4   Once you have worked through all of the syllabus sections, **attempt at least one of the Mock Exams under strict exam conditions**.

    If you don't have time to do both under exam conditions, have a look at the exam you didn't do to get an idea of the style of questions and the likely topics.

Topic	2005 Passcard chapter	Questions in this kit	Comments (NB key questions are shaded)	Done ✓
Revision period 1 *English legal system*				
Court system, arbitration and alternative dispute resolution	1	2, 3	You will have a 10 mark question on English legal system in the exam. In the sittings to date the examiner has set questions on most of the topics. The examiner is quite keen on areas of topical interest and development in the law, one of which is alternative dispute resolution. Also try question 5, for further practice on courts.	
Statutory interpretation and human rights	1, 2	6	This question is quite a good example of the examiner's style. It is identical to a question in the December 2004 exam.	
Delegated legislation	1	7	These are two important topics examined in June 2002 and June 2003. Try them if you have time – if not, produce a comprehensive answer plan for each.	
EC Law	1	8, 9		
Revision period 2 *Formation of contract*				
Contract formation	4, 5	11, 12	These questions comprehensively cover the issue of contract formation. They look at offer, acceptance and consideration and are the type of question you should expect in Part B of the exam in this area and are therefore very good practice for you.	
Offers	5	10	There is likely to be a 10 mark question on contract formation or discharge of contract in the exam (there has been in each sitting so far). This question is good practice for such a question.	
Consideration	5	16	This scenario question looking specifically at consideration is good practice as this can be a tricky area. Consideration features quite frequently in the exam as it is central to contract law. It sometimes features in both Part A and Part B, as for example in June 2003.	
Contract issues	5	17	If you find scenario questions about formation of contract tough, take the time to work through this question too. It covers a range of contract issues. It is important to feel confident tackling a contract scenario question, as one is bound to come up relating to formation, terms, discharge or a combination of each.	

Revision programme

Topic	2005 Passcard chapter	Questions in this kit	Comments (NB key questions are shaded)	Done ✓
Revision period 3 *Terms and discharge of contract*				
Terms of a contract	7	19	This pilot paper question covers the key issues in relation to the nature of the contents of contracts. A question like this could easily come up in part A, and indeed did so in December 2003.	
Express and implied terms and exclusion clauses	7	24	This question gives useful practice at both a 'state and explain the law' requirement (part (a)) and an 'explain and apply the law' requirement (part (b)) which largely correspond to Sections A and B of the exam. Exclusion clauses were examined in June 2002 and June 2004.	
Exclusion clauses	7	22	This is another useful look at a scenario where there is an exemption clause. If you found question 24 difficult, or want more practice in this area, try and put together an answer plan for this question.	
Performance of a contract	8	25	Discharge by performance was examined in December 2001. It could easily be examined in the form of a scenario question such as this one.	
Damages	8	28	Damages are an important remedy in relation to breach of contract. In June 2002, students were required to discuss the issue of damages in a scenario, although the question did not specifically refer to them. You must be able to spot when the issue of damages is relevant in a question. Question 29 (below) tackles damages in a practical way. Section A could have a similar question to this pilot paper question. The exams have included questions both on damages alone and remedies generally. Remoteness of damage and the measure of damages are other popular areas.	
Breach	8	27	This Part A question makes you think about breach and particularly anticipatory breach, which was examined in a similar way in December 2001. Try it if you have time, or alternatively, write a comprehensive answer plan.	

Topic	2005 Passcard chapter	Questions in this kit	Comments (NB key questions are shaded)	Done ✓
Remedies	8	29	This question looks at breach and remedies in a practical way. If you don't have time to complete a full answer for it, run through the issues in your head and do an answer plan. Remedies were examined in December 2004.	
Revision period 4 *Agency and business associations*				
Agents	9	31	This is the type of question on agents that could come up in Part A. In December 2003, the means of creation of agency were examined. Rights of an agent is another important issue.	
Partnership	10	36	You might find that agency is more likely to be examined in a practical way, for example, like this question in June 2002 on the liability of partners. This question is therefore excellent practice. In June 2004 partnership was examined in Part B.	
Incorporation	10	34	Try this question and see how many points you can make.	
Revision period 5 *Company formation*				
Company formation	11	40	This December 2002 question focuses particularly on plcs, but as you know, ltd companies are very similar except for the s117 requirement for plcs. This subject matter is very popular with the examiner, and has been examined a number of times.	
Public and private companies	10,11	41	Work through part (a) in full and then jot down answers in bullet point form for part (b). The distinction between plcs and ltd companies is important in practice and could affect your answer to a scenario question.	
Memorandum and articles	12, 13	45	This question is also typical and therefore good practice. This is a popular area; for example, there was a Section A question in December 2003 and again in June 2004. You might find scenario questions in company law draw on knowledge of what is contained in both of these documents. You will practise such questions below. Both names and objects clause were examined in December 2004.	

Revision programme

Topic	2005 Passcard chapter	Questions in this kit	Comments (NB key questions are shaded)	Done ✓
Company names	11	46	This is a good question, typical of what you should expect in Part B and it requires a quite detailed knowledge of the law. If this is an area you struggle with, work through this question in full.	
Alteration of articles	13	50	This past exam question is a good example of a Part B question examining the articles in some detail.	
Revision period 6 *Company administration*				
Resolutions	13	51	It is vital you know all about resolutions – they may be relevant in a scenario question where shareholders are taking various actions (see question 47) or in an explain question such as this. You should aim to get full marks on questions like this in Part A.	
Company administration	10, 14, 16	55	This is a good example of the type of Section B question that covers several areas of the syllabus. Think carefully about whether you can tackle all of the parts before you decide on a question like this.	
Revision period 7 *Company management*				
Company secretary Auditors	15	56, 57	You must be prepared to answer questions like these in Part A comprehensively. Try 56 in full and 57 in bullet point form	
Directors, articles of association, shares	13, 15, 16, 17, 18, 19	59, 60	Q59 is a comprehensive question on directors: extremely good practice for the type of company law question you should expect in the exam, drawing on a number of issues. There is invariably some type of question on directors in the exam, sometimes in both parts A and B, as was the case in December 2003 and December 2004. The same issues appeared also in June 2004. Q60 is also excellent practice.	
Duties of director, wrongful trading and disqualification.	17	61	This question looking at the duties of directors is also good practice and you should work through it in full.	

Topic	2005 Passcard chapter	Questions in this kit	Comments (NB key questions are shaded)	Done ✓
Insider trading	17	64	The duties of directors is an important issue and insider dealing is a favourite of the examiner. If you found question 64 tough you should take the time to work through Q65 too. In any case, you should put together a detailed answer plan for both questions 64 and 65, as the additional practice could be vital for your exam.	
Minority protection	18	68, 70	This is another favourite area for examiners, often combined with director issues, for example in a question in June 2003. You must work through these two questions. Unfairly prejudicial conduct is a feature that you can bring into many different exam answers.	
Meetings, directors, shares, articles	13, 14, 15, 17, 18	69	This question is also good practice and wide-ranging if you found question 68 hard. Produce at least an answer plan for this one.	
Revision period 8 *Company finance*				
Shares	19	71	If a question like this comes up, you should be looking to score highly. Work through this one to consolidate your answer on these relatively straightforward points.	
Debentures and charges	21	73	Similarly, you should be able to answer a part A question on loan capital well. Work carefully through this pilot paper question too. You may find an exam question asking you to compare and contrast shares and debentures. In June 2004 a question examined debentures and charges together.	
Dividends	20	76	Dividends were examined in June 2002. They are important, but can be complex, so produce an answer plan for this question.	
Revision period 9 *Company finance and winding up*				
Issue of shares	19	77	This is typical of the sort of question you can see in Section A on capital. It is an opportunity to score very easy marks. Notice that it requires consideration of both 'meaning and effect'.	

Topic	2005 Passcard chapter	Questions in this kit	Comments (NB key questions are shaded)	Done ✓
Capital maintenance	20	78, 81	Question 78 looks at some of the basic issues in capital maintenance. Even though you may find this a hard area, work through this question, as there are simple marks available to you and you should put yourself in a position to get them if a question like this comes up again. Try Q81 also: it is a good example of a Part B question on this area.	
Compulsory winding up	22	84	Winding up was examined in June 2002. It is again an area which might seem daunting, but where easy marks can be gained. Work through this in full.	
Voluntary winding up	22	85, 86	Question 85 gives good practice at the skills needed in both parts A and B. It would be useful to try if you have the time. If not, try (a) in full and do an answer plan for part (b). Q86 provides good practice at analysing the situation. It is quite a difficult question, so take your time.	
Revision period 10 *Employment law*				
Employees or independent contractors	23	90	This question covers this important practical issue and explores the importance of the distinction.	
Redundancy and constructive dismissal	24	91	The examiner has examined constructive dismissal in several sittings now, so it is clearly important. Make sure you can explain both the issues in this question.	
Rights at work	25	93	Focus on part (b) of this question. The examiner has examined disability discrimination, but has not yet looked at sex or race discrimination (which are similar). Run through part (b) so that you are prepared in this area.	

THE EXAM PAPER

The examination is a **three hour paper** divided into **two sections**.

Section A will contain short knowledge-based questions.

Section B will be problem-based and will test communication skills and the ability to appraise and analyse information.

		Number of Marks
Section A:	Choice of 6 from 8 questions (10 marks each)	60
Section B:	Choice of 2 from 4 questions (20 marks each)	40
		100

Additional information

Knowledge of new legislation will not be expected until at least six months after the last day of the month in which the Royal Assent (or similar procedure in other country) is given, or six months after the specific provision comes into effect, whichever is the later.

The Study Guide provides more detailed guidance on the syllabus. Examinable documents are listed in the 'Exam Notes' section of Student Accountant.

Analysis of past papers

The analysis below shows the topics that were examined in the first seven sittings of the current syllabus and in the Pilot Paper.

December 2004

Section A		*Question on this topic area*
1	Interpretation of statute; Human Rights Act	6
2	Offer, counter-offer and tender	11
3	Privity of contract	Mock exam 2: Q2
4	Remedies for breach of contract	Mock exam 2: Q4
5	Company names	44 (b)
6	Types of director	60
7	Insider dealing	65
8	Company winding up	84(b)

Section B		
9	Intention to create legal relations; consideration	Mock exam 1: Q3
10	Termination of contract of employment	Mock exam 1: Q10
11	Forms of business association	34
12	*Ultra Vires* rule and directors' fiduciary duties	47(a); 59

This exam can be downloaded from the ACCA's website at www.accaglobal.com/students

The exam paper

June 2004

This exam can be downloaded from the ACCA's website at www.accaglobal.com/students

---

Examiner's comments

Performance on this paper was poorer than for a number of sittings. A significant number of candidates did not answer the eight questions required, and this makes it more difficult to pass the paper. Nor should candidates do more than eight questions. Candidates should always fill in the question box on the front of the paper to keep track of the number of questions they have attempted. They should also start each question on a fresh page of the answer book, to assist the marker, and at all times try to write coherently and clearly.

December 2003

This exam can be downloaded from the ACCA's website at www.accaglobal.com/students

---

Examiner's comments

There were some extremely good performances on this paper, but in many cases this was as a result of candidates concentrating on the same limited number of questions. The questions that were less popular in general produced lower marks.

June 2003

		Question on this topic area
Section A		
1	English legal system: delegated legislation	7
2	Contract: acceptance and revocation of offer	13
3	Contracts in restraint of trade	92
4	Liquidated damages and penalty clauses; mitigation of losses	Mock exam 2: Q4
5	Fair and unfair dismissal in employment law	94
6	Company law: veil of incorporation	39
7	Company law: powers and duties of directors	58
8	Company law: auditors	57
Section B		
9	Contract law: consideration	17
10	Partnership law: duties owed between partners	Mock exam 2: Q10
11	Company law: minority protection; directors' duties	68
12	Company law: memorandum and articles, charges, guarantees and 'passing off	45, 50

This exam can be downloaded from the ACCA's website at www.accaglobal.com/students

Examiner's comments

The paper presented a fair test, but many candidates had neither the confidence nor the capacity to tackle the part B questions other than on a superficial level. Candidates should practise past papers to develop the required skills of legal analysis.

December 2002

		Question in this Kit
Section A		
1	English legal system: the civil courts	2
2	Contract law: consideration	15
3	Contract law: terms	18
4	Contract law: remedies for breach	Mock exam 2: Q4
5	Business association: termination of partnership	37
6	Company: promoters and pre-incorporation contracts	Mock exam 2: Q6
7	Company: class rights	80
8	Company: resolutions	Mock exam 1: Q6
Section B		
9	Contract: consideration	Mock exam 2: Q9
10	Employment: unfair dismissal/redundancy	Mock exam 1: Q10
11	Company: authorised capital	81
12	Company: directors and company secretary	60

Examiner's comments

This paper was reasonably well answered. It was apparent that some candidates had prepared general answers in relation to Section B questions and were determined to deliver them, even if they were not totally or even marginally relevant to the question actually set.

June 2002

Section A		*Question in this Kit*
1	English legal system: EC law	8
2	Contract law: offers and invitations to treat	10
3	Contract law: exclusion clauses	20
4	Employment law: common law duties, constructive dismissal	89
5	Business associations: types of company	Mock exam 2: Q7
6	Company: directors' duties	58
7	Company: dividends	Mock exam 2: Q8
8	Company: winding up	84

Section B		
9	Contract: remedies	Mock exam 1: Q9
10	Business associations: partnership	36
11	Company: formation and publicity	40
12	Company: directors, articles, meetings	50

Examiners' comments

Most candidates dealt with this examination well although the number of candidates who did not answer the full eight questions may show that the width of the syllabus has caused some difficulties.

December 2001

Section A		*Question in this Kit*
1	English legal system: statutory interpretation, Human Rights Act 1998	6
2	Contract: privity	Mock exam 2: Q2
3	Contract: discharge	26
4	Employment: constructive dismissal, disability discrimination	87
5	Business associations: names and legal implications	42
6	Agency: authority	31
7	Company: share capital	77
8	Company: general meetings	52

Section B		
9	Contract: agreement	12
10	Business associations: best options	34
11	Company: insider dealing	65
12	Company: minority protection	70

Examiners' comments

The first Corporate and Business Law paper under the new Professional Scheme was awaited almost with as much trepidation by the Examiners, as it no doubt was by the candidates who sat it. By and large levels of performance held up well, although there were fewer high marks awarded than was the case with the old law syllabus. Candidates and their tutors will now be aware that there is a significant shift from the knowledge to the analysis/application elements in the new exam.

One general point to make before offering a detailed consideration of the paper was the fact that the first time the usual form was reversed in that candidates rather poor performance in part (a) was salvaged by a better performance in part (b). It has to be recognised however, that even in this, the improvement was really only due to good performances in Questions 9 and 10, with the other two questions in part B being very poorly done, if they were done at all.

Pilot paper

Section A   *Question in this Kit*

1	English legal system: delegated legislation	7
2	Contract: intention to create legal relations	Mock exam 1: Q3
3	Contract: terms, conditions and warranties	19
4	Contract: damages	28
5	Employment: contracts of service/for service	Mock exam 2: Q5
6	Company: formation	38
7	Company: loan capital	73
8	Company: company secretary	56

Section B

9	Contract: formation	11
10	Partnership: rights and duties	Mock exam 2: Q10
11	Company: directors duties and appointment, articles	59
12	Company: directors duties/disqualification	61

EXAM TECHNIQUE

Passing professional examinations is half about having the knowledge, and half about doing yourself full justice in the examination. You must have the right approach at the following times.

> **Before the exam**
> **Your time in the exam hall**

Before the exam

1   Set at least one **alarm** (or get an alarm call) for a morning exam.

2   Have **something to eat** but beware of eating too much; you may feel sleepy if your system is digesting a large meal.

3   Allow plenty of **time to get to the exam hall**; have your route worked out in advance and listen to news bulletins to check for potential travel problems.

4   **Don't forget** pens, pencils, rulers, erasers, watch. Also make sure you remember **entrance documentation** and **evidence of identity**.

5   Put **new batteries** into your calculator and take a spare set (or a spare calculator).

6   **Avoid discussion** about the exam with other candidates outside the exam hall.

Your time in the exam hall

1   *Read the instructions (the 'rubric') on the front of the exam paper carefully*

Check that the exam format hasn't changed. Examiners' reports often remark on the number of students who attempt too few - or too many - questions, or who attempt the wrong number of questions from different parts of the paper.

2   *Select questions carefully*

Read through the paper once, underlining the key words in the question and jotting down the most important points.   Select the optional questions that you feel you can answer best. You should base your selection on:

- The **topics** covered
- The **requirements of the whole question**
- How easy it will be to **apply the requirements** to the details you are given
- The availability of **easy marks**

Make sure that you are planning to answer the **right number of questions,** all the compulsory questions plus the correct number of optional questions.

3   *Plan your attack carefully*

Consider the **order** in which you are going to tackle questions. It is a good idea to start with your best question to boost your morale and get some easy marks 'in the bag'.

4   *Check the time allocation for each question*

Each mark carries with it a **time allocation** of 1.8 minutes (including time for selecting and reading questions, and checking answers). A 10 mark question therefore should be selected, completed and checked in 18 minutes. When time is up, you **must** go on to the next question or part. Going even one minute over the time allowed brings you a lot closer to failure.

5   *Read the question carefully and plan your answer*

Read through the question again very carefully when you come to answer it. Plan your answer taking into account how the answer should be **structured**, what the **format** should be and **how long** it should take.

Confirm before you start writing that your plan makes **sense**, covers **all relevant points** and does not include **irrelevant material.** Two minutes of planning plus eight minutes of writing is virtually certain to earn you more marks than ten minutes of writing.

Remember that for law questions, particularly the 20 mark problem style questions in part B of the paper, the best approach is ISAC:

*   identify the **issue**
*   **state** the law
*   **apply** the law
*   **conclude** on the situation in the question

If you use this approach you will maximise your mark-earning potential by including those elements that the examiner wants to see.

6   *Answer the question set*

Particularly with written answers, make sure you **answer the question set**, and not the question you would have preferred to have been set.

7   *Gain the easy marks*

Include the obvious if it answers the question and don't try to produce the perfect answer.

Don't get bogged down in small parts of questions. If you find a part of a question difficult, get on with the rest of the question. If you are having problems with something, the chances are that everyone else is too.

8   *Produce an answer in the correct format*

The examiner will **state in the requirements** the format in which the question should be answered, for example in a report or memorandum.

9   *Follow the examiner's instructions*

You will **annoy** the examiner if you ignore him or her.

10   *Present a tidy paper*

You are a professional, and it should show in the **presentation of your work**. Students are penalised for poor presentation and so you should make sure that you write legibly, label diagrams clearly and lay out your work neatly. Markers of scripts each have hundreds of papers to mark; a badly written scrawl is unlikely to receive the same attention as a neat and well laid out paper.

11   *Stay until the end of the exam*

Use any spare time **checking and rechecking** your script. This includes checking:

*   You have **filled out** the **candidate details correctly.**
*   Question parts and workings are **labelled clearly.**
*   Aids to navigation such as **headers and underlining** are used effectively.
*   **Spelling, grammar** and **arithmetic** are correct.

12   *Don't discuss an exam with other candidates afterwards*

There's nothing more you can do about it so why discuss it?

13   *Don't worry if you feel you have performed badly in the exam*

It is more than likely that the other candidates will have found the exam difficult too. Don't forget that there is a competitive element in these exams. As soon as you get up to leave the exam hall, *forget* **that exam** and think about the next - or, if it is the last one, celebrate!

BPP's *Learning to Learn Accountancy* book gives further invaluable advice on how to approach the day of the exam.

CURRENT ISSUES

If you have been studying with the latest edition of the BPP *Corporate and Business Law* Study Text you will already be up to date for developments up to June 2004. Since then, however, there have been some developments of which you should be aware.

The contents of this section are as follows.

1   National minimum wage
2   Disability discrimination
3   Employment disciplinary and grievance procedures
4   New legal form: the European company
5   The Companies (Audit, Investigations and Community Enterprise) Bill
6   Implementing company law reform

1   National Minimum Wage

From 1 October 2004 the national minimum wage has been increased to:

- £4.85 per hour for those aged 22 and over
- £4.10 per hour for those aged 18 to 21.

In addition, a new minimum wage rate for young workers has been introduced. Workers aged 16 and 17, excluding apprentices, are entitled to a minimum of £3.00 per hour.

2   Disability Discrimination

Some amendments have been made to the Disability Discrimination Act, effective from 1 October 2004:

- Any business providing goods, services or facilities directly to the public is now required to make any reasonable adjustments that are necessary to ensure equal access for disabled people. This includes provision for those with limited mobility, such as wheelchair users, and also for those with other types of disability such as those affecting sight, hearing, speech and concentration. The concept of what is a reasonable adjustment will differ from business to business. A national chain of shops selling to the general public will probably have a greater responsibility than a small company with a specialist customer base.

- Previously only businesses with 15 or more employees were prohibited from discriminating against employees or job applicants with disabilities. From 1 October 2004 this prohibition extends to all businesses, including those with fewer than 15 employees.

3   Employment disciplinary and grievance procedures

The Employment Act 2002 (Dispute Resolution) has introduced a new set of mandatory procedures for dealing with workplace disputes with effect from 1 October 2004. **An employer who dismisses an employee without following the new dispute-resolution process will be automatically faced with a finding of unfair dismissal**.

The new rules require that employers and employees try to resolve all workplace disputes by following a three-step process:

- Employees with a grievance against their employer, or employers initiating disciplinary action against an employee, must set out the basis of their complaint in writing.

- The written statement must be followed by a meeting between the two parties. Employees have the right to be accompanied by a colleague or a trade union

representative. After the meeting the employer must tell the employee how the employee's grievance is to be dealt with or what disciplinary action is to be taken

- The employee has the right to take the matter to an appeal

If the grievance ends up at an employment tribunal and this procedure has not been followed, penalties may be imposed.

There are a small number of exceptions where the three stage process does not have to be followed, for example when fear of violence, harassment or vandalism on the part of one of the parties makes it unreasonable for the two parties to deal together in this way.

Additionally, employees will not now be able to raise a grievance at an employment tribunal without first raising a formal grievance at work. This is so that the employee and the employer can try to fix the dispute internally first, before incurring the time and expenses of a tribunal.

4 New legal form: the European company

From 8 October 2004 businesses that have operations in more than one EU member state are also able to incorporate using a new EU-wide company form, the European company. This is also known as by its formal Latin name, Societas Europaea (SE). European companies are public companies with limited liability and a minimum capital requirement of €120,000. They must be registered in the member state where the company's administrative headquarters are based.

There are four ways of setting up a European company:

- A merger between existing companies from at least two member states

- Formation of a holding company by companies from at least two EU member states

- Formation of a subsidiary of companies from at least two member states

- Transformation of a company that has had a subsidiary in another EU member state for at least two years

The legal and tax provisions governing European companies will be very complicated, reflecting the interaction of EU law and different national systems.

5 The Companies (Audit, Investigations and Community Enterprise) Bill

The DTI has been carrying out a long term and fundamental review of company law since 1998. In July 2002 the Government published a White Paper *'Modernising Company Law'* which set out the core proposals for reform. The intention is to modernise and simplify company law and renew trust in business, while at the same time minimising red tape for small companies. The White Paper includes proposals to set out directors' duties in statute for the first time.

In July 2003, after the consultation period on the White Paper, the Government announced its plans to change company law (see section 6 below), but it does not seem that legislation will be in place until at least the end of 2005. However the Government has moved more quickly in order to plug some perceived gaps in the law.

The **Companies (Audit, Investigations and Community Enterprise) Act** was given Royal Assent on 3 November 2004. It is designed to implement safeguards in the light of various recommendations in the aftermath of the Enron and Worldcom failures.

Its provisions include:

- Increasing DTI powers to investigate companies

- Tightening the regulation of auditing and strengthening the role and independence of auditors

- Increasing auditors' powers to obtain information from directors, employees and others

- Requiring directors to state specifically that there is no relevant information of which the directors are aware

- Making companies publish full details of the non-audit services provided by their auditor

- Allowing the Inland Revenue to pass on information about suspect accounts that it has acquired during tax investigations

- Strengthening the Financial Reporting Review Panel's role in enforcing accounting requirements

- Clarifying s 310 Companies Act 1985, to the effect that in some circumstances companies can indemnify directors

The Act also includes provisions for a new type of company, called the 'community interest company' (CIC). The primary purpose of such a company is the advancement of social objectives rather than the maximisation of profits, and the company will not be subject to the same rigorous constraints as charities.

6 Implementing company law reform

The main aims of the forthcoming company law reform, subsequent to the White Paper referred to in section 5, are as follows:

- Enabling better shareholder engagement

- Modernising and de-regulating the law to make it more accessible for business, especially small and medium sized companies

- Giving greater clarity to directors on their duties and responsibilities so that they do not inadvertently fall foul of the law

- Enabling better communication with shareholders

- Speeding up decision making

Specific proposals include the following:

- Written resolutions will become easier

- AGMs will become opt in rather than opt out

- Capital maintenance will be reformed, including repeal of the restrictions on financial assistance by private companies

- Removal of statutory controls on directors over 70

- Abolition of the requirement for a company to have an authorised share capital

- Simplification of detail and length of time that companies must maintain registers of past and present members

You need to bear in mind that these are just proposals at the moment, and have some way to go before they are enshrined in law. However these are interesting developments and it is worth keeping an eye on the business press for further details as and when they become available.

USEFUL WEBSITES

The websites below provide additional sources of information of relevance to your studies for *Corporate and Business Law.*

- ACCA www.accaglobal.com
- BPP www.bpp.com
- Financial Times www.ft.com
- The Times www.timesonline.co.uk
- The Economist www.economist.com
- Department of Trade and Industry www.dti.gov.uk
- Law Society www.lawsociety.org.uk
- UK Government www.open.gov.uk
- The Incorporated Council of Law Reporting www.lawreports.co.uk
- UK Law Online www.leeds.ac.uk/law/hamlyn
- Law Rights www.lawrights.co.uk

SYLLABUS MINDMAP

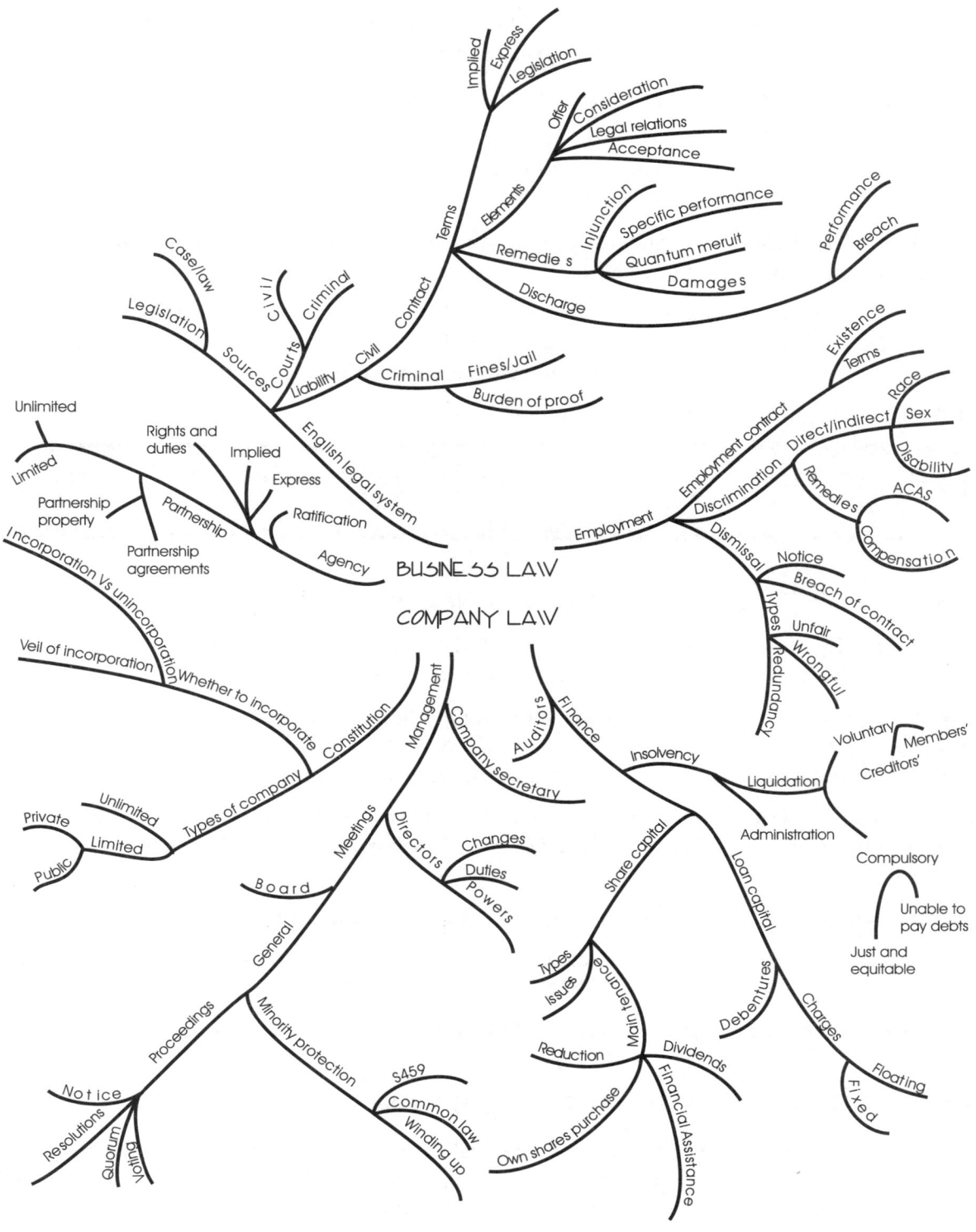

OXFORD BROOKES BSc (Hons) IN APPLIED ACCOUNTING

The standard required of candidates completing Part 2 is that required in the final year of a UK degree. Students completing Parts 1 and 2 will have satisfied the examination requirement for an honours degree in Applied Accounting, awarded by Oxford Brookes's University.

To achieve the degree, you must also submit two pieces of work based on a **Research and Analysis Project.**

- A 5,000 word **Report** on your chosen topic, which demonstrates that you have acquired the necessary research, analytical and IT skills.

- A 1,500 word **Key Skills Statement**, indicating how you have developed your interpersonal and communication skills.

BPP was selected by the ACCA and Oxford Brookes University to produce the official text *Success in your Research and Analysis Project* to support students in this task. The book pays particular attention to key skills not covered in the professional examinations.

BPP also offers courses and mentoring services.

> THE OXFORD BROOKES PROJECT TEXT CAN BE ORDERED USING THE FORM AT THE END OF THIS STUDY TEXT.

OXFORD INSTITUTE OF INTERNATIONAL FINANCE MBA

The Oxford Institute of International Finance (OXIIF), a joint venture between the ACCA and Oxford Brookes University, offers an MBA for finance professionals.

For this MBA, credits are awarded for your ACCA studies, and entry to the MBA course is available to those who have completed their ACCA professional stage studies. The MBA was launched in 2002 and has attracted participants from all over the world.

The qualification features an introductory module (*Foundations of Management*). Other modules include *Global Business Strategy, Managing Self Development,* and *Organisational Change & Transformation.*

Research Methods are also taught, as they underpin the **research dissertation**.

The MBA programme is delivered through the use of targeted paper study materials, developed by BPP, and taught over the internet by OXIIF personnel using BPP's virtual campus software.

For further information, please see the Oxford Institute's website: www.oxfordinstitute.org

CONTINUING PROFESSIONAL DEVELOPMENT

ACCA is introducing a new continuing professional development requirement for members from 1 January 2005. Members will be required to complete and record 40 units of CPD annually, of which 21 units must be verifiable learning or training activity.

BPP has an established professional development department which offers a range of relevant, professional courses to reflect the needs of professionals working in both industry and practice. To find out more, visit the website: www.bpp.com/pd or call the client care team on 0845 226 2422.

Questions

ENGLISH LEGAL SYSTEM

Questions 1 to 9 cover the English legal system, the subject of Part A of the BPP Study Text for Paper 2.2.

1   COUNTY COURT (6/98)   *18 mins*

Explain the importance of the county court in the English legal system.   **(10 marks)**

2   CIVIL COURTS AND TRACKS (12/02)   *18 mins*

(a) Briefly describe the main civil courts in the English legal system.   (6 marks)
(b) Explain the three track system for allocating cases between courts.   (4 marks)

                                                                               (10 marks)

3   ARBITRATION   *18 mins*

Explain the importance of arbitration as a means of alternative dispute resolution.

                                                                               (10 marks)

4   PREPARATION QUESTION: SOURCES OF LAW

What are the main sources of contemporary United Kingdom law?

Approaching the question

It is well worth spending three or four minutes of the time available in thinking around the subject and planning what to write. Identify the sources (statute, case law and European law) and then identify different categories within them eg legislation and delegated legislation.

5   BINDING PRECEDENT (6/00)   *18 mins*

Explain the doctrine of binding precedent in English law, paying particular regard to:

(a) The hierarchy of the courts.   (5 marks)
(b) The relative advantages and disadvantages of the doctrine.   (5 marks)

                                                                               (10 marks)

6   INTERPRETATION AND HUMAN RIGHTS (12/01)   *18 mins*

(a) Explain the powers of the courts in interpreting legislation, paying particular regard to the rules they use in so doing.   (7 marks)

(b) How has the Human Rights Act 1998 affected this process?   (3 marks)

                                                                               (10 marks)

7   DELEGATED LEGISLATION (Pilot paper)   *18 mins*

Explain the meaning and effect of delegated legislation, paying particular attention to its advantages and disadvantages, and how it is controlled by both Parliament and the Courts.

                                                                               (10 marks)

8   **EC LAW (6/02)**   *18 mins*

Explain the following in the context of European Community Law.

(a)   Regulations   (3 marks)
(b)   Directives   (3 marks)
(c)   The role of the European Court of Justice   (4 marks)

(10 marks)

9   **EU INSTITUTIONS**   *18 mins*

Explain the importance of each of the following bodies to the UK legal system.

(a)   The European Commission   (2 marks)
(b)   The Council of Ministers   (2 marks)
(c)   The European Parliament   (2 marks)
(d)   The European Court of Justice   (4 marks)

(10 marks)

LAW OF CONTRACT

Questions 10 to 29 cover the law of contract, the subject of Part B of the BPP Study Text for Paper 2.2.

---

10   OFFERS AND INVITATIONS TO TREAT (6/02)

(a) Explain and distinguish between an offer and an invitation to treat in the law of contract.   **(7 marks)**

(b) Explain why the distinction is important.   **(3 marks)**

(10 marks)

11   ADAM (Pilot paper)   *36 mins*

Adam is a secondhand car dealer. He places an advertisement in the Saturday edition of his local paper stating:

'Once in a lifetime opportunity: a one year old, low mileage, Mota Special: £5,000 cash. This is a serious offer – the car will go to the first person who accepts it – valid for one day only.'

When Ben sees the advert he immediately posts a letter of acceptance of Adam's offer.

Carol also sees the advert and after inspecting the car offers Adam a cheque for £5,000, but he refuses to accept the cheque and tells her she cannot have the car.

Later in the day Dave asks Adam if he will keep the offer open until he can get to his bank to arrange a loan. Adam agrees but later in the day when Eric says that he will pay £6,000 in cash for the car he agrees to sell the car to Eric.

On Monday morning Ben's letter arrives, and Dave returns to complete his purchase of the car. In the afternoon Eric phones Adam to say that he has had second thoughts and no longer wishes to buy the car.

Required

Consider the above situation with respect to the rules governing the creation of contracts.

In particular consider:

(a) The precise nature of Adam's advertisement   (4 marks)
(b) Whether Ben has entered into a binding contract with Adam.   (4 marks)
(c) Where Carol has any right of action against Adam.   (4 marks)
(d) Whether Dave has any right of action against Adam.   (4 marks)
(e) Whether Adam has any right of action against Eric.   (4 marks)

(20 marks)

12   ANN'S ART (12/01)   *36 mins*

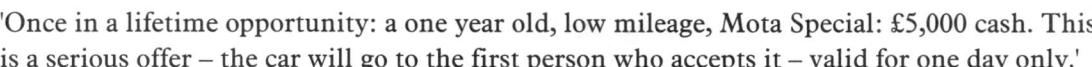

On Friday 10 December the following notice is placed in the window of Ann's art gallery: '2 copies of a very rare Blake print - £15,000 each'. Chas and Dave are very keen to acquire the prints but think that the price is too high. They each offer Ann £12,000 for a copy but she refuses to sell the prints at that price, although she says she will accept £13,500. Moreover she says she will keep her offer to them open until 12 o'clock on the following Monday, 13 December, if they each pay her £100. Chas and Dave agree and each hands over £100. On the Saturday before the deadline Chas and Dave have to leave the country on business but before they do so each posts a letter stating that he agrees to buy one of the prints at the

agreed price of £13,500. Chas's letter arrives at 9.30 on the Monday morning but Dave's letter is delayed and arrives on the morning of Tuesday 14 December. In any event Ann had already sold both prints to Eve on Saturday 11 December for a total price of £30,000.

Required

Analyse the above situation from the point of contract law. In particular advise the parties as to their rights, liabilities and the potential remedies available to them under contract law.

(20 marks)

13 ADAM AND BEN (12/00)
36 mins

Adam is sitting with a group of his friends outside a public house in a harbour. He says that he will give £100 to anyone who can swim across the harbour. Adam puts that amount of money on the table to show the seriousness of his challenge. Ben is not with Adam's group but is sitting at a table next to Adam. He hears the promise but does not say anything. Suddenly a child falls into the water from the other side of the harbour. Ben dives into the water and begins to swim to her rescue. As Ben is approaching the child, Adam shouts out:

'Don't think you are going to get my £100, because I am withdrawing my offer'.

Ben nonetheless rescues the child and climbs out onto the other side of the harbour.
Explain, with reasons, whether Ben can claim the £100 from Adam under the law of contract.

(20 marks)

14 PREPARATION QUESTION: CONSIDERATION
18 mins

(a) Define consideration as it is understood in contract law. (3 marks)

(b) Explain the following statements in relation to the law of contract:

    (i)   Consideration must be sufficient but need not be adequate; (3 marks)
    (ii)   Past consideration is not good consideration. (4 marks)

(10 marks)

Approaching the question

It is important that you allocate your time appropriately to the parts of the question. You should give no more than 5½ minutes each to part (a) and part (b)(i) and then 7 minutes to part (b)(ii). You need to cite cases in support of your answer, to illustrate the meaning of concepts such as sufficiency and adequacy of consideration.

15 FORMS OF CONSIDERATION (12/02)
18 mins

(a) Define consideration as it is understood in English contract law. (3 marks)

(b) Explain and distinguish between the following terms:

    (i)   executory consideration; (2 marks)
    (ii)   executed consideration; (2 marks)
    (iii) past consideration. (3 marks)

(10 marks)

16 AXEL (6/99)
36 mins

Axel publishes a weekly magazine using specialist computer equipment. He employs journalists to produce text and printworkers to produce the actual magazine. He has a service contract with Ben which provides that Ben must always be available to repair any faults in the equipment when the magazine is being printed.

On the day of publication the computer which controls the printing broke down, after the journalists had produced their text. However, Ben refused to fix it unless his payment was increased. Axel agreed to pay Ben an additional £1,000 per week and Ben fixed the machine. The repair took a considerable time and there was a danger that the magazine would not be published in time to permit its distribution. Axel promised his printworkers that he would pay each of them an extra £100 if the magazine was produced in time.

The magazine was produced in time and, in a celebratory mood, Axel also offered to pay his journalists an additional £100 for the work they had done. However, on the following day Axel decided not to meet any of his promises.

Required

Can either Ben, the printworkers, or the journalists enforce Axel's promise?   **(20 marks)**

17   **CONTRACT ISSUES (12/99)**   *36 mins*

In 20X8, Ann, an artist, decided to have an extension built onto her house. She agreed to pay Belle £500 to produce the architectural plans for the work and Chas £3,000 for carrying out the work. Ann provided all the materials, which she bought from Dan for an agreed price of £5,000. After the work was completed Ann discovered that she did not actually have the money to pay the various people concerned. Consequently she made the following arrangements with each of them:

(a)   She gave Belle one of her paintings instead of payment.

(b)   When she failed to pay Chas he threatened to sue her, until her friend Eric offered to pay him £1,500 if he withdrew his action, which he did.

(c)   She told Dan that he would have accept £3,000 as she could not afford to pay him any more money and he reluctantly agreed to accept it in full and final payment of her debt.

Three months later Ann inherited £100,000.

Required

Advise the parties whether Ann can be made to pay her original debts.   **(20 marks)**

18   **EXPRESS AND IMPLIED (12/02)**   *18 mins*

In relation to the law of contract:

(a)   distinguish between express and implied terms;   (4 marks)
(b)   explain the circumstances under which terms may be implied in contracts. (6 marks)

                                                                             (10 marks)

19   **TERMS OF A CONTRACT (Pilot paper)**   *18 mins*

In relation to the contents of a contract explain the following.

(a)   Terms   (2 marks)
(b)   Conditions   (3 marks)
(c)   Warranties   (3 marks)
(d)   Innominate terms   (2 marks)

                                                                             (10 marks)

| 20 | **EXCLUSION CLAUSES (6/02)** | *18 mins* |

(a) Explain the meaning of exclusion clauses, also known as exemption clauses, in contract law. (2 marks)

(b) How are such clauses controlled:

    (i)   at common law; (4 marks)

    (ii)   by statute? (4 marks)

(10 marks)

| 21 | **SELLER LTD AND TRANSPORT LTD** | *36 mins* |

Seller Ltd had used the services of Transport Ltd for a number of years. On this occasion, the managing director of Seller Ltd telephoned the offices of Transport Ltd and arranged for the transportation of some expensive machinery to a customer. Transport Ltd confirmed the order by sending a notice to this effect. Unfortunately, due to driver error, the vehicle carrying Seller Ltd's equipment crashed and the equipment was badly damaged. Transport Ltd has advised Seller Ltd that it intends to rely on the following clause:

'Transport Ltd will not accept any liability for loss or damage caused to customers' property during transportation, no matter how the loss or damage was caused. Customers are advised to take out their own insurance.'

Transport Ltd has pointed out that the clause appears in a notice prominently displayed outside the entrance to the company's offices, and is reproduced on the back of all invoices, receipts and confirmation of order notices issued by the company.

Required

Advise Seller Ltd whether Transport Ltd will be able to use the clause to avoid liability for the damaged goods.

(20 marks)

| 22 | **PREPARATION QUESTION: LAPTOP LTD** |

After several successful deals with Laptop Ltd, David entered into a contract with the company to install a new computer network, including the provision of some new workstations, in his offices. On the seven previous occasions in the last two years when David has contracted with Laptop Ltd the contract was always in writing and contained a clause stating that Laptop Ltd is not liable for any financial or other losses caused by using any products supplied and installed by the company, howsoever caused.

The present contract between David and Laptop Ltd is not in writing, but when the new workstations were delivered to David by Laptop Ltd, David was handed a delivery note by a Laptop Ltd employee which contained a clause worded in exactly the same terms as the one quoted above. David did not read the delivery note.

The first time the new network was used after installation a fire broke out in the office because of the negligent installation of the new workstations by a Laptop Ltd employee. David suffered serious burns as he escaped from the office and incurred expenses of £100,000 in refurbishing the damaged premises.

David sues Laptop Ltd for breach of contract, but the company denies liability on the basis of the exclusion clause in the contract.

Advise David on the following matters:

(a) Whether the exclusion clause is incorporated into the contract with Laptop Ltd.

(b) Whether the exclusion clause exempts Laptop Ltd from liability for the losses and personal injuries suffered by David.

Approaching the question

The key to this type of question is careful reading, so that you understand the scenario fully. It is worth reading it through twice or even three times. The best approach in answering each part is to identify the **issues** involved, **state** the law relating to the issues, **apply** the law and then **conclude** on the case in question.

23   MINA   *36 mins*

Mina is a self employed accountant who works from her home. Because she deals with some sensitive accounts, she decided that she should install a security alarm system and entered into a contract with Nemo Security Ltd to install security equipment in her house. The brochure from which Mina selected her system contained a statement that 'Nemo Security Ltd accepts no liability whatsoever for any injury or loss sustained as a consequence of the wrongful installation or operation of any equipment supplied or fitted by it'. Mina did not see that particular notice nor did she read a similar notice in the form which she signed to confirm her order.

The installation of Mina's security system was carried out incorrectly. During the first night it short-circuited and caused a fire which destroyed Mina's house. As a consequence of the fire, Mina was badly burned and will not be able to work for six months. Additionally all the papers she had been dealing with were lost and she is now faced with a claim from one of her clients for the value of some unique documents left in her possession. Nemo Security Ltd admits negligence, but is refusing to compensate Mina for any of the losses she has sustained, relying on the exclusion clause.

Required

Advise Mina, giving reasons:

(a) Whether the exemption clause had been incorporated into her contract with Nemo Security Ltd.   (10 marks)

and assuming it has

(b) Whether the exemption clause exempts Nemo Security Ltd from any or all of the losses suffered by Mina.   (10 marks)

(20 marks)

24   EXPRESS AND IMPLIED TERMS   *36 mins*

(a) Terms in a contract may be express or implied.

Explain how terms can be implied into a contract and give examples.   (10 marks)

(b) Worldwide Computers plc supplied and installed a database facility for Barchester Council. The software packages proved defective causing the local authority to underestimate the revenue they would receive from council tax payers. The deficiency amounted to £1,500,000.

Worldwide Computers plc relied upon a limitation of liability clause in the contract restricting their liability to £100,000. Enquiries have revealed that the company carry

product liability insurance throughout the world totalling £50,000,000 and their global sales for 20X6 amounted to £2.5 billion.

Prepare a memorandum to Barchester Council explaining whether they are bound by the limitation of liability clause, and if not, what legal arguments can be put forward to enable them to recover their loss.

(10 marks)

(20 marks)

25 PERFORMANCE   *36 mins*

(a) Explain to what extent is it correct to say that each party to a contract must perform precisely all the terms of the contract.

(12 marks)

(b) Andrew instructed Builder Ltd to construct an extension to his house for £20,000. The contract specified that the work had to be completed by 1 July 20X7. The company completed part of the extension by 1 April 20X7 but then stopped work before a roof had been added to the building. Andrew has now been notified that Builder Ltd is in creditors' voluntary liquidation, and he has received a demand from the liquidator for £12,000 in respect of the work completed prior to the company going into liquidation.

Explain to Andrew whether he is obliged to pay the £12,000 demanded by Builder Ltd.

(8 marks)

(20 marks)

26 TERMINATION OF CONTRACTS (12/01)   *18 mins*

Explain the meaning of the following in relation to the termination of contracts:

(a) discharge by performance.   (5 marks)
(b) anticipatory breach and the remedies available in such a situation.   (5 marks)

(10 marks)

27 BREACH (12/99)   *18 mins*

Explain the general meaning and effect of breach of contract, paying particular attention to anticipatory breach.

(10 marks)

28 DAMAGES (Pilot paper)   *18 mins*

In the law of contract describe the rules relating to:

(a) Remoteness of damage   (5 marks)
(b) The measure of damages   (5 marks)

(10 marks)

29 EMMA AND SIDNEY   *36 mins*

Emma, an accountant, agreed with Sidney that Sidney would redecorate Emma's business premises for £2,000. The written contract provided that:

(a) All woodwork would be properly prepared for painting prior to the application of paint.

(b) No paint containing lead or lead compounds would be used. (Note that in this context it is not illegal for paint to contain lead.)

The work was completed but, contrary to the terms of the contract, Sidney used paint containing lead in one of Emma's offices. As a consequence Emma suffers a serious allergic reaction and is off work for three months, during which she loses £6,000 in income. Emma knew of her allergy to lead, and that was the reason she had specified that no paint containing lead or lead compounds was to be used. She had not mentioned this reason to Sidney.

Emma has also discovered that in three of her offices the woodwork was not prepared for painting before paint was applied.

Emma now seeks your advice as to whether she is able to:

(a) Sue successfully for damages for breach of contract in respect of her loss of earnings.

(b) Obtain an order for specific performance to compel Sidney to prepare and repaint the woodwork as agreed in the contract.

Required

Advise Emma.   **(20 marks)**

> **AGENCY AND BUSINESS ASSOCIATIONS**
>
> Questions 30 to 37 cover agency and business associations, the subject of Part C of the BPP Study Text for Paper 2.2.

30   RIGHTS OF AN AGENT   *18 mins*

Brian is about to enter into an agency agreement with Patrick. He has been told by Patrick of his duties but has not been advised of his rights.

Advise Brian of his rights.   **(10 marks)**

31   TYPES OF AUTHORITY (12/01)   *18 mins*

Explain the meaning of the following terms with regard to the law of agency:

(a) express authority   (3 marks)
(b) implied authority   (3 marks
(c) ostensible/apparent authority.   (4 marks)

                                                                     (10 marks)

32   FREDERICK AND GEORGE   *36 mins*

Frederick asks his agent George to sell 10 computers for him. He instructs him that they are not to be sold for less than £500. What is the legal position if:

(a) George sells the computers for £450   (7 marks)

(b) George buys the computers himself for £500 without informing Frederick and later sells them to Harry for £550   (6 marks)

(c) George sells the computers to Jonathan for £550 and also receives 'commission' from Jonathan of £50?   (7 marks)

                                                                     (20 marks)

33   PREPARATION QUESTION: PERSONALITY AND PARTNERSHIPS

(a) Explain how the concept of legal personality relates to partnerships and companies.

(b) Describe the advantages and disadvantages of the limited company and unlimited partnership as forms of business organisation.

Note. Do not discuss limited liability partnerships in detail in your answer.

Approaching the question

Allocate your time to the two parts of the question, ie 18 minutes each. Take a moment to think what part (a) is asking you, ie the impact of legal personality on partnerships (where it does not separate) and on companies (where it gives a separate identity). In comparison questions it is usually more effective to give a point by point comparison on each issue. Make sure that you try to identify some advantages **and** disadvantages for both companies **and** partnerships.

34   FRAN, GAIL, HANNAH AND IAN (12/01)   *36 mins*

Fran, Gail, Hannah and Ian have just been made redundant and have received payments of £50,000 each. They were highly skilled workers and believe that they could carry on their own business successfully.

Required

Consider the advantages and disadvantages of the registered company as against the partnership as a form of business organisation and advise them as to which form best suits their situation.

(20 marks)

35   UNLIMITED AND LIMITED PARTNERSHIPS   *18 mins*

(a)   What are the rights and duties of partners in an unlimited partnership?   (4 marks)

(b)   What is meant by 'apparent authority' in the context of partnership law?   (3 marks)

(c)   What are the main requirements of a limited liability partnership with regard to formation and publicity of information?   (3 marks)

(10 marks)

36   CLARE, DAN AND EVE (6/02)   *36 mins*

Clare, Dan and Eve formed a partnership 10 years ago, although Clare was a sleeping partner and never had anything to do with running the business. Two years ago the partnership employed Frank as its manager and last year Dan retired from the partnership. Eve subsequently has left much of the day-to-day work to Frank who has let it be known generally that he has become a partner, although he has not. In January of this year Frank entered into two large contracts. The first one was a longstanding customer Greg who had dealt with the partnership for some five years. The second contract was with a new customer Hugh. Both believed Frank's claim that he was a partner in the business. Both contracts have gone badly wrong leaving the partnership still owing £50,000 to both Greg and Hugh. Unfortunately the business assets will only cover the first £25,000 of the total debt.

Required

Consider and explain the potential liabilities of Clare, Dan, Eve and Frank.   **(20 marks)**

37   TERMINATION OF PARTNERSHIPS (12/02)   *18 mins*

Detail the grounds upon which a partnership can be terminated.   **(10 marks)**

> **COMPANY FORMATION AND CONSTITUTION**
>
> Questions 38 to 50 cover company formation and constitution, the subject of Part D of the BPP Study Text for Paper 2.2.

38   COMPANY FORMATION (Pilot paper)   *18 mins*

What documents and procedures are involved in a public limited company being registered and starting to trade?

(10 marks)

39   TOM'S COMPANY   *36 mins*

Tom has carried on business for a number of years as a sole trader selling electrical goods to the public. Tom has now decided to incorporate his business.

Required

(a)   Explain the concepts of corporate personality and lifting the veil of incorporation.

(10 marks)

(b)   Explain the advantages and disadvantages of purchasing an 'off the shelf' company (that is, a company already registered but not trading) compared with registering a new company.   (7 marks)

(c)   Describe the extent to which Tom needs to bring in another person in order to satisfy the law relating to the membership and management of a private company limited by shares.   (3 marks)

(20 marks)

40   IMRAN AND JANE (6/02)   *36 mins*

Imran and Jane have established a successful publishing business which they have run as a partnership. They now wish to turn it into a public limited company.

Required

(a)   Explain the procedure required and the forms that have to be submitted before the public company can begin trading.   (10 marks)

(b)   List and explain the purpose of the various registers that will have to be kept by the company.   (5 marks)

(c)   Describe what accounting records will have to be maintained by the company. (5 marks)

(20 marks)

41   IKE, JAN AND KIT (12/99)   *36 mins*

Ike, Jan and Kit have been told that if they form a private, rather than a public company it will benefit from significantly less rigorous control under the Companies legislation.

Required

(a)   Advise them generally as to the difference between public and private companies.

(5 marks)

(b) Give a specific explanation of the following:

   (i)   Elective resolutions   (5 marks)
   (ii)   Written resolutions   (5 marks)
   (iii) The payment of dividends   (5 marks)

                                                                   (20 marks)

42   BUSINESS TERMS (12/01)   *18 mins*

Explain the meaning of the following terms when found at the end of the names of business organisations:

(a) & Co.   (3 marks)
(b) Ltd.   (3 marks)
(c) plc.   (4 marks)

                                                                   (10 marks)

43   PREPARATION QUESTION: INCORPORATION AND PROMOTERS

(a) Explain what is meant by the following in company law:

   (i)   A promoter
   (ii)   A pre-incorporation contract

(b) Describe the liability of a promoter on a pre-incorporation contract.

Approaching the question

In this question you are discussing two things in the first part, and bringing them together in the second. Try to set out the basic law and then bring in more recent developments, like the Contracts (Rights of Third Parties) Act 1999.

44   CLAUSES AND NAMES   *18 mins*

(a) What clauses are required to be contained in a company's memorandum of association?
                                                                        (5 marks)

(b) Explain what legal limitations there are on the names that may be adopted by companies.   (5 marks)

                                                                   (10 marks)

45   COMPANY CONSTITUTION (12/00)   *18 mins*

Distinguish between a company's memorandum of association and its articles of association, and describe briefly what is included in both documents.

                                                                   (10 marks)

46   NATIONAL HAIR BRUSHES   *36 mins*

National Hair Brushes plc was incorporated in June 20X2.

Required

(a) The company wishes to trade under the business name 'Wave Oh'. State the statutory requirements with which the company must comply.   (5 marks)

(b) The directors have received a letter from another company, Lancashire Hair Brushes plc, stating that it was incorporated seven years ago in 20W5, that its business is being

adversely affected by the use of the new company name and demanding that National Hair Brushes plc changes the company name.

Advise National Hair Brushes plc. (5 marks)

(c) Explain what is meant by a company's registered office, and describe how its address might be changed. (5 marks)

(d) Describe the extent to which the directors may seek to alter the objects clause in the company's memorandum of association should they wish in the future to change the nature of its business. (5 marks)

(20 marks)

47   NORTH OF ENGLAND   *36 mins*

The main object of the North of England Private Housing plc is to develop private housing in the north of England. Recently the government has offered some very attractive financial incentives to those firms who are willing to invest in commercial development in the south west of England.

The board of directors is anxious to diversify the company's activities and take advantage of the opportunities in the south west. The directors believe that they have the support of some 80% of the company's shareholders, although there is a substantial minority group of shareholders opposed to any form of diversification.

Required

Advise the directors on the following points.

(a) What alteration(s) might it be desirable to make to the company's memorandum of association to enable it to carry out its policy of diversification? Describe the steps which will have to be followed to give effect to such alteration(s). (10 marks)

(b) State the rights of the minority who are opposed to the proposed diversification and, in consequence, may wish to withdraw their capital from the company. (6 marks)

(c) Set out the rules which have to be followed in respect of the appointment of proxies and the rights of proxies once appointed. (4 marks)

(20 marks)

48   ARTICLES   *18 mins*

Explain the content and effect of a company's articles of association. **(10 marks)**

49   STATUTORY RECORDS   *18 mins*

In the absence of a company taking advantage of alternative provisions under the Companies Act 1985, what statutory records must be kept at a company's registered office?

(10 marks)

50   LAX LTD (6/02)   *36 mins*

Kath owns 76% of the share capital in Lax Ltd. There are only two other shareholders in Lax Ltd. Matt owns 10% and also operates his own separate business in direct competition with Lax Ltd. Norm owns the remaining 14%. All three shareholders are on the board of directors. However, Owen has been the effective chief executive of the company for the past three years and, although he does not own any shares in it, he has a service contract to act as the company's managing director until 20X8.

Kath has received a very generous offer from Prime plc to buy her shares in Lax Ltd but only on the understanding that she is the sole shareholder and that Owen is removed from his position as managing director of the business. Unfortunately for Kath the articles of association of Lax Ltd contain a pre-emption clause requiring that members wishing to sell their shares must first of all offer them to the other members and only on their refusal to buy them can they be sold to an outsider.

Kath intends calling an extraordinary general meeting and proposing the following resolutions:

(a)   that Owen be removed from the board of directors and replaced by Kath's son Ron;

(b)   that the articles of association be altered in the following ways:

   (i)   to remove the exiting pre-emption right so as to permit members to sell their shares to outsiders;

   (ii)   to require any member conducting business in competition with Lax Ltd to sell their shares to the company at fair value;

   (iii)   to require any shareholder to sell their shares to the company at fair value on receipt of a resolution of the directors to that effect.

Kath then intends to use the new articles to require Matt and Norm to sell their shares back to the company and sell her shares to Prime plc.

Required

Advise the parties as to the legality and effectiveness of Kath's proposed actions.

(20 marks)

> **COMPANY ADMINISTRATION AND MANAGEMENT**
>
> Questions 51 to 70 cover company administration and management, the subject of Part E of the BPP Study Text for Paper 2.2.

51   RESOLUTIONS (12/00)   *18 mins*

Explain what is meant by:

(a) Extraordinary resolutions   (2 marks)
(b) Special resolutions   (2 marks)
(c) Elective resolutions   (3 marks)
(d) Written resolutions   (3 marks)

(10 marks)

52   MEETINGS AND VOTES (12/01)   *18 mins*

Explain the following within the context of company general meetings:

(a) Who has the power to call meetings?   (6 marks)
(b) How are votes taken?   (4 marks)

(10 marks)

53   MEETINGS   *18 mins*

Explain and distinguish between the following.

(a) Annual general meeting
(b) Extraordinary general meeting
(c) Class meeting   **(10 marks)**

54   PREPARATION QUESTION: HYDRANGEA

The directors of Hydrangea Ltd, a recently incorporated company selling garden furniture and regulated by Table A, wish to increase the authorised share capital of the company to £100,000 and to change the name of the company to Motormowers Ltd.

Required

(a) (i)   The directors seek your advice on the statutory requirements which apply to the calling of the meeting and the resolutions required to give effect to the above proposals.

(ii) The first annual general meeting of Hydrangea Ltd is due to be held in September 20X5 and the directors seek your advice on how the votes of members and proxies should be taken and counted at the meeting.

(b) You have also been approached by Diana, who holds 60% of the shares in Rake Ltd, a company regulated by Table A, which manufactures greenhouses. She wishes to propose a resolution at the next annual general meeting of the company to remove the four directors, who between them hold 40% of the shares.

Advise Diana as to her right to have this resolution on the agenda of the annual general meeting and on the action she would take if the four directors fail to attend the meeting.

Approaching the question

Make sure that you read through the question thoroughly at least a couple of times. In this question, the topics are separate and not linked to each other, so you can regard each part as a small question in its own right. Try to tackle the question in the right order:

- identify the issue
- state the law relating to the issue
- apply the law in this situation
- conclude by advising whoever the question tells you to advise

55 FRAN, GWEN, HILARY AND INA (12/98)

36 mins

Fran, Gwen and Hilary and Ina have all recently been made redundant from their jobs as machine operators and intend setting up their own business as independent clothes designers and manufacturers. They have been advised to establish it as a private limited company. However, they are unsure as to precisely what this means or what it involves.

Required

Paying particular regard to the fact that the company will be a private one, advise them about the following:

(a) The meaning of limited liability   (6 marks)
(b) The appointment and dismissal of company directors   (6 marks)
(c) The need to hold company meetings   (8 marks)

(20 marks)

56 COMPANY SECRETARY (Pilot paper)

18 mins

Explain the rules relating to the appointment, duties and powers of a company secretary in a public limited company.

(10 marks)

57 AUDITORS (12/99)

18 mins

Explain the role of the company auditor. In answering the question pay particular regard to the following issues relating to auditors:

(a) Qualification
(b) Appointment
(c) Removal
(d) Rights and duties   **(10 marks)**

58 FIDUCIARY DUTIES (6/02)

18 mins

Explain the fiduciary duties owed by directors to their companies.   **(10 marks)**

59 FRAN, GILL AND HARRY (Pilot paper)

36 mins

In 20X5 Fran, Gill and Harry formed a private limited company to pursue the business of computer software design. They each took 100 shares in the company and each of them became a director in the new company. The articles of association of the company were drawn up to state that Fran, a qualified lawyer, was to act as the company's solicitor for a period of five years, at a salary of £2,000 per year.

In 20X8 Gill and Harry found out that Fran had been working with a rival software company and has passed on some of secret research results to that rival.

Required

Advise Gill and Harry as to the legality of the following proposals and how they may be achieved.

(a)   They wish to remove Fran from the board of directors.   (5 marks)

(b)   They have told Fran that they no longer wish her to be the company solicitor and have refused to pay her for the work she has done previously. Fran, however, claims that she has a contract in the articles of association and that they cannot remove her before the five year period is completed.   (5 marks)

(c)   They would like to alter the articles to force Fran to sell her shares to them.   (5 marks)

(d)   They would also like to take an action against Fran for breach of fiduciary duty.

(5 marks)

(20 marks)

60   **KING LTD (12/02)**   *36 mins*

King Ltd is a property development company. Although there are five members of its board of directors, the actual day to day running of the business is left to one of them, Lex, who simply reports back to the board on the business he has transacted. Lex refers to himself as the Managing Director of King Ltd, although he has never been officially appointed as such. Lex is assisted in the running of the business by Mary, King Ltd's company secretary.

Six months ago Lex entered into a contract on King Ltd's behalf with Nat to produce plans for the redevelopment of a particular site that it hoped to acquire. However King Ltd did not acquire the site and due to its current precarious financial position, the board of directors have refused to pay Nat, claiming that Lex did not have the necessary authority to enter into the contract with him.

The board are also refusing to complete a contract with Owen for the supply of new office furniture that Mary had ordered on King Ltd's behalf. They have also learned that Mary has entered into a contract on King Ltd's behalf to have an extension built onto her own house.

Required

Analyse the situation with regard to the authority of both Lex and Mary to make contracts on behalf of King Ltd and in particular advise the board of directors if the company is liable for each of the contracts.   **(20 marks)**

61   **LUXOR LTD (Pilot paper)**   *36 mins*

In 20X0 Jack became a director of Luxor Ltd, a company set up by his friend Ken. At the time Ken told Jack that there was nothing involved in being a company director and that he need not get involved in the day to day business of the company. Since then, however, Jack, with increasing concern, has read in the newspaper that things might not be as carefree as Ken originally suggested.

Required

Generally he seeks advice about the following matters.

(a)   (i)   The meaning and effect of wrongful trading under s 214 of the Insolvency Act 1986.   (6 marks)

       (ii)   The effect of the Company Directors Disqualification Act 1986.   (6 marks)

(b) In particular he wishes to know:

    (i)   The requirements placed on directors in relation to attending board meetings.

             (4 marks)

    (ii)   Whether, and if so how, he can withdraw his agreement to be a director.

             (4 marks)

             (20 marks)

62   LEN AND MOD PLC   *36 mins*

Len is a director of Mod plc, but he also owns a majority interest in Nim Ltd.

Last year Mod plc entered into a contract to buy new machinery from Nim Ltd. Len attended the board meeting that approved the contract and voted in favour of it, with revealing any link with Nim Ltd.

At the same meeting the board of Mod plc decided not to pursue the development of a new product that had been offered to them by its inventor. Len, however, liked the new product and arranged for it to be produced by Nim Ltd. It has proved to be a great success and Nim Ltd has made a great deal of money from its production.

Required

Owen is a shareholder in Mod plc and has found out about Len's links with Nim Ltd. He seeks your advice on the following matters:

(a) The precise nature of the fiduciary duties that directors owe to their companies.

             (8 marks)

(b) Whether any action can be taken against Len in relation to either:

(i)	The purchase of the machinery from Nim Ltd, or	(6 marks)
(ii)	The development of the new product by Nim Ltd.	(6 marks)

             (20 marks)

63   FRAUD ON MINORITY   *18 mins*

In company law what is meant by fraud on the minority?

How does the law control such behaviour?   **(10 marks)**

64   EWAN, FRANK AND GENE (12/00)   *36 mins*

(a) Dome plc is listed on the Stock Exchange. Ewan works for Dome plc as an accountant. Whilst drawing up the annual accounts Ewan notices that Dome plc's profits are better than anyone could have expected. As a consequence of this knowledge he buys shares in Dome plc before the good results are announced. He makes a substantial profit on the share dealing. Ewan also tells his friend Frank about the results before they are announced. Frank also buys shares in Dome plc.

    Have either Ewan or Frank done anything illegal and, if so, how is their action regulated?   (12 marks)

(b) Gene is a director of Dome plc. When he receives a preliminary draft of Ewan's report he also buys more shares in Dome plc before the results are released.

Consider Gene's position with specific regard to the effect of the Company Directors Disqualification Act 1986.   (8 marks)

(20 marks)

65   JEFFREY (12/01)   *36 mins*

Jeffrey lives with Kim. Kim is on the Board of Directors of Large Television plc which has been considering a take-over bid from Megacorps TV plc. One Friday Kim tells Jeffrey that she has to attend a very important board meeting of Large Television plc, the outcome of which could have a crucial impact on the future of the company. At the Board meeting it is agreed that, subject to some final negotiations to be carried out by the Managing Director of Large TV, the take-over bid should be accepted. That evening the Managing Director phones Kim and leaves a message on the answering machine confirming that the negotiations have been successful and that the take-over bid will therefore be accepted. When Jeffrey comes home, before Kim, he hears the message.

The following events subsequently take place:

(i)   Jeffrey buys shares in Large Television plc;

(ii) Jeffrey tells his friend Nat about the likelihood of the take-over and Nat buys shares in Large Television plc;

(iii) Nat in turn passes on the information to his friend Owen who also buys shares in Large Television plc;

(iv) At a dinner party Jeffrey, without actually telling him about the take-over proposal, advises his brother Pete to buy shares in Large, and Pete does so.

Required

Consider the position of the various parties under the legislation regulating Insider Trading.

(20 marks)

66   FRANK (12/99)   *36 mins*

Frank is managing director of Good plc, a company listed on the London Stock Exchange. The memorandum of association of Good plc states that the company's area of business operation is to be restricted to the production and sale of non-alcoholic soft drinks, and its articles of association provide that any contract above £50,000 requires the prior approval of the full board of directors. In January, Frank entered into a contract on behalf of Good plc to purchase £100,000 worth of a new type of alcoholic drink for sale in Good plc's shops. He did not inform the board of directors of his intentions. The alcoholic drinks were hugely successful and increased Good plc's profits substantially. A few weeks before the declaration of the company's improved results Frank secretly bought more shares in it.

Required

Advise Henry who is a shareholder in Good plc, as to whether any action can be taken against Frank, and if so, what action can be taken.

(20 marks)

67   PREPARATION QUESTION: BALANCE OF POWER

(a)   Explain how power and responsibility within a limited company is divided between the board of directors and the shareholders.

(b)   Explain the powers that are given to minority shareholders by common law and statute to prevent them from being unfairly treated by the board and the majority shareholders.

Approaching the question

You must have a firm understanding of these issues, in order to be able to **apply** the concepts in scenario questions such as the following two questions.

68   JACK AND KEN (12/98)   *36 mins*

Jack and Ken started a business as carpet salesmen in 20T0. They ran it successfully as a partnership until 20V0 when they converted it into a private limited company. The company was formed with an authorised capital of 200 £1 shares and Jack and Ken each took 100 shares and were appointed as the directors of the company. In 20W0 Jack and Ken each gave Jack's son Liam 25 shares in the company and he joined the board of directors.

The company continued to be financially successful but in 20W5 Jack and Liam fell out with Ken about how the business should be run and since then they have overruled Ken's wishes at board meetings.

Ken found out that Jack and Liam sold some carpets at undervalue to a separate company owned by themselves. When he challenged them they used their majority voting power to pass a resolution ratifying the sale and another resolution to remove Ken from his position as director.

Required

Advise Ken, as a minority shareholder:

(a)   As to whether he can challenge the transaction involving the sale of the carpets to the company owned by Jack and Liam, and if so, how he can do it.   (10 marks)

(b)   How he can use the following provisions to remedy his situation:

   (i)   s122 Insolvency Act 1986 relating to just and equitable winding up.   (4 marks)
   (ii)   s459 Companies Act 1985 relating to unfairly prejudicial conduct.   (6 marks)

                                                                          (20 marks)

69   HARVEY   *36 mins*

Harvey Ltd has an issued share capital of 5,000 ordinary 50p shares. Alexander, the company's sole director, owned 55% of the shares, Suzanne owned 25% and Tina 20%. Alexander wanted to sell his shares directly to Peter who had offered him a high price. However, under the articles of Harvey Ltd Alexander was compelled to offer his shares to the other shareholders first.

Alexander called an extraordinary general meeting to alter the articles, but the other two shareholders voted against the resolution, and thus Alexander was unable to obtain the necessary majority. An ordinary resolution authorising the board to issue further shares was then put to the extraordinary general meeting and passed on Alexander's vote, Suzanne and Tina voting against the resolution. Subsequently Alexander issued a number of shares to a friend Margaret. He then called a second extraordinary general meeting, at which his and Margaret's votes were sufficient to pass a resolution making the following amendment to the articles.

'Any member can sell his shares directly to a non-member if the sale is authorised by an ordinary resolution.'

Suzanne and Tina are unhappy about what has happened and are contemplating legal action.

Required

Advise Suzanne and Tina:

(a)   Of the legality or otherwise of the issue of shares to Margaret.   (12 marks)

(b)   Whether they can challenge the new provision in the articles on the grounds that it is 'unfairly prejudicial to members' under s 459 of the Companies Act 1985.   (8 marks)

(20 marks)

70   **QUENTIN (12/01)**   *36 mins*

Quentin started business as a sole trader in 1976. In 1990 he formed a partnership with his two most senior workers Raj and Sam, although Quentin provided all of the capital. In 1990 they transformed the partnership into a private limited company, Trio Ltd. Quentin holds 76% of the issued share capital in Trio Ltd and Raj and Sam each hold 12% of the issued share capital. The three of them form the board of directors of Trio Ltd. Quentin has never really recognised the change of business form and still treats the company as his personal business, taking decisions without consulting Raj or Sam or holding board meetings. Recently some of Quentin's decisions have caused the company to lose a considerable amount of money and Raj and Sam are unhappy about this situation. When they raised the issue with Quentin he said that it was his company and if they objected he would simply remove them from the board of directors.

Required

Analyse the above situation from the perspective of the minority position of Raj and Sam. In particular advise them as to any statutory remedies they might seek as a consequence of Quentin's actions in the context of a private limited company.

(20 marks)

COMPANY FINANCING AND INSOLVENCY

Questions 71 to 86 cover company financing and insolvency, the subject of Part F of the BPP Study Text for Paper 2.2.

71   SHARES (12/99)   *18 mins*

    (a)   What is a company's share capital?   (4 marks)

    (b)   Explain the meaning of the following:

         (i)   Authorised capital   (2 marks)

         (ii)   Issued capital   (2 marks)

         (iii)   Paid up capital   (2 marks)

                                       (10 marks)

72   ISSUE OF SHARES   *18 mins*

Explain the meaning of the following:

    (a)   Pre-emption rights   (4 marks)

    (b)   The issue of shares at a premium   (3 marks)

    (c)   The prohibition on the issue of shares at a discount   (3 marks)

                                       (10 marks)

73   DEBENTURES AND CHARGES (Pilot paper)   *18 mins*

In relation to companies' loan capital explain the following terms.

    (a)   Debenture   (3 marks)

    (b)   Fixed charge   (3 marks)

    (c)   Floating charge   (4 marks)

                                       (10 marks)

74   REGISTRATION OF CHARGES   *18 mins*

State the requirements of the Companies Acts in respect of charges requiring registration. What are the effects of non-registration?

                                       (10 marks)

75   INHERITANCE (12/00)   *36 mins*

Under the will of her late uncle, Clare has just inherited the following:

    (a)   £10,000 of ordinary shares in A Ltd, 75% paid up

    (b)   £10,000 of ordinary shares in B Ltd, fully paid up

    (c)   £5,000 of preference shares in C plc

    (d)   £5,000 debenture stock secured by a fixed charge against the assets of D plc

    (e)   £5,000 debenture stock secured by a floating charge against the business and assets of E plc.

Explain the meaning of each of these inheritances to Clare, who knows nothing about company law.

                                       (20 marks)

76   DIVIDENDS

18 mins

(a) What are dividends?

(2 marks)

(b) What are the rules governing the payment of dividends in relation to:

    (i)   Private companies

    (ii)   Public limited companies?

(8 marks)

(10 marks)

77   ISSUE AND PREMIUM (12/01)

18 mins

With regard to payment for shares explain the meaning and effect of the following:

(a)   issuing shares at a discount

(6 marks)

(b)   the share premium account.

(4 marks)

(10 marks)

78   PURCHASE OF OWN SHARES

18 mins

(a) In what circumstances can a company purchase its own shares?

(3 marks)

(b) What are the rules governing transfers of amounts to the capital redemption reserve when a company purchases its own shares?

(3 marks)

(c) What are the possible uses to which the balance on the share premium account may be put?

(4 marks)

(10 marks)

79   PREPARATION QUESTION: CAPITAL MAINTENANCE

It is a fundamental principle of company law that a company maintains its share capital.

You are required to explain how the provisions of the Companies Act 1985 below help to achieve this objective:

(a) S 135: reduction of share capital

(b) S 151 financial assistance.

Approaching the question

1   Capital maintenance is a technical area, but one which is important and examined regularly. The fundamental point is that the creditors' buffer must be maintained.

2   In part (a), remember to state that creditors must be invited to object to the scheme.

3   Part (b) is asking for an explanation of the rules governing financial assistance given *to others* to allow *them* to purchase the company's shares: it is not asking for the rules on the company *itself* purchasing its own shares.

80   CLASS RIGHTS (12/02)

18 mins

In company law:

(a) explain the meaning of class rights in relation to company shares providing examples of such rights;

(6 marks)

(b) state how such rights can be altered.

(4 marks)

(10 marks)

81   IMPROVE LTD AND JUDDER LTD (12/02)   *36 mins*

Hank is a director in two companies. The first, Improve Ltd, has an authorised and issued capital of 100,000 shares at a nominal value of £1. It has been very successful and is looking to increase its share capital by £50,000 in order to finance its future development.

The second, Judder Ltd, also has an authorised and issued capital of 100,000 shares at a nominal value of £1. It, however, has not traded profitably and has consistently lost capital for a number of years. Although the company has shown a profit on its current year's trading its accounts still show a deficit of £50,000 between assets and liabilities. The board of directors thinks it would be beneficial if the company were to write off its previous losses and to that end are looking to reduce its authorised and issued capital by £50,000.

Required

Advise Hank as to the procedure involved in:

(a)   increasing Improve Ltd's authorised share capital;   (8 marks)
(b)   reducing Judder Ltd's authorised/issued capital.   (12 marks)

(20 marks)

82   PREPARATION QUESTION: DTI INVESTIGATIONS

What are the statutory obligations of the Department of Trade and Industry to appoint an inspector to investigate (a) the affairs of a company (b) the ownership of a company (c) share dealings within a company? What are the powers of an inspector so appointed?

Approaching the question

1   DTI investigations are most commonly used as a last resort remedy by disgruntled shareholders.

2   The Paper 2.2 syllabus contains questions for only 10 marks which are a straightforward demand for information. This tutorial question is good practice for this type of exam question.

83   COMPULSORY WINDING UP   *18 mins*

What is the immediate legal effect of an order of the court for the compulsory winding up of a company?

(10 marks)

84   EXPLAIN WINDING UP (6/02)   *18 mins*

(a)   Explain what is meant by 'winding up' in company law.   (2 marks)

(b)   Distinguish between:

(i)   voluntary winding up;   (4 marks)
(ii)   compulsory winding up.   (4 marks)

(10 marks)

85   KEN AND DORIS   *36 mins*

(a)   What are the distinguishing characteristics of a creditors' voluntary winding up?
                                                                                (10 marks)

(b)   Ken and Doris, a husband and wife, have traded as a private registered company, Kendor Ltd, of which they were the sole shareholders and directors. The company has adopted Table A articles of association. Doris has also acted as company secretary. Ken

has died leaving all his estate to Doris. Although the company has always been and still is profitable, Doris has decided that she no longer wishes to carry on the business or sell it as a going concern but wishes to wind the company up.

As her accountant, advise Doris on the steps she must take and the procedures she must follow to wind up the company as far as and including the appointment of a liquidator. Your attention is particularly drawn to the fact that at the present moment she is the sole shareholder, director and secretary of the company.   (10 marks)

                                                                                          (20 marks)

86   **FABULOUS FOODS**   *36 mins*

Simon, James and Emily are the directors of Fabulous Foods Plc, a long-established supplier of organic foods and wines to the restaurant and catering trades. In recent years the company has been struggling, and by 31 December 20X3 the company was technically insolvent, in that it was unable to pay its debts, although it was continuing to trade.

On 2 August 20X3, the company had issued a fixed charge in favour of Borset Bank. The charge was secure a loan of £1 million made to the company by the bank and was secured on the company's freehold warehouse. The charge was registered by the company on 31 March 20X4.

On 1 February 20X4, the company repaid to Simon a loan of £100,000 that he had made to it several years before.

On 15 February 20X4 James left the company and resigned as a director. On his departure he bought his company car from the company for £10,000, although at that date the market value of the car was £17,500.

On 1 April 20X4, the company ceased to trade and a liquidator was appointed by the creditors. In the period from 1 January to 1 April the company had made losses of £500,000 and at the date of liquidation it owed its creditors £2,500,000. Borset Bank is demanding that the warehouse be sold immediately in order to enable the secured loan to be repaid.

Required

Analyse the above situation and advise the liquidator as to whether he has to repay the secured loan to the Bank and whether he has any course of action against the directors of the company.   **(20 marks)**

PROFESSIONAL EDUCATION

LAW OF EMPLOYMENT

Questions 87 to 94 cover the law of employment, the subject of Part G of the BPP Study Text for Paper 2.2.

---

87   **CONSTRUCTIVE DISMISSAL AND DISABILITY**
   DISCRIMINATION (12/01)   *18 mins*

   Explain the following in the area of employment law:

   (a)   constructive dismissal.   (7 marks)
   (b)   the defence of justification under the Disability Discrimination Act 1995.   (3 marks)

                                                                          (10 marks)

88   **PREPARATION QUESTION: THE EMPLOYMENT CONTRACT**

   (a)   What are the implied duties owed by an employee under a contract of employment?

   (b)   Carol is employed as a clerk by a firm of accountants. She is approached by George, a garage owner, who asks Carol if she will 'do his bookkeeping' in her spare time. Explain whether Carol will be breaking her contract of employment if she accepts this offer.

   Approaching the question

   The duties owed by an employer and an employee to each other are key areas of employment law. This question requires statements of fact in part (a) and the application of the law in part (b). Try to provide an illustration or a case example for each duty you cite in part (a).

89   **COMMON LAW DUTIES (6/02)**   *18 mins*

   Explain in the context of employment law:

   (a)   the common law duties imposed on employers;   (6 marks)
   (b)   constructive dismissal.   (4 marks)

                                                                          (10 marks)

90   **CAROL**   *36 mins*

   Carol ran a business in Glasgow which specialised in producing computer software programs. Dan and Eve both worked for Carol for a period of three years. They were both described as self-employed and both paid tax as self-employed persons. Carol provided all of their specialist computer equipment. Dan was required to work solely on the projects Carol provided, and he had to attend at her premises every day from 9 am till 5 pm. Eve usually worked at home and was allowed to work on other projects. Eve could even arrange for her work for Carol to be done by someone else if she was too busy to do it personally. When Carol lost her most important contract, which Dan had been working on, she decided to relocate the business to be closer to her one remaining large contract in London some 500 miles away. As a result she told Dan and Eve that there would be no more work for them.

   Dan and Eve are concerned.

   You are required to advise them:

   (a)   Why it is important to distinguish between contracts of service and contracts for services;

(b) How the courts decide whether someone is self-employed or is an employee;

(c) Which category each of them is likely to fall into.

(20 marks)

91   REDUNDANCY AND CONSTRUCTIVE DISMISSAL (12/99)   *18 mins*

In employment law explain:

(a) What is meant by redundancy, and what an employee has to show in order to be able to claim redundancy repayments   **(6 marks)**

(b) Constructive dismissal   **(4 marks)**

(10 marks)

92   EMPLOYEES AND RESTRAINT OF TRADE   *36 mins*

A business selling fresh fruit and vegetables was owned by Mr Cox. He hired Mr Bean as his sales manager. Mr Bean was very capable and successful in expanding the business of selling to the wholesalers.

Mr Bean, working on commission based upon sales, spotted an opportunity to miss out the wholesalers, and using a team of salespersons in vans sold direct to retail outlets. Mr Cox became concerned at the high level of commissions payable and on several occasions tried unsuccessfully to get Mr Bean to accept a conventional salary.

After a heated argument Mr Bean resigned and set up his own business having recruited a number of Mr Cox's salespersons. Before leaving they had all familiarised themselves with such things as customer lists, pricing structures and delivery routes. Mr Cox's business suffered dramatically and he decided to sue Mr Bean and the others for breach of contract. He contended that it was a term of all employment contracts that they would not take with them vital secrets and work in direct competition after terminating their employment. Although nothing had been expressly included in their original contracts Cox argued that it was implied by law.

Advise Mr Cox and his former employees of their respective legal positions.   **(20 marks)**

93   RIGHTS AT WORK   *36 mins*

(a) The Employment Rights Act 1996 sets out five 'reasons' which an employer can rely on in order to justify dismissing an employee fairly.

Explain the 'reasons', supported by appropriate case references.   **(10 marks)**

(b) The Sex Discrimination Act 1975 provides that discrimination is not unlawful where a person's sex is a genuine occupational qualification for a job.

Explain the circumstances under which lawful discrimination may occur.   **(10 marks)**

(20 marks)

94   GRACE AND HILDA   *36 mins*

Grace has worked for Hilda for the past 12 years and they have always been on extremely friendly terms, frequently socialising together. Recently, however, they had an argument outside of work and totally unrelated to it. Grace now believes that Hilda is going to dismiss her from her job at the end of the week.

Required

Advise Grace in relation to the law relating to unfair dismissal. In particular advise her as to:

(a) The grounds on which dismissal may be fair   (8 marks)
(b) The grounds which dismissal would be automatically unfair   (6 marks)
(c) The remedies she would have if she were to be unfairly dismissed.   (6 marks)

(20 marks)

Answers

1 COUNTY COURT

> **Tutor's hint**. Do not be tempted to write anything about criminal law issues! Be clear about the court structure – the diagram in the Study Text should be in your memory, showing the routes of appeal.

In the English legal system the county court is the local court for the trial of **civil cases**, underpinning a system for the resolution of civil disputes. The county courts now deal with the majority of civil litigation in England and Wales, their jurisdiction having been expanded by the High Court and County Court Jurisdiction Order 1991 and further dealt with by the **Woolf Reforms** of April 1999 (see below).

Judges

A **circuit judge** presides. A circuit judge must be a barrister of at least ten years' standing or have served as a recorder in a Crown Court for at least three years. A recorder must in turn be a solicitor or barrister of at least ten years' standing.

A **district judge** (formerly a registrar) may try small claims (see below) or other minor cases where the parties consent to this. The district judge, who must be a solicitor or barrister of at least seven years' standing, also assists the circuit judge, acting as clerk of the court and dealing with administrative matters. In a limited number of civil cases (such as fraud, libel and slander) a jury of eight persons may sit but usually the circuit judge sits alone.

Jurisdiction

The county court exercises its **jurisdiction** in the following types of case.

(a) **Contract** and **tort** claims

(b) **Equitable matters** concerning trusts, mortgages and partnership dissolution up to £30,000, unless the parties waive the limit

(c) Disputes concerning **land** where the capital value of the land is less than £30,000, although its jurisdiction is unlimited where the Rent Acts are concerned, or where the parties agree

(d) Undefended **matrimonial** cases

(e) **Probate matters** where the estate of the deceased is estimated to be less than £30,000

(f) **Miscellaneous matters conferred by various statutes**, for example the Consumer Credit Act 1974 (no limit on jurisdiction)

(g) Some **bankruptcy, company winding-up** and **admiralty** cases

(h) **Small claims**

The High Court and County Court Jurisdiction Order 1991 made new arrangements for the **distribution of proceedings** between the High Court and the county courts. Criteria are laid down for determining where proceedings are to be commenced and tried and where judgements are to be enforced. For example, actions in respect of personal injuries are to be commenced in a county court unless the claim is worth £50,000 or more.

Actions in contract and tort worth less than £25,000 must normally be tried in a county court and those exceeding £50,000 in the High Court. Those in between may be tried in either court. Relevant factors include the '**financial substance**' of the action, whether questions of **public interest** are raised, the **complexity** of the facts, the **legal issues, procedures** or **remedies** involved and the likely **speed of proceedings** in either case.

Small claims court

Claims not exceeding £5,000, or where the parties agree, will normally be referred by the county court registrar to the small claims court. Litigants usually conduct their case in person without legal representation. Proceedings are more **informal, cheaper** and **quicker** and the small claims procedure is frequently used in consumer cases, motor accident and personal injury claims, employment, tenancy, travel and debt disputes. The arbitrator is usually the district judge but may be some other person selected by the parties. His award is recorded as a county court judgement.

Woolf Reforms

The **Woolf Reforms** of 1999 revised the civil justice procedures by allocating cases to one of three 'tracks', depending on the sums involved and the issues in the case. Cases under £5,000 go to arbitration and are dealt with in a small claims procedure as described above, while those under £15,000 go on a 'fast track', to enable speedier justice. More complex cases over £15,000 are allocated to a 'multi-track'. The High Court and County Court are still separate, but are administered together outside London. Fast track and small claims cases are held at local county courts.

Appeal

From a decision of a county court there is a **right of appeal** to the Civil Division of the Court of Appeal. In bankruptcy cases an appeal goes to the Chancery Division of the High Court.

2   CIVIL COURTS AND TRACKS

> **Tutor's hint**. Before you start a question like this it is worth drawing a rough diagram of the civil court system to use as a plan. This will help to ensure that you don't forget any of the courts involved. Notice that part (b) asks you specifically about the track system for allocating cases, so there is no need to go into detail about that in part (a). Keep to the civil courts in this question: you will gain no marks for discussing the criminal courts.
>
> **Examiner's comments**. This was not a very popular question and it was not very well-answered. Most candidates dealt adequately with the County Court and the High Court, but less well with the Court of Appeal and the House of Lords, tending to discuss precedent rather than the role of the courts. Part (b) was poorly answered, and candidates seemed to have little knowledge in this area.

(a)   The courts in the English Legal System which have a civil jurisdiction are as follows.

The magistrates' court is mainly a criminal court, but it also has original jurisdiction in a number of civil cases, particularly family proceedings. It hears many domestic issues such as proceedings for the financial provision for parties to a marriage and children, the custody or supervision of children and guardianship, and adoption orders. Various types of licensing are the responsibility of the magistrates' court and it will also hear claims for recovery of unpaid local authority charges and council tax.

The county court hears only civil cases, but deals with virtually every type of civil matter arising within the geographical area which it serves. In some types of case, its jurisdiction is concurrent with that of the High Court. The main limits to its jurisdiction are financial. It is involved in hearing the following.

(i)   Actions in contract and tort, not exceeding £50,000;

(ii)   Equitable matters concerning trusts, mortgages and partnership dissolution up to £30,000, unless the parties waive the limit;

(iii)   Disputes concerning land where the capital value of the land is less than £30,000;

(iv)   Undefended matrimonial cases;

(v)   Probate matters where the estate of the deceased is estimated to be less than £30,000;

(vi)   Miscellaneous matters conferred by various statutes, for example the Consumer Credit Act 1974 (no limit on jurisdiction); and

(vii)   Some bankruptcy, company winding-up and admiralty cases.

The High Court also deals with civil cases at first instance. It is divided into three sections.

(i)   The Queen's Bench Division deals with common law matters, such as contract and tort. It also includes a Commercial court and an Admiralty Court (to deal with shipping cases). A Divisional Court of the QBD has an appellate jurisdiction on cases from magistrates' courts and tribunals.

(ii)   The Chancery Division of the High Court deals with equity matters such as trusts, mortgages, bankruptcy, taxation, probate and partnerships. It also has a special Companies Court which deals with liquidations and other company proceedings, and a Patents Court.

(iii)   The Family Division of the High Court deals with matrimonial cases, family property and proceedings relating to children. The Family Division also has a limited appellate function in that it hears some appeals on domestic matters from the Magistrates' Courts.

The civil courts which have an exclusively appellate jurisdiction are the Civil Division of the Court of Appeal and the Judicial Committee of the House of Lords. The Court of Appeal hears appeals from the High Court, county courts and several special tribunals. It reviews the evidence and the legal opinions and makes its decisions based on them. Cases are heard by three judges sitting together (known as Lord Justices of Appeal).

The House of Lords is the highest court of appeal in the English legal system. Cases are heard by five Law Lords sitting together. The court hears appeals from the Court of Appeal and also appeals from the High Court, under the 'leapfrog procedure' where the House of Lords gives leave to appeal.

In certain circumstances the decisions of the European Court of Justice are binding on all English courts. This is the case for all legal proceedings where the meaning or effect of any EC treaties or the validity, meaning or effect of any community instrument is questioned. The ECJ does not consider itself bound by its own previous decisions.

There are also a number of specialised courts and tribunals, established by statute to deal with disputes between individuals or between individuals and government agencies. They have particular jurisdictions and include the Social Security Appeals Tribunal, Employment Tribunals, the Employment Appeals Tribunal and the Lands Tribunal.

(b)   The Civil Procedure Rules introduced a three track system for the allocation of civil cases. Generally speaking, county courts hear small claims and fast track cases and the High Court hears multi-track cases.

Under the small claims track, cases are heard where the claim is for less than £5,000 (or £1,000 in the case of personal injury claims, claims for possession of land, housing disrepair claims and harassment claims). If the claim is for more than the stated amount, the parties may still elect to use the small claims track, subject to the court's approval. The small claims track is intended to permit litigants to conduct their case in person if they so wish as the procedure is less formal, cheaper and quicker than court proceedings. The arbitrator is usually the district judge or may be appointed by the parties.

Cases under £15,000 may be allocated to the 'fast track'. This is a strictly limited procedure, designed to enable cases to be brought to trial within a short but reasonable timescale. Costs are fixed and hearings are designed to last no longer than one day.

Finally, the multi track approach is intended to provide a new and more flexible regime for the handling of claims over £15,000 in value. These are the cases that tend to be more complex. An initial 'case management conference' will be held to encourage the parties to settle the dispute or to consider the merits of alternative dispute resolution. The trial judge sets a budget and a final timetable for the trial.

Marking Guide		Marks
(a)	Magistrates court	1
	County Court (with examples)	2
	High Court (3 divisions)	1½
	Court of Appeal	1
	House of Lords	½
		6
(b)	County Court and High Court	1
	Small claims track	1
	Fast track	1
	Multi track	1
		4
		10

3 ARBITRATION

> **Tutor's hint.** Arbitration and the whole concept of alternative dispute resolution are becoming increasingly popular in practice, and hence are a likely area for exam questions. The examiner has written two articles in *Student Accountant* in June and August 2004, and it would be worth reading them to gain his perspective on this issue.

This is increasingly becoming a popular alternative to litigation in the courts, and it is now quite common for contracts, especially large commercial contracts, to contain provision for voluntary arbitration in the event of a dispute arising between the parties to the contract. This can be very helpful as referring the dispute to arbitration means that it will be handled by an independent expert who fully understands the legal ramifications. It also provides advantages such as privacy for the parties involved.

Proceedings in arbitration are less adversarial in nature than court hearings (where one party is 'opposed' to the other) so it is more likely that a compromise will be found, meaning that the concept of 'winners and losers' is less pronounced.

Unless otherwise agreed, a hearing before an arbitrator follows the same essential procedure as in a court of law. However, following the Arbitration Act 1996, the arbitrators and parties can settle on the **form** of the arbitration.

The Arbitration Act 1996

The Arbitration Act 1996 aimed to introduce **greater speed and flexibility** into the arbitration process, in particular by conferring upon the parties the right to make their own agreement on virtually all aspects of the arbitration (s 1). It contains provisions for the **appointment and removal** of arbitrators, and the power to appoint **experts** (s 37), advisers and assessors. It turned the courts' role into a **supervisory** rather than an interventionist

one. Under this Act, the parties may choose to dispense with formal hearings and strict rules of evidence and procedure (s 46).

Under the 1996 Act, an arbitration agreement is a **separate agreement** which can outlive the original contract that gave rise to the arbitration proceedings.

The main advantage of the arbitration procedure is **privacy**, since the public and the press have no right to attend a hearing before an arbitrator.

Compulsory arbitration

In addition to voluntary arbitration as described above, compulsory arbitration may be enforced in the following circumstances.

(a)   Certain statutes (Acts of Parliament) provide for arbitration on disputes arising out of the provision of the statute.

(b)   The High Court may order that a case of a technical nature shall be tried (or investigated with report back to the court) by an Official Referee or other arbitrator.

(c)   A county court may order that a small claim (not exceeding £5,000) shall be referred to arbitration, under the small claims court procedure.

4   PREPARATION QUESTION: SOURCES OF LAW

> **Tutor's hint.** There are many sources of English law as shown in the answer below. It is important to cover all of the different sources. Do not worry if you feel that you are not describing the different sources in as much depth as you would like. It is more important to cover all the sources of law than to deal with one or two of them in great detail.

There are **three main sources** of English law, namely **statute**, **case law** and directly applicable **EC law**. There are also a number of **subsidiary sources**, the most important of which is **custom**.

Legislation

Statute law is made by **Parliament**. Subject to various overriding principles of EU law, Parliament may make law as it sees fit. It may repeal earlier statutes, overrule case law developed in the courts or make law in new areas which have not been regulated previously.

Generally speaking, a proposal for legislation is passed through various stages in the House of Commons and, when approved by the commons, it is introduced into the House of Lords. After both houses have approved the legislation, it must receive royal assent before becoming an Act of Parliament.

Statute law may be 'fresh' legislation or it may be a **consolidation** of existing statutes and their amendments, for example the Companies Act 1985, or a **codification** of existing statutory and case law, for example the Sale of Goods Act 1979.

The **courts are bound to apply relevant statute law** and cannot choose to disregard or rewrite it. Whatever the nature of the legislation the role of the judges to interpret and apply it is the same. Judicial interpretation might be needed because of ambiguity in drafting or uncertainty as to whether a particular set of facts are within the scope of a statute, or where unforeseeable developments have occurred since the statute was passed.

Delegated legislation

The complexity of much modern legislation means that, in many instances, there is a great deal of detail which cannot conveniently be included in an Act. Therefore, much **modern legislation** expressly gives power to a minister or public body, such as a local authority, to

make laws for specified purposes in the form of **statutory instruments, bye-laws and Rules of Court**. Such **delegated legislation** has the same legal force and effect as the empowering Act itself.

Case law

Case law is law which is made in the courts according to the rules of **common law and equity** which, historically, were combined and clarified when the courts were amalgamated by the Judicature Acts 1873-1875. Both common law and equity are the product of decisions in the courts made by judges who interpret and apply previous cases based on a principle of consistency, the **doctrine of binding precedent.**

Doctrine of binding precedent

This doctrine provides that once a principle of law has been decided in court, it becomes a precedent which, generally speaking, binds the lower courts in cases with materially the same facts.

In order to be a binding precedent, a **decision must be based on a proposition of law and not a question of fact**. It must form part of the **ratio decidendi**, or reasoning behind the decision of the case. Statements which announce legal principle but which do not form part of the ratio decidendi and statements which are based only on hypothetical facts are not binding precedents but are obiter dicta (literally other words) and of persuasive authority only.

European law

The **Treaty of Rome 1957** is one of the foundation treaties of the European Community. It is a **primary source of law, self-executing and directly applicable**, which needs nothing further than ratification in order to become law in the member states. The same is true of the other foundation treaties, the Treaty of Paris 1951 and the Second Treaty of Rome 1957. Most articles of the treaties have direct effect, creating rights which must be protected by the courts in the member states.

The European Community generates much law by means of its own legislative process, which is independent of national legislatures of member states including the United Kingdom Parliament. **EC law may be enforced either by the national courts of individual member states or by the European Court of Justice.**

In the event of a conflict between EC law and the national law of a member state, then EC law prevails. EC law acts, therefore, as a separate legal system, independent of UK law, but overriding it in certain circumstances.

The treaties establish four main institutions: the European Parliament, Commission, Council and the European Court of Justice. The ECJ has a wide jurisdiction over EC law including member states' actions or inactions in fulfilling their treaty obligations. In the same way as English courts must apply UK statutes, they must also apply statutes which originate from or have been enacted in order to comply with EC law, the foundation treaties, regulations which are directly applicable and rulings from the ECJ on the interpretation of EC law.

In addition to the treaties, there is also **secondary legislation**. This comprises **regulations, directives and decisions**. This comprises regulations, directives and decisions.

(i) Regulations (unless expressed to the contrary) have effect as law throughout the European Community as soon as they are made.

(ii) Directives are statements of principle to which the member states must adapt their own law by their national legislative process, usually within a given time frame.

(iii) Decisions of an administrative nature are made by the EC Commission and are immediately binding on the government or person to whom they are addressed.

5   BINDING PRECEDENT

> **Tutor's hint**. Remember to answer both parts of the question to maximise your marks. You can make general points in a couple of introductory paragraphs.

The doctrine of binding precedent dictates that in determining any case, **where the facts of the case are materially the same as in a previous case heard by a superior (or sometimes equal) court, then the court will be bound by any proposition of law which formed part of the ratio decidendi of that previous case.**

Obiter dicta, statements which do not form part of the ratio decidendi, to not constitute binding precedents but are of persuasive authority only.

Previous decisions which can be said to rest on materially different facts can be distinguished and not followed and, in some cases, previous decisions can be declared too wide or obscure to be followed.

(a)   **The hierarchy of the courts**

Decisions of the **Magistrates' Courts** and **County Courts** are not binding as precedents but these courts are bound by decisions of the High Court, Court of Appeal and House of Lords. The **Crown Court** is bound likewise by the superior courts and its decisions are of persuasive authority only.

A decision of a **High Court** judge sitting alone binds all lower courts but not other High Court judges. A decision of two or more High Court judges sitting together as a divisional court of the High Court is binding on any other divisional court and on a High Court judge sitting alone.

Decisions of the **Court of Appeal** bind all inferior English Courts and the Court is bound by the House of Lords. In *Young v Bristol Aeroplane Co*, it was held that the civil decision of the Court of Appeal is bound by its own pervious decisions except where

(i)   Two previous decisions are in conflict,

(ii)   The previous decision is in conflict with the subsequent House of Lords decision, or

(iii)   The previous decision was made per incuriam.

The **House of Lords**' decisions bind all English Courts. The House of Lords generally regards itself as bound by its own decisions although it is entitled to depart from an earlier decision when it considers it to be just. The House does not exercise this discretion lightly.

Decisions of the **European Court of Justice** are binding on all English courts (including the House of Lords) where they concern the interpretation of Community treaties or the validity or interpretation of secondary community legislation. The ECJ is not bound by its own decisions.

(b) **Advantages and disadvantages**

The relative advantages and disadvantages of the doctrine may be summarised as follows.

Advantages

(i) **Certainty**. The primary purpose of the doctrine of judicial precedent is to create certainty, fairness and predictability. Litigation can even be avoided where the facts of a case are so materially similar to those of a previous case (from a suitable court) that the outcome can be foretold or, in any event, legal advice can be given more wisely when it is known how much weight will be attached to previous decisions. In either case, costs and time are reduced. The doctrine also gives guidance to the judges and leads to consistency in decisions from different judges in different courts and in different parts of the country.

(ii) **Clarity**. Since only propositions of law forming part of the ratio decidendi of a case constitute binding precedent, it should be the case that the doctrine gives rise to a healthy source of statements of legal principal that can helpfully and clearly be applied to new cases generally. This is strengthened by the fact that the Court of Appeal and the House of Lords will normally follow their own previous decisions.

(iii) **Flexibility**. The doctrine allows the law to grow and be developed in accordance with changing needs and circumstances of society and allows much more flexible judge-made law than Parliament-generated legislation. Judges can avoid having to apply a previous decision as a precedent by distinguishing it on the facts or, in certain cases, by overruling decisions.

(iv) **Detail**. In applying propositions of law to the facts of the case, judges often go into a great deal of detail. This has the advantage of encouraging flexibility, by assisting the distinguishing of later cases on the facts.

(v) **Practicality**. Another advantage of the doctrine of judicial precedent sometimes put forwards is that it has its roots in tied and tested cases and not in theory, as is often the case with new legislation. As a result, there should perhaps be less uncertainty and misunderstanding in its application. It is much less likely (than in the case of legislation) that principles of law will become binding on other courts which are essentially hypothetical or obscure.

Disadvantages

It can be argued that with certainty comes **rigidity, inflexibility and undesirable decisions** being reached because judges are obliged to apply earlier decisions (where they are unable to distinguish them on the facts). This makes the law more complicated especially where judges are clearly at pains to avoid being bound by a precedent which would cause such a result.

The possibility of precedents not being applied because the court is persuaded that the facts are not sufficiently similar also causes uncertainty.

Although possibly not strictly a 'disadvantage' of the doctrine, the criticism is sometimes made that these propositions of law are often not clear enough and there may appear to be **conflicting propositions** in the same judgement or discrepancies between propositions reached in more than one case.

It may also be argued that the doctrine in fact produces **inflexibility** and **limits the discretion of judges**, sometimes producing unfair or undesirable results that do nothing to encourage confidence in the doctrine itself as a suitable tool in producing a fair legal system. The need to pass new legislation in order to alter law established on

the strength of precedents which are (at the time or subsequently) considered to be unjust is clearly unattractive. It can also be argued that the flexibility given to judges who are not elected democratically is too great as it effectively allows them to make law not just to apply law.

The disadvantage of the level of detail often contained in judgements is that the bulk of material makes subsequent reading, digesting and application of judges' decisions unnecessarily difficult and complicated. The distinguishing of cases can also become more tenuous the more detail is included.

Marking Guide	Marks
Definition of doctrine	2
Summary of lower courts	1
Summary of higher courts	2
Role of ECJ	1
2 clearly explained advantages	2
2 clearly explained disadvantages	2
	10

6 INTERPRETATION AND HUMAN RIGHTS

Tutorial note. You should have been able to gain good marks in part (a) of this question if you have revised this area properly. Notice what the examiner says (below) about the depth of answers given. To pass this exam, you are required to demonstrate an understanding of the law and legal process, not just list the facts or rules you have read in your Study Text. This is why making reference to case law can assist your answers as cases illustrate the law in practice. This is not to say you will fail if you don't refer to cases. Just make sure you explain how the law works in practice; using cases is one way of doing that. Part (b) may have seemed more difficult if the Human Rights Act seems daunting. You should have been able to make reference to the requirements to interpret English law in a way that is compatible with the convention. Revise this area using the suggested answer if not.

Examiner's comments.

(a) Although most candidates could identify the three main rules of interpretation used by the courts, there were wide differences in the level of understanding of them and the ability to do any more than merely naming them. Where candidates mentioned the other rules of and aids to interpretation, they were given credit. Most candidates appreciated the fact that although in principle Parliament is the supreme source of law, judges continue to play an important part in the interpretation of legislation to solve problems of ambiguity and uncertainty.

(b) Not many candidates were able to demonstrate other than a basic knowledge of the Human Rights Act 1998. Very few could explain the effect that the Act has on the role of the UK courts in their capacity as interpreters of legislation.

(a) **Need for statutory interpretation**

Although the wording of a **piece of legislation is carefully scrutinised** at all stages of its development, from its initial drafting through to the various stages of its passage through the two Houses of Parliament, **difficulties may nonetheless be encountered in its application.**

When the statute comes to be applied in the courts, there may be uncertainty over the **precise meaning** of a word or whether a particular term applies to the circumstances of the case. The applicability of legislative provisions may be uncertain when **unforeseeable or unforeseen developments** have occurred since the legislation was enacted.

It is the **role of the judiciary to apply the law made by Parliament as legislation**. The courts are thus required to determine the meaning of such legislation. In doing so, they will apply a number of well-established rules and principles to interpret the statute.

Rules of statutory interpretation

The following rules of statutory interpretation have been developed by the courts:

(i)   *The literal rule*

The most important guide to the purpose of the statute is the wording of that statute. Under the literal rule, words are to be given their literal, or plain and ordinary, meaning and to be interpreted in the same way throughout the statute. This means that if the words used are clear, the courts must apply them even if they find the consequences distasteful. Thus in *Whitely v Chapell 1868*, a statute made it an offence to impersonate any person entitled to vote at an election. The accused was acquitted because he impersonated a dead person (who clearly was not entitled to vote).

(ii)   *The golden rule*

The 'golden rule' requires a statute to be construed in such a way as to avoid a manifest absurdity or contradiction which would result from an application of the literal rule. Thus a statute which was designed to clarify the rules on intestacy was not applied literally when the heir had in fact murdered the deceased (*Re Sigsworth*).

(iii)   *The mischief rule*

The mischief rule provides that if there is any ambiguity or uncertainty the courts will consider the mischief at which the statute is aimed by reference to the preamble of the statute (where the purpose is stated) and will adopt the interpretation best suited to remedying that wrong. Thus in *Gardiner v Sevenoaks RDC*, the Act in question sought to regulate the safe storage of inflammable film on 'premises'. It was held that 'premises' included a cave, since the purpose was clearly to protect the safety of persons wherever the film was stored.

The mischief rule is also known as the rule in Heydon's case in which it was laid down that the judges should consider the following matters:

- What the law was before the statute was passed
- What 'mischief' the statute was seeking to remedy
- What remedy Parliament was trying to provide

Presumptions of statutory interpretation

In addition to these main rules of statutory interpretation, the courts will also apply a number of other **principles and maxims**, for example the *eiusdem generis* rule, which provides that where a statute appends general terms to a list of specific words, the general words are to be limited in their meaning to other things of the same type as the preceding specific word (*Evans v Cross*).

Interpretation of EC law

EC legislation is drafted in a different way from UK legislation by stating broad principles and leaving the judges to develop the detail. The English courts follow the European approach to statutory interpretation in order to avoid the law being interpreted differently in different member states.

The national courts are required to interpret and apply EC law in order to achieve **consistency between states**. In part as a result of EC law, English courts have shown a tendency to adopt a more **purposive approach** to the interpretation of English statutes.

(b)   **The Human Rights Act 1998**

The Human Rights Act 1998 incorporates the European Convention for Human Rights and Fundamental Freedoms and came into operation on 2 October 2000. The extent of the impact of the legislation will become clearer as case law develops.

The effect that this Act has on statutory interpretation is that UK courts are now required to **interpret UK law in a way compatible with the Convention so far as it is possible to do so** (s3). They must also take into account previous decisions, judgments, declarations and adverse opinions of the European Court of Human Rights.

Where a court considers that any legislative provision is incompatible with the Convention, it cannot disregard it but may make a **declaration of that incompatibility**. The provision remains valid in domestic law until amended by legislation or statutory instrument (s4).

Marking Guide		Marks
(a)	Explanation of interpretation	1
	Literal rule (1 for explanation; ½ for example)	1½
	Golden rule (1 for explanation; ½ for example)	1½
	Mischief rule (1 for explanation; ½ for example)	1½
	Presumptions	1
	Interpretation of EC law	½
		7
(b)	Background to HRA	1
	UK interpretation to be compatible	1
	Declaration of incompatibility	1
		3
Total		10

7   DELEGATED LEGISLATION

> **Tutor's hint.** Be sure that you answer all the aspects of this question. It specifies several things that you should cover. This means that as it is only a 10 mark question, the marks allocated against each one will be few and therefore that you will not score highly if you concentrate your answer in one area.

Delegated legislation means **rules of law**, often of a detailed nature, **made by bodies which are subordinate to Parliament** to whom the power to do so has been given by statute. Validly enacted delegated legislation properly authorised by the Act of Parliament under which it arises has the same legal force and effect as the Act itself.

The complexity of much modern legislation means that, in many instances, there is a great deal of **detail** that **cannot conveniently be included in an Act**. Therefore, much modern legislation provides a general framework and enables Parliament's delegates (who are normally ministers, government commissions or local authorities) to produce detailed provisions within the purpose and aim of the enabling Act. This is the means by which delegated legislation is made.

There are various forms of delegated legislation:

(a)   **Statutory instruments**. This is the most common form of delegated legislation. Power to make the legislation is delegated by Act of Parliament to a government minister. The Insolvency Act 1986, for example, gave rise to a number of statutory instruments.

(b)   **Orders in Council**. These include rules made by the Queen, usually in times of national emergency.

(c) **Bye-laws**. These are made by local authorities and apply within a specific locality.

(d) Parliament also gives powers to various **professional bodies,** such as the Chartered Association of Certified Accountants, in connection with the regulation by the professional body of the conduct of its members.

(e) **Rules of Court**. These may be made by the judiciary to control court procedure (for example the rules under the Supreme Court Act 1981).

Advantages

Delegated legislation is important for a number of reasons. Without delegated legislation, Parliament would be overwhelmed by the volume of work. Even now, the government of the day is frequently unable to fulfil all its proposals for new legislation within the allotted period. The advantages of delegated legislation explain the increased frequency with which it is used. It **enables new laws to be passed much more quickly than would otherwise be the case**.

The subject of new legislation is often **highly detailed, technical and complex**. It makes sense, therefore, for the exact content and wording to be arrived at by consultation with professional, commercial or industrial groups outside parliament.

Delegated legislation also means that the primary legislation is less voluminous because the details are left to other delegated legislation documentation. Delegation leads to **greater flexibility,** because regulations can be altered later without the need to revert to Parliament.

Disadvantages

There are also several disadvantages.

- Delegated legislation causes a resulting **increase in the volume of legislation**.

- The different types of delegated legislation which may derive from a single statute can be **confusing** and **difficult to monitor**.

- It can be said that the system is **unrepresentative** in that it passes power to **civil servants** and others who are **not democratically elected**.

There is a disadvantage inherent in passing legislative powers into the hands of persons outside Parliament itself. It is therefore important that delegated legislation is properly controlled.

Control

The power to make delegated legislation is conferred by the enabling Act of Parliament and this also defines the extent of that power.

Control is exercised by the **judiciary**. For example, a statutory instrument may be challenged in the courts by judicial review on the grounds that it is ultra vires - in other words that it exceeds the prescribed limits or that it has been made without due compliance with the correct procedure.

Control may also be exercised by means of judicial interpretation of the enabling Act of Parliament and/or delegated legislation.

Control over delegated legislation is also exercised by **Parliament**. This is achieved by means of providing for statutory instruments to be laid before Parliament for 40 days before they take effect and for members to propose (within forty days) a resolution of veto if there are objections. Alternatively, some regulations must be affirmatively approved by Parliament before they take effect.

In addition, there are **standing committees** ('Scrutiny Committees') of both Houses of Parliament whose duty it is to examine statutory instruments with a view to raising objections if necessary (usually on the grounds that the instrument is obscure, expensive or retrospective).

Marking guide. To get full marks you need to address the six specific issues mentioned in the question, ie:

- Meaning of delegated legislation
- Effect of delegated legislation
- Advantages
- Disadvantages
- Control by Parliament
- Control by the Courts

With 1½ marks available for each element, there is one further 'floating' mark available for additional points or overall impression.

---

8   EC LAW

Tutor's hint. This question is clearly structured and should present few problems. Make sure you have sufficient knowledge of the European Court of Justice. The Teaching Guide refers specifically to the need to 'understand the significance of the European Community as a source of law'. Given the increasing importance of this source of law, it is likely to feature regularly on the paper.

In questions like this, don't forget to give the appropriate amount of time to each part. Three marks worth of a question should take you just above five minutes, so make sure that you don't get carried away, spend too much time on the first section and then not leave yourself enough time for the others.

Examiner's comments. Most candidates coped well with parts (a) and (b) but were not then able to discuss the role of the European Court of Justice, and many confused it with the European Court of Human Rights. This indicates a fairly fundamental failure of understanding.

(a)   There are a number of sources of European law. The primary sources are the foundation treaties themselves, namely the Treaty of Paris 1951, the First Treaty of Rome 1957 and the Second Treaty of Rome 1957. These three treaties are self-executing, in that they do not require any other legal process, beyond ratification, in order to become law in the member states. There are three forms of secondary legislation, namely regulations, directives and decisions.

Regulations (unless expressed to the contrary) are binding and enforceable throughout the European Community as soon as they are made. They are self-executing or 'directly applicable' and do not require any UK Act of Parliament since the regulation is already legally binding (although, very rarely, national legislation might be required, eg *EC Commission v UK (re Tachographs) Case*). Regulations are usually employed for areas of law-making within the basic aims of the Treaty of Rome, for example, in connection with the establishment of a single unrestricted market in the EC territory in manufactured goods.

(b)   **Directives** are statements of principle to which the member states must, by their national law-making process, adapt their own law within a specified period, usually two years. For example, the several directives on company law require that company law in each member state shall conform to certain principles, such as the law on company securities now contained in the Financial Services Act 1986.

Although directives are mainly statements of principle to be absorbed into national law by a national law-making process, it is sometimes permissible for an EC national in court proceedings to rely on the principles of a directive where this has not been done (*Van Duyn v Home Office*). (Individuals may even seek damages against the state where they have suffered as a result of the state's failure to implement a directive into national law (*Francovich v Italy*).)

(c) **European Court of Justice**

The ECJ is one of the four principal institutions of the European Community (and is not connected in any way with the European Court of Human Rights). It is a court of first instance from which there is no appeal. The court's jurisdiction empowers it to make rulings on legal issues of the following types.

(i) Legal matters arising from the acts or omissions of member states, including the failure of a member state to fulfil its obligations under a European treaty;

(ii) Rulings on legal issues arising from EU law which affect persons from member states;

(iii) Actions brought against EU institutions by member states, individuals or corporations;

(iv) Disputes between the Communities and their employees.

If EU law conflicts with the national law of a member state, then EU law prevails. EU law should therefore be seen as a separate legal system, independent of UK law, but overriding it in certain circumstances. Judgments of the ECJ overrule those of national courts. In *Factortame Ltd v SS Transport (No. 2)*, the House of Lords acknowledged the supremacy of EU law and laid down that it must be fully and uniformly applied in all member states. In the case of matters arising under (b) above, the House of Lords is bound to refer the case to the ECJ for a ruling and lower courts may do so. Proceedings in the English courts must be stayed while the decision of the ECJ is awaited and interim relief should be granted (as it was in the *Factortame case*). Once a ruling is given, it must be applied to the case before the national court.

Marking Guide		Marks
(a) Regulations:		
Binding as soon as they are made		1
Self executing and directly applicable		1
Example of type of area they affect		1
		3
Directives:		
Members must enshrine in own law		1
Examples: company legislation in the UK		1
Individuals can rely on directives if not in own domestic law		1
		3
(c) European Court of Justice:		
A court of first instance: no appeal		1
Examples of types of issues it rules on (½ each)		1
EU law is supreme if conflict		1
Re Factortame		1
		4
		10

9   EU INSTITUTIONS

> **Tutor's hint.** This is one of those areas of the syllabus where you can score good marks with some basic knowledge. It is worth learning areas like this.

There are four main **institutions** established by the Treaties. Three are political institutions: the **Commission**, the **Council of Ministers** and the **European Parliament**. The fourth is the **European Court of Justice**.

Institution	Activities and personnel
The European Commission	The European Commission is the **executive** body of the EC. Its main activities are 'formulating proposals for new community policies, mediating between the Member States to secure the adoption of these proposals, co-ordinating national policies and overseeing the execution of existing community policies'. There are twenty Commissioners appointed by mutual agreement of the member governments. The Commission has a wide legislative function. It is responsible for drafting most EC legislation, and puts its proposals before the Council for enactment.
The Council of Ministers	The Council is the Community's **decision-making body**. It 'takes the final decision on most EC legislation, concludes agreements with foreign countries and decides on the Community budget'. The Council comprises **representatives of the member states**; each government sends a relevant minister as its delegate. Different voting arrangements apply in different situations. Sometimes a unanimous vote is required; more usually a 'qualified majority' will suffice. This involves the use of a **weighted voting system**, based on the relative population of member states.
The European Parliament	The **European Parliament** is a directly elected body. Members sit in political groupings rather than by country. The Parliament has consultative and advisory functions which are exercised through standing committees dealing with specialist topics.
The European Court of Justice	This is a court of first instance from which there is no appeal. The jurisdiction of the European Court falls under four main heads. • Legal matters arising from the acts or omissions of member states, such as failure of a member state to fulfil its treaty obligations. • Rulings on legal issues affecting persons which arise from EC law. • Actions brought against EC institutions by member states, individuals or companies. • Disputes between the Communities and their employees.

10   OFFERS AND INVITATIONS TO TREAT

> **Tutor's hint**. Notice that part (a) of the question asks you to both explain **and** distinguish between the two terms. This means that you have to define and also explain what the difference is between them, ie one, once accepted, gives rise to a contract, while the other merely sets the contractual ball rolling. Make sure that you leave enough time at the end to earn the three marks available in part (b).
>
> **Examiner's comments**. This was the most frequently attempted question in Part A of the paper, reflecting the centrality of the issue of offers and invitations to treat to the contract part of the syllabus. It was generally well-answered, although some candidates merely defined an invitation to treat as an offer, without explaining what an offer was. The best answers focussed on the importance of intention, as demonstrated in *Carlill's case*.

(a)   The distinction between an offer and an invitation to treat may be illustrated as follows.

Offer

In the law of contract an offer is a definite promise to another to be bound on specific terms. It cannot be in vague terms, for example a promise to buy a horse if it is 'lucky' (*Gunthing v Lynn*). An offer can be made to an individual, a class of persons or to the world at large and it can be accepted by the conduct of the offeree (*Carlill v Carbolic Smoke Ball Co*). A mere supply of information is not an offer, because there is no intention to be bound. For example, stating the minimum price that one would consider if a sale were to be agreed does not constitute an offer (*Harvey v Facey*). Similarly, a mere statement of intention, for example, that an event such as an auction is to take place, is not the same as an offer (*Harris v Nickerson*). Only an offer made with the intention that it shall become binding when accepted may be accepted so as to form a binding contract.

Invitation to treat

An invitation to treat is an indication that someone is prepared to receive offers with a view to forming a binding contract. There is no binding contract until such an offer is made and accepted.

An auctioneer's request for bids is not a definite offer to sell to the highest bidder but an invitation to treat. The bid itself is the offer, which the auctioneer is then free to accept or reject (*Payne v Cave*). As a general rule, an advertisement is not of itself an offer capable of acceptance but is usually regarded as an attempt to induce offers and therefore is an invitation to treat (*Partridge v Crittenden*). Similarly, the circulation of a price list constitutes an invitation to treat (*Grainger v Gough*). In limited circumstances, an advertisement may constitute an offer as in *Carlill v Carbolic Smoke Ball Co*, where the words of the advertisement were held to be sufficiently clear to constitute an offer to the world at large, capable of being accepted by anyone fulfilling the necessary conditions.

It is also established that the display or exhibition of goods for sale on self-service shelves amounts to an invitation to treat (*Pharmaceutical Society of Great Britain v Boots Cash Chemists (Southern)*). Similarly, the display of an article in a shop window was in no sense an offer for sale, but constituted an invitation to treat (*Fisher v Bell*).

(b)   As has been stated in part (a) of this answer, only an offer made with the intention that it shall become binding when accepted may be accepted so as to form a binding contract. An invitation to treat is rather an indication that someone is prepared to receive offers with the view to forming a binding contract. There is no binding contract until such an offer is in turn made and accepted. The invitation to treat cannot be 'accepted' and give rise to a contract.

Marking Guide

		Marks	
(a)	Offer a promise to be bound	1	
	Make to one person or the world at large	1	
	Carlill v Carbolic Smokeball Co.	1	
	Invitation: willingness to accept an offer	1	
	Examples (1 mark each)	1	
	Cases (½ mark each)	2	
			7
(b)	Offer is indication of willingness to be bound	1	
	Invitation indicates willingness to open negotiations	1	
	No binding contract until offer is accepted	1	
			3
			10

11 ADAM

Tutor's hint. This question is very rigidly structured indeed, with 'bite-size' pieces which should be easy to address. The specific parts do, however, require specific knowledge. You must be prepared to analyse different possibilities in relation to the various problems set out. There is more to this question than a discussion of invitation to treat.

Marking guide. Each part of the question is only worth 4 marks. To maximise the marks you earn, make sure that you:

- Identify the issue involved
- State the law relating to the issue and cite a case or a piece of statute in support of the law
- Apply the law to the specific scenario
- Conclude on the situation in the question

If you cannot remember a case to cite, don't worry too much about it, as it is the identification of the point of law and the application of the law to the scenario that are critical.

(a) **Advertisement.** In the law of contract an **offer** is a definite promise to another to be bound on specific terms. Only an offer made with the intention that it shall become binding when accepted may be converted into a contract by acceptance. An offer can be made to a particular person or persons or to the public at large. An **invitation to treat**, by contrast, is an indication that someone is **prepared to receive offers** with the view to forming a binding contract. An invitation to treat is not capable of being accepted so as to form a legally binding contract.

Case law has established a number of accepted principles which apply to determine whether something is an offer or merely an invitation to treat. As a general rule, an **advertisement** is not of itself an offer capable of acceptance but is usually regarded as an attempt to induce offers and therefore is an invitation to treat (*Partridge v Crittenden*). Similarly, the circulation of a price list also constitutes an invitation to treat. In limited circumstances, an advertisement may constitute an offer as in *Carlill v Carbolic Smoke Ball Co*, where the words of the advertisement were very clear and precise and were held to be an offer to the world at large, capable of being accepted by anyone fulfilling the necessary conditions.

Adam's advertisement may be regarded as an offer rather than an invitation to treat, owing to the very clear and categorical language used (following Carlill's case). His advertisement is 'a serious offer', clearly stating the price and open to acceptance by the first person to respond.

(b) There is a general rule in the law of contract that **acceptance** must be express (oral or written) or implied and must be **communicated** to the offeror before it can be effective, unless the offeror expressly waives the need for communication (Carlill's case). The offeror may stipulate the exact means of communication in which case only compliance with his or her terms will suffice.

The **postal rule** provides an exception to this. The postal rule provides that where the use of the post is in the contemplation of both parties and the acceptance is correctly put in the post, then acceptance will be valid once posted, whether or not the offeror actually receives the letter: *Adams v Lindsell*. Whether the use of post was in the contemplation of the parties may be deduced from the circumstances, for example if the offer was itself made by post (*Household Fire and Carriage Accident Insurance Co v Grant*).

In this case it is clearly not appropriate for acceptance to be made by post. The offer is valid for one day only and the car will be sold to the 'first person who accepts it'. It is implicit that a more immediate communication of acceptance was required. Ben has not entered into a binding contract with Adam.

(c) Acceptance must be **unqualified agreement** to the terms of the offer. Where the 'acceptance' actually introduces some new term it constitutes a **counter-offer**. A counter-offer operates to reject the original offer and is itself open to acceptance or rejection by the original offeror (*Hyde v Wrench*).

In purporting to accept Adam's offer contained in the advertisement, Carol is altering the terms by seeking to pay by cheque rather than cash. The offer clearly requires payment in cash. The decision in *D & C Builders v Rees* to the effect that payment by cheque is equal to payment by cash would not be applied in this case, where payment by cash and not by cheque is expressly intended and required. Carol has made a counter-offer that Adam is free to accept or reject.

(d) The offeror may revoke the offer, by communicating revocation to the offeree, at any time up to acceptance (*Payne v Cave*) unless by a separate option agreement, for which consideration has been given, he has agreed to keep the offer open for a certain period of time (*Routledge v Grant*). A simple promise, unsupported by consideration, to keep the offer open is not binding.

It appears that Dave provided no consideration in return for Adam's promise to keep the offer open and so no contract arose and Adam's promise was not binding. Dave could argue, however, that his entering into a loan with his bank constituted consideration. If successful, Adam would be in breach of contract if he refused to sell the car to Dave.

(e) Eric introduced a new term as to price and his counter offer is accepted by Adam. Thus a binding contract comes into existence and by refusing to pay for and accept the car, Eric is in breach of contract. Adam is entitled to sue Eric for the price. He might be better advised to sell the car to Dave for £5,000 and sue Eric for the remaining £1,000.

12 ANN'S ART

Tutorial note. This scenario question is typical of the type of question you must expect in this part of the exam. It requires you to analyse the scenario and apply principles of contract law to it. As the examiner points out, the situation is not clear cut despite the volume of information given, and it is a key skill to be able to recognise that several answers are possible and discuss the merits of each. You must not expect there to be one simple and obvious answer to a question like this. Comparing this situation to case law you are aware of will help you identify what is most likely to be the case here. Imagine the process (say) Dave's solicitor will go through – analysing case law, trying to build up his own case. He would compare the facts to *Carlill v Carbolic Smokeball Co*, etc … so must you. In this instance you must consider the scenario from each person's point of view (Ann, Chas, Dave, Eve). What case would each try to build? Each point raised would be relevant in this answer. You will probably find it useful, as we have in our answer, to consider the various elements of contract separately: agreement (offer and acceptance), consideration, intention (if relevant … in this commercial situation it is a fair assumption that the parties intended legal relations and it does not merit being mentioned).

Examiner's comments. This was a popular question which was attempted by the great majority of candidates. It raised basic issues in relation to the formation of contracts and required discussion of the law relating to offers, counter-offers, acceptance and aspects of consideration. The problem did not present an absolutely clear-cut situation on several of these aspects. Those candidates who saw this and then:

(a) offered alternative solutions;
(b) argued which was to be preferred;
(c) supported their analysis with reference to case law;

obtained the best marks.

Agreement

For an agreement to constitute a valid and binding contract, it must comprise a valid **acceptance** of a valid **offer** made with the **intention of creating legal relations** and being supported by valid **consideration**.

Offer

An offer is a definite promise to be bound on specific terms. It must be certain in its terms (*Gunthing v Lynn*) and can be made to a particular person or to a class of persons, in which case it is only open for those persons to whom the offer is made to accept it.

However, an offer can be made to the **world at large** (*Carlill v Carbolic Smoke Ball Co*) in which case anyone can accept it. It must be more than a mere supply of information (*Harvey v Facey*) or statement of intention (*Harris v Nickerson*).

Invitation to treat

An invitation to treat, on the other hand, is an indication that a person is prepared to receive offers with a view to entering into a binding contract. It is generally accepted that an advertisement constitutes an invitation to treat (*Partridge v Crittenden*) although in special circumstances it may be held to constitute an offer (*Carlill v Carbolic Smoke Ball Co*).

Similarly, goods displayed in a shop window give rise to an invitation to treat rather than an offer (*Fisher v Bell*).

Application to Ann

In this case the notice in Ann's window is almost certainly an invitation to treat and not an offer under the generally accepted principle that advertisements are invitations to treat. An offer is made in response to this invitation to treat when Chas and Dave offer £12,000 for the prints.

Acceptance

Acceptance must be an **unqualified agreement** to the terms of the offer and must not introduce new terms (in which case it is a counter offer). Similarly, a purported acceptance which is actually a request for further information or one which is made 'subject to contract' will not constitute valid acceptance.

Acceptance of an offer may be by express words or be inferred from conduct (*Brogden v Metropolitan Rly Co*). Mere passive inaction is not capable of constituting acceptance (*Felthouse v Bindley*).

Acceptance of an offer may only be made by a person authorised to do so, usually the offeree or his authorised agent.

Application to Ann

Ann is entitled to accept or reject Chas's and Dave's offers and she rejects them, but at the same time makes a **counter-offer** that she will sell the prints for £13,500 each. Likewise, Chas and Dave are free to accept or reject this counter offer which destroys the original offer of £12,000 (*Hyde v Wrench*).

The arrangements whereby Ann agrees to keep the offers open until noon on Monday amount to separate option agreements supported by consideration in Chas and Dave each paying £100. These collateral contracts are binding on both parties. The offer to sell at £13,500 has still to be accepted in order to make the main contract of sale binding also.

Communication of acceptance

Generally speaking, **acceptance must be communicated to the offeror** before it can be effective, unless the offeror expressly waives the need for communication (as in Carlill's case). The offeror may stipulate the sole means of communication in which case only compliance with his or her terms will suffice.

If the offeror specifies a means of communication but does not make it absolutely compulsory, then acceptance by another means which is equally expeditious and does not disadvantage the offeror in any way will be sufficient (*Yates Building Co v R J Pulleyn and Sons (York)*).

The postal rule

Communication of acceptance by post is subject to the **postal rule** established in *Adams v Lindsell*. This provides that where the use of the post is in the contemplation of both parties and the acceptance is correctly addressed and stamped and is actually put in the post, then **acceptance will be valid and effective once posted** and it is irrelevant whether the offeror actually receives the letter.

There is no need for the offer specifically to state that acceptance must be communicated by post - whether this was in the contemplation of the parties may be deduced from the circumstances, for example if the offer was itself made by post (*Household Fire and Carriage Accident Insurance Co v Grant*).

Clearly if it is evident that the parties did not intend the postal rule to apply - for example where the offer requires 'notice in writing'- then the rule will be excluded (*Holwell Securities v Hughes* where it was held that the stipulation for 'notice in writing' meant that notice of acceptance actually had to be received by the offeror).

Application to Ann

In this case, Ann does not stipulate the means by which acceptance of her offer is to be communicated. It can be argued, however, that since the parties so far have communicated face to face, it was to be expected that Chas and Dave would again visit the shop by Monday

if they wished to purchase the prints at £13,500 a piece. In the case of Chas, his acceptance arrives within the stipulated time in any event and a binding contract for sale exists from this point. It is submitted that Dave, however, has not entered into a binding contract for sale with Ann because his acceptance has not been communicated by noon on Monday and the postal rule was not in the reasonable contemplation of the parties.

It transpires of course that Ann actually sold the prints to a third party on the Saturday before the time for expiry of the option contracts. She is therefore in breach of both those contracts and Chas and Dave are entitled to recover the £100 paid in respect of them. The sale implies a revocation of her offer but such revocation is invalid, as she has failed to communicate it to Chas and Dave.

Whether a **revocation** is express or implied, it must be communicated to the offeree in order to be effective (*Dickinson v Dodds*). She is therefore also in breach of the contract for the sale of goods to Chas and is liable in damages. The measure of damages would be made according to the available market rule and amount to £1,500, that being the difference between the contract price of £13,500 and the market price of £15,000 (as evidenced by the sale to Eve). The same remedy might be available to Dave if it is concluded that his acceptance of the offer is valid. However, as noted above, it is probable that Dave's acceptance would be found not to be valid, hence a contract has not been formed and he has no remedy.

Marking Guide	*Marks*
Definition of agreement	1
Definition of offer	1
Can be made to the world at large	1
Distinguish invitations to treat	2
Application to situation	1
Definition of acceptance	1
Express or implied	1
Application to situation	2
Communication of acceptance	2
Means might be specified	1
Postal rule	2
Application to situation	2
Revocation rules	2
Application to situation	1
	20

13   ADAM AND BEN

> **Tutor's hint.** This question asks you to consider whether a contract has been formed. It is necessary for you to work through the elements which are essential for a contract to have been formed and consider whether they are present. The fact that a reward is involved may remind you of some precedent in case law, but don't let it confuse you, concentrate on the essential elements of contract.
>
> Remember:
>
> - identify the **issue** (agreement in contract law)
>
> - **state** the law (rules on offers; rules on acceptance)
>
> - **apply** the law (are there offer and acceptance here?)
>
> - **conclude** (can Ben claim the £100 from Adam?)

An agreement must be constituted by

- An **offer and acceptance of that offer,**
- **Consideration** must (normally) be given, and
- There must be an **intention** to create legal relations.

Offer

An offer is a **definite promise to be bound on specific terms**. It must be certain in its terms (*Gunthing v Lynn*) and can be made to a particular person or to a class of persons, in which case it is only open for those persons to whom the offer is made to accept it.

However, **an offer can be made to the world at large** (*Carlill v Carbolic Smoke Ball Co*) in which case **anyone can accept it**. It must be more than a mere supply of information (*Harvey v Facey*) or statement of intention (*Harris v Nickerson*). An offer is also more than an invitation to treat, such as an auctioneer's request for bids or (usually) an advertisement (*Partridge v Crittenden*).

A typical circumstance involving an invitation to treat would be the placing of an advertisement. However, **an advertisement may, depending on the particular circumstances, constitute an offer or an invitation to treat.**

It is necessary to consider the intention with which the advert is made. If the words of the advertisement are **clear and precise,** the advertisement **may constitute an offer** (*Carlill v Carbolic Smoke Ball Co*). Here the defendants advertised that they would pay £100 to anyone who caught influenza while using their product. This was held to be an offer to the world at large capable of being accepted by anyone fulfilling the necessary conditions.

Acceptance

The acceptance must be an **unqualified agreement** to the terms of the offer and not propose new terms (*Hyde v Wrench*) or simply amount to a request for further information (*Stevenson v McLean*).

The acceptance may be by **express words or by action** or **be inferred from conduct** (*Brogden v Metropolitan Rly Co*). There must be some act on the part of the offeree, however, as mere silence or passive inaction is not capable of constituting acceptance (*Felthouse v Bindley*).

The acceptance **must be communicated** to the offeror before it can be effective **unless the offeror expressly waives the need for communication.** Such waiver can either be **express or inferred** from the circumstances. In the case of a **unilateral contract**, where (typically) an offer is made to pay money in return for an act, **the offeree is not required to perform the act but if he does, he is entitled to claim the payment.** In such cases, there is no need for the offeree to notify his acceptance of the offer beforehand, rather **acceptance by conduct is sufficient.**

Carlill's case is one example of a unilateral contract, as are cases where **rewards** are offered. **Performance of the act may still constitute valid acceptance even if the offer is not the sole reason for it and there is another motive** (*Williams v Carwardine*).

End of offer

An **offer can be revoked at any time before acceptance** and, once revoked, can no longer be accepted (*Routledge v Grant*). Revocation may be express or implied but **must be communicated** to the offeree. In the case of a unilateral contract, the courts have held that an **offer cannot be revoked once the offeree has begun to perform whatever act is necessary.**

Consideration

Consideration must also be present unless an agreement is made by deed. **Performance of an act in response to an offer of payment constitutes executed consideration**. The promise becomes binding when the act is performed (as in Carlill's case).

Intention

Although in **social arrangements**, there is a **presumption that legal relations are not intended**, this presumption is **rebuttable** and the courts will consider all the evidence presented to see whether an intention can be said to have existed (as in *Merritt v Merritt* and *Simpkin v Pays*).

In the present case, it appears that a unilateral contract may have arisen. The first question is whether Adam made the offer just to his group of friends, in which case only one of them could accept it, or to the world at large (as in Carlill's case). This will turn on the facts and evidence of, for example, how loudly Adam spoke and what was intended.

Application to this case

If, and only if, the **offer** is treated as having been made to the world at large, then it appears to follow that Ben can claim the £100 promised for the following reasons.

Acceptance of the offer is made by performance of the act required, namely swimming to the other side of the harbour. Other communication of acceptance is not necessary (*Carlill's case*). It does not matter that Ben had another primary motive for the act; he was aware of the offer (*Williams v Carwardine*).

The **offer cannot be revoked once performance of the act has begun**. An **intention** to create legal relations can be **inferred** from the way Adam put the cash offered down on the table 'to show the seriousness of his challenge' and also, perhaps, by the way he tried to revoke the offer as Ben swam.

14   CONSIDERATION

> **Tutor's hint**. The first part of this question is straightforward, so do not spend too long on it. Divide your time fairly equally between all the three parts, do not run out of time on the last part which is worth an extra mark.

(a)   **Definition**

Consideration is an **essential element** of all binding contracts, except those made by deed. This is based on the idea that the contractual promise should not be gratuitous but should have an **element of bargain** about it, even though the courts will not weigh up the relative values of each party's promise or act.

Broadly speaking, the doctrine of consideration provides that one party must know that he has bought the other party's promise, either by performing some act of his own or by offering a promise of his own.

Consideration has been defined as follows: 'an act or forbearance of one party, or the promise thereof, is the price for which the promise of the other is bought, and the promise thus given for value is enforceable': *Dunlop v Selfridge*. An alternative definition was given in *Currie v Misa*. 'A valuable consideration in the sense of the law may consist either in some right, interest, profit or benefit accruing to one party, or some forbearance, detriment, loss or responsibility given, suffered or undertaken by the other.'

Consideration may validly be executed or executory but cannot be past. Executed consideration is a performed, or executed, act in return for a promise. Executory consideration is a promise given for a promise (and will be valid before either party performs his promise).

Consideration must 'move from the promisee' which means that the price of a promise must be paid by the person who seeks to enforce the promise: *Tweddle v Atkinson*.

(b) **Rules of consideration**

(i) **Sufficiency and adequacy**

Consideration need **not be adequate** in that it does not have to be of a value appropriate to the promise. The **courts will not seek to weigh up the comparative values** of the promises, nor will they provide a remedy for someone who simply makes a poor bargain.

In *Chappell & Co v Nestle Co*, chocolate wrappers were held to be good consideration because they were identifiable even though they had no economic value to Nestle. A nominal rent is sufficient consideration even if it is inadequate as rent in the open market: *Thomas v Thomas*.

Forbearance can be consideration provided it has **some value** or **amounts to giving up something of value**. Additional incentives from the promisee to encourage performance of existing contractual or statutory obligations are not good consideration: *Stilk v Myrick*. However, in *Williams v Roffey Bros & Nicholls (Contractors) Ltd*, where the promise to pay extra was given (without duress) to avoid liability under a penalty clause, the courts held that the **mutual benefit derived** was sufficient to constitute valid consideration.

(ii) **Past**

Subject to some exceptions, **anything which has already been done when the promise is made is 'past consideration' and is not enforceable**: *Re McArdle*. Where one party to an existing contract makes a further promise, even if it is directly related to the previous bargain, it will be held to have been made on past consideration: *Roscorla v Thomas*.

There are some **exceptions** where past consideration will suffice to make the promise enforceable, including:

- s 27 bills of Exchange Act 1882. Past consideration is sufficient to create liability on a bill of exchange

- Where a request for services is made, it may be implied that the person requesting them was also promising to pay for them, in which case where that person promises a specific reward after the services have been performed, that promise will be treated as fixing the amount promised rather than as a new promise: *Lampleigh v Braithwait*. The courts will need to be satisfied, however, that both parties must have assumed, during their negotiations, that the services being requested would have to paid for: *Re Casey's Patents*.

```
  Marking Guide
                                                                     Marks
  (a)  Definition (eg Currie v Misa, Dunlop v Selfridge)              1
       Essential element of a contract                                1
       Executory or executed                                          1
                                                                     ─
                                                                      3
  (b)  (i)   Meaning of sufficient                                    1
             Meaning of adequate                                      1
             Cases or examples (½ mark each; max. 1)                  1
                                                                     ─
                                                                      3
       (ii)  Explanation of past consideration                        1
             Cases or examples                                        1
             Exceptions (1 mark each; max. 2)                          2
                                                                       ─
                                                                       4
                                                                      ──
                                                                      10
```

15   FORMS OF CONSIDERATION

Tutor's hint. It is important to notice the mark allocation in this type of question, as there are four separate parts and it is all too easy to overrun on one of them, limiting the time available on the others.

Examiner's comments. This was the most popular question on the paper. Candidates tended to score higher marks where they gave definitions, cases or examples. Some candidates were confused between executory and executed consideration, and in part (b)(ii) some just cited *Re McArdle* without explaining the legal principle.

(a)   Consideration, like a valid offer and acceptance and an intention to create legal relations, is an essential element of all binding contracts, except those made by deed. This is based on the idea that the contractual promise should not be gratuitous but should have an element of bargain about it, even though the court will not concern itself with the fairness of the bargain made. Broadly speaking, the doctrine of consideration provides that one party must know that he has bought **the other party's promise,** either by performing some act of his own or by offering a promise of his own.

In *Dunlop v Selfridge*, consideration was defined as follows: 'an act or forbearance of one party, or the promise thereof, is the price for which the promise of the other is bought, and the promise thus given for value is enforceable'. An alternative definition was given in *Currie v Misa*. 'A valuable consideration in the sense of the law may consist either in some **right, interest, profit or benefit** accruing to one party, or some **forbearance, detriment, loss or responsibility** given, suffered or undertaken by the other.'

Consideration must be **sufficient but it need not be adequate.** That is to say that it does not have to be of a value appropriate to the promise. The courts will not seek to weigh up the comparative values of the promises, nor will they provide a remedy for someone who simply makes a poor bargain. In *Chappell & Co v Nestle Co*, chocolate wrappers were held to be good consideration because they were identifiable even though they had no economic value to Nestle. A nominal rent is sufficient consideration even if it is inadequate and not equal to rent in the open market (*Thomas v Thomas*).

(b)   It is often said that consideration may validly be **executed or executory but cannot be past.** Both executed and executory consideration are provided at the time when the promise is given.

BPP
PROFESSIONAL EDUCATION

(i)   **Executory consideration** is a promise given for a promise (and will be valid before either party performs his promise). Thus the consideration in support of each promise is the other party's promise rather than a performed act. If one party agrees to pay for goods which the other party agrees to deliver, that constitutes sufficient consideration so that if either party withdraws without the other's consent, that is breach of contract.

(ii) **Executed consideration** is a performed, or executed, act in return for a promise. Thus in reward cases, for example, a promise to pay a reward when an act is done becomes enforceable only when that act is performed.

(iii) Subject to some exceptions, anything which has already been done when the promise is made is '**past consideration**' and is not enforceable (*Re McArdle*). Where one party to an existing contract makes a further promise, even if it is directly related to the previous bargain, it will be held to have been made on past consideration (*Roscorla v Thomas*).

There are, however, some exceptions where past consideration will suffice to make the promise enforceable, including:

(i)   under s 27 bills of Exchange Act 1882, past consideration is sufficient to create liability on a bill of exchange; and

(ii) where a request for services is made, it may be implied that the person requesting them was also promising to pay for them, in which case where that person promises a specific reward after the services have been performed, that promise will be treated as fixing the amount promised rather than as a new promise (*Lampleigh v Braithwait*). The courts will need to be satisfied, however, that both parties must have assumed, during their negotiations, that the services requested would be paid for (*Re Casey's Patents*).

Marking Guide		
		Marks
(a) Price of the other person's promise (or similar explanation)		1
Cases or examples		2
		3
(b) *Executory consideration*		
A promise for a promise		1
Example		1
		2
Executed consideration		
Definition and example		2
Past consideration		
Explanation		1
Cases or example		1
Exceptions to the rule		1
		3
		10

16   AXEL

Tutor's hint. This question is about consideration for promises. It deals with Axel's promises to several different people, which will help you to structure your answer. Remember to state the basic principles of law as this will gain you easy marks, but try not to repeat yourself as you will only get marks for one point once. Once you have **identified the issue** and **stated the law**, apply it to the situation and then **conclude** for all three groups of people.

Current situation

In this case, there are already **contractual relations in existence** between the various parties. Under the terms of the contract between Axel and Ben, Ben must be available to repair any faults in the equipment when the magazine is being printed. Under the terms of the contract between Axel and his employees, there is a set of existing contracts under which the employees have agreed to provide, respectively, journalistic and printworking services.

Axel appears to make a new promise to each of these three individuals, or groups of individuals. Each new promise consists of the promise of an additional payment to do something which the promisee appears already to have agreed to do or has already done. The **question** therefore arises as to **whether these actions can amount to consideration for the new promises**.

Consideration is an essential element of all binding contracts, except those made by deed. This is based on the fundamental idea that the **contractual promise should not be gratuitous but should have an element of bargain about it**. The promisor agrees to do something; in return the promisee gives consideration.

Rules concerning consideration

There is a long-established rule is that additional incentives from the promisee to encourage **performance of existing contractual or statutory obligations are not good consideration** since the promisor is only doing what he has agreed to do (*Stilk v Myrick*).

If, however, **additional actions beyond those duties** are performed, this is **good consideration** (*Hartley v Ponsonby*).

More recently, the courts appear to have qualified the basic principle. In *Williams v Roffey Bros & Nicholls (Contractors) Ltd*, the plaintiffs agreed to do carpentry work for the defendants, who were engaged as contractors to refurbish a block of flats, at a fixed price. The work ran late and so the defendants, concerned that they might have to pay money under a penalty clause in the main contract, agreed to pay the plaintiffs an extra sum to ensure the work was completed on time. They later refused to pay this extra amount.

It was held that the defendants were **obtaining a benefit** by avoiding the need to make other provision for the works to be finished on time and by avoiding having to make penalty payments under their contract. These **benefits were sufficient to provide consideration** for the defendant's promise to make additional payments and so that promise was enforceable by the plaintiffs. It was significant that the defendants' promise was extracted by duress or fraud but rather the defendant offered the extra money on his own initiative to avoid a penalty.

Although the Court of Appeal did not overrule *Stilk v Myrick*, it is apparent that the basic principle has been somewhat curtailed. Now it appears that the **performance of an existing contractual duty can amount to consideration for a new promise where both parties obtain practical benefit from the promise** and where there is no suggestion of duress or fraud.

Application to Ben

In relation to the contract between Axel and Ben, **Ben will argue that Axel received practical benefits**, in that the magazine was duly published on time. However, the **facts** described **suggest duress** in that Ben refused to fix the machine unless his payment was increased.

Axel was left with no choice other than to agree to Ben's demands. For this reason it is submitted that *Williams v Roffey Bros* **would not be applied**, that **Axel's new promise is not binding** and that Ben will be unable to recover the additional £1,000 per week.

Application to the printworkers

In relation to the printworkers, Axel will argue that they were merely **performing their existing contractual duties** and, therefore, that there is no consideration for his promise of the extra £100.

The printworkers will argue, however, that due to the computer breakdown and the considerable time taken in its repair, they actually had to work a great deal harder to achieve production of the magazine on time and therefore they were **required to do more than merely perform existing contractual duties** . It is submitted that *Hartley v Ponsonby* would be applied and the **printworkers could enforce Axel's promise** to pay more.

Application to the journalists

In relation to the journalists, they had completed their tasks before the promise was made (*Stilk v Myrick*) and that amounts to **past consideration**. As shown in the case of *Re McArdle*, **past consideration is not sufficient to make a promise binding** and so the claim of the journalists is likely to fail.

17 CONTRACT ISSUES

> **Tutor's hint**. This question requires you to apply your knowledge of consideration and waiver of rights to the given scenario. As always, with application questions, it is vitally important to identify the **issue**, **state** and explain the law, then **apply** it to the facts given and then **conclude**.

Ann is seeking to rely on the separate agreement of each of the parties with whom she contracted to accept something other than the consideration originally agreed as satisfying the whole contractual debt.

The situations described raise three separate questions:

- Can payment in kind (here, a painting) constitute consideration?
- Can payment of a lesser sum by a third party constitute consideration?
- Can a party who has accepted a lesser amount be estopped from claiming the full amount?

Consideration

Consideration was defined in *Currie v Misa* as follows: 'A valuable consideration...may consist either in some right, interest, protection or benefit accruing to one party, or some forbearance, detriment, loss or responsibility given, suffered or undertaken by the other'.

Thus forbearance, or the waiver, of existing rights can amount to consideration. As in all cases, **one party's promise must be supported by consideration on the part of the other party**. Hence if a party to a contract agrees to waive his right to a part of a debt, it is clear under the general principles of contract law that this promise must itself be supported by consideration.

In *Foakes v Beer*, the defendant had obtained judgement against the claimant for a debt. By written agreement, the defendant agreed to accept payment by instalments of the sum due, with no mention being made of interest which was also due.

The claimant paid off the amount and the defendant then claimed the interest as well, arguing that her written agreement (promise) did not prevent her from claiming the interest as this promise was not supported by consideration. It was held that she was indeed entitled to the debt with interest, as the claimant had provided no consideration for any waiver of rights.

There are **situations**, however, **in which a waiver may be binding** even if the debtor apparently gives **no consideration** (known as exceptions to the rule in Pinnel's case), including the following:

(i)   Where the debtor offers and the creditor accepts anything to which the creditor was not originally entitled, for example,

- **Goods instead of cash**
- **Payment before the date on which settlement is due** (*Pinnel's case*)

(ii) Where the debtor makes an arrangement with his creditors that they will each accept part payment in full settlement, the debtor can hold the creditors individually to the agreed terms

(iii) Where a **third party offers part payment** and the creditor agrees to waive his rights against the debtor, the creditor has received consideration from the third party against whom he had no previous claim (*Welby v Drake*)

(iv) Where the principle of **promissory estoppel** applies.

Promissory Estoppel

The principle of promissory estoppel is, if a creditor makes a promise which is not supported by consideration to the debtor that the creditor will release the debtor from some of the debt, the creditor intends the debtor to act on this and the debtor does so, then the creditor may be estopped from retracting his promise unless the debtor can be restored to his original position.

The principle was developed in the case of *Central London Property Trust v High Trees House*. In this landmark case, the claimants had, in September 1939, let a block of flats to the defendants, agreeing an annual rent of £2,500 per annum. As it was difficult to let the flats during wartime, the claimants agreed in January 1940, in writing, to accept a reduced rent of £1,250. No stipulation was made as to the duration of this arrangement, but it was clear that it related to wartime conditions.

The defendants paid the reduced rent from 1940 to 1945, subletting flats at rents set on the basis of their own expected liability to pay rent under the revised agreement with the claimants. In 1945, when the flats were fully let, the claimants demanded the original rent of £2,500 per annum for the final two quarters of 1945.

It was held that the agreement of January 1940 was a temporary expedient only and had ceased to apply in early 1945. The claimants' claim was therefore upheld. However, in an important obiter dictum which forms the basis of the principle of promissory estoppel, Denning J (later Lord Denning) said that had the claimants sued for the full rent in respect of the earlier periods, the 1940 agreement would have served to defeat the claim and they would not have been allowed to go back on their promise.

> **Tutor's hint.** In an answer you would not be expected to go into the facts of a case in quite so much detail, as it is the point of law that is important. We include the facts here so that you can understand the principles involved.

The **defendants had relied on the promise given**. The doctrine of promissory estoppel operates as a **shield only and not a sword**, that is, the defendants could not have sought to sue on the promise relying on the doctrine (*Combe v Combe*). Promissory estoppel applies only to a waiver of rights that is **given voluntarily**. If the creditor agrees to waive existing rights reluctantly or under pressure the doctrine does not apply and he can later claim the full sum (*D and C Builders v Rees*).

Application to Ann

Applying these principles to the facts of the three cases, the following conclusions can be drawn:

(a) **Belle**. As Belle accepts a painting in place of the £500 owed to her, she falls within one of the exceptions to the rule in Pinnel's case and cannot claim payment of the original debt.

(b) **Chas**. Chas also falls within one of the exceptions as he accepts a lesser sum from a third party as consideration for releasing his entitlement to the full sum as in *Welby v Drake*. He cannot, therefore, claim payment of the balance of £1,500.

(c) **Dan**. Dan's agreement to accept £3,000 rather than £5,000 must be supported by consideration on Ann's part to be enforceable and this does not appear to be the case. Applying *Foakes v Beer* he may claim the balance.

None of the exceptions to the rule apply given that his **agreement was given reluctantly** as in *D and C Builders v Rees*. This means that promissory estoppel does not apply.

Even if promissory estoppel did apply, Ann would need to argue not only that Dan promised to waive his entitlement to the full debt but also that she acted on his promise to her detriment. There is nothing to suggest that this is the case.

18   EXPRESS AND IMPLIED

> **Tutor's hint**. The key to the difference between express and implied terms is the court's approach to them. Don't dwell too much on implied terms in part (a) as you can discuss them at length in part (b).
>
> **Examiner's comments**. Not many candidates were able to explain the importance of the court's approach, and many just rephrased the question, adding little else. A significant minority confused representations and implied terms. Few candidates referred to case law or gave examples in part (b).

(a) As a general principle, the parties to a contract may include in their contract whatever terms they choose. The agreement reached on the terms must be **complete** in order to be legally binding and those terms must be sufficiently **clear and precise** (*Scammell v Ouston*). However, it is always possible for the parties to leave an essential term to be settled by specified means outside the contract, for example by agreeing to sell at open market value on the day of delivery or to invite an arbitrator to determine a fair price (*Hillas & Co Ltd v Arcos Ltd*). If, however, the parties defer an essential term for later negotiating (rather than specifying a means for its ascertainment), there is no binding agreement.

An **express term** may be defined as any term which has been included by the parties. It may be written or unwritten and the court will ascertain as a question of fact whether any oral statement constitutes a term of the contract or simply a representation. However, if a contract exists and contains all necessary terms to make it an effective contract, generally speaking oral evidence will not be admitted in order to add to, vary or contradict any of the written terms.

An **implied term** is one which is deemed to form part of a contract even though not expressly stated by the parties, whether orally or in writing. Some terms are implied by the courts as necessary to give effect to the parties' presumed intentions or by statute or in accordance with relevant trade practices. Implied terms can normally be excluded or varied by the parties save where this is prevented by relevant statutory provisions.

(b) The usual reason for a court to imply a term in a contract is in order to give **business efficacy** to that contract. In such cases the term which is implied will be one which, it appears to the court, the parties inadvertently omitted or which is so obvious that it goes without saying and it can be assumed that the parties simply took it for granted that such a term would apply. The courts will be **keen to prevent the failure of an otherwise sound contract** and to implement the manifested intention of the parties (*The Moorcock*).

The test, commonly referred to as 'the bystander test' was formulated in *Shirlaw v Southern Foundries*: 'Prima facie that which in any contract is left to be implied and need not be expressed is something so obvious that it goes without saying; so that, if while the parties were making their bargain an officious bystander were to suggest some express provision for it in their agreement they would testily suppress him with a common 'Oh, of course' '.

The court may imply terms which it considers to be required implicitly by the nature of the contract itself. In *Liverpool City Council v Irwin*, the defendants were tenants of a maisonette in a tower block owned by the claimants with no formal tenancy agreement. The defendants withheld rent, alleging that the claimants had breached implied terms because (*inter alia*) the lifts did not work and the stairs were unlit. The court concluded that since tenants could only occupy the building with access to stairs and/or lifts, therefore terms needed to be implied on these matters, including an implied obligation on the landlord's part to keep these parts reasonably safe.

The courts have also established a number of **implied terms into employment contracts** concerning employers' and employees' duties.

(i) Terms will be implied by statute where that is the expressed intention of the legislation, for example under The Sale of Goods Act 1979, terms are implied as to the vendor's **title** and the **description** and **quality** of the goods in a contract for the sale of goods. In some cases, the statute provides that the implied terms cannot be overridden (there are several instances of this in SGA 1979, but in others, express provisions to the contrary will prevail).

(ii) The parties may be considered to have entered into a contract subject to a **custom or practice of their trade**. In *Hutton v Warren*, the defendant landlord gave the claimant, a tenant farmer, notice to quit the farm. He insisted that the tenant should continue to farm the land during the period of notice. The tenant asked for 'a fair allowance' for seeds and labour from which he received no benefit (as he left before harvest time). It was held that by custom he was bound to farm the land until the end of the tenancy, but he was also entitled to a fair allowance for seeds and labour. However, any express term overrides a term which might be implied by custom (*Les Affreteurs v Walford*).

Marking Guide		Marks	
(a)	Terms can be settled by the court	1	
	Cases/examples	1	
	Express terms description	1	
	Implied terms description	1	
			4
(b)	Desire to maintain the contract	2	
	The Moorcock (or example)	1	
	'Bystander test' (or example)	1	
	Terms implied by SOGA 1979	1	
	Terms implied by custom	1	
			6
			10

19   TERMS OF A CONTRACT

> **Tutor's hint.** The fact that this question was broken into four parts should have helped you to focus on what was required. Ensure that you answer all parts of the question.
>
> **Marking guide.** The mark allocation in the question provides an indication of the time and depth required for each part of the question, so parts (b) and (c), each attracting 3 marks, would require a:
>
> * Definition
> * Description of the impact of each
> * Case in support
>
> to earn full marks.
>
> However, the examiner has indicated that in questions such as this the marker will look at a student's answer as a whole to assess the degree of thoroughness of coverage, so it could be possible to gain full marks without necessarily addressing every point in every part.

(a)   **Terms**

Contractual terms are **statements** or promises which are **incorporated into a contract**. The terms of a contract must be **precise** enough for agreement on their interpretation to be reached, although the parties to the contract **may leave specific terms to be settled by means outside the contract**, for example market price on a certain date.

Express terms are those which are specifically stated in the contract. It is also possible that some terms will be **implied** by the context of the contract or by law. Law may imply conditions by custom (for example a trade practice), statute (such as the Sale of Goods Act) or the courts.

The courts will imply terms where they conclude that the parties intended certain terms to apply but failed to include them because they were taken for granted or because they were inadvertently omitted.

Some statements do not form part of a contract. A **representation** is a statement which induces the other party to contract but does not itself become a term of the contract. In the event that such a representation turns out to be false, the plaintiff has a cause of action for misrepresentation (whether fraudulent, negligent or innocent) not for breach of contract.

If, however, such a statement is construed as a contract term, the parties (as appropriate) will be contractually bound to observe and perform it. In the event of breach, the injured party's remedies will depend on whether the term is classified as a condition or a warranty.

(b)   **Conditions**

A condition is a **contractual term which goes right to the heart of the contract, breach of which allows the innocent party to treat the agreement as terminated and sue for damages**. Alternatively, he **may elect to affirm the contract**, in which case he can still sue for damages for any loss but must continue with his own obligations.

In *Poussard v Spiers* it was held that failure by an opera singer to appear on the opening night of a series of performances amounted to breach of a condition and the producer had been entitled to treat the contract for the remaining performances as discharged.

(c)   **Warranties**

A warranty is a contractual **term which is less fundamental to the contract than a condition. Breach** of a warranty **gives** the injured party **a right to damages only**, not a right to treat the contract as discharged.

If a party to the contract attempts to repudiate the contract following a breach of warranty, this will amount to a **wrongful repudiation**. This would therefore make the party initially in breach open to a claim for breach of contract.

This means that it is important for the wronged party to distinguish clearly between breach of condition and breach of warranty before deciding what action to take.

In contrast to the *Poussard* case, above, *Bettini v Gye* involved an opera singer who was booked to arrive six days before the first performance in order to attend rehearsals. He arrived three days before the first performance and it was held that this was a breach of a warranty. The defendants were not entitled to treat the contract as discharged and were ordered to compensate the plaintiff, whose services they had refused to accept.

(d) **Innominate terms**

When there is no express provision describing a contractual term as a condition or warranty (or any statutory provision which implies certain conditions and warranties, as for example may be found in the Sale of Goods Act), the term is described as an innominate term. This means that it must be interpreted in the light of the parties' express or implied intentions and the actual effect of the breach.

If the effect of the breach is to deprive the injured party of substantially the whole benefit then the term will be treated as a condition. This gives the injured party a right to treat the contract as repudiated and sue for damages. If the effect of the breach is not so severe, the injured party's rights will be the same as for breach of an express warranty.

In the case of *Hong Kong Fir Shipping Co Ltd v Kawasaki Kisa Kaisha Ltd*, there was a breach of an innominate term. The breach was that a ship was not available for 7 out of 24 months. This was held to be insufficient to be regarded as breach of condition.

20   EXCLUSION CLAUSES

> **Tutor's hint**. It is important to spend a little time planning before embarking on this question, especially for part (b). You need to clarify in your own mind the differences between statutory and common law control of exclusion clauses, so that you can produce a logical and well-structured answer.
>
> **Examiner's comment**. Candidates did not pay heed to the mark allocations for the different parts of this question, and did not equate their efforts in relation to the marks indicated for each part of the question. Candidates tended to score better marks on parts (a) and (b)(i) and seemed happier dealing with the common law rather than the statutory points. The Unfair Contract Terms Act and the Unfair Terms in Consumer Contracts Regulations were essential for a full discussion of this area of the law.

(a)   An exclusion clause, or exemption clause, can be defined as '**a clause in a contract which purports to exclude liability altogether or to restrict it by limiting damages or by imposing other onerous conditions**'. As a general principle of contract law, the courts will not usually interfere where two parties negotiate a contract from positions of comparable bargaining strength. However, the law will seek to **protect a weaker party**, for example in the case of standard term contracts put forward by the party in the stronger bargaining position. The validity of exclusion clauses is governed by the common law, the Unfair Contract Terms Act 1977 and a number of other statutory regulations.

(b)   (i)   The common law provides that an exclusion clause must be properly incorporated into a contract, or in a document which is an integral part of the contract, before it can be effective (*Chapelton v Barry UDC*). Provided this is the case, a term cannot usually be disputed if the **document has been signed**, even if the signatory could not read the terms (*L'Estrange v Graucob*), unless the party putting forward the document gives a misleading explanation of the term's effects (*Curtis v Chemical Cleaning Co*).

In the case of an unsigned contract, then it must be shown either that the party affected actually **knew of the clause** or that the person seeking to rely on the exemption clause has taken reasonable steps to bring the existence of the clause to the attention of the other party at the time of or before the contract was made. Thus a sign on a hotel room wall was not incorporated into the contract between hotel and client since it was not seen until after the contract was made (*Olley v Marlborough Court*). The court will have regard to the nature of the liability which is being excluded when deciding whether a clause has been effectively incorporated. If the terms are particularly unusual or wide, a more prominent notice may be necessary (*Thornton v Shoe Lane Parking Ltd*). Prior notice of the terms is not necessary, however, where the parties have had previous consistent dealings and the documents used previously contained similar terms (even if the claimant has never read them (*Spurling v Bradshaw*)). Where there have been previous dealings, but not on a consistent basis, then the party to be bound by the term must be sufficiently aware of it at the time of making the latest contract (*Hollier v Rambler Motors*). A particularly unusual or onerous term must be highlighted if it is to be incorporated into the contract (*Interfoto Picture Library Ltd v Stiletto Visual Programmes Ltd*).

At common law, under the *contra proferentem* rule, the courts interpret exclusion clauses strictly and in favour of the weaker party. They presume that the clause is not intended to defeat the main purpose of the contract. A general exemption will not be interpreted so as to cover negligence (*Hollier v Rambler Motors*) unless to do so is the only means by which the clause is given meaning (*Alderslade v Hendon Laundry*).

(ii)   The scope of the common law in governing exclusion clauses has been significantly curtailed by extensive statutory provisions. The main statutory limitations on exclusion clauses are contained in the Unfair Contract Terms Act 1977. The Act applies to clauses inserted into most agreements by commercial concerns or businesses (there are some exceptions, such as insurance contracts) and provides that some clauses shall be void and some valid only as far as they are reasonable.

Thus liability for personal injury or death due to negligence may never be excluded (s 2(1)). An exemption for loss due to negligence in other circumstances will be valid only insofar as it is reasonable (s 2). 'Negligence' covers breach of contractual obligations of skill and care and the common law duty of skill and care. Reasonableness is to be considered with reference to the factors in s 11 and Schedule 2. The court will consider the relative strength of the parties' bargaining power, whether an inducement was offered to the customer, whether the customer knew or ought to have known of the exemption clause and whether compliance with the contract's terms (so that the exemption clause would never be needed) was practicable (Sch 2). The burden of proof lies with the person relying on the clause and the court will consider the factors outlined above in reaching a decision. This will be a matter of fact.

A term in a guarantee of goods which excludes or limits liability for loss or damage caused by a defect of the goods in consumer use (s 5) will be void, as will a clause in any contract for the sale of goods which excludes the condition that

the seller has a right to sell the goods (s 6). Likewise a clause which purports to exclude or limit liability for breach of the conditions relating to description, quality, fitness or sample (ss 6 and 7) will be void in a consumer contract and subject to the reasonableness test in a non-consumer contract.

In addition to UCTA, the Unfair Terms in Consumer Contracts Regulations 1999 apply to consumer contracts for the supply of goods and services and to terms which have not been individually negotiated. An unfair term is any term which causes a significant imbalance in the parties' rights and obligations under the contract to the detriment of the consumer. The courts will have regard to similar factors as those under UCTA and whether the supplier dealt fairly and equitably with the consumer.

Marking Guide		Marks	
(a)	Definition	1	
	Aim of law is to protect the weaker party	<u>1</u>	
			2
(b) (i)	Proper incorporation into contract	1	
	If document signed	½	
	Effect of misrepresentation	½	
	Cases (½ each)	1	
	Contra proferentem rule	<u>1</u>	
			4
(ii)	Unfair Contract Terms Act	1	
	No exclusion for death or injury	1	
	Other examples of terms	1	
	Unfair Terms in Consumer Contracts Regulations	1	
			<u>4</u>
			<u>10</u>

21   SELLER LTD AND TRANSPORT LTD

Tutor's hint. This is quite a straightforward problem if you have revised this area thoroughly. A lack of technical knowledge will cost you marks. There is plenty of case law on the topic and you should refer to it.

- identify the **issue** (validity of exclusion clauses)

- **state** the law (what makes them invalid)

- **apply** the law (is the clause valid?)

- **conclude** (advise Seller Ltd)

A general principal of contract law is that the courts will not interfere where two parties negotiate a contract from positions of more or less **equal bargaining strength**. However, in some situations one party is in a much stronger bargaining position, particularly where there are few suppliers of the goods or services which are the subject of contract. As a result, the weaker party (who may be a consumer) may be presented with a **standard form contract** which he has no choice but to take.

The party which introduces the standard form contract may seek to abuse its position or include **onerous terms** which may disadvantage the weaker party in the event of default. One way in which this is frequently done is by means of the **exclusion clause**. This is a clause which purports to exclude liability altogether or to restrict it by, for example, limiting the amount of damages payable. The clause which Transport Ltd seeks to rely on is such an example.

BPP
PROFESSIONAL EDUCATION

In deciding whether or not Transport may rely on the clause to escape liability, the courts will consider whether the clause is properly **incorporated** into the contract, its **interpretation** and its **validity** under relevant legislative provisions.

Incorporation

There are three ways in which exclusion clauses can be incorporated into contracts: by **signature**, by **notice** and by a **course of dealing**.

The terms may be incorporated into the contract by the **signature** of the other party on a document bearing the terms. The signatory is taken to know of the terms, even if he could not read them (*L'Estrange v Graucob*).

With regard to incorporation by **notice**, it must be shown that the person seeking to rely on the exclusion clause has taken reasonable steps to bring the existence of the clause to the attention of the other party **at the time the contract was made**. Only in limited circumstances will the courts allow the incorporation of a term after the contract has been made. Thus a sign on a hotel room wall was not incorporated into the contract between hotel and client since it was not seen until after the contract was made (*Olley v Marlborough Court*).

The court will have regard to the **nature of the liability** which is being excluded when deciding whether a clause has been effectively incorporated. If the terms are particularly unusual or wide, a more prominent notice may be necessary (*Thornton v Shoe Lane Parking Ltd* where a notice excluding liability for injury in an automatic car park was not sufficiently displayed or referred to at the time the contract was made).

Where the parties deal frequently in **transactions of a similar nature** and on the **same terms**, the courts are ready to hold that the exclusion clause has been incorporated into the latest agreement by virtue of its being present in the previous dealings, even if the plaintiff had never read it. The position is not as straightforward where the previous dealings have not been on a consistent basis (eg *Hollier v Rambler Motors* which concerned a consumer contract).

In the case of Seller and Transport, the court will consider each of these tests. There is no evidence that Transport's exclusion clause has been incorporated by signature. With regard to incorporation by notice, it seems that visitors to Transport's premises will be made aware of the clause by virtue of the 'notice prominently displayed', however as the order was placed by telephone, it is unlikely that Transport can use this in its defence. Equally, the notice provided with the confirmation of order is provided too late to be incorporated into the contract, as the contract has already been concluded by this stage. Following *Olley v Marlborough Court*, this precludes incorporation of the clause by notice to the other party.

The court will also consider the fact that there have been previous dealings between the parties and will need to determine whether unspecified dealings over 'a number of years' are enough to constitute a regular and consistent course of dealing. In *Hollier v Rambler Motors* a course of dealing which amounted to 3 or 4 transactions over 5 years was held not to be sufficient. On the facts given it is not possible to conclude on this point.

Interpretation

As well as controlling the incorporation of exclusion clauses into contracts, the courts tend to interpret them strictly, in favour of the weaker party. This is the **contra preferentem** rule. They presume that the clause is not intended to defeat the main purpose of the contract. If the clause limits liability in general terms, the courts will construe its scope so as to give the party relying on it the minimum opportunity to escape liability. A general exclusion will not usually be interpreted so as to cover **negligence** (*Hollier v Rambler*

Motors). However, if the exclusion clause only has meaning if it is interpreted to include negligence, this will be covered (*Alderslade v Hendon Laundry*).

The clause used by Transport appears to be all-encompassing and so would appear to include an exclusion of liability for negligence. On the assumption that it has been incorporated into the contract by the course of previous dealings and that it has been drafted so as to permit interpretation in favour of Transport, the possible effect of statutory provisions should be considered.

Statute

Statute law imposes some very important restrictions on the use of exclusion clauses. The **Unfair Contract Terms Act 1977**, which applies to clauses covering business liability, divides these clauses into two types; those which are **void** and those which are valid only as far as they are **reasonable**.

Conclusion

There has been a clear breach of contract here by Transport Ltd, including breach of its implied duty to exercise reasonable care and skill in supplying a service under the **Supply of Goods and Services Act 1982**. Liability for personal injury or death due to negligence may never be excluded. An exclusion for loss due to negligence in other circumstances, in a business contract such as this one, will be valid only insofar as it is reasonable (s 2 of the 1977 Act).

The court will consider the relative strength of the parties' bargaining power, whether an inducement was offered to the customer, whether the customer knew or ought to have known of the exclusion clause and whether compliance with the contract's terms so that the exclusion clause would never be needed was practicable (Sch 2).

The burden of proof lies with the person relying on the clause and the court will consider the factors outlined above in reaching a decision. This will be a matter of fact.

Marking Guide	Marks
Standard form contracts	1
Explanation of what an exclusion clause is	1
Incorporation of the clause	1
– By signature	1
– Notice/nature	3
– Course of dealings	4
Interpretation of the clause	2
– *Contra preferentem*	1
– Negligence	2
– Statute	2
Conclusion	2
	20

22   PREPARATION QUESTION: LAPTOP LTD

> **Tutor's hint**. In a question with a fairly complex scenario and lots of 'ifs and buts' like this one it is essential to follow the basic rule of identifying the issue, stating the law, applying the law and concluding

(a)   The issue here is whether David is bound by the exclusion clause in the contract he has entered into with Laptop Ltd. This in turn will depend on whether the exclusion clause is incorporated into the contract and whether, on its true construction, it exempts the company from the loss which has happened. In addition it will also depend on the possible effects of the Unfair Contract Terms Act 1977 and Unfair

Terms in Consumer Contracts Regulations 1999. It must be remembered that **an exclusion clause is only relevant if there is some liability from which to be exempted**. This answer is based on the assumption that Laptop Ltd would be liable for breach of contract but for the exemption clause.

Under the common law there are strict rules of incorporation which need to be satisfied before an exclusion clause is incorporated into a contract and then the strict rules of interpretation which the courts apply in determining the meaning and scope of such clauses.

The first question which needs to be answered on the facts of the problem in the present case is whether the exclusion clause is incorporated into the contract.

Essentially there are three ways in which exclusion clauses can be incorporated into contracts: **by signature, by notice and by course of dealing**. On the facts of the problem there is no question of such a clause being incorporated by signature; the only issues are whether it may have been incorporated by notice or by a course of dealing.

In so far as incorporation by notice is concerned the essential issue is **whether Laptop Ltd has taken reasonable steps to bring the existence of the clause to the attention of the other party at the time of, or before the time of, contracting**. The facts of the problem indicate that the notice, in this case, was contained in the delivery note which was handed to David when the workstations were delivered, but that he did not read it. The fact that David did not read the exclusion clause is not fatal to its efficacy, if Laptop Ltd has done what is reasonably necessary to draw it to David's attention. However, what is fatal in this case is that the notice containing the clause was only given **after the time when the contract was entered into**. *Olley v Marlborough Court Ltd* is clear authority for the proposition that notice which is given after the contract has been formed is ineffective to incorporate an exclusion clause; see also *Thornton v Shoe Lane Parking Ltd*. It should also be noted that, even if the notice was brought to David's attention at the correct time, it would still only be effective to incorporate the exclusion clause if the documents containing the notice were contractual documents: see *Chaplton v Barry Urban District Council*; however, it is clear on the fact of the problem that the clause has not been incorporated by notice because of the principle enunciated in *Olley v Marlborough Court Ltd*.

However, it is open to Laptop Ltd to argue that the clause has been incorporated by virtue of the **previous course of dealing** between the parties. In order for an exclusion clause to be incorporated in this way a number of criteria need to be satisfied:

(i)   The previous course of dealings between the parties must have been regular and consistent. The essential issue on the facts of the problem is whether the seven previous dealings within the last two years constitute a sufficiently regular and consistent course of dealings for the purposes of the rule. In the case of *Hollier v Rambler Motors (AMC) Ltd* the court depended that a series of four transactions over a five year period was not sufficient. Seven dealings over two years implies a much more consistent course of dealing than in the *Hollier* case, and it is strongly arguable that the test would be satisfied.

(ii)   Where one of the parties to a contract deals as a consumer then the courts will generally require much more in relation to a previous course of dealings, but on the facts of the problem we are told that the relationship between David and Laptop Ltd is a commercial one.

(iii) The facts of the problem do not disclose whether David was aware of the inclusion of the exemption clause in the previous written contracts, and the case

law is not conclusive as to whether, if the clause is to be binding against David, such knowledge is necessary or not.

On the basis of the facts of the problem it is likely that the court would consider that the exclusion clause is incorporated in the contract with David on the basis of the previous course of dealings. Accordingly it is necessary to consider whether, on its true construction, the clause is capable of excluding liability for the losses which have occurred.

(b) The courts interpret exclusion clauses very restrictively. The essential issue is whether the **wording of the clause is appropriate to exclude liability for negligence** – the facts of the problem make it clear that the losses which occurred followed the negligent installation by Laptop Ltd. The general operative principle is that clear words are necessary to exclude liability for negligence. The facts of the problem disclose that Laptop Ltd is seeking to exclude losses caused by using the company's products howsoever caused. Prima facie these words are appropriate to exclude liability for losses caused following negligent acts.

Accordingly, on the basis that the exclusion clause is incorporated in the contract as result of a previous course of dealing and that on its true construction it is sufficiently widely drafted to protect Laptop Ltd against liability for the losses which have occurred, the remaining issue to consider is **whether the operation of the clause is affected by the provisions of the Unfair Contract Terms Act 1977**. Under s. 1 of the Act it is provided that the Act applies to business liability; accordingly the Act is applicable to the facts of the present problem. By virtue of s.2(1) any purported exclusion of liability for death or personal injuries caused as a result of negligence is ineffective. Accordingly, although the clause seeks to exclude liability for 'other losses' caused by negligence (see above), such attempted exclusion is invalid. Laptop Ltd will, therefore, be liable to David for the personal injuries he has suffered.

What of the £100,000 damage caused to David's premises? Under s.2(2) exemption clauses must satisfy the test of reasonableness in relation to such losses, and s.11(2)0 and Schedule 2 of the Act detail the matters to be taken into account in determining whether the clause is reasonable or not. **The burden of proving reasonableness rests on the person relying on the clause.** The factors which the courts will consider will include the relative bargaining position of the parties, whether the customer ought to have known about the nature and extent of the term.

Determination of the above matters will essentially be a matter of fact for the courts to decide, but there are no factors disclosed on the facts of the problem to indicate that the clause would be regarded, on the basis of the factors mentioned above, as unreasonable.

Marking Guide	
	Marks
Definition of agreement	1
Definition of offer	1
Can be made to the world at large	1
Distinguish invitations to treat	2
Application to situation	1
Definition of acceptance	1
Express or implied	1
Application to situation	2
Communication of acceptance	2
Means might be specified	1
Postal rule	2
Application to situation	2
Revocation rules	2
Application to situation	1
Total	20

23   MINA

> **Tutor's hint.** The whole of this question is a scenario question. However, it asks you to consider two aspects of exclusion clauses, incorporation and validity. It is unlikely that you would put facts into the wrong half of the answer or repeat yourself in each part as the topics are fairly distinct, but guard against it. Spending five minutes putting together an answer plan will help you to avoid that error. In the plan, make sure that you identify the issues, state the law, apply the law and then conclude.
>
> In part (b), it is important to consider the general attitude of the courts to exemption clauses, any prevailing exemptions against negligence and, of course, Mina's protection by The Unfair Contract Terms Act 1977.

(a)   **Exclusion clauses**

As exemption (or exclusion) clauses are open to abuse by a stronger party where the persons making the contract are of **unequal bargaining power**, the law departs from its usual position of allowing parties to govern their own contractual relations and imposes some restrictions on their use.

Certain types of clause are **void** by statute, while others will be examined by the courts firstly to ensure that they are properly **incorporated** into the contract, and secondly to **interpret** the clause.

Incorporation of the exclusion clause

There are three ways in which exemption clauses can be incorporated into contracts: by **signature**, by **notice** and in **course of dealing**.

Incorporation by signature

The terms may be incorporated by signature of the other party on a document bearing the terms. The signatory is taken to know of the terms, even if he could not read them: *L'Estrange v Graucob.*

The only exception to this (which does not seem to apply here) is where the party is misled into signing the document by the other party: *Curtis v Chemical Cleaning and Dyeing Co.*

Incorporation by notice

With regard to incorporation by notice, it must be shown that the person seeking to rely on the exemption clause has taken reasonable steps to bring the existence of the

clause to the attention of the other party at the time of or **before the contract was made**: *Olley v Marlborough Court*.

The court will have regard to the nature and extent of the liability which is being excluded when deciding whether a clause has been effectively incorporated. If the terms are particularly unusual or wide, a more prominent notice may be necessary: *Thornton v Shoe Lane Parking Ltd*.

Incorporation through previous dealing

Incorporation due to a previous course of dealing is not relevant here as there is no suggestion that Mina has dealt with Nemo Securities Ltd before.

In this case, Nemo has included notice of its exclusion of liability in the brochure and on the form signed by Mina. The document containing the exclusion clause must be an **integral part** of the contract and **sufficiently prominent** for the other party to see it. Mina did not see the clause (it may have been in very small print, for example) and the brochure was not made a part of the contract or given when the contract was entered into.

Conclusion

Considering the scope of the exclusion clause it is unlikely that including notice in the brochure would be regarded as sufficient to make it a part of the contract.

However, **Mina's signature** on the order form which contains the exclusion clause would be **sufficient to incorporate the clause into the contract** (assuming that the order form constitutes a sufficient statement of contractual terms to be regarded as the contract). She is bound by her signature to all contractual terms including the exclusion clause.

(b) **Validity of the exclusion clause**

Once incorporated into the contract, the exclusion clause may still be invalid. As well as controlling the incorporation of exemption clauses into contracts, the courts have developed other restrictions on their use.

The courts tend to **interpret them strictly,** in favour of the weaker party. This is the **contra proferentem** rule. They presume that the clause is not intended to defeat the main purpose of the contract.

General exemptions

If the clause limits liability in general terms, the courts will construe its scope so as to give the party relying on it the minimum opportunity to escape liability. A general exemption will not usually be interpreted so as to cover **negligence:** *Hollier v Rambler Motors*.

However, if the exemption clause only has meaning if it is interpreted to include negligence, this will be covered: *Alderslade v Hendon Laundry*.

The clause in question is clearly worded to cover the liability and losses suffered. It must therefore be considered in the light of the **Unfair Contract Terms Act 1977** and the Unfair Terms in Consumer Contracts Regulations 1994.

Statutory protection

The Unfair Contract Terms Act 1977, which applies to clauses covering **business liability,** divides these clauses into two types; those which are **void** and those which are **valid only as far as they are reasonable.** Liability for personal injury or death due to negligence may never be excluded.

An exemption for loss due to **negligence** in other circumstances will be valid only insofar as it is reasonable (s 2 of the 1977 Act). Negligence covers breach of **contractual obligations** of skill and care and the **common law duty** of skill and care.

When considering reasonableness, the court will consider:

(i) The **relative strength** of the parties' bargaining power

(ii) Whether an **inducement** was offered to the customer

(iii) Whether the customer **knew or ought to have known** of the exemption clauses

(iv) Whether compliance with the contract's terms so that the exemption clause would never be needed was practicable

The burden of proof lies with the person relying on the clause.

Thus in this case, Nemo Securities Ltd **cannot rely** on the exclusion clause **to avoid liability for the injury to Mina**. In respect of the damage to premises, the exclusion clause must be considered in the light of whether or not it is **reasonable**, and it is submitted that the **company** would be most **unlikely to succeed** (*Smith v Eric S Bush*) and, therefore, would be liable to Mina for damages.

The **Unfair Terms in Consumer Contracts Regulations 1999** apply to terms in consumer contracts which have not been individually negotiated, such as this exclusion clause. If considered to be unfair and contrary to the requirements of good faith, the court can declare a term to be not binding. In this case the Regulations provide no further benefit than UCTA save that a complaint to the DGFT may result in his taking action against the company.

Marking Guide

		Marks
(a)	Definition of exclusion clause	1
	Incorporation by signature	1
	Example or case	1
	Incorporation by notice	1
	Examples or cases	2
	Incorporation by previous dealing	1
	Application to situation	2
	Advice to Mina	1
		10
(b)	Contra proferentem rule	1
	Effect if liability limited in general terms	1
	UCTA 77 applies	1
	Never exclude liability for death or personal injury	1
	Clauses either void or valid if reasonable	1
	Effect of negligence	1
	Factors courts will consider	1
	Application to Mina's situation	2
	Unfair Terms in Consumer Contracts Regulations 1999	1
		10
		20

24   EXPRESS AND IMPLIED TERMS

Tutor's hint. In part (a), the answer is structured around the three places that terms can be implied from.

Structure is important when tackling the scenario question in part (b). Stating the current situation at the beginning will not only focus your answer, it will focus you on the important issues. The rest of the answer follows on logically from a consideration of UCTA 1977.

(a) **Implied terms**

There are occasions where certain terms are not expressly adopted by the parties, but may be implied from the context of the contract. Additional **terms** of a contract **may be implied by custom, statute or the courts.**

Terms implied by custom

The parties may be deemed to **enter into a contract subject to a custom** or practice of their trade.

In *Hutton v Warren*, the courts held that a farmer required to work a farm during his notice period was entitled to a fair allowance for seeds and labour as a matter of custom which also provided the fact that he should farm the land until the notice expired.

Any express term will override a term which might otherwise be implied by custom.

Terms implied by statute

Some terms are **implied by statute** and are **obligatory**. There are sometimes terms **implied by statute** which the **parties can choose to exclude** if they wish.

Terms implied by the courts

The court may conclude that **the parties intended certain terms to apply**. The parties may have failed to include them expressly in the contract because they were **taken for granted** or because they were **omitted in error**. In such circumstances the court may imply those terms into the contract to prevent the failure of the agreement and to implement the clear intention of the parties.

An example of this is *The Moorcock*, where the owners of a wharf agreed that a ship should be moored alongside to unload its cargo. The court held that it was an implied term that the ground alongside the wharf (which did not belong to the wharf owners) was safe at low tide since both parties knew that the ship must rest on it.

The concept of terms implied by the court can be summed up in an idea put forward in *Shirlaw v Southern Foundries* which is that it covers terms which, if parties were making an agreement and an eavesdropper suggested an express provision to include in the contract, they would say '**why should we put that in? That's obvious!**'

The court may also imply some terms in order to maintain a **certain standard of behaviour**, even though the parties may not have intended them to be included. For example, in *Liverpool City Council v Irwin*, the court decided that it was necessary to consider the obligations which 'the nature of the contract itself implicitly requires'. Tenants could only occupy the building with access to stairs and/or lifts, so terms needed to be implied on these matters including one that the landlord would keep these parts reasonably safe.

(b)

> **Tutor's hint**. As always, for this part of the question, identify the **issues**, **state** the law, **apply** the law and **conclude**.

BPP PROFESSIONAL EDUCATION

Memorandum

To: Barchester Council
From: Adviser
Date: 5.12.X0
Subject: Liability of Worldwide Computers plc

The current situation

Worldwide Computers plc has committed a breach of its contract with Barchester Council by installing defective software in the database facility. There is an exclusion clause in the contract which Worldwide Computers are seeking to rely on.

As the clause has been inserted by a business it falls within the scope of the Unfair Contract Terms Act 1977 (UCTA). Therefore the clause must be examined to see if the clause is valid in accordance with the act.

The Unfair Contract Terms Act 1977

UCTA limits the extent to which it is possible to exclude or restrict business liability. It relates to **businesses dealing with businesses**.

In order to be valid and enforceable, the exclusion clause relied upon by Worldwide Computers plc must satisfy the **test of reasonableness** laid down by UCTA. This says that the term must be fair and reasonable having regard to all the circumstances which were, or ought to have been, known to the parties at the time the contract was made.

The test of reasonableness

The burden of proof lies on the company, the party seeking to rely on the exclusion clause. The court may consider the following:

- The relative **strengths** of the **parties' bargaining positions**
- Whether any **inducement** was offered to accept the limitation
- Whether the **customer knew** (or ought to have known) **of the clause**
- Whether goods were made or adapted to the **purchaser's special order**.

This case is similar to *St. Albans City and District Council v International Computers Ltd.* In that case it was held that the limitation was very low in relation to the potential loss, that the parties were not of equal bargaining strengths and that it was unreasonable having regard to the company's insurance.

Effectiveness of the exclusion clause

The factors that were relevant in the St Albans case are relevant here. This implies that Barchester will not be bound by the liability clause because it is **unreasonable** in the light of all the facts: the potential loss, the strength of the bargaining parties and the level of Worldwide Computer's insurance cover.

Recovery of the loss

Barchester should be able to recover their loss in **damages,** which aim to place the injured party in the same position he would have been in if the contract had occurred. The general principle of damages is to **compensate for actual financial loss,** which in Barchester's case appears to be **£1.5 million.**

Conclusion

Barchester Council should not be bound by the exclusion clause which appears unreasonable. If they take action against Worldwide Computers for breach of contract, the court are likely to follow the precedent of the St Albans case and conclude that the exclusion clause is not valid.

In this case, Barchester should be able to claim damages in the sum of £1.5 million, being the loss sustained by Barchester.

25   PERFORMANCE

> **Tutor's hint**. This is a fairly standard style of question where in part (a) you are asked to explain the law and in part (b) you are asked to apply it. This is a question based on exceptions to a rule. You must state the rule, ie that performance must be complete and exact, and then run through the exceptions.
>
> Having stated the exceptions in part (a), try not to repeat yourself in part (b) but state which ones apply and why they apply. Draw a conclusion as to whether Andrew will have to pay or not.

(a) **Complete and exact**

The general rule is that a contract is discharged by performance only if all contractual obligations are performed **completely and exactly**.

A party who fails to perform perfectly is not entitled to claim payment or performance from the other party. Thus in *Cutter v Powell*, C was employed as second mate on a ship at a wage for the complete voyage. After his death, C's widow was unable to claim a part of the agreed wage since he died 19 days before the end of the voyage.

Exceptions

A number of **exceptions** to the complete and exact rule have been developed by the courts:

(i) **Substantial performance**. Where a party has completed the essential part of a contract but has left relatively minor work outstanding, he may be able to claim the contract price less a deduction for the unfinished work: *Sumpter v Hedges*.

Thus in *Hoenig v Isaacs*, the plaintiff was employed to decorate and furnish the defendant's flat for £750 and did so but there were defects in the furniture which could be remedied at a cost of £56. The defendant's argument that the plaintiff was entitled only to reasonable remuneration failed and he was required to pay the full sum less the £56 needed to remedy defects.

(ii) **Partial performance**. Where the promissor only partially fulfils his contractual obligations and the promise chooses to accept it, this will be sufficient to discharge the contract and the promissor will be entitled to payment for the extent of his partial performance.

(iii) **Prevention of performance**. Where the promise prevents performance, the offer or tender of performance by the promissor will be sufficient, provided the tender is precise (and, where it is an obligation to pay money, the correct amount is paid into court in order to show a continuing willingness to perform).

If the promissor is prevented by the promise from performing, he may sue for damages for breach of contract or bring a **quantum meruit** claim for the amount of work done. Thus in *Planche v Colburn*, where the defendant abandoned a commission after part of it had been completed by the plaintiff, the plaintiff was entitled to a quantum meruit.

(iv) **Time not of the essence**. 'Time is of the essence' may be an express provision or it may be implied, for example in a commercial contract (other than where the performance required is payment of money).

(v) **Severable contracts**. Where the contract provides for performance by instalments with separate payments for each, it is said to be severable or **divisible** and performance of some will entitle the promissor to payment for

each. Thus in *Taylor v Laird,* where the plaintiff agreed to captain a ship at a rate of £50 per month but abandoned the job before it was completed, he was entitled to £50 for each completed month.

(b) **Andrew**

Applying the basic rule means that Builder Ltd's contractual obligations can only be discharged once complete and exact performance has taken place. This would require completion of the entire extension to Andrew's house.

Exceptions

There are exceptions to this rule. In this case the contract is not severable, no issue of whether delayed performance is still within the contract arises and there is no question of Andrew preventing performance by Builder Ltd.

Builder Ltd is likely to claim that it has substantially performed the contract and is therefore entitled to £12,000 as a fair proportion of the original contract price.

Substantial performance

In *Sumpter v Hedges,* the plaintiff agreed to build on the defendant's land for £565. After completing work to the value of £333 he abandoned the works. The defendant completed the works using materials left behind by the plaintiff.

It was held that the defendant should pay for the materials since he had elected to use them but he was not required to pay for the work that had been done. The contract had not been substantially performed.

Partial performance

In this case it seems unlikely that building an extension with no roof would be regarded as substantial performance. Andrew was not in a position to choose whether to accept or reject the partial performance. Even in *Sumpter v Hedges,* where the defendant used the builder's materials to complete the work, it was said that although this appeared to be an acceptance of the plaintiff's work, this was meaningless since he had no way of rejecting it.

Conclusion

Thus this seems not to be a case of substantial performance but of **partial performance with no acceptance.** As in *Sumpter v Hedges* there would appear to be no obligation on Andrew's part to pay the sum demanded in respect of the work.

26   TERMINATION OF CONTRACTS

Tutorial note. At the time when this question was set in a real exam, it was not altogether clear whether performance of a contract was included on the syllabus, hence the disappointing performance (excuse the pun) of candidates in the exam (see Examiner's comments below). If this happens again in any area and you are faced with a subject which has not been covered in detail in your study materials, our advice is not to choose that question. However, do not panic! This paper was the first sitting of a new syllabus and the examiner has clarified the syllabus. Such a problem should not happen again.

Examiner's comments. Although this question was a popular option, less than half of the candidates who attempted it scored a pass mark. The major problem appeared to be with part (a) of the question on performance. As outlined above, this was due to uncertainty over the scope of the syllabus, which has now been resolved. A small number dealt with the issues of part performance. Part (b) was dealt with most successfully by candidates. Most discussed breach and all the possible remedies. The good answers discussed the claimant's options when a breach is anticipated.

(a) **Discharge by performance**

The general rule is that a contract is discharged by performance only if all contractual obligations are performed completely and exactly. A party who fails to perform perfectly is not entitled to claim payment or performance from the other party.

Thus in *Cutter v Powell*, C was employed as second mate on a ship at a wage for the complete voyage. After his death, C's widow was unable to claim a part of the agreed wage since he died 19 days before the end of the voyage.

Similarly, in *Bolton v Mahadeva*, the defendant installed a central heating system in the plaintiff's house that failed to heat adequately and gave off fumes and was held not to be entitled to claim any part of the contract sum.

Exceptions to the rule

A number of exceptions to this rule have been developed by the courts (in an attempt to ensure that one party does not profit to an undue degree by taking substantial benefit from an incomplete performance by the other party):

(i) **Substantial performance**: where a party has completed the essential and major part of a contract but has left relatively minor work outstanding, he may be able to claim the contract price less a deduction for the unfinished or defective work (*Sumpter v Hedges*). Thus in *Hoenig v Isaacs*, the plaintiff was employed to decorate and furnish the defendant's flat for £750 and did so but there were defects in the furniture which could be remedied at a cost of £56. The defendant's argument that the plaintiff was entitled only to reasonable remuneration failed and he was required to pay the full sum less the £56 needed to remedy defects.

(ii) **Partial performance**: where the promisor only partially fulfils his contractual obligations and the promisee, having the choice of either accepting or rejecting such partial performance, chooses to accept it, then partial performance will be sufficient to discharge the contract and the promisor will be entitled to payment for the extent of his partial performance.

(iii) **Severable (or divisible) contracts**: where the contract provides for performance by instalments with separate payments for each of them, it is said to be severable or divisible and performance of some but not all of the instalments will entitle the promisor to payment for each of them. Thus in *Taylor v Laird*, where the plaintiff agreed to captain a ship at a rate of £50 per month but abandoned the job before it was completed, he was held to be entitled to £50 in respect of each completed month.

(iv) **Prevention of performance**: If the promisor is prevented by the promisee from performing his contractual obligations completely, he may sue for damages for breach of contract or bring a quantum meruit claim for the amount of work done (*Planché v Colburn*).

(b) **Anticipatory breach**

An anticipatory breach is a breach of contract which occurs before the due date for performance of the contract. It may be either express or implied. An express anticipatory breach occurs where one party declares that he has no intention of complying with the terms of the agreement.

Thus in *Hochster v De la Tour*, the defendant cancelled a trip for which he had already engaged the plaintiff as a courier, before the trip was due to take place. It was held that the plaintiff was entitled to sue as soon as the anticipatory breach occurred (that is, when he was told he was no longer required) and there was no need to wait until the time for performance of the contract.

Anticipatory breach may be implied from the circumstances, for example where one party does something which makes subsequent performance of the contract impossible.

When an anticipatory breach occurs, the innocent party may treat the contract as discharged immediately and sue for damages or he can elect to affirm the contract but must then wait until the due date for performance before he can sue for breach. In these circumstances, he is entitled to continue to prepare for performance and recover the agreed price for his services (contrary to the normal duty to mitigate losses).

It was made clear in *White & Carter (Councils) v McGregor* that repudiation does not of itself bring the contract to an end but it merely gives the innocent party the option of affirming or rejecting it.

However, by allowing the contract to continue, the innocent party runs the risk of the contract being frustrated (or discharged for some other reason) and thus of losing his rights to sue in respect of the anticipatory breach.

Marking Guide		*Marks*
(a)	General rule of complete performance	1
	Case or example	1
	Exceptions (1 mark each: max. 3)	3
		5
(b)	Definition of anticipatory breach	1
	Case or example	1
	Express or implied	1
	Options of innocent party	1
	Case or example	1
		5
		10

27   BREACH

Tutor's hint. This question asks you to define breach of contract and explain the results of it. It also asks you to cover anticipatory breach – so make sure you do!

A party is said to be in breach of contract where he fails to perform his contractual obligations precisely and where there is no lawful excuse for non-performance.

In the event of a breach of contract, the party not in breach may, in certain circumstances, treat the contract as discharged and, in all cases, may sue for damages.

Anticipatory breach

Breach of contract normally becomes apparent at or following the time for performance under the contract. Anticipatory breach, on the other hand, **occurs before the due time of performance** and may be express or implied.

Thus, for example, anticipatory breach occurs where one party declares that he will not perform the contract when the appointed time arrives (*Hochster v de la Tour*). It also occurs when a party renders himself unable to perform the contract at the appointed time, for instance by selling specific contract goods to a third party before the date of delivery under the contract.

Actions of the injured party

In the event of anticipatory breach, the injured party **may treat an anticipatory breach as if the breach had already occurred** and sue for breach of contract form that date without having to wait until the actual date of performance under the contract.

The injured party **may allow the contract to continue and not treat it as discharged**. However, the party in anticipatory breach may subsequently change his mind and perform his part of the contract after all.

If the injured party permits the contract to continue and incurs expense by preparing to perform it, he **may recover the agreed price for his services** (*White & Carter (Councils) Ltd v McGregor*). Thus **anticipatory breach does not of itself bring the contract to an end** but simply **gives the innocent party the choice of affirmation or rejection** and the normal duty to mitigate losses does not apply.

28 DAMAGES

> **Tutor's hint.** The rule in *Hadley v Baxendale* is central to part (a). In part (b), you might have considered mitigation of losses, liquidated and unliquidated damages, and damages for injured feelings. We also discuss 'expectation' and 'reliance' interest.
>
> **Marking guide.** The two parts of the question each attract the same number of marks. You cannot earn a good mark for the question without tackling both parts. Marks are available both for definitions of the two terms and then a description of the rules, supported by cases wherever possible.

Damages are a common law remedy primarily intended to restore the person who has suffered loss to the **same position he would have been in had the contract been performed**. Where there is no contractual provision for **liquidated damages**, the courts will determine the damages payable with reference to the following factors: the **remoteness of damage** and the **measure of damages**.

(a) **Remoteness of damage.** With regard to remoteness, the courts are considering how far down the chain of cause and effect the consequences of breach should be traced before they become so remote that no compensation should be awarded in respect of them.

First, damages may be awarded only in respect of **losses which arise naturally** from the breach or losses which arise in a manner which the parties may reasonably be deemed to have **contemplated as the probable result** of breach of contract. Secondly, if the resulting loss is of an **unusual** type, that is, outside the natural course of events, it may be claimed only if the **defendant was aware** of the circumstances which might give rise to that abnormal loss. This two-part ruling was established in *Hadley v Baxendale*.

Both parts of the rule are concerned with **what the defendant must have known**. Under the first head of the rule, he is deemed to accept any normal consequence which might be expected. Under the second head, if the consequence of his breach is abnormal, he is liable only if he knew of the special circumstances from which the abnormal consequence of breach could arise. The application of the rule is illustrated by *Victoria Laundry v Newman Industries*.

(b) **Measure of damages.** Damages are intended to restore the wronged party to the position he would have been in if the contract had been performed, but not to put him in a better or more profitable position. This is sometimes referred to as protecting the **expectation interest** of the claimant. A claimant may alternatively seek to have his **reliance interest** protected; this refers to the position he would have been in had he not relied on the contract. Because they compensate for wasted expenditure, damages for reliance loss cannot be awarded if they would put the claimant in a better position than he would attain under protection of his expectation interest.

Measurement of financial loss may be made with reference to the **available market rule**. Thus if a buyer refuses to take delivery of goods which he has contracted to buy, and the seller sues for loss of profit on the transaction, the existence of a market in which there is an excess of supply over demand will lead to a successful claim (as in *Thompson Ltd v Robinson (Gunmaker) Ltd*), whereas if there is an excess of demand over supply, only nominal damages will be payable (*Charter v Sullivan*).

The amount of damages payable is usually quantified as a **financial loss**, based on the actual loss suffered, although some types of **non-financial loss** are recoverable, for example personal injuries or distress caused by a holiday failing to match the brochure's promises (*Jarvis v Swan Tours*).

The claimant must take reasonable steps to **mitigate** his loss or he may not receive his full losses (*Payzu v Saunders*). This means that he must take reasonable steps to put himself in as good a position as if the contract had been performed. For example, where goods are not delivered the buyer must take steps to buy the same goods from elsewhere as cheaply as possible. He does not have to take discreditable or risky measures to mitigate his loss (*Pilkington v Wood*).

The parties to a contract may seek to avoid complicated calculations of loss and disputes as to damages by providing a **formula for the calculation of damages** in the contract itself, for example a daily rate of payment in the event of late completion. A **liquidated damages clause** will be upheld by the court, provided it is a genuine attempt to anticipate the appropriate level of damages (*Ford Motor Co (England) Ltd v Armstrong*). Any term which amounts to a **penalty clause** will be void.

In determining whether the clause in question is a penalty clause or a liquidated damages provision the courts will look to see if the cause represents a **genuine pre-estimate of loss** (*Dunlop Pneumatic Tyre Co Ltd v New Garage & Motor Co Ltd*). If so, the clause will be upheld, even if the actual loss is greater or smaller.

29 EMMA AND SIDNEY

> **Tutor's hint**. The topic of remedies for breach comes right at the end of your studies of contract law, but this does not mean that it is unimportant. The examiner has said that 'this topic is of great importance both in the law of contract as a whole and for the parties involved in a breach of contract. Candidates should be urged not to neglect this topic in the future'. Remember the approach to questions like this: identify the **issues**, **state** the law, **apply** the law and then **conclude**.

(a) There is a clear breach of contract by Sidney in his use of paint not containing lead in some of Emma's offices. As a result, Emma may sue for and recover damages for breach from Sidney.

The type and **measure of damages** awarded by the court will be such as are intended to restore the party who has suffered loss to the same position as he or she would have been in if the contract had been properly performed and no breach had occurred. Damages will not be punitive nor put the injured party in a better position than he or she would have been in the event of there being no breach.

It is a fundamental principle in the law relating to damages that damage or loss which is considered to be too **remote** cannot be recovered. This is concerned with the type of

damage which can be claimed for. Furthermore, the court will assess the **measure** of damages, for which the principle of law is **restitutio in integrum**.

With regard to remoteness of damage, the case of *Hadley v Baxendale* established that damages may only be awarded in respect of losses which arise naturally, in the usual course of things, from the breach and/or losses which arise in a manner which would have been in the reasonable contemplation of the parties at the time the contract was made as a probable consequence of the breach. In that case, the claimant was not entitled to damages for loss of profits which arose as a result of a delay in the repair of some equipment needed to operate his business.

In *Victoria Laundry (Windsor) v Newman Industries*, failure to deliver certain goods to the claimant meant that he lost ordinary business profits and additional profits from another contract which, as a result, he was prevented from entering into. The defendant was not aware of the second contract. The claimant was entitled to recover for loss of normal earnings, but not the additional profits.

Unlike in *Hadley v Baxendale*, the loss of ordinary profits in *Victoria Laundry* was the inevitable result of the breach of the supply contract. In the *Hadley* case, it was not reasonably foreseeable that the claimant's business would be closed until the repair was carried out - it was not a natural consequence of the breach.

It follows that a loss **outside** the normal course of events may only be recovered if the exceptional circumstances surrounding the loss are within the defaulting party's **actual or constructive knowledge.**

Sidney and Emma

Emma is claiming financial loss, ie loss of earnings arising as a result of her illness caused by an allergic reaction to lead. Sidney was not aware of her allergy, nor can it be said to be a probable consequence of the breach which ought reasonably to have been in the contemplation of both parties at the time of the contract was made. Clearly it was not something which would arise in the normal course of events either. As a result, a court is liable to consider that Emma's loss of earnings is too remote (for an award of damages to be made in respect of it).

(b) Specific performance is an equitable remedy, entirely within the discretion of the court, which may be awarded where the common law remedy of damages is inadequate or inappropriate (such as where there has been a breach of a contract to supply land or goods which are unique).

The court is unlikely to grant an order of specific performance where performance is required to be made over a period of time and the court is unable to supervise or ensure that the defendant complies fully with the order. A court is, therefore, unlikely to order specific performance of a contract of employment or personal services or a contract for services such as building works. The court will make exceptions in this latter instance where, for example, the redecoration work required is clearly defined, the claimant is in possession of the relevant land and where damages would be inadequate.

Sidney and Emma

In this case there has been a clear breach of contract in Sidney's failure to prepare the woodwork properly, and Emma is entitled to claim for damages as a result of that breach. It does not appear that this remedy of damages is in any way inappropriate or inadequate, those criteria applied by the courts. The court would be unlikely to order specific performance because of its inability to supervise due performance. Consequently, Emma would appear to be restricted to her remedy in damages which could include a sum in respect of her losses in needing to contract with another decorator to re-do the work.

30   RIGHTS OF AN AGENT

> **Tutor's hint**. In this straightforward question, deal with each of the agent's rights briefly, in turn.

Brian should be made aware that an agent has certain rights against his or her principal.

Expenses

The agent is entitled to **repayment of expenses and an indemnity against losses** and liabilities incurred in the course of his duties.

Expenses properly incurred may be recovered even if the agent was not legally bound to pay them. The indemnity operates only against those expenses incurred when the agent is acting within the scope of his authority. His entitlement will be lost if he acts in an unauthorised manner or negligently.

Remuneration

The agent is also entitled to any **agreed remuneration** for his services. This may have been agreed expressly or by implication (eg by trade or professional practice). If the amount of the remuneration has not been fixed the agent is entitled to a reasonable amount.

Commissions

There are special considerations where the agent is appointed to carry out a task and is to be paid by commission. This is particularly relevant to estate agents. As a general rule, it is considered that the commission is payable only on an actual sale of property to a person introduced by the agent. The principal is free to withdraw from the contract as there is no implied term that he will not prevent the agent from earning his commission.

If the principal has agreed to pay a fee on the introduction of a purchaser, then it is a question of construction as to whether the fee has been earned. If the purchaser introduced enters into a contract and does not withdraw his offer at any stage, then this is likely to earn the agent his fee. Anything less (for example, even an unconditional offer) is unlikely to amount to fulfilment of the condition.

31   TYPES OF AUTHORITY

> **Tutor's hint**. This was another reasonably straightforward 'explain' requirement, although some students find the authority of the agent a tricky area. When faced with a question with three parts of (nearly) equal marks, make sure that you read through the question and are confident that you can gain at least some marks in all the parts. If you had looked at part (a) of this question and thought 'express authority – that's easy' but not been able to answers parts (b) and (c), even if you had scored full marks on part (a), you would have failed the question. If you had been able to write even a one line definition for both parts (b) and (c), you might have been able to pick up enough marks (2 or more) to get a pass on this question. This illustrates the importance of reading through and getting to grips with the key terms and definitions given in the Study Text. You can then build on your understanding of these by seeing the law in practice – in the case examples given in the Text.
>
> **Examiner's comments**. Candidates generally did not do well on this question, possibly because agency was a new topic in the syllabus at the time the question was set. However many candidates did not seem to have grasped the essential principles, especially of implied authority.
>
> Many candidates failed to answer part (c) of the question despite the fact that it was worth 4 marks. The candidates who did attempt part (c) often repeated material that they already produced for part (a).

Authority of an agent

As a general rule, in order to be valid and binding on the principal and third party, a contract entered into by an agent must be entered into within the bounds of the agent's authority. However, that authority need not be express for the contract entered into by the agent to bind the principal. It may be implied actual authority or apparent authority.

Agency may also arise by operation of law, most significantly agency of necessity, resulting in the principal being bound by a contract entered into by the agent. There are also a number of very specific circumstances where an agent can bind his principal without express authority as a consequence of statutory provisions (for example, Disposal of Uncollected Goods Act 1952).

(a) **Express authority**

Express authority is the extent of authority which it is agreed (between the principal and agent) the agent shall have to enter into contracts on the principal's behalf. The precise scope and extent of 'express actual authority' will depend on the proper construction of the written document in which the appointment or conferring of authority is contained or on the evidence supporting an oral giving of actual express authority. If the agent acts outside his express authority, he will be liable to the principal for breach of contract and to the third party for breach of warranty of authority.

(b) **Implied authority**

Actual authority may be implied rather than express:

(i) **'Implied incidental authority'** will be deemed to exist where it is reasonable to suppose that the principal also gave the agent authority to enter into transactions which are necessarily incidental or subordinate to the matter of the express authority, for example, the authority to advertise goods when the agent is expressly authorised to sell them.

(ii) **'Implied customary authority'** is that which an agent shall be deemed to have by reason of his operating in a particular market or business, for example an estate agent may have implied authority to show potential buyers round a house.

(iii) **'Implied usual authority'** is that which an agent shall be deemed to have by reason of his occupying a particular position or engaging in a particular trade.

In cases of implied actual authority, the third party who contracts with the agent is entitled to assume that the agent has implied authority unless he knows to the contrary.

In *Watteau v Fenwick*, the principal was held to be bound by a contract entered into by his agent with implied usual authority (as a hotel manager, he bought cigars on credit) even though the third party did not know that the agent, as the other contracting party, was the agent of the principal. As between the agent and the principal, however, the agent is not entitled to contravene the principal's express authority or instructions by claiming implied authority.

(c) **Apparent authority**

'Apparent' or 'ostensible' authority is that which the principal represents to other parties he has given to his agent. Although matters of apparent authority and implied usual authority often appear to be co-extensive, it is the conduct of the principal (expressly or by inference) which creates apparent authority. It also arises where the principal is aware that an agent is claiming to be his appointed agent and yet does nothing to correct that impression. In either case, the principal will be bound by the actions of the ostensible agent.

In *Freeman & Lockyer v Buckhurst Park Properties (Mangal) Ltd*, a company was bound by the acts of one of its directors who acted like a managing director even though he had not been appointed formally to that position. By its mere acquiescence, the company had led the third party to believe that he was the managing director and the third party had relied on that impression.

There need not be a pre-existing agency relationship. Apparent or ostensible authority (or 'agency by estoppel') requires a representation which is relied upon thereby causing an alteration in the position of the representee. The representation may be express or implied from previous dealings or implied from conduct.

Where the principal has subsequently revoked an agent's authority, he will continue to be bound by acts entered into by that agent within his former authority with third parties who dealt with him previously, until he informs those third parties that the agent is no longer so authorised (*Willis Faber and Co Ltd v Joyce*).

The representation must be made either by the principal or by another agent acting on his behalf (*Armagas Ltd v Mundogas SA, The Ocean Frost*) but not by the agent claiming to have the authority. It must be one of fact and not of law and it must be made to the third party. If the third party knew that the agent had no authority or did not believe him to have, he cannot claim agency by estoppel. Unless the alteration of position also causes damage or detriment, any damages awarded will be nominal although, strictly speaking, it is not necessary to show that reliance resulted in such damage or detriment.

Marking Guide		
		Marks
(a) Definition of express authority		1
Depends on terms of agency agreement		1
Breach of warranty of authority		1
		3
(b) Implied incidental authority		1
Implied customary authority		1
Implied usual authority		1
		3
(c) Explanation		1
Case or example		1
Agency by estoppel requirements		2
		4
Total		10

32 FREDERICK AND GEORGE

> **Tutor's hint**. Each of the situations in this question relates in some way to an agent not complying with his principal's instructions. It is a good idea when answering such questions to set out the common principles first before proceeding to analyse each of the particular situations. This follows our suggested approach of: identify the **issues, state** the law, **apply** the law and then **conclude**.

Authority

An agent is a person authorised to make a contract between his principal and a third party. For this purpose the agent has authority from his principal which may be actual or apparent (also called ostensible authority). In determining how much authority of either kind is given to an agent much depends on what is usual.

If, for example, the principal employs a business agent, such as a stockbroker, a bank, a solicitor or an estate agent to make a contract for him, he gives him actual authority to do on his behalf what it is **usual** for such an agent to do for his clients.

Apparent authority

Anyone dealing with such an agent is entitled to assume, unless he has notice to the contrary, that the agent has authority of the usual kind. This is the agent's apparent authority as perceived by the person with whom he deals.

A principal may restrict the actual authority of his agent by giving him appropriate instructions but in doing so he does not restrict apparent authority unless notice has been given to those who deal with the agent that his (apparent) authority has been reduced to less than normal: *Watteau v Fenwick*.

Merely entrusting the goods to another person to sell implies that the agent is authorised to sell at or above a stipulated but undisclosed price. It is not in any way a representation that the agent may sell at a particular price, if that price is less than the undisclosed minimum fixed by the principal. The agent has no apparent authority in excess of his actual authority.

(a) **Sale at £450**

On the facts given the purchaser from George does not know what is the limit set on George's authority (not to sell for less than £500) but he should anticipate that there is a limit and he has no obvious grounds for claiming that George is authorised to sell at a price below his actual authority. On that basis the sale is void since it is made without actual or apparent authority.

The purchaser will have to give up the computer (or pay the extra £50) and his remedy is against George for breach of warranty of authority.

However a sale of ten computers is more than a normal private agency transaction. The mere size of the consignment suggests that George carries on a business of selling computers (and perhaps other articles).

If George is in business with Frederick selling computers, it would appear to the third party that George has authority to sell them at an agreed price.

Therefore, Frederick will be bound by the contract as he has not expressly communicated the price restriction on George's authority.

(b) **Sale to agent himself**

It is an implied duty of an agent not to secure any profit from his position as agent except such as is disclosed to and approved by his principal. He is also prohibited from engaging in any transaction, unless it is similarly disclosed and approved, in which the agent's personal interest is in conflict with the principal's interest.

For this reason an agent may not, without the knowledge and consent of his principal, buy the goods of the principal delivered to the agent for a sale even though he pays the full market price.

Frederick has no remedy against Harry who is an innocent purchaser for value from George. The sale to Harry must stand. But Frederick may recover from George his undisclosed profit of £50, terminate his position as agent and withhold any commission to which George is normally entitled for his services as agent.

(c) **Sale with commission**

The question does not state whether the commission of £50 is paid before the sale to Jonathan as an inducement to George to make the sale to Jonathan, or whether it is

simply a payment made after the sale without any prior arrangement for it between George and Jonathan.

If it is the latter case George owes a duty to disclose to Frederick that George has obtained this payment for which he is accountable to Frederick, unless after disclosure Frederick agrees that George may keep it. This is the position even though George has obtained for Frederick a higher price than Frederick prescribed as a minimum, so that Frederick has already benefited by receiving an extra £50 from the sale in excess of his expectations.

Bribe

If on the other hand the £50 commission is paid to George by Jonathan as a corrupt inducement – a bribe – Frederick may dismiss George from his position as agent and recover the £50 from him: *Boston Deep Sea Fishing & Ice Co v Ansell*.

Frederick may also sue Jonathan to recover from Jonathan damages for a £50 loss. Frederick would argue that if Jonathan had not paid £50 commission to George, Jonathan would have been willing to pay the whole £600 (which is the real cost to Jonathan of the purchase) to Frederick.

In this answer, we set out the law to start with, and then apply it to each of the situations in the question. This marking guide includes the relevant points of law in the parts of the answer.

Marking guide

		Marks	
(a)	Explanation of apparent authority	2	
	Illustration or case	1	
	If purchaser aware no apparent/actual authority: void	1	
	Size of consignment a factor?	1	
	Apparent authority may be valid	1	
	Frederick bound	1	
			7
(b)	Implied duty not to make a secret profit	2	
	Agent must disclose conflicts of interest	1	
	Sale to Harry is valid	1	
	Frederick can recover from George	1	
	Agency can be terminated	1	
			6
(c)	Issue of uncertainty of when commission paid	1	
	If post sale, George has duty to disclose	1	
	Unless Frederick agrees	1	
	Even though price is higher	1	
	If a bribe: agent can be dismissed	1	
	Case or illustration	1	
	Recovery from Jonathan also possible	1	
			7
			20

33   PREPARATION QUESTION: PERSONALITY AND PARTNERSHIPS

> **Tutor's hint.** Make sure that you can write equally confidently about partnerships and companies.
>
> The answer to (a) starts off by defining companies and partnerships, and then discusses the main issue of the question, the concept of separate legal entity. After that it goes on to talk about the main consequences of being a separate legal entity. Note that (a) is a **point-by-point comparison** of companies and partnerships; this is the best way to answer a comparison question, rather than spending the first half of the answer discussing limited companies and the second discussing partnerships.
>
> In (b) there is a danger of using material that you have already used in (a). What you should have done is concentrate on the **legal aspects** in (a) and the **practical implications** of these in (b). You may need to cross-refer to the other part as we have done briefly in (b). It is also important that you include a similar number of points in both parts because the marks for each part are virtually the same.
>
> You are likely to be given a couple of marks in (b) for indicating the importance of the advantages and disadvantages discussed.
>
> *Other points.* This question does not ask for a detailed discussion of **limited liability partnerships** but you need to be aware of the law relating to limited liability partnerships, since it is now possible to conduct business in this way.

(a)   **Definition**

A **registered company** is a concern which is incorporated and registered under the **Companies Act 1985**.

A partnership is a relationship which subsists between persons carrying on a business **in common** with a view of **profit**. A company need not be carrying on a business (it could be dormant or just exist to hold assets). In addition some companies limited by guarantee do not exist to make profits for their members.

Legal personality

A company is a distinct **legal entity,** meaning that a company is distinct as a separate legal person from its owners or members. Hence a **'veil' of incorporation** exists between them. This distinction between a company and its members was first established in *Salomon v Salomon and Co Ltd.* Since then it has been developed in both case law and statute. The **assets, rights and liabilities** associated with a company's business belong to the company itself and not to the members: *Macaura v Northern Assurance Co Ltd.*

Partnerships, other than limited liability partnerships, are **not separate legal entities**. In a partnership, the partners agree on the joint ownership and use of partnership property and property owned by individual partners but used by the partnership.

Written constitution

A registered company always has a written constitution comprising a **memorandum** and **articles** of association.

A partnership can exist with **no express agreement** or constitution. It will arise where there is the necessary relation between persons. If a partnership has a **written partnership agreement,** it serves to fill in any details which are not implied by law (notably the **Partnership Act 1890**). It may also specifically override any terms which would otherwise be implied by statute.

Formation

To incorporate a company, certain specified documents should be prepared and delivered to the Companies Registry to obtain **registration**. Once these have been checked and found to be in order by the Registrar, a **certificate of incorporation** is issued. This is conclusive evidence that the formalities of registration have been complied with.

A partnership is formed when the partners **enter** into the **relationship** of partnership. In doing this they are agreeing to act in a way which establishes the partnership from that time. There are no required formalities and registration procedure.

Liability

For a limited liability company the principle of independent legal personality is particularly apparent in the area of **liability** for company debts. If the company becomes insolvent, the shareholders are **not liable** for the company's debts. They are liable only to the company for that **amount**, if any, which remains **unpaid** on their shares.

In contrast, a partner (other than a partner in a limited liability partnership) has **unlimited liability** for all the debts of the firm and could lose all his or her personal assets.

Changes in membership

Perpetual succession applies in the case of companies, there is no cessation brought about by a change in the membership.

Any change of partners in a partnership operates as a **termination** of the old partnership and the beginning of a new one. In practice, a **partnership agreement** will often provide that for so long as there are two or more surviving partners, on the death of one partner the partnership shall continue between them.

Winding up

A company is 'dissolved' by **liquidation**, which has to follow a precise procedure and must be conducted by a licensed insolvency practitioner.

Dissolution of the partnership can be effected by the agreement of the partners or according to the terms of the partnership agreement. There are no specified rules governing how dissolution must be done.

(b)   The choice of whether to set up a company or a partnership may be affected by some or all of the following factors.

Limited liability

As noted above, the liability of a member of a limited company is **limited** to the amount unpaid on the shares held.

The liability of a partner is **unlimited** and can extend to the whole of his personal wealth. Under the principle of **joint and several liability**, he may also be responsible for the acts and defaults of his fellow partners. A creditor can sue any, or all, of the partners until his debt has been satisfied. Partners remain liable for debts incurred during their period as partners even after leaving the partnership.

Formalities of establishment and operation

Companies are subject to the many **rules and regulations** contained in the Companies Acts.

A partnership can exist with **no written formalities** or constitution and partners can decide informally how the partnership is going to operate.

Privacy

A company must **file annual accounts** and **returns** and many other notices to the registrar of companies. It must keep available for inspection a number of **statutory registers**.

A partnership need only **declare** the **names** of its partners on its business documentation.

Involvement in management

The management of a company is undertaken by **directors**. **Members** (who are not also directors) will not be involved in the day to day running of the business.

In a partnership, subject to anything contained in the partnership agreement, **every partner** is entitled to participate in the **management** of the business. Every partner is treated as an **agent** of the firm and his other partners. Thus all acts carried out by him in the usual course of the firm's business will bind the firm and his partners.

Transferability of interest

Subject to any restrictions imposed by the company's constitution, a company member's shares constitute a form of **property** and are transferable to another person who thus becomes a member of the company.

Although a partner can **assign** his **interest**, the assignee of it will not as a result become a partner in the partnership.

Raising finance

A company may be helped when raising finance by being able to provide **security** by way of a **floating charge** over its assets. However a company is able to **borrow** only for the **purpose(s)** set out in its memorandum of association.

Partnerships may find it more difficult to raise finance than companies. A partnership is **not able** to grant a **floating charge**. A partnership can however **mortgage** the firm's assets for the purpose of borrowing, and its ability to borrow is not necessarily limited by the partnership agreement.

34 FRAN, GAIL, HANNAH AND IAN

> **Tutorial note.** This was a straightforward question on the benefits and disadvantages of incorporation, which scarcely needed a scenario attached to it. However, bear in mind that you might get a similar question in the exam, in which specific requirements of the parties are given. You will need to incorporate such factors into your answer. Read through the examiner's comments below, as he gives useful guidance on how to approach questions like this.
>
> **Examiner's comments.** Many candidates limited their options in answering this question by merely setting out in point form the advantages and disadvantages of trading as a partnership or a limited company. They did not make the necessary comparisons between the two or discuss the relative merits. This meant that many candidates were repetitive in their answers. More thought and planning would have enabled candidates to apply their knowledge in this area, thus gaining more marks.
>
> In this type of question the best approach would be:
>
> (a) Describe partnership and company status.
>
> (b) Identify the key headings which would enable you to deal with the points in a logical and cohesive manner, for example 'limited liability' or 'personal risk'. Under each heading explain and apply the relevant points.
>
> (c) Apply the points identified to the specific situation in the question, dealing with each of the parties in turn.

Advantages of incorporation

There are a number of advantages offered by incorporating the business into a private limited company:

(a) **Legal entity**: Probably the most important factor which distinguishes a company from other forms of organisation is that a company is a distinct legal entity separate from its members whereas in a partnership there is no separate legal person as distinct from the partners. This means that the assets and liabilities of the business belong to the company itself.

(b) **Limited liability**: If the company becomes insolvent, the shareholders are not liable for the company's debts which belong to the company. They are liable only to the company for that amount, if any, which remains unpaid on their shares. In contrast, a partner is normally jointly and severally liable for all the debts of the firm to the extent of his or her personal wealth. (However, directors of private companies are often required to give personal guarantees to lenders so the distinction is not always so great.)

(c) **Perpetual succession**: In the case of companies, there is no cessation brought about by a change in the membership, but any change of partners in a partnership (by death, bankruptcy or resignation) operates as a termination of the old partnership and the beginning of a new one. In practice, a partnership agreement will often provide that for so long as there are two or more surviving partners on the death of one partner the partnership shall continue between them. Dissolution of the partnership can be effected by the agreement of the partners or according to the terms of the partnership agreement. A company is 'dissolved' by liquidation.

(d) **Transferability**: Subject to any restrictions imposed by the company's constitution, a company member's shares constitute a form of property and are freely transferable. Although a partner can assign his interest, the assignee of it will not as a result become a partner in the partnership (whereas a transferee of a member's shares thereby becomes a member of the company).

(e) **Capital and security**: A company may find it easier to raise capital for the expansion of the business than a partnership since the liability of potential investors is limited as described above and a company can borrow by debentures and loan stock. Furthermore, a company can raise capital by providing a fixed or floating charge as security but a partnership cannot provide security by way of a floating charge. There are, for the benefit of shareholders, various rules and regulations, contained in the Companies Act and the company's constitution, which are stringently applied relating to the reduction or distribution of a company's capital whereas in the case of a partnership partners may, by mutual agreement, withdraw capital from the partnership as they wish

Application

Fran, Gail, Hannah and Ian should also consider the advantages offered by incorporating their business as a partnership. Generally speaking, the formalities and regulation concerning the formation and running of companies are greater than those concerning partnerships. A partnership requires no formal documentation and simply comes into existence wherever persons are carrying on a business together with a view to making a profit. A company, on the other hand, is required to submit prescribed documents to the Registrar of Companies. However, in practice, business partners are advised to enter into a formal written agreement.

Once established, a company also has to comply with a number of statutory requirements concerning the calling and conduct at company meetings, the submission of returns and annual accounts and restrictions on reduction of capital and alteration of capital structure.

A partnership is not subject to any such regulation. However, it should be noted that there has been considerable deregulation of the activities of private companies, particularly smaller ones, in recent years.

A private company may be formed and operated with only a single member and there has been simplification of the requirements of company meetings with the introduction of elective resolutions and written resolutions. Companies whose turnover is below a certain threshold may take advantage of various audit exemptions.

Conclusion

In conclusion, it might appear preferable for these four workers to incorporate their business as a private limited company, taking advantage of the lesser regulations for small companies and the significant benefits of the business being a separate legal entity offering them limited liability.

Marking Guide

	Marks
Separate legal personality	2
Contrast with partnership	1
Limited liability	2
Contrast with partnership	1
Perpetual succession	1
Contrast with partnership	1
Transferability of interest	2
Contrast with partnership	2
Capital	2
Security	1
Statutory requirements for companies: examples	2
Easier for smaller companies	1
Conclusion: advice	2
Total	20

35 UNLIMITED AND LIMITED PARTNERSHIPS

> **Tutor's hint.** This is a straightforward factual question and is nicely broken down so that you should be able to gain good marks on each part. Notice that part (c) is asking specifically about limited liability partnerships, so you should restrict your answer to consideration of those.
>
> There is half a mark available for each right or duty in a question like this, so you should aim to think of at least four of each. Try to think of a similar number of each, to demonstrate the breadth of your knowledge. In part (b) there are two marks for an explanation of apparent authority and a further mark for an example. In part (c) assume a mark and a half for each of the two requirements.

(a) Unlimited partnerships are governed by the **Partnership Act 1890,** which sets out the basic rights and duties of the partners. However, a partnership can (and usually does) implement its own partnership agreement, which can overrule some or all of the provisions of the Act. The key rights and duties of partners are these:

Rights

- To be involved in decision making which affects the business
- To share equally in the profits
- To examine the partnership accounts
- To expect openness and honesty from the other partners
- To veto the admission of new partners

Duties

- To share in any losses
- To show the utmost good faith to fellow partners
- To indemnify fellow partners against bearing more than their share of losses or expenses of the partnership

(b) Partners in a firm are regarded as having both actual and apparent authority to bind the firm. Their actual authority is the authority given to them by the partnership agreement to carry out certain acts.

Their apparent authority is defined by the Partnership Act 1890. This states that every partner is an agent of the firm and the other partners for the purpose of the business of the partnership. The partner's actions in the normal course of business, of a sort that the firm would normally be expected to do, bind the firm and the other partners, so that they too are liable to the third party. However, if the partner does not have the

authority to make the contract, and the **third party knows that to be the case or does not know or believe him to be a partner**, then the firm will not be bound.

For example, X is a partner in a firm that runs a garage buying and selling second hand cars, but the partnership agreement states that the firm is not to trade in new cars. If X enters a contract for the purchase of a new car from a third party who is not aware of the prohibition in the partnership agreement, then the firm as a whole would be bound by that contract, as X had apparent authority to enter into it.

The purpose of the law is the protection of third parties, and the nature of the authority often depends on the perception of the third party involved. If the third party genuinely believes that the partner has authority, the firm is likely to be bound by the partner's actions.

(c)   A limited liability partnership (LLP) formed under the Limited Liability Partnership Act 2000 is a corporate body with separate legal personality from its members, but it retains some of the features of a partnership.

In order to be incorporated, the subscribers must file details with the Registrar of Companies:

- The name of the LLP

- The location of its registered office (ie England and Wales, Wales or Scotland)

- The address of the registered office

- The name and address of all the members of the LLP

- Which members are to be designated members, who take responsibility for the publicity requirements of the LLP.

The designated members of a LLP are required to:

- File notices with the Registrar of Companies, for example when a member leaves
- Sign and file accounts
- Appoint auditors if appropriate

Marking Guide

		Marks	
(a)	Governed by PA 1890 or by partnership agreement	1	
	Rights (½ mark each; max 1½)	1½	
	Duties (½ mark each; max 1½)	1½	
			4
(b)	Definition in PA 1890	1	
	Example, case or illustration	1	
	Purpose the protection of third parties	1	
			3
(c)	Definition	1	
	Examples of filing requirements	1	
	Examples of publicity	1	
			3
			10

36   CLARE, DAN AND EVE

> **Tutor's hint**. This is a perfect example of the type of question that you have to read at least twice, if not three times, to pick up all of the relevant information. Given the number of 'characters' in the question it would be worth drawing a little plan of the inter-relationships between them. Notice that the question requires you to consider the potential liabilities of four different people. You can reasonably assume that each is worth about a quarter of the marks, so make sure that you don't miss anyone out!
>
> **Examiner's comments**. The question was generally dealt with fairly well, but some candidates tended to deal with general issues rather than focus on the specific issues identified in the question. Some candidates were confused between 'sleeping' and 'limited' partners, and very few identified the issue of partnership by estoppel.

A partnership is the relationship which subsists between **persons carrying on a business in common with the intention of making a profit**. A partnership does not have a separate legal identity distinct from the partners. Being a partnership gives rise to a number of legal duties, for example of mutual indemnity and good faith, and rights, such as being involved in the decision-making affecting the business and sharing in the profits. Partners are **jointly liable** for debts and liabilities arising under any contracts made which bind the partnership. Generally speaking, if the third party genuinely believes that the party making the contract was a partner with authority, then all partners are likely to be jointly liable.

It is possible (but not commonly done) to register a limited partnership in which individual partners have limited liability but the limited partners are not permitted to take part in the management of the business. However, the partnership in question is not a registered limited partnership under the Limited Partnership Act 2000 (it was formed ten years ago). In any other partnership, every partner is personally liable without limit for the debts of the partnership.

(a) **Clare**

A **sleeping partner** is someone who invests in a partnership but who takes no part in the day to day running of the partnership business. A sleeping partner is not recognised by law as having any lesser liability or responsibility than a fully active partner. **Clare is thus jointly liable** without limit with the other partners for the partnership's liabilities.

(b) **Dan**

When a partner retires, **he remains liable for any outstanding liabilities incurred while he was a partner** unless the creditor has agreed to release him from liability. He also shares the firm's liabilities incurred after his retirement if the creditor knew him to be a partner and has not been notified of his retirement. (This is the effect of s 36 PA 1890 which provides that a partner continues to be an 'apparent member' of a partnership and liable for all its debts until notice is given that he is no longer a partner.) To avoid being an 'apparent member' following retirement, the retiring partner should give **actual notice** of his retirement to creditors who had dealings with the firm while he was a partner (correspondence with the creditor on letterhead which no longer bears the retired partner's name is sufficient). He should also advertise his retirement in the London Gazette in order to give general notice to other creditors who may have begun dealings with the firm after his retirement but who knew him to be a partner.

Thus **Dan will be jointly liable for debts** owed to Greg unless has given him notice of his retirement. (If Hugh did not know that Dan was once a partner, then Dan will have no liability towards him. If he did know him to be a partner, then Dan will be liable in respect of the debt owed to Hugh unless he gave general notice in the Gazette.)

(c) **Eve**

Eve remains fully liable jointly with Clare and, according to the principles mentioned above, Dan. She cannot avoid any liability by leaving the daily running of the partnership to Frank.

(d) **Frank**

Frank is described as a manager rather than as a partner and it is necessary to consider whether he had authority to bind the partnership by entering into contracts with Greg and Hugh. Only if this is the case will Clare, Dan and Eve have any potential liability in respect of the debts owed to them in any event.

As a general rule, in order to be valid and binding on the principal and third party, a contract entered into by an agent must be entered into within the bounds of the agent's authority. However, that authority need not be express for the contract entered into by the agent to bind the principal. It may be implied actual authority or apparent authority.

Even in the absence of express authority, Frank clearly has **implied usual authority**, namely the authority which an agent shall be deemed to have by reason of his occupying a particular position or engaging in a particular trade. He acts as managing director even if he has not been formally appointed as such. The contracts entered into with Greg and Hugh were within the usual scope of the business and as both third parties believed his claim to be a partner, the partnership is liable and the individual partners liable to the extent described above.

In cases of implied actual authority, the third party who contracts with the agent is entitled to assume that the agent has implied authority unless he knows to the contrary. In *Watteau v Fenwick*, the principal was held to be bound by a contract entered into by his agent with implied usual authority (as a hotel manager, he bought cigars on credit) even though the third party did not know that the agent, as the other contracting party, was the agent of the principal. It appears that none of the partners has done anything to deny Frank's claim of being a partner and, therefore, they will be estopped from denying their own liability (*Freeman & Lockyer v Buckhurst Park Properties (Mangal) Ltd*).

Similarly, **Frank would be liable**. Having held himself out to be a partner, he would be **estopped** from denying his own liability as a contracting party on the basis that he was not actually a partner.

(Greg and Hugh are entitled to take action against any one or more of the partners and Frank. Under the Civil Liability (Contributions) Act 1978, the one sued would be able to seek a proportionate indemnity from the remaining liable parties.)

Marking Guide

	Marks
Principle of joint liability	1
Clare	
Definition of a sleeping partner	1
Same amount of liability as any other partner	1
Clare is jointly liable with the others	1
Dan	
Retired partner still liable unless released by creditor	2
Creditor must be notified of retirement	1
S36 PA 1890	1
How to avoid being liable	2
Dan liable unless has notified Greg	1
Position relating to Hugh	2
Eve	
Fully liable	1
Irrelevant that she is not involved in running	1
Frank	
Issue is apparent or implied authority	2
Frank has implied actual authority as MD	1
Cases	2
Frank is a partner by estoppel	1

$\underline{\underline{21}}$ (max 20)

37 TERMINATION OF PARTNERSHIPS

Tutor's hint. Think carefully before choosing a question like this: it requires a detailed knowledge of a fairly narrow area of the law on partnership.

Examiner's comments. This was a popular question and was relatively well-answered. The main criticism is that some candidates just listed the grounds as bullet points, and did not explain how the circumstances would arise. Many candidates did not make the point that the dissolution can occur at the volition of either the partners or in some instances the court.

Dissolution is the term used to describe when a partnership comes to an end. A partnership can always be dissolved by agreement of the partners. In addition the Partnership Act 1890 provides that a partnership will be dissolved in the following circumstances.

(a) Where the partnership was entered into for a **specific venture or a fixed time period** and that venture or fixed period comes to an end. If in fact the partners decide to continue even after such time, the partnership is thereafter referred to as a 'partnership at will' and like any other partnership can be brought to an end by the partners' wishes.

(b) On the **death or bankruptcy of one of the partners**. Since a partnership has no separate legal personality but is the relationship that subsists between its partners, it follows that the death or bankruptcy of one of its partners will bring the partnership to an end (this is not the case with partnerships created under the Limited Liability Partnerships Act 2000). In practice, however, a partnership agreement will usually provide for the partnership business to continue under the control of the remaining partners who automatically constitute a new partnership.

(c) In the case of **supervening illegality**. Where the business of the partnership becomes illegal, it is automatically dissolved, for example where the outbreak of war means that the partnership is thereafter trading with the enemy (*R v Kupfer*). Where a solicitor in a partnership failed to renew his practice certificate, as required by law, this too rendered the partnership practice illegal and brought the partnership to an end, although a

partnership was treated as continuing to exist between the remaining partners (*Hudgell, Yeates and Co v Watson*).

(d) Where one partner gives **notice of dissolution** to the remaining partners, provided the partnership is for an unlimited duration.

(e) Where the partners decide to dissolve the partnership following one of the partners' interest in the property or profits of the partnership in relation to any judgment debt becoming subject to a **charge**.

(f) By order of the **court**. The court may order dissolution of a partnership where, for example, a partner becomes a patient under the Mental Health Act 1893 or otherwise permanently incapacitated; or where one partner carries on activities prejudicial to the partnership business or is persistently in breach of the partnership agreement; or where the partnership business can only be carried on at a loss; or where it is just and equitable to do so on any other grounds.

Marking Guide	
	Marks
Dissolution by agreement of partners	2
Partnership Act 1890 grounds:	
Specific venture/fixed period ends	2
Death or bankruptcy of one of the partners	1
Supervening illegality	2
Notice by a partner	1
By court order	2
	10

38   COMPANY FORMATION

> **Tutor's hint.** The key point to note with this question is that it refers to a public limited company. Answers which refer to private companies will not score highly. This is a very fact based question. If you did not know the rules concerning registration and starting to trade, you would have been ill-advised to try this question in the exam.
>
> **Marking guide.** Marks are available for discussing both documents and procedures, and for discussing both registration and starting to trade.
>
> Since the question is quite wide-ranging, only a mark would be available for each of the items to be filed on registration, and then the remaining four marks are for a discussion for the requirement of a s117 certificate.
>
> One final mark available for mentioning the impact of a private company re-registering as public.

A registered company is a commercial concern which is incorporated and registered under the Companies Act 1985. A registered company always has a written constitution comprising a memorandum of association and articles of association. Any company not registered as a public company is a private company.

Under the Companies Act, the following **documents** should be prepared and **delivered to the Companies Registry to obtain registration of a public limited company** and a certificate of incorporation:-

(a) **The memorandum of association.** This must be signed (with witnesses) by two or more subscribers. The memorandum defines what the company and its business are and how its external business and affairs are to be conducted.

The memorandum sets out the company's name, location of registered office, its objects and limited liability, its authorised share capital, a declaration of association and a statement that it is a public company.

(b) **The articles of association**. Alternatively, the memorandum may be endorsed 'registered without articles of association', in which case the company will adopt Table A (1985 edition) as its articles) signed in the same way as the memorandum.

The articles deal with matters affecting the internal conduct of the company's affairs, including the issue and transfer of shares, the conduct of meetings, dividends and the appointment, powers and proceedings of directors.

(c) **Form 10**. This gives particulars of the company's first directors and secretary (with their signed consent to act) and the address of the registered office.

(d) **A statutory declaration**. This is made by one of the persons named as directors or secretary or by a solicitor that there has been compliance with the requirements of the Companies Act 1985 on company formation (s 12(3)).

(e) **Form 117**. This must be signed by a director or secretary with a statutory declaration stating that the nominal value of the allotted share capital is at least £50,000, the amount paid up on the allotted shares (which must be at least 25% of the nominal value and entire premium if any). It must also state particulars of preliminary expenses and payments and benefits to promoters.

(f) **A registration fee**. This fee is £20.

A public company must state in its memorandum that it is a public company, its name must end with the words 'public limited company', the nominal value of its issued share capital must be £50,000 or more and the company must be registered as a public company.

Once the submitted documents have been checked and found to be in order by the Registrar of Companies, a certificate of incorporation is issued. This is conclusive evidence that the formalities of registration have been complied with (s 13 CA 1985).

A public company cannot commence business or borrow money until the Registrar has issued a trading certificate under s 117. The Registrar must notify receipt of form 117 in the Gazette and a trading certificate is conclusive evidence, once issued, that the company is entitled to do business.

Trading in contravention of s 117 is an offence punishable by fine (the other party is protected as the transaction is not invalidated) and **failure to obtain a trading certificate** constitutes **grounds for a compulsory winding up** under s 122 IA 1986.

A private company may re-register as a public company under s 43 CA 1985 by passing a special resolution to that effect altering the memorandum and articles as appropriate and applying to the Registrar in the prescribed form. The Registrar then issues a certificate of re-registration of the company as a public company. The company must still obtain a trading certificate under s 117.

39   TOM'S COMPANY

> **Tutor's hint**. (a) represents core knowledge for company law. You should be able to discuss the facts of the *Salomon* case in detail. Your answer should also clearly have distinguished statutory and common law lifting of the veil.
>
> (b) requires wide-ranging knowledge of company procedures, and the question should also have prompted you to draw a conclusion bearing in mind that Tom was about to take action to form a company.
>
> (c) deals with single member private companies, a topic that may well be covered as part of a larger question. The question highlights certain points about the way such companies should do business, and also that you cannot have a single member company where the single member is both director and secretary.

(a) **Corporate personality**

A company limited by shares is distinct as a **separate legal person** from its owners or members. One of the consequences of this is that a **'veil' of incorporation** exists between the company and its members. The term refers to the distinction between the members and the company.

Salomon case

The distinction between a company and its members was confirmed in *Salomon v Salomon and Co Ltd*. In this case, the court held that Salomon, although he owned 20,001 out of 20,007 shares in Salomon & Co Ltd, was under no personal liability to the failed company or to its creditors. Debentures issued to him by the company created a valid security over the company's assets which ranked before the claims of unsecured creditors of the company. Since then the distinction has been developed in both case law (*Macaura v Northern Assurance Co Ltd*) and statute.

Implications of corporate personality

The implications of this distinction are that the company (not its members) **owns** its **assets** (*Macaura v Northern Assurance*) and **incurs liabilities**. Most importantly the separation of the company and its members means that **members' liability** can be **limited** even though the company's liability is unlimited.

Lifting the veil of incorporation

However, the Courts and statute will on occasion 'lift' the metaphorical veil and identify a company with its members, and hence treat the actions of the company as those of its members.

Case law exceptions to Salomon

In each of the following cases the veil was lifted to identify a company with its members or directors, as members and directors were trying:

(i)   To **escape liability** for tax, excise duty or other liabilities: *Re H and Others*

(ii)   To **evade** a **valid agreement** restricting an individual's activities: *Gilford Motor Co v Horne*

(iii) To **disguise** an **enemy** in time of war

(iv)   To **commit** a **fraud**: *Re FG Films Ltd*

(v)   To **conceal** the **nationality** of the company: *Unit Construction Co Ltd v Bullock*

Groups

The veil can also be raised so as to eliminate the distinction between companies, that is, to treat groups as a **single legal entity**.

However group companies have to carry on substantially a single business before they may be identified as one and they may not be identified as one even then. In *Adams v Cape Industries* the judgement observed that English law recognised **subsidiaries** as **separate legal entities**. Lifting the veil cannot thus generally be used by creditors to make a holding company liable for its subsidiary's debts.

Statutory exceptions to Salomon

Statute also provides instances of lifting the veil.

(i)   Insolvency can lead to directors and other officers becoming personally liable for a company's debts, if they engage in **fraudulent** or **wrongful trading**: s 213-214 IA 1986.

(ii) Generally a company's name must be correctly and completely displayed on documents (s 349); an individual who signs a cheque bearing an **incorrect name** becomes **personally liable**: *Penrose v Martyr*.

(iii) If a public company enters into a trading transaction in contravention of the provisions which require it to obtain a **certificate before doing business**, the directors of the company may be jointly and severally liable: s 117-8.

(b) Most of the advantages and disadvantages of purchasing an off the shelf company relate to the **formalities** required to incorporate a company and to **alter various details** that relate to existing companies.

Advantages

The principal advantages are as follows.

(i) Tom will **not need to file** the following documents with the Registrar of Companies:

(1) A **memorandum** and **articles**
(2) A **statement** in the **prescribed form**
(3) **Statutory declaration**

This will be a quicker, and very possibly cheaper, way of incorporating his business.

(ii) There will be **no risk** of **potential liability** arising from pre-incorporation contracts. Tom will be able to continue trading without needing to worry about waiting for the registrar's certificate of incorporation.

(iii) The **need to use** the services of **professionals** will be **decreased**, making incorporation cheaper.

Disadvantages

The disadvantages relate to the changes that will be required to the off-the-shelf company to make it compatible with Tom's needs.

(i) The **objects** set out in the company's memorandum may **not** be **appropriate** for Tom's business. They may need to be altered. However, if, as is likely, the memorandum describes its objects as those of a '**general commercial company**', it is unlikely that any change would be needed.

(ii) The off-the-shelf company is likely to have **Table A articles**. Tom may wish to amend these, for example to give the shares he owns rights which ensure he retains control. Revised articles would need to be filed with the registrar.

(iii) Tom may want to **change** the **name** of the company and, if so, would need to pass a special resolution.

(iv) The **subscriber shares** will need to be **transferred**, and the transfer recorded in the Register of Members. Stamp duty will be payable.

(v) **Tom** will have to have himself **appointed** as **company director**, and someone else as company secretary.

(vi) Tom may wish to have the **authorised share capital increased**. If so, an ordinary resolution sanctioning the increase would need to be passed.

With the exception of the transfer of the subscriber shares, details of all the above changes would need to be **filed** with the **Registrar**.

On balance it is likely to be easier and quicker to purchase an off-the-shelf company, but it depends on how many changes will be required to make the company compatible with Tom's needs.

(c)   Private companies may be formed with only one member.

Formalities

Single member companies have to fulfil certain formalities. The fact that it is a single member private company must be stated in the register of members and the member's name and address given. Company resolutions or decisions which are normally decided in general meeting must be evidenced in writing. Any contract between the company and the sole member/director not made in the ordinary course of business must also be in writing.

Directors and secretary

S 282 provides that a private company need only have one director but a sole director cannot be the company secretary: (s 283(2)). Therefore Tom will need to bring in another person and appoint him or her to be company secretary though he may be sole member and sole director. The secretary does not need to own shares in the company.

Marking Guide

			Marks
(a)	Company is a separate legal person	1	
	'Veil of incorporation'	1	
	Salomon case or other example	1	
	Effect on asset ownership and liabilities	1	
	Possible to set aside the veil	1	
	Examples of case law exceptions (½ each; max. 2)	2	
	Examples of statutory exceptions (½ each; max. 2)	2	
	Groups	1	
			10
(b)	Advantages (1 mark each; max. 3)	3	
	Disadvantages (1 mark each; max. 4)	4	
			7
(c)	Formalities of single member companies	1	
	No need for another director	1	
	Needs a company secretary	1	
			3
			20

---

40   IMRAN AND JANE

Tutor's hint. This is an unusually straightforward question for Section B of the paper, as unusually it does not require much application of the law. Given that students traditionally tend to find the application questions more difficult, it would be a good question to choose in the exam.

Examiner's comments. This was a very popular question and was generally very well done. Some candidates struggled with the order in which the steps are taken to register as a plc. It was part (c) of the question that caused the most difficulty, as few candidates were familiar with the requirements of s 221 CA85 to keep accounting records; some candidates adopted a 'write all you know' approach in the hope of gaining a few marks.

(a)   A registered company is a commercial concern which is incorporated and registered under the **Companies Act 1985**. A registered company always has a written constitution comprising a **memorandum of association and articles of association**. Any company not registered as a public company is a private company.

Companies can be formed by Royal Charter, Act of Parliament or by delegated legislation but by far the most common is incorporation under the Companies Act 1985. Under this Act, the following documents should be prepared and delivered to the Companies Registry to obtain registration of a company and a certificate of incorporation.

(i)   A **memorandum of association** signed and witnessed by two or more subscribers. The memorandum includes an **objects clause** limiting the scope of its legal powers to actions which further the stated objects. Any purported legal obligation outside the scope of those powers is ultra vires and void, although in practice, the amendments to s 35 of the 1985 Act by the Companies Act 1989, have lessened the effects of this rule. The memorandum must also detail the **name** and **capital structure** of the company, state that the company is a **public company** and that **the members liability shall be limited**;

(ii)   **Articles of association** (or the memorandum may be endorsed 'registered without articles of association', in which case the company will adopt Table A (1985 edition) as its articles). The articles will govern the **procedures for the daily running of the company,** including the voting rights attached to shares and the calling and conduct of meetings;

(iii)   **Form 10** giving particulars of the company's first directors and secretary (with their signed consent to act) and the address of the registered office;

(iv)   **Form 12** containing a statutory declaration by one of the persons named as directors or secretary or by a solicitor that the requirements of the Companies Act 1985 on company formation have been fully complied with; and

(v)   A £20 **registration fee.**

Once these have been checked and found to be in order by the Registrar of Companies, a **certificate of incorporation** is issued under s 117 (1) CA 1985. This is conclusive evidence that the formalities of registration have been complied with. Alternatively, a company may be bought 'off the shelf' from an appropriate enterprise which has already incorporated a range of companies for sale. In such cases, the name of the company and the directors will need to be changed (as a minimum).

In addition, as their company is to be a public limited company, Imran and Jane must obtain a **trading certificate** by submitting Form 117 signed by a director or secretary to the Registrar of Companies. The submission should include a statutory declaration that the nominal value of the allotted share capital is at least £50,000 and that the amount paid up on the allotted shares exceeds one quarter of the nominal value and the entire premium, if any.

(b)   Under the Companies Act, companies are bound to keep a number of **statutory registers** available for public inspection and normally held at the company's registered office.

(i)   A **register of members** containing the name and address of each member and (if more than one and not apparent from the particulars of his shareholding) the class to which he belongs, the number of shares held by him and the date on which he became and (when appropriate) ceased to be a member (s 352);

(ii)   A **register of charges** containing details of all fixed and floating charges affecting the company property or undertaking, setting out brief descriptions of property charged, the amount secured and the name of the chargee. The register, and copies of all instruments creating charges, *must* be kept at the company's registered office;

(iii) A **register of directors and secretary** containing details of the individuals' names and addresses, nationality, business occupation, other current or former directorships during the last 5 years and (directors only) dates of birth;

(iv) A **register of directors' interests** containing details of directors' interests as disclosed by them pursuant to other provisions in the Act (s 324) and of rights granted to directors;

(v) A **register of written resolutions** (s 382A); and

(vi) A **register of substantial interests in public limited company shares** of 3% or more of the nominal value of any class of shares (s 211).

(c) Under s 221 CA85, a company is required to keep accounting records **sufficient to show and explain the company's transactions,** so that it is possible at any time to determine the company's financial position and to ascertain that any balance sheet or profit and loss account complies with the Act. The records must contain daily entries of sums paid and received (describing the nature and source of the transactions), and a record of assets and liabilities. Where the company deals in goods, the accounts must also contain statements of stocktaking and the stock held at the end of each financial year and statements of goods bought and sold (except retail sales).

Marking Guide		*Marks*	
(a)	Documents to deliver to the Registrar:		
	Memorandum	1	
	Articles	1	
	Form 10	1	
	Form 12	1	
	Registration fee	1	
	Registrar issues certificate of incorporation	1	
	Or could buy off the shelf	1	
	Requirement for S117 certificate	1	
	Minimum capital requirement	2	
			10
(b)	Register of members	1	
	Register of charges	1	
	Register of directors and secretaries	1	
	Register of directors' interests	1	
	Register of written resolutions	½	
	Register of substantial interests in shares	½	
			5
(c)	Sufficient to show company's transactions	2	
	Daily entries of cash	1	
	Record of assets and liabilities	1	
	Statement of stocks	1	
			5
			20

41   IKE, JAN AND KIT

Tutor's hint. This appears to be a relatively straightforward question. However, beware writing too much on part (a). There is plenty that you could write, but it is only worth five marks and it would be wrong to concentrate your answer on this part too heavily to the detriment of the rest of your answer.

(a) **Difference between public and private companies**

Companies are either public companies or private companies. A public company must:

- State in its memorandum that it is a public company
- Its name must end with the words 'public limited company'
- The nominal value of its issued share capital must be £50,000 or more
- It must be registered as a public company.

If any of these requirements is not satisfied then the company is a private company. Public companies tend to be large scale concerns with a broad base of shareholders whereas private companies tend to be small enterprises in which some, if not all, shareholders are also directors.

The main differences between public and private companies are as follows:

- A public company can raise capital from the public but a private company cannot

- A public company must have a minimum allotted share capital of £50,000 but a private company has no minimum requirement

- A public company must obtain a trading certificate from the Registrar of Companies before it can commence business but a private company may begin trading immediately

- A public company must state in its memorandum that it is a public company and its name must end with the words ' public limited company' or 'PLC' or 'plc' - a private company name must end with 'limited' or 'ltd'

- The rules on distribution of profits as dividends are quite different for public and private companies

- A public company must file its statutory audited accounts within 7 months from the end of its accounting referencing period whereas a private company has 10 months and some private companies will be exempted from various accounting provisions on account of size

- A public company must have at least two directors but a private company need only have one

- The rules on loans to directors are much more stringent in relation to public companies

- The rules relating to consideration given in return for shares are different for the two types of company

- The necessary qualifications of a company secretary are also different

- Unlike public companies, private companies may use the written resolution procedure and can pass elective resolutions on certain matters.

(b) **Resolutions**

(i) **Elective resolution**

An elective resolution may be passed **only by a private company** in particular circumstances. These are:

- Conferring of authority to issue shares indefinitely or for a fixed period (s 80A CA 1985)

- Dispensing with the laying of accounts before a general meeting, unless required by a member or the auditors (s 366A)

- Dispensing with the annual appointment of auditors (s 386)

- Dispensing with the need to hold an AGM unless required by a member (s 366A)

- The reduction to 90% or more of the 95% majority required to consent to short notice under s 369(4) or s 378(3).

All members who are entitled to attend meetings and vote must agree to the passing of an elective resolution, in person or by proxy. 21 days notice must be given (this can be waived if all members entitled to attend and vote at the meeting agree). The resolution must be registered within 15 days (s 379) and it can be revoked by ordinary resolution (which must also be registered):s 379A.

(ii)   **Written resolutions**

The written resolution procedure was introduced by the 1989 Companies Act. A written resolution is **a resolution signed by all members entitled to attend and vote** (s 381A) and can be **any resolution which could ordinarily be passed in general meeting**, including a special resolution and including an elective resolution.

The Act provides that the written resolution shall be 'equivalent' to a resolution passed in general meeting and it can be used notwithstanding any contrary provisions in the company's articles. The resolution need not be contained in a single document so long as all documents signed set out the resolution. The date of the resolution is the date on which the last member signed it.

The procedure cannot, however, be used to remove a director or auditor from office under s 303 or s 391 respectively, since both have a right to attend and speak at a meeting where any proposal for removal is to be discussed. No notice is required but any information which would have had to be sent with the notice of a meeting must still be supplied to members before they sign the resolution

A copy of any proposed written resolution or details thereof must be sent to the company's auditors at or before the time they are sent to shareholders. Breach of this requirement renders the directors and secretary liable to a fine but the resolution remains valid.

(iii) **Payment of dividends**

A company's **power to declare dividends is given in its articles**. Table A provides that the company in general meeting may declare dividends by ordinary resolution subject to a maximum amount which is recommended by the directors.

Dividends are usually declared payable on the paid up amount of share capital (Article 104) and are usually paid in cash. Under Article 105 of Table A, dividends can be paid wholly or partly by the distribution of non-cash assets. Table A permits the directors to 'pay interim dividends if it appears to them that they are justified by the profits of the company available for distribution'. (Article 103). There is no requirement for shareholder approval.

The general rule on payment of dividends applicable to both private and public companies is set out in s 263 which provides that '**dividends may only be paid by a company out of profits available for the purpose**'.

In addition, a **public company** can only make a distribution if **its net assets at the time are equal to or greater than the aggregate of its called up share capital and undistributed reserves** and the amount of any dividend cannot exceed such amount as would leave its net assets at not less than that aggregate amount (s 264). This means that a public company is required to maintain its capital to a greater extent than a private company.

42 BUSINESS TERMS

> **Tutorial note.** This is an extremely straightforward question and if a similar one came up in your exam, you should attempt it. A well-prepared student should score extremely well on a question like this. However, as the examiner points out (below) there is also scope to make mistakes on simple questions like this, for example, thinking plcs are all listed companies. Of course, this is not the case. You must ensure that you have a good understanding of the basics of these legal entities. Also note the comments made below about the style of answers. The examiner prefers an 'essay' style to a highly bulleted approach, so may sure you oblige.
>
> **Examiner's comments**. This was a very popular question, answered by the vast majority of candidates, and in general it was done competently with most candidates earning a clear pass mark. The main weakness was the failure of some candidates to cite case law and statute in support of their arguments. Candidates must try to quote the relevant legal authority to substantiate the points that they make. A discursive essay style is preferable to a list of bullet points, although appropriate credit was given for the latter.
>
> One of the main errors was to state that a public company and a listed company are effectively the same thing. Candidates should expect this type of question to feature frequently in forthcoming exams, and they provide an excellent opportunity for earning high marks.

(a) **Partnership**

The words '& Co' show that the business organisation is a **partnership**. A partnership is the relation which subsists between persons carrying on a business in common with a view of profit (Partnership Act 1890 s 1).

A partnership is not a separate legal entity but merely the partners as a group working in a particular relationship with each other. In a partnership, **every partner is liable without limit for the debts of the partnership**. A partnership may exist without any written agreement - though it is normal practice to have a written agreement – in fact a partnership may even arise without the persons concerned intending it to do so.

There must be at least 2 partners and no more than 20, save where an exception applies, as in the case of professional partnerships, such as accountants and solicitors.

The **Limited Liability Partnership Act 2000** provides for new limited liability partnerships which are to have separate legal personality and therefore some of the attributes of registered companies.

(b) **Private company**

'Ltd' shows that the business organisation is a limited company, and, in particular, a **private limited company** as opposed to a public limited company. The essential characteristic of a company is the distinction between the corporation and its members (*Salomon v Salomon & Co Ltd*) which means that its assets and liabilities are its own and a company can enter into and enforce contracts in its own right without members into the bargain. Following on, therefore, a company is liable for breach of contract and may have to pay damages or suffer some other remedy against it.

The significance of the word 'limited' is that the **liability of the company's members is limited to such amount as is unpaid on their shares**. Once shares are fully paid up, the owners of those shares have no further liability in respect of the debts of the company. A company will not cease to exist on a change in its membership.

If it is a private limited company, it must end with the word 'limited' or 'ltd' (except in the case of private companies limited by guarantee and companies licensed to do so before 25 February 1982 where the word 'limited' may be omitted if certain conditions are satisfied). Appropriate Welsh wording may be used by companies having a registered office in Wales. (s25).

(c) **Public company**

'Plc' denotes a **public limited company** which is also a separate legal entity distinct from its members, whose liability is limited to the amount outstanding on their shares. A public company must state in its memorandum that it is a public company and its name must end with the words ' public limited company' or 'PLC' or 'plc' or its Welsh equivalent.

Unlike a private company, a public company can raise capital from the public. Many are listed on the Stock Exchange. Generally speaking, a public limited company is subject to more stringent accounting and other regulations than a private limited company.

Marking Guide		*Marks*	
(a)	Identification of '& Co.'	1	
	Definition of a partnership	1	
	Limited liability partnerships	1	
			3
(b)	Identification of private limited company	1	
	Explanation of limited liability	1	
	Required wording for ltd company	1	
			3
(c)	Public limited company	1	
	Memo must state a plc	1	
	Can offer shares to the public	1	
	Examples of more stringent regulations	1	
			4
Total			10

43   PREPARATION QUESTION: INCORPORATION AND PROMOTERS

> **Tutor's hint.** The question is very specific about the information required for each part. You should follow a similar approach if you are asked to write generally about pre-incorporation contracts. Remember that pre-incorporation contracts cannot be ratified when a company is incorporated; evidence of a new contract is required.

(a) (i) **Definition**

A company is usually formed by a **promoter,** who is 'one who undertakes to form a company with reference to a given project and to set it going and who takes the necessary steps to accomplish that purpose': *Twycross v Grant*. It is a promoter who enters into pre-incorporation contracts.

Pre-incorporation expenses

A promoter cannot enter into a contract to be paid for expenses incurred before incorporation, such as drafting legal documents, because the company does not possess legal capacity prior to being incorporated. However, he can generally arrange that the first directors, of whom he may be one, should reimburse him or pay the bills.

(ii) **Definition**

A **pre-incorporation contract** is a contract made in a company's name before it is formed. Companies are not bound by such contracts as they do not exist when the contracts are made.

Company cannot ratify

It follows that a company can never ratify a pre-incorporation contract made on its behalf. Since it did not exist when the pre-incorporation contract was made, it cannot be made a party to it. In *Natal Land and Colonisation Co v Pauline Colliery Syndicate* it was held that a company could not enforce an option granted to it before it existed.

Need for novation

Once the company is incorporated there must be **novation** for a pre-incorporation contract to be enforced. This means that a new contract is made with the same subject matter, or the terms of the contract modified to the extent that it constitutes a new offer: *Howard v Patent Ivory Manufacturing Co*.

Contracts (Rights of Third Parties) Act 1999

This legislation has had an impact on the position of the promoter with regard to a pre-incorporation contract. The Act provides that a third party to a contract may enforce a contractual term if the contract itself expressly provides for it, and identifies the promoter by name, class or description. Therefore a promoter may be able to enforce a pre-incorporation contract if these conditions are met.

(b) **Liability of promoter**

Although a company is not liable on a pre-incorporation contract the promoter may nevertheless incur personal liability both at common law and statute. In *Kelner v Baxter* it was held that **promoters** who signed a contract on behalf of a company which had not at that time been incorporated were **liable** on the contract.

S 36C

S 36C contains the statutory provisions relating to pre-incorporation contracts. It states that where **a person contracts in the name of, or as agent for, a company before its incorporation, that person will be personally liable unless there is agreement to the contrary**. The application of s 36C was illustrated by *Phonogram Ltd v Lane*. In this case, a sum was advanced to a company before incorporation. It was held that the promoter was personally liable for repayment of the sum.

44 CLAUSES AND NAMES

> **Tutor's hint**. You should be able to list the clauses in the memorandum fairly easily. In your answer to part (b), split your answer up by considering the requirements first under statute and second under common law.

(a) **Memorandum of Association**

The memorandum of association of every registered company must contain the following clauses.

(i) The **name of the company** (dealt with in (b) below).

(ii) The **registered office**. Whether the company's registered office is in England and Wales, or in Scotland. The registered office fixes the domicile of the company which (unlike other details in the memorandum) cannot be altered. The specific address of the registered office can, however, be altered at any time by the directors, provided the new address is in the same country. The registered office is where the company's statutory registers, records and minutes must be maintained and it is the address for service of legal documents on the company.

(iii)   The **objects clause**. Under s 2 Companies Act 1985, every company is required to state its objects so defining the purpose of the company and its capacity to act with the consequence that activities outside the scope of the objects clause are ultra vires. The Companies Act 1989 abolished the application of ultra vires in respect of outsiders but retained the power of members to bring proceedings to restrain acts on the grounds of their being ultra vires. It is sufficient for the memorandum to state that the object of a company is to carry on business as a 'general commercial company'.

(iv)   **Limited liability**. This should state that, if this is the case, the liability of the members is limited. If the company is limited by guarantee rather than by shares, the amount guaranteed by the members will be stated.

(v)   The **authorised share capital**. Setting out the amount of share capital including the division of that capital into shares of a fixed amount and the nominal value of each share.

(vi)   The **association** clause. The memorandum will end with a declaration of association, which is a statement by the subscribers that they wish to join together to form a company.

(vii)   If a company is a **public limited company**, an additional clause is required, stating that the company is a public limited company.

Other **optional clauses** may sometimes be included, for example clauses setting out details of class rights (although these are more usually found in the articles of association). The memorandum may be amended only in accordance with the provisions of the Companies Acts.

(b)   **Company name**

The name of a company must be specified in the company's memorandum of association and serves to identify the company, distinguishing it from any other company. The registrar of companies has statutory powers of control over the choice of names in order to ensure that they comply with both statutory and common law restrictions and requirements. These apply both on the initial registration of a company by its promoters and on any subsequent change of name by the company.

Statutory restrictions

If the company is a **public company**, it must end with the words 'public limited company' or 'plc'. If the company is a **private limited company**, it must end with the word 'limited' or 'ltd'. Appropriate Welsh wording may be used by companies having a registered office in Wales: s 25.

A company **cannot share the name of any existing company** which appears in the statutory index at the Companies Registry. Non-essential differences will be disregarded for the purposes of working out what constitutes 'the same' so that, for example, John Smith Limited will be deemed to be the same as John Smith & Company Ltd: s 26(3).

A company cannot bear a name which, in the registrar's opinion, suggests a connection with the **government or a local authority**: s 26(2). Words such as 'British' or 'National' will only be permitted if the nature and size of the company is appropriate.

A name which suggests some **professional expertise** will be permitted only if that expertise is in the company and appropriate professional bodies have no objection.

A name will not be permitted if the registrar considers it to be **offensive** or if it constitutes a **criminal offence**: s 26(1).

Written application can be made to the Secretary of State to approve proposed names in advance. The Secretary of State can compel a company to **change its name** if it is the same as or, in the registrar's opinion, too like the name of another company which is or should have been on the register at the time or if misleading information was given to secure registration.

Likewise he can require a change of name where the name gives so misleading an indication of the company's activities as to be likely to cause harm to the public: s 32. A company can elect to change its name by passing a special resolution to that effect: s 28.

Common law restrictions

In addition, at common law, a company can be prevented from using its registered name if the use of that name causes the company's goods to be confused with those of another company.

The court may grant an injunction in a passing-off action brought by that other company and may also force the defendant company to change its name: *Ewing v Buttercup Margarine Co Ltd*.

Marking Guide	Marks
Name	½
Registered Office	1
Objects	1
Limited liability	½
Authorised share capital	½
Association	½
Plc requirement	½
Optional clause	½
Statutory restrictions	3
Passing off	2
	10

45 COMPANY CONSTITUTION

> **Tutor's hint**. A question like this should be bread and butter marks for you. If you have revised the area of the company's constitution you should have no problem scoring high marks on this question.

There are two documents which are sometimes described as the **'written constitution'** of a limited company and which each registered company is required to have. These are

- The **articles of association**, which set out the internal regulations of the company, and

- The **memorandum of association**, which sets out the company's basic constitution and its relationship with the outside world.

Provisions in the articles may be invoked to clarify any uncertainties in the memorandum, but in the event of any **inconsistency** between the memorandum and articles, the **memorandum prevails**. A company's articles of association, along with its memorandum, bind its members to the company, the company to its members and its members to each other (s 14 CA 1985).

Memorandum of Association

Before a company can be incorporated, the original memorandum, signed by at least two subscribers from the company's first shareholders, must be submitted to the Registrar of companies to obtain registration.

The memorandum of association of every limited company must contain the following clauses (and may contain additional clauses):

(a) **The name of the company**. This must comply with both statutory and common law restrictions and requirements. If the company is a public company, it must end with the words 'public limited company' or 'plc'. If it is a private limited company, it must end with the word 'limited' or 'ltd'. The name of the company must not be the same as any company already registered, nor may it be offensive nor constitute a criminal offence, nor suggest an unauthorised connection with the Government or a local authority (s 26). The name can be altered by a special resolution (s 28).

(b) **The registered office of the company** and whether the company's registered office is in England and Wales, or in Scotland. The registered office fixes the **domicile** of the company which (unlike other details in the memorandum) cannot be altered. The specific address of the registered office can, however, be altered at any time by the directors, provided the new address is in the same country. The registered office is where the company's statutory registers, records and minutes must be maintained and it is the address for service of legal documents on the company.

(c) **The objects clause**. Under s 2 Companies Act 1985, every company is required to state its objects so defining the purpose of the company and its capacity to act. Prior to the 1989 Companies Act the basic rule was that an act outside the objects clause was *ultra vires* and void and could not therefore be enforced by the company or by an outsider. The Companies Act 1989 abolished the application of *ultra vires* in respect of outsiders, thus giving security to commercial transactions, but retained the power of members to bring proceedings to restrain acts on the grounds of their being *ultra vires*.

Under s 3A CA 1985, it is now sufficient for the memorandum to state that the object of a company is to carry on business as a **'general commercial company'** ie the object of the company is to carry on any trade or business whatsoever and the company has the power to undertake such activities as are incidental or conducive to the carrying on of any trade or business by it.

(d) **Limited liability**. This clause states, if applicable, that the liability of the members is limited. If the company is limited by guarantee rather than by shares, the amount guaranteed by the members will be stated.

(e) **The authorised share capital**. In the case of a company limited by shares, this clause must include the amount of share capital including the division of that capital into shares of a fixed amount and the nominal value of each share. The company's capital can be increased by ordinary resolution.

If a company is a **public limited company**, an additional clause is required, stating that the company is a public limited company.

Finally, the memorandum will end with a **declaration of association** (the 'association clause'), which is a statement by the subscribers that they wish to join together to form a company. Other optional clauses may sometimes be included, for example clauses setting out details of class rights (although these are more usually found in the articles of association).

The memorandum may be **amended** only in accordance with the provisions of the Companies Acts.

Articles of Association

A company's articles of association deal mainly with matters affecting the **internal conduct of the company's affairs** including

- The issue and transfer of shares and class rights
- Dividends
- Alterations of capital structure
- Convening and conduct of general meetings
- The appointment, powers and proceedings of directors
- Company accounts.

A company may have its own full-length special articles or it **may adopt Table A** of the Companies Acts. **Table A will be deemed to apply to the extent that the company does not submit its own articles in substitution**. Where a company incorporates Table A but also has special articles which cover the same ground, the special articles will prevail. The relevant Table A will be that which was in force at the time of the company's incorporation.

The provisions of the **Companies Acts will override a company's articles** where they prohibit something which, on the face of it, is permitted by the articles or where the Companies Acts require a special procedure to be followed.

A company's **articles of association may be altered by the company by passing a special resolution** to that effect in general meeting (s 9 CA 1985). An article cannot be retrospective or made unalterable by declaring it to be unalterable in the articles or by requiring a greater majority vote than is required by s9 or by means of a separate contract under which the company undertakes not to alter it. An alteration will be void if it conflicts with the Companies Acts or with the memorandum. Equally it will be void if it compels any member to subscribe for additional shares or if the majority who approve it are not acting bona fide in what they deem to be the interests of the company as a whole.

In *Greenhalgh v Arderne Cinemas Ltd* the Court of Appeal made it clear that the 'bona fide for the benefit of the company as a whole' test referred to above is a single test and also a subjective test (ie what did the majority believe?). The **company as a whole** in this context means the general body of shareholders and the test is whether every 'individual hypothetical member' would in the honest opinion of the majority benefit from the alteration.

46 NATIONAL HAIR BRUSHES

> **Tutor's hint.** A common error when answering questions like (b) about confusion of names is solely to discuss passing-off. Don't forget there are statutory remedies available as well.
>
> For (c) you must distinguish between changing the **address** of the registered office within the same country (which is fairly easy) and changing the **domicile** (which can only be achieved by Act of Parliament).
>
> In (d) you are not told what the objects clause actually says, so it is certainly legitimate to speculate that the company might have a '**general commercial company**' objects clause; if so, they will not need to alter the objects clause at all if they wish to change the nature of the company's business. If you know that there is a right of objection, but are not sure of the % shareholdings that the objecting minority need to possess, you will still get credit for mentioning a right of objection even if you do not give further details. (Remember however that the % limits might be tested in an objective test question.)

MEMORANDUM

To: Board of Directors, National Hair Brushes plc
From: Company Secretary
Date: 30 June 20X2
Subject: Formation matters

(a) In order to carry on its business under the name 'Wave Oh', National Hair Brushes plc must comply with certain requirements as follows: s 4 Business Names Act 1985.

  (i)   It must **state** its **registered name** and address legibly on all business letters, invoices, receipts, written orders for goods and services and written demands for payment of debts.

  (ii)   It must **display** its **registered name** and address in a prominent position in any **business premises** to which its customers or suppliers have access.

  (iii) It must **give notice** of its **registered name** and address to **anyone who does business** with the company and who requests that information.

  (iv)   The **address** must be one at which **service of a document** relating to the business will be **legally effective** and must be within Great Britain.

(b) **Passing-off action**

Lancashire Hair Brushes plc may seek to bring a '**passing-off action**', a common law action which applies when one company believes that another's conduct (here the use of a company name) is causing **confusion** in the minds of the public over the goods which each company sells. Lancashire Hair Brushes plc would apply to the court for an injunction to prevent National Hair Brushes plc from using its name.

However, in order to be successful, Lancashire Hair Brushes plc will need to satisfy the court, that:

  (i)   **Confusion** has arisen because of National Hair Brushes use of its registered name.

  (ii)   It lays claim to **something exclusive** and distinctive and not something in general use: *Aerators Ltd v Tollit*. The courts are unlikely to rule that the name is exclusive and distinctive here.

Appeal to Registrar

Alternatively Lancashire Hair Brushes plc might object to the Registrar of Companies that the name National Hair Brushes is too like its own name and is causing confusion, thus appealing to the **Registrar of Companies** to exercise its power under s 28 to compel a change of name. In these circumstances, the Registrar would invite written submissions from each company, on which he would base his decision (against which there is no appeal).

(c) **Purpose of registered office**

The registered office is the legal address of the company, which means that documents served at the registered office have been served on the company.

First registered office

The first **registered office** of a company must be set out in the prescribed documents presented to the Registrar on **incorporation** under s 10. The address will not be set out in the memorandum of association but only the **country** of the registered office, ie England and Wales or Scotland. This fixes the **domicile** of the company which (unlike other details in the memorandum) cannot be altered.

Alteration of address

The address of the registered office can, however, be **altered** at any time by the directors, provided the new address is in the same domicile. The address need not have any close connection with the company.

Notice of the **new address** must be sent to the registrar within **15 days** and the alteration will be effective after the registration (s 287(3)). The registrar must give notice of the change in the London Gazette and the company's letterheads and annual returns must be amended to reflect the change.

Documents may still be served on the former address for **14 days following** registration of the alteration.

(d) General commercial company

In the **objects clause** in the company's memorandum of association the company may be registered with the objects of being 'to carry on business as a **general commercial company**' as permitted by s 3A. The clause then would be so wide as to mean that the company can carry on any trade or business whatsoever and that the company has power to do all such things as are incidental or conducive to the carrying on of any trade or business by it.

Alteration of objects

However, if the registered objects clause is more detailed (which may be preferable with regard to securing investment in the company for example), it can be altered by the company in general meeting by passing a **special resolution**. The alteration can be for any reason. Provided no objection is made under s 5 a **copy** of the **resolution** and amended **memorandum** must be submitted to the Registrar within **15 days** of the period for making an application under s 5.

Right of objection

S 5 provides that, within **21 days** from the date of the special resolution, members holding in aggregate at least **15% of the issued share capital** or **15% of any class of shares** may apply to the court to modify an otherwise valid alteration of the objects clause. They must not have originally voted in favour of the alteration or consented to it. The court may make such order as it deems fit.

47 NORTH OF ENGLAND

> **Tutor's hint**. Do not limit your answer in part (a) to alteration of the objects clause. The name will need to be altered as well.

(a) Objects clause alteration

Because of the extent of the diversification and the relocation, the company should **alter** its **objects clause**. A company can now alter its objects for any reason whatsoever, and, by taking advantage of s 3A provide that 'the object of the company is to carry on business as a general commercial company'.

It might be desirable to change the company's name, if it has changed the area of its operations. The existing name does not reflect the proposed new area of the company's activity.

To carry out the proposed alterations, the directors must call an extraordinary general meeting, or place the matters on the agenda of the annual general meeting. Both the name and the objects clause may be altered by **special resolution** (75% majority).

The company must deliver to the Registrar of Companies:

- A **signed copy** of the **resolution** by which the alteration is made (s 380)
- A **copy** of the **altered memorandum** itself

This must be done within **15 days** of making the alteration. The registrar gives notice of receiving it in the *London Gazette*: s 711. The company cannot rely on the alteration against a person ignorant of it if this notification procedure is not observed.

(b) **Minority objection**

S 5 provides a procedure for a dissenting minority to apply to the court to modify an otherwise valid alteration of the objects clause. The conditions are that:

- Application to the court must be made within **21 days** from the passing of the special resolution to alter the objects.

- The applicants must hold in aggregate at least **15 per cent** of the **issued share capital** or 15 per cent of any class of shares. They must not originally have voted in favour of the alteration, nor consented to it.

The court may do any one of the following:

- **Confirm** the **resolution** to alter the objects clause (possibly subject to certain conditions)

- **Cancel** the **alteration**

- **Adjourn the proceedings** to allow the majority shareholders the opportunity of purchasing the shares of the dissenting minority

- **Provide for the purchase** by the company of the dissenting minority's shares and for the consequent reduction of the company's capital

(c) **Proxies**

Any member of a company which has a share capital, if entitled to attend and vote at a general or class meeting of the company, has a statutory right (s 372) to appoint an agent, called a '**proxy**', to attend and vote for him. This right must be stated in the notice calling the meeting.

The directors may, at the company's expense, issue **proxy cards** to members, but if they do so they must issue them to all members and not just to their supporters.

The articles may require that the proxy appointment cards shall only be valid if received in advance of the meeting, but may not fix an **interval longer than 48 hours** before the meeting for receipt of proxies.

A member of a **private company** may only nominate **one proxy**. However, the proxy has the **right to speak** at the meeting. A member of a **public company** may appoint **more than one proxy**, but his proxy has **no** statutory **right to speak** at the meeting. Whether it is a private or public company, the proxy may demand and vote on a poll, but not on a show of hands.

48   ARTICLES

> **Tutor's hint.** It is essential that you have a good understanding of the articles of association, since reference to them is needed when considering many aspects of company law. The examiner commented that many candidates failed to explain how the articles constituted a binding contract, and some candidates confused the articles with the memorandum. Notice that the question asks for content **and** effect.

Content of articles

A company's articles of association lay down **rules governing its internal management** and the rights of its shareholders and directors.

The principal areas covered will be the issue and transfer of shares, alterations of the company's capital structure, voting rights and the conduct of general meetings, the appointment, powers, duties and proceedings of company directors, dividends, class rights and the procedure for their variation, accounts, audit and the issue of notices.

Where a company does submit its own articles on incorporation, these must be signed by the subscribers to the memorandum of association but not where new or altered articles are submitted at a later date. In the event of any conflict between a company's memorandum and articles, the memorandum shall prevail.

Legal effect of articles

S 14 states that the memorandum and articles of a company **bind the company and its members** to the same extent as if they had been signed and sealed by each member and each member had covenanted to observe all their provisions. Thus the articles are treated as a **binding contract** between the company and its members and as a binding contract between the shareholders.

Thus the company's articles were enforceable by the company against one of its shareholders in *Hickman v Kent or Romney Marsh Sheepbreeders Association* and by the members against the company in *Pender v Lushington*. The role applies only where the shareholders' rights affected are their rights as members and not in any personal capacity or capacity as director: *Beattie v ECF Beattie Ltd*.

Rayfield v Hands illustrates the existence of a contract between company members under s 14. In this case the articles required that the directors should purchase the shares of any member wishing to transfer his shares and also that the directors should also be shareholders. When the directors claimed that their liability was not as members and that the article was not enforceable by members, it was held that the article created an enforceable contract between the claimant members and directors as members of the company.

The **articles do not constitute a contract with any third party** by virtue of s 14: *Eley v Positive Government Security Life Assurance Co*. However, where a contract between a company and a third party fails to address an issue which is covered in the company's articles, the relevant provisions may be taken to supply a missing contract term: *Re New British Iron Co, ex parte Beckwith*.

If legislation enables a company to do something provided its articles contain appropriate authority, the company, in the absence of such authority, will need to alter its articles first of all before doing the thing permitted. The alteration must be *bona fide* for the benefit of the company as a whole, meaning the individual hypothetical member. **Alterations cannot be made if their effect is to place the articles in conflict with the memorandum or statute**. The courts will look with suspicion upon changes that give some members the power to expel others (*Dafen Tinplate Co Ltd v Llanelly Steel Co (1907) Ltd*), unless the benefit to the company is clear (for example expulsion of a member who is competing with the company: *Sidebottom v Kershaw Leese*). The fact that a contract with a third party may be broken by a change in the articles does not invalidate that change, however damages may be payable: *Southern Foundries v Shirlaw*.

In some cases, provisions of a statute may prohibit a company from doing something notwithstanding anything to the contrary in its articles of association.

Where a company fails to submit its own articles of association or where its articles fail to deal with a particular issue, **Table A** will apply. Table A applies only to companies limited by shares.

A company may alter any of its articles (usually) by the passing of a special resolution to that effect.

Marking Guide	
	Marks
Set out internal regulations	1
Examples of contents	1
Signed by subscribers	1
Effect of S14 CA 85	2
Cases or examples of binding members and company	1
Binding members to members	1
Not a contract with a third party (plus case or example)	1
Bona fide alteration possible	1
If no articles Table A applies	_1_
	10

49   STATUTORY RECORDS

> **Tutor's hint**. The wording of the question means that you do not need to mention alternative locations. However, you should be aware that the register of members may also be kept at the place where it is made up, and the register of directors' interests and substantial members may be kept at the same location as the register of members. The register of debentureholders may be kept elsewhere provided the Registrar is informed of its whereabouts.

The Companies Act 1985 requires the following documents to be kept at a company's registered office:

- **Register of members** (s 352) and an index of members if there are more than 50

- **Register of directors and secretaries** (s 288) containing the details specified

- **Register of directors' interest in shares** and debentures of the company and its associates: s 325

- **Register of fixed and floating charges** over the company's property and undertakings, together with copies of the charges: s 411

- **Minutes** of general meetings of the company's members: s 382

- **Register of notifiable interests** in shares

- **Register of debenture-holders** if there is one

Other documents

In addition to these registers, a number of other documents must be kept at the registered office if circumstances bring about their existence; for instance, if a company wants to approve or release a **contract** or option for the **purchase** of its own shares in an off-market purchase, a copy of such a contract must be kept at the registered office for at least 15 days before the required resolution: s 164(6). If a scheme such as this is implemented the contract must be kept there for 10 years: s 169(4).

Also in relation to maintenance of capital, a company which intends to redeem or purchase its shares out of capital must keep a copy of the requisite **declaration of solvency** and auditors' report at the registered office: s 175.

Finally, except in limited circumstances, a copy or memorandum of a director's **service contract** must be kept at the registered office (or two other specified locations): s 318(3).

Marking Guide	Marks
Register of members	1
Register of directors and secretaries	1
Register of directors' interests in shares	1
Register of fixed and floating charges	1
Minutes of general meetings of members	1
Register of notifiable interests in shares	1
Register of debenture holders	1
Other documents	
1 mark for each; max.	3
	10

50 LAX LTD

Tutor's hint. As with most Section B questions, the way to tackle this question is to:

- Identify the **issue**
- **State** the law
- **Apply** the law in the situation
- **Conclude**

Examiner's comments. This was the least popular question on the paper. Answers tended to be either very good or very bad, with marks to correspond. The question relied on analysis of the problem scenario, a recognition of the legal problems raised and a proposed solution to those problems. Weaker candidates tended to focus just on s 459 CA85 as a solution to all the issues, while the alteration of the articles should have been addressed more immediately.

S 303 CA85 provides that a director may be removed from office at any time by **ordinary resolution of which special notice** (28 days) has been given to the company by the person proposing it. Neither the articles nor any service agreement can override this statutory power. On receipt of the special notice, the company must send a copy to the relevant director who may require that a memorandum of reasonable length be issued to the members. He also has a right to address the meeting at which the resolution is considered (s 304).

(a) Since Kath owns 76% of the shareholding, she may pass the ordinary resolution required (which needs only a simple majority of 51%) to remove Owen. Likewise, she is able to pass a resolution appointing Ron, since only an ordinary resolution of the members is needed to appoint a new director.

As Owen is not a member of the company, he has no right to protest under s 459. However, his removal would constitute a **breach of his service contract** with Lax Ltd that is expressed to run until 2005. As a consequence, he would be entitled to sue for damages for breach of contract. He may also consider an action for unfair dismissal.

A company's articles of association **bind its members to the company, the company to its members and its members to each other** (s 14 CA 1985). The members are contractually bound by the articles in their dealings with one another as if each had separately agreed to be bound by them (*Rayfield v Hands*).

A company's articles of association may be altered by the company by passing a **special resolution** to that effect in general meeting (s 9 CA 1985). The articles once properly altered are binding on the company and its members in the same way as the original articles. An article cannot be made unalterable by declaring it to be unalterable in the articles or by requiring a greater majority vote than is required by s 9 or by means of a separate contract under which the company undertakes not to alter it. An alteration will be void if it conflicts with the Companies Acts or with the memorandum. Equally it will be void if it compels any member to subscribe for additional shares or if the majority who approve it are not acting bona fide in what they deem to be the interests of the company as a whole. An alteration cannot have retrospective effect. Any alteration which varies class rights must be made according to the correct rights variation procedure.

In *Greenhalgh v Arderne Cinemas Ltd* the Court of Appeal made it clear that the 'bona fide for the benefit of the company as a whole' test referred to above is a single test and also a subjective test (ie what did the majority believe?). The company as a whole in this context means the general body of shareholders. The test is whether every 'individual hypothetical member' would in the honest opinion of the majority benefit from the alteration. Provided the purpose is to benefit the company as a whole, the alteration does not become invalid by reason of the minority suffering special detriment or some members escaping loss (*Allen v Gold Reefs of West Africa Ltd*).

(b) (i) Kath's proposed resolution to remove the existing pre-emption rights is the same as that made in *Greenhalgh's case*. Following that case, where it was held that the variation would be to the advantage of 'the hypothetical member' (notwithstanding that it reduced the rights of real members), it is likely that the proposal would be deemed to be legitimate. Since she holds 76% of the shares in Lax Ltd, she can pass the necessary special resolution.

(ii) The proposed resolution to require any member who carries on a competing business to sell his shares to the company at a fair value is questionable because it is 'discriminatory' against a minority. However, the courts will regard such an alteration as valid provided the majority was concerned to benefit the company or to remove some detriment to its interests. The alteration would not be valid if the majority was clearly seeking to secure an advantage to itself.

In *Sidebottom v Kershaw, Leese & Co Ltd*, the articles were altered in the way proposed by Kath. The court held that the 'expulsion' resulting from the alteration was valid. It was justifiable and made bona fide in the interests of the company as a whole, in removing a competitor who had knowledge of the company.

Following the *Sidebottom case*, it appears that Kath will also be able to alter the articles in this respect lawfully.

(iii) This proposed alteration cannot be argued to be bona fide in the interests of the company as a whole but is simply the oppressive use of majority power. A similar alteration in *Brown v British Abrasive Wheel Co*, which required any member to sell his or her shares to the majority (rather than to the company) on demand, was held invalid since it was purely for the benefit of the majority. It was not 'directly concerned with the provision of further capital' and was not for the benefit of the company. Following the *Brown case*, this resolution would appear to be unlawful and so Norm cannot be forced to sell his 14% shareholding.

Marking Guide	
	Marks
Removal of director	1
Articles and service contract cannot override s 303	1
Kath can pass ordinary resolution	1
Kath can appoint Ron	1
Owen has no rights under s 459 CA85	1
Effect of s 14 CA85	2
Alteration of articles procedure	2
Situations when alteration void	2
Cases	1
Effect on pre-emption rights	2
Discussion of compulsory sale at fair value	2
Cases	1
Effect on Kath	1
Impact of a non bona fide alteration	2
	20

51 RESOLUTIONS

> **Tutor's hint**. You should be familiar with all the types of resolution a company can pass. This question should therefore hold no fear, as it is an ideal opportunity to earn easy marks.

(a) An extraordinary resolution is one carried by **a majority of 75%** or more of votes cast. A **14 days' notice** period applies (s 378)

An extraordinary resolution is required, for example, where the company is to be put into creditors' voluntary liquidation (where it may be advantageous to have the 14 day notice period rather than the 21 days required for a special resolution).

An extraordinary resolution may also be required where there is to be variation of class rights.

(b) A special resolution requires **a majority of 75%** or more to pass it and also requires a **special notice period of 21 days** (s 378).

A special resolution will be required for a change of name (s 28), reduction of share capital (s 135), alteration of the objects or articles (ss4 and 9), a voluntary winding up (in most cases) and for the presentation of a petition by the company for a compulsory winding up.

A **signed copy** of all special and extraordinary resolutions must be **delivered to the Registrar** of Companies for filing, usually within 15 days of their being passed. Also the **text** of special and extraordinary resolutions must be **set out in full in the notice convening the meeting** and they must be described as such.

(c) An elective resolution is one which may be passed only by a **private company** in particular circumstances. These are:

(i) The conferring of **authority to issue shares** indefinitely or for a fixed period which may exceed 5 years (s 80A)

(ii) The **dispensing with the laying of accounts** before a general meeting, unless required by a member or the auditors (s 252)

(iii) The **dispensing with the annual appointment of auditors** (s 386)

(iv) The dispensing with the need to hold an **AGM** unless required by a member (s 366A), and

(v) The reduction to 90% or more of the **majority required to consent to short notice** under s 369(4) or s 378(3).

All members who are entitled to attend meetings and vote must agree to the passing of an elective resolution, in person or by proxy. 21 days notice must be given The resolution must be registered within 15 days (s 379)

An elective resolution can be **revoked by ordinary resolution**, which must also be registered (s 379,380).

(d) A **written resolution** is a resolution **signed by all members entitled to attend and vote** and can be any resolution which could **ordinarily be passed in general meeting**. The Act provides that the written resolutions shall be 'equivalent' to resolutions passed in general meeting. **Essentially, they enable the company to carry on business without the need to call meetings.** A written resolution need not be contained in a single document so long as all documents signed set out the resolution.

A written resolution can be used notwithstanding any provision in the company's articles. **A written resolution cannot, however, be used to remove a director or auditor** from office under s 303 or s 391 respectively, since both have a right to attend and speak at a meeting where any proposal for removal is to be discussed. A copy of any proposed written resolution or details thereof must be sent in advance to the company's auditors at or before the time notice is sent to shareholders. Failure to comply with this requirement renders the company liable to a fine but the validity of the resolution is not affected.

The date of a written resolution is the date of the last member's signature and the company is required to keep a record of all written resolutions.

52 MEETINGS AND VOTES

> **Tutorial note.** This is another two-part 'explain' question and is therefore typical of Part A on the paper. Part (b) of this question is probably more tricky than part (a), particularly because it might be tempting to talk about resolutions (as the examiner regrets candidates did (below)) as this is an area you were very likely to be very well prepared, while you were less so about the mechanics of voting. However, good marks can be gained for relatively simple and short explanations of polls and show of hands. Use the answer to this question in your revision. Remember, no matter how learned you are on your chosen specialised subject, always, always, always answer the question set. Answers which sadly do not answer the question will win no marks at all.

(a) **Meetings**

Annual general meeting

An annual general meeting ('AGM') must be called by the directors **once in each calendar year** (not more than 15 months elapsing between meetings) save that private companies are permitted to dispense with holding an AGM by passing an elective resolution. If the directors fail to call an AGM, the members may apply to the DTI which may call the AGM instead.

Extraordinary general meeting

An extraordinary general meeting ('EGM') may be called in any of the following ways:

(i)   By the **directors** whenever they see fit (Art 37)

(ii) By the directors on the requisition of **members holding at least one-tenth of the paid up share capital carrying voting rights** or (if there is no share capital) one-tenth of the voting rights, in which case the meeting must be called within 28 days of the requisition being deposited. If the directors fail to call the meeting

within 21 days of the members' requisition being issued, the members may themselves convene the meeting for a date within 3 months of the requisition

(iii)   By the **court,** on the application of a director or member (s371 CA). This is usually in the case of deadlock (for example where one member of two refuses to attend and so provide a quorum)

(iv)   By an **auditor** who gives a statement detailing the circumstances for his resignation or other loss of office and requires his explanation to be considered by the company (s394 CA) and

(v)   **Compulsorily,** by the directors of a public company where the **net assets fall to half or less of the amount of its called up share capital** (s142 CA).

(b) **Votes**

Unless a poll is demanded, a resolution is decided upon by a **show of hands**, where every person present has one vote and proxies do not vote. On a poll, each share normally carries one vote, so a member or his proxy may use as many votes as his shareholding grants him. It need not be held at the time, but can be postponed so that arrangements to hold it can be made. In either case, the number of votes cast determines the result and votes which are available but not used are disregarded.

A poll may be demanded by not less than 5 members (unless the articles provide for a lesser figure) or members representing at least one tenth of the total voting rights or members holding shares which represent at least one tenth of the paid up capital. When a poll is held, any previous vote on a show of hands is disregarded and the votes cast are checked against the register of members.

Marking Guide		Marks
(a) AGM called by directors		1
Timing requirements		1
Members can fall if directors fail		1
EGMs (1 mark for each possibility)		3
		6
(b) Show of hands		1
One person one vote		1
Poll		1
Depends on shareholdings		1
		4
Total		10

53   MEETINGS

> **Tutor's hint**. This should be a straightforward question to answer, as all it requires is statement of fact.

(a) **Annual general meeting**

Every company must hold an annual general meeting ('AGM') in each **calendar year:** s 366. Provided that the first AGM is held within eighteen months of incorporation, the company need not hold another AGM within the year of incorporation or in that following year, otherwise **not more than 15 months may elapse between meetings.**

Under s 366A, a **private company** can pass an **elective resolution** to dispense with the holding of an AGM. Such a resolution will be effective for the year in which it is made and subsequent and any member is entitled to require the holding of an AGM at any

time while such a resolution is in place by notice to the company not later than 3 months before the end of the year.

In the event of default, the DTI on application of any member may call an AGM and give such directions as he deems necessary, including fixing a quorum of one.

At least 21 days' written **notice** must be given for each AGM unless all members entitled to attend agree to shorter notice: s 369. The notice must specify the meetings as an AGM. Ordinary business to be transacted at an AGM includes the consideration of the directors' and auditors' reports and the company accounts, the election of directors and appointment of auditors, the fixing of auditors' remuneration and the declaration of dividends. The full text of any proposed resolution concerning special business is set out in the notice.

(b) **Extraordinary general meeting**

Other meetings of the company are extraordinary meetings ('EGM's), and 14 days' written notice (or 21 days where a special resolution is proposed) must be given. The meeting may be called in any of the following ways.

(i) By the **directors** whenever they see fit

(ii) By the **directors on the requisition of members** holding at least one-tenth of the paid up share capital carrying voting rights or (if there is no share capital) one-tenth of the voting rights, in which case the meeting must be called within 28 days of the requisition being deposited.

(iii) By the **court**, on the application of a director or member, usually in the case of deadlock (for example where one member of two refuses to attend and so provide a quorum)

(iv) By an **auditor** who gives a statement detailing the circumstances for his resignation or other loss of office and requires his explanation to be considered by the company

(v) **Compulsorily,** by the directors of a public company where the net assets fall to half or less of the amount of its called up share capital

(c) **Class meetings**

A class meeting may be called by the directors for the holder of one class of shares to approve a proposed **variation of rights** attached to those shares.

The standard general meeting rules on issuing **notices** and on voting apply to a class meeting. The **quorum** for a class meeting is two persons who hold at least one third in nominal value of the issued shares of the class except that a quorum of one is permissible where all the shares are held by one member.

Marking Guide		Marks
AGM –	timing	
	private co	
	DTI	
	notice	4
EGM –	explanation	1
	various callers	3
	(directors, members, court)	
Class meeting	– variation of rights	1
	– quorum	1
		$\overline{10}$

54   PREPARATION QUESTION: HYDRANGEA

Tutor's hint. The marks in (a) would have been weighted towards giving details of what the **notice** of the meeting should contain; as the directors are unsure about the requirements, it is quite possible that the notice would not contain sufficient details if you just told them that they had to give notice.

To pass (a)(i), you would also have had to identify correctly the **types of resolution** required; special for a change of name, whatever the articles specify (generally ordinary) for an increase in share capital.

In (a) (ii) your answer should have stated that votes are normally taken on a show of hands. Because a holding of a poll depends on certain conditions being fulfilled, you needed to describe what these conditions were. You also needed to make the position of proxies clear; because we are told that Hydrangea is a **private** company with **Table A** articles, s 372 applies and proxies cannot vote except on a poll.

The 5% limit mentioned in (b) for requisitioning a resolution is an important one to remember, as you may be set a question where the requisitionists failed to fulfil the limits. However Diana clearly fulfils the requirements here. We are also told that the meeting will be held, so there is no question of forcing the directors to hold the meeting. As the company has Table A articles, it will not have a *Bushell v Faith* clause giving the directors weighted voting rights to prevent their removal.

The key issue is therefore how a quorate meeting can be held, and application to the courts offers Diana her best chance.

(a)   (i)   **Calling of the meeting**

You must call an **extraordinary general meeting** in order that both resolutions might be passed. You are empowered to call an EGM at any time by Table A Art 37.

Notice of the meeting

Notice of the EGM must be sent to every **member** of the company who is entitled to attend and vote at the meeting. It should also be sent to the directors and auditors. The notice should:

(1)   Give adequate information concerning the **date, time and place** of the meeting

(2)   Describe the proposed **special resolution** as such

(3)   Give sufficient **details** of the **proposed business** at the meeting to enable recipients of the notice to understand what it is proposed to be done at the meeting

Length of notice

The length of notice required is **21 clear days** notice because of the special resolution: s 369.

If the notice is posted, it shall be deemed to have been **received 48 hours after posting**. 'Clear days notice' means that the day the notice is received and the day of the meeting are excluded in calculating the notice period.

Increasing the authorised share capital

Under Table A, authority to **increase the authorised share capital** of a company needs to be given by an **ordinary resolution** of the company in general meeting, which is carried by a simple majority (over 50%) of votes cast.

Changing the company's name

Authority to **change the name** of a company requires a **special resolution** of the company in general meeting (s 28), which means a 75% majority of votes cast is needed to pass it.

(ii)   **Voting rights**

The **rights** of members **to vote** and the **number of votes** to which they are entitled will be **determined by** the company's **articles**.

Show of hands

Voting is normally done by a **show of hands** by each member present in person who each has **one vote**. Proxies cannot vote in this way.

The chairman's declaration of the result on a show of hands (in the absence of it being fraudulent or manifestly wrong) will be conclusive. **Voting** by **show of hands** will **not be effective**, however, where a poll is properly demanded.

Polls

S 378 provides that there is a statutory right to a poll wherever a special (or extraordinary) resolution is proposed. Voting on a poll may be demanded by at least **five members** or by **members representing at least one tenth of the voting rights** or by members holding **at least one tenth of the paid-up capital** conferring voting rights. (A company's articles cannot make these criteria more onerous from the shareholders' point of view.)

Where voting is on a poll, every member and proxy present may cast the **full number** of votes to which they are entitled.

Proxies

Under s 372 every member entitled to **attend** and **vote** at a meeting may instead appoint a proxy to attend and vote for him. The proxy need not be a member.

Notice of the meeting must contain a statement which explains each member's **right to appoint** a non-member proxy. It also provides that a proxy **may only vote on a poll**, though (s 373) he has the same right to demand a poll as the member whom he represents. Most companies issue **two-way proxy cards** under Art 61 on which the member instructs his proxy to vote either for or against each resolution.

An appointment of a proxy is **revocable** by the member. It will be deemed to have been revoked where the member himself attends the meeting in person and votes.

(b) **Right to give notice**

Under s 376 any member or members holding at least **one twentieth of the total voting rights** is entitled to give notice in writing to the company of his or her requisition to require the company to give notice to members of a resolution they wish to move at the next AGM.

Diana holds 60% of the shares and is thus entitled to make a requisition under s 376 to have a resolution to remove the directors at the AGM. She must follow the procedure laid down in the Act strictly: *Pedley v Inland Waterways Association Lt*.

Giving notice

A copy of the requisition must be deposited at the company's registered office **not less than six weeks** (where notice of a resolution is required) before the meeting. The requisitionist, at the same time, must also deposit a sum reasonably sufficient to meet the company's expenses: s 377.

After receipt of a requisition, the company must give **notice** of the proposed resolution, and any related statement of up to 1,000 words, to all members of the company entitled to receive notice of the meeting: s 376.

Resolution for removal of director

S 303 provides that a director may be removed from office by an **ordinary resolution** subject to **special notice** of the resolution being given to the company by the member proposing the resolution. Thus Diana must notify Rake Ltd that she intends to propose the resolution at least **28 days** before the forthcoming meeting. The company must then give notice to the members of the proposed resolution at least **21 days** before the meeting.

Failure by directors to attend the meeting

If the four directors fail to attend the meeting, the meeting will be **inquorate** since **one member cannot be a quorum** except by order of the court or DTI. Art 40 requires a quorum of two persons present entitled to vote. The meeting would automatically be **adjourned** when inquorate.

Diana would be advised to **apply to the court** for an order stating that one member will constitute a quorum where it is impractical to call or conduct a meeting (under s 371). In these circumstances, if the directors remained absent in order to frustrate the business at the meeting proposed by Diana, it seems likely that the court would grant such an order.

55   FRAN, GWEN, HILARY AND INA

> **Tutor's hint.** Note the examiner's comment that answers needed to mention provisions applicable to private companies. It is important that you understand the concept of limited liability, as the examiner has stressed its importance. It is one of the cornerstones of company law.

(a) **Limited liability**

The fact that a company has **limited liability** means that, in the event of the company becoming insolvent, the shareholders of the company cannot be required to contribute more than the **amount outstanding** (if any) on their shares. So where the shareholders have already paid the nominal value of their shares plus any premium, they have no further liability.

If their shares are only partly paid up then their liability is up to the amount outstanding on those shares but no further. A company has **unlimited liability** for **its own debts,** being a distinct legal entity, separate from the identity of its members from the moment of its incorporation: *Salomon v Salomon and Co Ltd.*

Limited liability as described is one of the main advantages of incorporating a business rather than setting up a partnership (where the partners are **personally liable** for the debts of the partnership) In practice, however, creditors of a private limited company will often require personal guarantees from the company directors over and above their limited liability as members.

(b) **Appointment of directors**

On formation of a company, particulars must be filed of the company's first directors on a form which must be signed by those named to signify their consent. They shall be deemed to have been appointed as the **first directors** of the company even if the articles state otherwise: s 13.

A company's articles will govern the appointment of subsequent directors. The following summary applies where Table A applies.

(i) At a company's **first AGM all directors** must retire.

(ii) At subsequent AGMs, **one third** (in rotation) of the directors must retire (so that those retiring are those who have been in office longest since their election). If there is disagreement as to who should retire, it must be decided by lot.

(iii) Retiring directors are **eligible for re-election** and will be deemed to be re-elected unless the meeting decides otherwise.

(iv) **Casual vacancies** may be filled by the directors **co-opting** a new member, who must then retire and may stand for election at the next AGM. (He will not be included in determining which directors are due to retire in rotation.)

(v) The **company in general meeting** may decide to appoint new directors by passing an ordinary resolution.

Dismissal of directors

A director can be dismissed by retirement, removal, disqualification or on the dissolution of the company.

Retirement of directors

A director retires every third year according to the **retirement by rotation** procedure (assuming his re-election) and in the case of a public company, is deemed to retire at the AGM following his seventieth birthday: s 293.

Removal of directors from office

A director may be removed from office by an **ordinary resolution** of the company in general meeting: s 303. **Special notice** of this notice must be given to the company by the person proposing removal.

Disqualification of directors

A director may be disqualified from his office by virtue of some provision in the company's articles or for breach of certain provisions of Companies Acts or under the Company Directors Disqualification Act 1986. Under this Act, a director may be disqualified.

- Where he is **convicted** of an **indictable offence** in connection with the promotion, formation, management or liquidation of a company

- Where it appears that he has been **persistently** in **default** in relation to provisions of company legislation requiring the filing of documentation

- Where, in the course of winding up, it appears that he has been guilty of **fraudulent trading** or has participated in **wrongful trading**

- Where the Secretary of State applies to the court for a **disqualification order**.

A court **must** disqualify a director (for between 2 and 15 years) where it is satisfied that he has been the director of a company which has at any time become insolvent and that his conduct as a director makes him **unfit** to be concerned in the management of a company.

Here as membership does not confer the automatic right to be on the board, all members should ensure that they are appointed directors. If there is a subsequent breakdown in relationships resulting in one or more directors being voted off the board, the aggrieved directors may be able to obtain relief under s 459 on the grounds that the company is a **quasi-partnership**.

(c) **Annual general meeting**

Every company must hold an **annual general meeting** in **each calendar year** not more than **15 months** after the previous AGM, which meeting is in addition to any

extraordinary meetings held in that year and which is **described** as an AGM in the **notices** calling it: s 366. At least **21 days' written notice** must be given for each AGM although all members entitled to attend may agree to shorter notice: s 369.

Under s 366A, a private company can pass an **elective resolution** to **dispense** with the **holding** of an **AGM.** Such a resolution will be effective for the year in which it is made and subsequent years. Any member is entitled to require the holding of an AGM at any time while such a resolution is in place by notice to the company not later than 3 months before the end of the year.

Table A Art 36 provides that 'all general meetings other than AGMs shall be called **Extraordinary General Meetings'.** Normally 14 days notice is required unless a special resolution is proposed in which case 21 days notice is required. The directors are entitled to convene an EGM whenever they see fit (Art 37) and must convene an EGM if a **requisition** is made by the members in accordance with a procedure set out in s 368.

This section states that the requisitionists must hold at least **one-tenth** of the **paid up share capital** carrying voting rights or, if there is no share capital, represent at least **one-tenth** of the **voting rights.** They must deposit at the registered office a **signed requisition** stating the resolutions that they intend to propose, and the EGM must be held within **28 days** of the issuing of the notice.

A private company, such as this one need not hold formal general meetings. By means of **elective resolutions,** where all members entitled to attend and vote agree (s 379A) they can confer authority to issue shares, dispense with the laying of accounts before general meeting, dispense with the need for the annual appointment of auditors and (as mentioned) dispense with the holding of an AGM.

Under s 381A, anything that a private company could do by a resolution of the company in general meeting can be done by **written resolution** (except removal of a director or auditor from office) provided **all members** entitled to attend and vote **agree** and **sign** the resolution.

56 COMPANY SECRETARY

> **Tutor's hint.** The question asks you to outline the rules in three areas. That should help to structure your answer, and you should attempt all three parts. Notice that the question relates to a public limited company and answer it accordingly. Try to focus on a plc.
>
> **Marking guide.** 3 marks are available for each of the requirements of the question (appointment, duties and powers) with an additional mark for overall impression or a particularly good attempt at one of the parts.

Appointment

Section 283 CA 1985 states that **every company must have a secretary** and that a sole director shall not also be the company secretary. A corporation can fulfil the role of secretary to a company. A company may also have two or more joint secretaries.

The **directors of a public company must take all reasonable steps to ensure that the secretary is suitably qualified** for his post by his knowledge and experience (s 286 CA 1985). A public company secretary may be anyone who:

(a) **Was the secretary or his assistant on 22 December 1980** (the date on which the rules came into effect)

(b) Has been a public company secretary for at least **three out of the five years prior to his or her appointment**

(c) **Is a member of the ACCA or one of a number of other professional bodies:** ICAEW, ICAS, ICAI, CIMA, ICSA or CIPFA

(d) Is a **barrister, advocate or solicitor** in the UK

(e) **Is a person who,** by virtue of holding or having held any other position or being a member of any other body, **appears to the directors to be capable of the post.**

Duties

The **duties of the secretary** are not defined by the 1985 Act but are **laid down by the company's board of directors,** thus varying according to the size and nature of the company. Generally, the company secretary is seen as the person who is charged with ensuring that the company and its officers comply with statutory and regulatory requirements. More specifically, the secretary's duties will include the following:

(a) **Convening meetings** under Table A Article 88 and **making all arrangements incidental to meetings of the Board of Directors.** This will include matters such as issuing the agenda, collating or preparing papers to be submitted to the meeting, attending the meeting, taking minutes of the meeting and communicating decisions of the meeting as appropriate to persons inside and outside the company.

(b) **Signing forms and returns** as required and (usually) any document to which the **company seal** is applied

(c) **Maintaining the register of members,** recording transfers of shares and issuing share certificates to members

(d) Maintaining the **other statutory registers** and ensuring that all necessary **documents, returns and notices** are delivered to the **Registrar of Companies**

(e) Ensuring that **accounts are kept** in accordance with the requirements of the Companies Act (unless the company has an accountant or a finance department)

Powers

Under the general principle of the law of agency, a **company secretary may be treated as having apparent authority to bind the company** (as his principal) by his actions on its behalf, unless the company has denied him that authority and the other party has notice of the restriction.

Thus, in *Panorama Developments (Guildford) Ltd v Fidelis Furnishing Fabrics Ltd*, the Court of Appeal recognised that it is the normal function of the company secretary to enter into contracts **connected with the administration of a company** (in this case ordering cars from a car hire firm purportedly for the company's business).

In obiter dicta the court said that it would probably not have regarded the company secretary as having any authority to enter into commercial contracts such as the buying or selling of trade goods since that would not normally be the duty of the company secretary.

This new outlook by the courts contrasts with the position accepted for a long time before the Panorama case. Historically the courts have accepted that a company secretary could not bind the company in the absence of express authority for the relevant act (borrowing money, issuing a writ).

57 AUDITORS

> **Tutor's hint**. The fact that this question is split into four parts should help you structure your answer and gain high marks on this question.

Every company, with the exception of certain dormant and small private companies, **is required to appoint auditors** (s 384).

(a) Qualification

In order to be an auditor, a person must be eligible for appointment as an auditor under the rules of a recognised supervisory body and must be a **member** of such **a recognised supervisory body**. As a result, only those persons recognised as qualified by the Association of Chartered Certified Accountants, by one of the United Kingdom's three Chartered Institutes or authorised by the DTI as having similar qualifications to one of these (but obtained outside the UK) is qualified to act as an auditor.

Several types of person are **specifically not qualified** to act as a company auditor:

- Officers and employees of the company
- Anyone employed by or in partnership with such a person
- Anyone who holds such a position in respect of an associated company.

The auditor must be neither a member of nor connected with the management of the company (s 27 CA 1989). As a result of s 25(2) of the same Act, corporate bodies are now allowed to act as auditors. Acting as an auditor to a company while ineligible is a criminal offence.

(b) Appointment

The **first auditors** are **appointed by the directors** of a new company. They are appointed to hold office until the conclusion of the first meeting at which the accounts are considered (s 385).

The **directors** or the company in general meeting **may** also **appoint** an **auditor to fill a casual vacancy** (s 388).

In normal circumstances, the members appoint the auditors at each general meeting at which the accounts are considered, to hold office until the next such meeting, that is, to audit and report on the accounts to be prepared for that subsequent meeting. This will often consist of reappointing the existing auditors or new auditors may be appointed.

If the members fail to appoint auditors at the general meeting at which the accounts are considered, the company must, within 7 days of the meeting, give notice to **the Secretary of State, who has the power to appoint auditors** (s 387).

A **dormant private company may be exempted from the requirement to appoint auditors** and have an annual audit if it passes a special resolution to this effect (s 388A and s 250). Certain small companies may also be exempt provided certain conditions are fulfilled.

A private company may dispense with the requirement to appoint auditors annually, by elective resolution in accordance with s 379A. In this case the auditors are deemed to be reappointed for each subsequent financial year while the election is in force.

(c) **Removal**

Auditors may **resign** from office by giving written notice to that effect or they may decline re-appointment or not be re-elected. Together with notice of resignation, the auditor must deposit at the company's registered office a written statement of any circumstances which he believes should be brought to the attention of members and creditors or a statement that there are no such circumstances (s 394).

Where a statement of circumstances is given, the auditor may also request an extraordinary general meeting and/or attend and speak at any meeting at which his resignation or the appointment of his successors is to be considered.

Auditors may be **removed** at any time by the **members passing an ordinary resolution** in general meeting in which case **special notice** is required (s 391). Any auditor who is to be removed or not re-appointed is entitled to make written representations which can be circulated or read out at the relevant meeting.

Auditors removed before their term of office expires are also entitled to attend and speak at any meeting at which their term of office would have expired or at which the appointment of their successors is to be considered (s 392).

(d) **Rights and duties**

Auditors have **statutory powers** which entitled them to obtain whatever information they require for the purposes of the audit. Under s 389 they may **inspect books and records** and call on officers of the company for **explanations and information**.

Under s 390 auditors are also **entitled to receive notices** and other documents relating to all **general meetings** (or written resolutions as appropriate (s 381) and to **attend and speak** at such meetings **when the business affects their role as auditors**.

The **statutory duty** of auditors is to **report** to the members of the company on whether the **accounts** which they have audited give a **true and fair view** and have been **properly prepared** in accordance with the Companies Act (s 235). This report covers the profit and loss account and balance sheet of the company. To fulfil this duty, the auditors must be aware of their duties under relevant companies legislation and the company's articles of association.

The auditors must form an opinion as to whether proper accounting records have been kept, whether proper returns adequate for the audit have been received from branches, whether the accounts are in agreement with the underlying accounting records, whether the information given in the directors' report is consistent with the accounts and whether Sch 6 relating to disclosure of directors' emoluments and other benefits has been obeyed.

The auditors' report must be read before any general meeting at which the accounts are considered and must be open to inspection by the members.

Auditors may also have duties in particular circumstances, for example in connection with the valuation of non-cash consideration for share allotments by a public company (ss 44 and 108), financial assistance for the purchase of he company's own shares (s 156) and the purchase or redemption of the company's own shares by a payment out of capital (s 173).

58   FIDUCIARY DUTIES

> **Tutor's hint**. This question requires you to set out the law in this area. You could also get a Section B question on these lines in the exam, where you are required to apply this law to a given scenario.
>
> **Examiner's comments**. Although this was a popular question, the majority of candidates who attempted it did not deal with it well. Candidates did not appreciate the difference between fiduciary and other duties of directors, and poorer candidates did not quote cases in support of their answers.

There are a **number of duties** imposed upon company directors including a **duty of care**, certain specific duties imposed by **statute** and **fiduciary duties**.

At **common law**, directors' duties **are owed primarily to the company** as the general body of shareholders rather than to individual shareholders: *Percival v Wright*. Since they make contracts as agents of the company and have control of its property, **directors are said to be akin to trustees** and thus owe **fiduciary duties** to the company in the same way as agents owe fiduciary duties to the principal.

Act bona fide in the interests of the company

First, a director must **act within the powers given to him** and must **exercise those powers bona fide in what he honestly considers to be the interests of the company**: *Re Lee Behrens & Co Ltd*. (The test is not entirely subjective, however, and if it is considered that no reasonable person could have held such a belief, the court may intervene.)

In *Hogg v Cramphorn* it was held that if an issue of shares to prevent a takeover bid was done honestly by the directors in the best interests of the company, the improper act could be ratified by the shareholders.

Proper purpose

Secondly, a director must **exercise his powers for a proper purpose**. Directors' powers are restricted to the purposes for which they were given. If a director exercises his powers for a collateral purpose, the transaction will be invalid unless ratified by the company in general meeting.

In *Howard Smith v Ampol Petroleum Ltd*, directors allotted new shares to a prospective bidder in order to reduce the majority of dissenting shareholders since they honestly believed the proposed bid to be in the company's best interests. It was held that the allotment was void. **Notwithstanding the directors' attempt to act honestly in the interests of the company, the use of their power for an improper purpose was breach of this fiduciary duty**.

The **company** in general meeting may, however, elect to **approve** of the transaction (in advance or retrospectively) by passing an ordinary resolution to that effect. Ratification will not be effective where it constitutes a fraud on the minority or involves a misappropriation of assets or prejudices creditors' interests when the company is insolvent.

Avoid conflicts of interest

Thirdly, a director must **avoid any conflict of duty and personal interest**, must **not obtain any personal advantage** from his position as director without the consent of the company (*Regal Hastings v Gulliver*) and must not fetter his discretion by agreeing to vote as some other person directs.

In the Regal Hastings case, the directors funded the creation of a subsidiary company in order to purchase two more cinemas. This resulted in profits on a later sale of the company.

It was held that they had only made the profits because of their position as directors of the parent company and they were therefore required to account for the profits.

The **possibility of a conflict is sufficient, it is not necessary to prove an actual conflict**: *Aberdeen Rly Co v Blaikie Bros*. A transaction entered into in breach of this fiduciary duty may be ratified by the company in general meeting. Directors are permitted to enter into or be interested in contracts with the company, despite conflicts of interest (which may be inevitable), subject to certain rules requiring disclosure of those interests, eg s 37 CA 1985.

Marking Guide	
	Marks
Basic duties of directors: *Percival v Wright*	1
Act bona fide in interests of company	1
Re Lee Behrens and Co Ltd	1
Hogg v Cramphorn	1
Exercise power for proper purpose	1
Howard Smith v Ampol Petroleum Ltd	1
Avoid conflicts of interest	1
Regal Hastings v Gulliver	1
No personal advantage from position as director	1
Possibility of conflict is sufficient	1
	10

59   FRAN, GILL AND HARRY

> **Tutor's hint.** The fact that this question is broken down into four, five mark questions should make it fairly straightforward to answer and therefore a sensible one to tackle. In an exam, ensure that you feel you can attempt an answer to all parts of the question before you begin. This is essential because there will be marks available in every section for stating fairly basic principles of law. Sometimes the parts of a question build on one another, so you need a knowledge of all of the elements.
>
> **Marking guide.** Equal application of marks to each part of the question.
>
> To maximise marks for each part, include:
>
> - The issue
> - Statement of the law (including case or statute)
> - Application of the law to the situation
> - Conclusion in this situation

(a)   **Removing Fran from the board of directors**

Procedure under s 303 Companies Act 1985

S 303 CA85 provides that a director may be removed from office at any time by **ordinary resolution with special notice**. This means that the resolution will require a **simple majority** to be passed, but that the proposer of the motion must give the company **28 days notice** of the resolution.

On receipt of the special notice, the company must send a **copy to the relevant director** who **may require that a memorandum** of reasonable length **be issued to the members**. He also has a **right to address the meeting** at which the resolution is considered (s 304).

Section 303 **cannot be overridden by the articles or by any service agreement although the articles can provide for weighted voting rights** (*Bushell v Faith*) or permit an easier procedure, for example a resolution of the board of directors.

Impact on Gill and Harry

Gill and Harry are therefore in a position to serve special notice on the company proposing Fran's removal from the board. As they hold 2/3 of the shares and voting rights they **will be able to pass the ordinary resolution required by s 303.** Any resulting breach of service contract will not render the dismissal unlawful but could render the company liable for breach of contract (*Southern Foundries Ltd v Shirlaw*)

(b) **Legality of Fran's protection in the Articles**

Section 14 CA provides that a **company's memorandum and articles** shall have the effect of a **contract between the members** and **between the company and its members**. However, this rule applies only to rights and obligations affecting members **in their capacity as members**.

Thus in *Eley v Positive Government Security Life Assurance Co*, the company's articles included provision for Eley to be employed as the company's solicitor. When he later sued the company for breach of contract in not employing him as a solicitor, it was held that he could not rely on s 14 since he was not asserting any rights qua member only in his role as solicitor.

In this case, **Fran might seek to rely** on s 14 to protect her appointment and contract contained in the articles but she will be **unable to do so in the light of Eley's case.** However, she may be entitled to payment resulting from **breach** of any other **service contract** (Shirlaw's case, above) on a **quantum meruit** basis, which contract can be implied from the parties' conduct and evidenced by the terms of the articles (*Re New British Iron Co, ex parte Beckwith*).

(c) **Altering the articles**

Statutory power to amend

A company has a statutory power to alter its articles by **special resolution** (s 9(1)) Such an alteration can be made in an **extraordinary general meeting** by a **seventy five percent majority** or by the **unanimous consent of all members under the assent principle** (*Cane v Jones*).

Generally, if the majority alter the articles but are **not acting bona fide** in what they deem to be the interests of the company as a whole, the **alteration may be void.** If the alteration is in fact intended to benefit the majority rather than the company, the minority will be entitled to protection.

In *Greenhalgh v Arderne Cinemas Ltd*, it was said that the test was whether the majority honestly believed that the alteration would be beneficial to the company as a whole, that is, the general body of shareholders or every individual hypothetical member. In *Sidebottom v Kershaw, Leese and Co Ltd*, an alteration providing for the mandatory sale of shares by any member who competed with the company was upheld as bona fide in the interests of the company as a whole.

Impact on Harry and Gill

Sidebottom's case (above) suggests that **alteration** of the articles to force Fran to sell her shares **would be legal** as she has been working for a rival company. However, **Gill and Harry have only 66% of the voting rights.**

In practice in this case, that although alteration would be legal, they would be **unable to pass the resolution required as it needs to be passed by a special resolution.** This is a 75% majority.

(d) **Action for breach of fiduciary duty**

The principal fiduciary duties of the directors of a company are to **act bona fide in the interests of the company, to use their powers for a proper purpose** (that is, not for any collateral purpose) and to **avoid conflicts of duty and personal interest.**

A director **cannot obtain personal advantage** from his position as director unless permitted by the company. A director must show **undivided concern for the company's interests,** regardless of whether or not the company is prejudiced by a conflict of interests (*Aberdeen Rly Co v Blaikie Bros*).

These duties are **owed to the company as a separate legal person** and not the shareholders. Any action for breach of duty must therefore be brought by the company (*Foss v Harbottle*). Fran appears to be in clear breach of her fiduciary duties and so it is open to the **company to bring proceedings against her** to recover any losses suffered as a result of her actions.

60   KING LTD

> **Tutor's hint**. The question asks you to consider the authority of both Lex and Mary, so make sure that you address both. In a complex question like this it is important to follow the correct approach: identify the **issues**, **state** the law, **apply** the law and **conclude**.
>
> **Examiner's comments**. Separate mark allocations were not given in the question, but the split should probably be about 12 to discuss Lex and 8 at the most to discuss Mary. The better candidates recognised the issues of agency and apparent authority, and could cite supporting cases. Some candidates strayed into the area of breach of directors' duties, not really relevant to the question. Some candidates were weaker on the area of a company secretary's authority and could not provide evidence to support the points that they made.

As a general rule, in order to be valid and binding on the principal and third party, a contract entered into by an agent must be entered into **within the bounds of the agent's authority**. However, that authority need not be express for the contract entered into by the agent to bind the principal. It may be implied actual authority or apparent authority.

Lex

Lex has not been formally appointed as managing director but has regularly carried on the day to day business of the company. It is necessary to examine whether he has sufficient authority to enter into a contract that is legally binding on King Ltd.

(a) **Express authority** is the extent of authority which it is agreed (between the principal and agent) the agent shall have to enter into contracts on the principal's behalf. The precise scope and extent of 'express actual authority' will depend on the proper construction of the written document in which the appointment or conferring of authority is contained or on the evidence supporting an oral giving of actual express authority. If the agent acts outside his express authority, he will be liable to the **principal for breach of contract** and to the **third party for breach of warranty of authority**.

It appears that Lex has not been given any express authority to enter into contracts on the company's behalf.

(b) Actual authority may be implied rather than express.

    (i) **'Implied incidental authority'** will be deemed to exist where it is reasonable to suppose that the principal also gave the agent authority to enter into transactions which are necessarily incidental or subordinate to the matter of the express authority, eg the authority to advertise goods when the agent is expressly authorised to sell them;

(ii) **'Implied customary authority'** is that which an agent shall be deemed to have by reason of his operating in a particular market or business (*Dingle v Hare*);

(iii) **'Implied usual authority'** is that which an agent shall be deemed to have by reason of his occupying a particular position or engaging in a particular trade (*Howard v Sheward*).

In cases of implied actual authority, the third party who contracts with the agent is entitled to assume that the agent has implied authority unless he knows to the contrary (*Watteau v Fenwick*). (As between the agent and the principal, however, the agent is not entitled to contravene the principal's express authority or instructions by claiming implied authority.)

Lex would appear not to have actual implied authority either, in part since he has not been appointed to any particular office.

(c) **'Apparent'** or **'ostensible'** authority is that which the principal represents to other parties he has given to his agent. Although matters of apparent authority and implied usual authority often appear to be co-extensive, it is the **conduct of the principal (expressly or by inference) which creates apparent authority**. It also arises where the principal is aware that an agent is claiming to be his appointed agent and yet does nothing to correct that impression, as appears to be the case here. In either case, the principal will be bound by the actions of the ostensible agent.

In *Freeman & Lockyer v Buckhurst Park Properties (Mangal) Ltd*, a company was bound by the acts of one of its directors who acted like a managing director even though he had not been appointed formally to that position. By its mere acquiescence, the company had led the third party to believe that he was the managing director and the third party had relied on that impression.

Following the *Freeman & Lockyer* case, therefore, Lex can be said to have had the necessary authority to bind King Ltd on entering into the contract with Nat, a contract well within the expected scope of a managing director's role. The company is therefore required to perform its part of the contract or be liable for damages for breach of contract.

Mary

For many years, a company secretary was treated as a mere subordinate of the company with no authority to enter into contracts or speak on the company's behalf. However, in *Panorama Developments (Guildford) Ltd v Fidelis Furnishing Fabrics Ltd*, the Court of Appeal recognised the general nature of a company secretary's duties and made it clear that a **company secretary has apparent authority to enter into contracts connected with the administration of the company** (in that case, ordering cars from a car hire firm).

With regard to Mary, it is likely that King Ltd is liable under the contract with Owen, since the purchase of new office furniture is clearly within the scope of a company secretary's duties. However, the contract to have a house extension built is clearly not related to her role as company secretary and King Ltd has no liability in respect of it.

Marking Guide	
	Marks
Principle of agent's authority	2
Lex	
Discussion of express authority	2
Lex does not have express authority	1
Discussion of implied authority	2
Lex does not appear to have implied authority	1
Discussion of apparent authority	3
Freeman & Lockyer case	1
Lex has apparent authority; co. is bound	2
Mary	
Nature of apparent authority	2
Panorama Developments or example	1
Co. liable for furniture purchase	1
Co. not liable for house extension	1
Mary personally liable for that	1
	20

61 LUXOR LTD

> **Tutor's hint**. This question should be reasonable to tackle because it is broken down into small parts. Ensure that you can answer all the sections. Parts (b)(i) and (ii) may be a little harder than the first two parts, but you should attempt all the sections.

(a) **Advice re director issues**

    (i) **Wrongful trading**

S 214 Insolvency Act 1986 provides that a director of an insolvent company shall be guilty of wrongful trading where:

(1) He **knew or should have known** that there was no reasonable prospect that the company could have avoided going into **insolvent liquidation** and

(2) He **failed to take sufficient steps to minimise the potential loss to the company's creditors.**

The Act also provides that the **director will be deemed to know** that the company could not avoid insolvent liquidation, if that would have been the **conclusion of a reasonably diligent person** who had the general knowledge, skill and experience that might reasonably be expected of a person carrying out that particular director's duties.

Where a court finds a director guilty of wrongful trading, it may order that **director to make such contribution to the company's assets as the court thinks proper,** taking into account the date from which the director ought to have realised that insolvent liquidation was inevitable.

The director may also be **disqualified for up to 15 years under the CDDA 1986**. The relieving provision, under s 727, does not apply in cases of wrongful trading (*Halls v David and Another*). In order to **escape liability**, the director must show that the above test is not satisfied or that he did take steps to minimise potential losses.

    (ii) **The Company Directors Disqualification Act 1986**

The Company Directors Disqualification Act 1986 (CDDA) provides that a court may disqualify a person from being a director, shadow director, liquidator,

141

administrator, receiver or manager of a company's property or in any way being directly or indirectly concerned or taking part in the promotion, formation or management of a company (s 1).

The court has a discretion to make such an order on the following grounds:

(1)   Where a person is convicted of an indictable offence in connection with the promotion, formation, management or liquidation of a company or with the receivership of management of a company's property (maximum 15 years if tried at crown court, 5 years if tried at magistrates' court)

(2)   Where a person appears to have been persistently in default in relation to company legislation (max 5 yrs)

(3)   Where a person appears to have been guilty of fraudulent trading (max 15 yrs)

(4)   Where the Secretary of State applies for a court order believing it to be expedient in the public interest, acting on a report made by the inspectors or from information or documents obtained under the Companies Act (max 15 yrs)

(5)   Where a director has participated in wrongful trading (max 15 yrs).

The court is **obliged to make such an order** where it is satisfied that a **person has been a director of a company which has at any time become insolvent** and that **his conduct** as a director **makes him unfit** to be concerned in the management of a company (s 6).

Jack faces possible disqualification under this Act since he appears generally unfit to be a director. A director can be disqualified under s 6 even though he may take not active part in the running of the business.

(b)   (i)   **Requirement to attend board meetings**

At common law, a director's duty to show **reasonable competence and care** was set out in *Re City Equitable Fire Insurance Co Ltd*. In this case it was laid down that a director is **required to attend board meetings when he is able to do so** but he need not concern himself with the affairs of the company at other times unless he has undertaken to do so. His duties are of an **intermittent nature**.

Generally, in the absence of any grounds for suspicion and subject to normal business practices, he is entitled to leave the routine conduct of the business in the hands of its management provided they appear to be honest and competent.

However, if Jack has any intention of remaining involved with the company, he should continue to bear in mind the **provisions of s 214 IA** concerning wrongful trading. This makes it very advisable that he begins to acquaint himself with the business of the company and, as a director, that he attends board meetings.

(ii)   **Withdrawal of agreement to be a director**

A director is **entitled to resign** either by one of its **articles of association** or under **general law**. His resignation should be in accordance with any relevant article (Art 81 prescribes written notice) or in a manner agreed by the parties.

Jack would be well advised to resign with immediate effect. However, such resignation would not absolve him of any liability for wrongful trading which might already have accrued.

Marking Guide

				Marks	
(a)	(i)	Definition of wrongful trading		2	
		Conclusion of a reasonably diligent person		2	
		Requirement to contribute to assets		1	
		Possibility of disqualification		1	
					6
	(ii)	Disqualification from various offices		1	
		Grounds for disqualification (examples)		2	
		Periods of disqualification (examples)		1	
		Explanation of unfit conduct		1	
		Application to situation		1	
					6
(b)	(i)	Basic duty of skill and care		1	
		Requirement to attend		1	
		Function of management		1	
		Risk of wrongful trading		1	
					4
	(ii)	Entitled to resign		1	
		Articles or law		1	
		Advice to Jack		1	
		May still be liable for wrongful trading		1	
					4
					20

62   LEN AND MOD PLC

Tutor's hint. This question asks you to explain the nature of **fiduciary** duties of a director, so you should limit your answer to his fiduciary duties. The question then asks you to apply your knowledge about directors' duties to two scenarios. Ensure you allow enough time to answer part (b) sufficiently for 12 marks. The pattern for your answer should be the usual: identify the **issues, state** the law, **apply** the law and then **conclude**.

(a)   **Fiduciary duties**

There are a number of duties imposed upon company directors including a **duty of care**, certain **specific duties imposed by statute** and **fiduciary duties**.

At common law, directors' duties are owed primarily to the company as the general body of shareholders rather than to individual shareholders: *Percival v Wright*. Since they make contracts as agents of the company and have control of its property, directors are said to be akin to trustees and thus owe **fiduciary duties to the company** in the same way as trustees owe fiduciary duties to the trust.

First, a **director must act within the powers given to him** and must **exercise those powers bona fide** in what he honestly considers to be the **interests of the company**. In *Re W & M Roith Ltd*, a director's service agreement included provision for his widow to receive a pension for life on his death. It was held that it had been done for the benefit of the widow and not the company. He had therefore acted in breach of this fiduciary duty.

Secondly, a director must exercise his powers for a **proper purpose**: *Howard Smith v Ampol Petroleum Ltd*. Directors' powers are restricted to the purpose for which they were given. If a director exercises his powers for a collateral purpose, the transaction will be invalid unless ratified by the company in general meeting. In the Howard Smith case directors allotted new shares to a prospective bidder in order to reduce the majority of dissenting shareholders since they honestly believed the proposed bid to be in the company's best interest. It was held that the allotment was void.

Notwithstanding the directors' attempt to act honestly in the interests of the company, the use of their power for an improper purpose was breach of this fiduciary duty.

Thirdly, a **director must avoid any conflict of duty and personal interest**, must **not obtain any personal advantage** from his position as director **without the consent of the company** *(Regal Hastings v Gulliver)* and must not fetter his discretion by agreeing to vote as some other person directs.

In the Regal Hastings case, the directors funded the creation of a subsidiary company in order to purchase two more cinemas. This resulted in profits on a later sale of the company. It was held that they had only made the profits because of their position as directors of the parent company and they were therefore required to account for the profits. The court said that the possibility of a conflict was sufficient, it was not necessary to prove an actual conflict. A transaction entered into in breach of this fiduciary duty may be ratified by the company in general meeting.

(b) **Application to Len**

   (i) **Purchase of machinery**

   Len is in a position of **potential conflict** here between his position as director of the purchasing company and as a majority shareholder in the selling company in a contract for the sale of goods. At common law, such a conflict would render the contract voidable by the company: *Aberdeen Rly Co v Blaikie*. However, provided the articles of association of Mod plc make the necessary relieving provisions as in Articles 85 and 94 of Table A, Len will not be liable so long as he **disclosed the nature of his interest** as required by s 317 and **does not vote on the issue**.

   S 317 CA 1985 requires a director to **declare the nature of his interest**, directly or indirectly, in a contract or proposed contract with the company. This disclosure can be a general declaration of interest in a particular company. The director is not required to volunteer detailed information of his interest. It must be made at the **board meeting at which the contract is first considered** (for if the interest arises after that board meeting then at the next board meeting).

   Article 94 of Table A prohibits a director from voting (or being counted as part of the quorum) in respect of a contract in which he has an interest. Failure to comply with these provisions renders the director liable to a fine and makes the contract voidable at the instance of the company. It also means that the director may be liable to account to the company for any profits made as a result.

   In this case, assuming (as appears to be the case) that Len did not make the necessary disclosure of his interest in Nim Ltd in accordance with s 317 and Article 85, he may be held liable to account to Mod plc for any secret profit he made on the transaction and be liable to conviction under s 317.

   (ii) **Development of new product**

   A director owes a **fiduciary duty not to use information which he obtains by virtue of his being a director to the detriment of the company** or for personal advantage without the consent of the company *(Regal Hastings v Gulliver*, the facts of which are outlined above).

   In this case, Len knows of the successful product only because of his position as director of Mod plc and, without disclosing his interest or obtaining the approval of the company, he has obtained personal advantage as a result of having that information and Nim Ltd producing the product.

   Applying *Regal Hastings v Gulliver*, he may be held liable to account to Mod plc for all the profits he made on the new product.

Marking Guide

				Marks	
(a)	Duties owed to company			2	
	Powers conferred/bonafide			2	
	Proper purpose			2	
	Conflict of duty/personal interest			2	
					8
(b)	Len				
	(i)	–	Potential conflict	1	
		–	Need for disclosure	1	
		–	When to declare	1	
		–	Table A voting requirement	1	
		–	Conclusion	2	
	(ii)	–	Duty not to use information to detriment of company	3	
		–	Application	2	
		–	Conclusion	<u>1</u>	
					<u>12</u>
					<u><u>20</u></u>

63   FRAUD ON MINORITY

> **Tutor's hint**. You may want to deal with different aspects of a fraud on the minority separately, stating how the law controls each, rather than answering these two questions in order. Remember however to include the role of the DTI in your answer.

General rule

The basic rule of law is that the **majority shareholders have the ultimate control** in a company and the **minority has no grounds for complaint** when a decision is taken by a majority which is unfavourable in some way to the minority.

Even in the event of a wrong being alleged to have been done by the directors (who may hold a majority of the voting rights or represents a majority shareholder), the **proper plaintiff is the company itself** and not a minority shareholder: *Foss v Harbottle*.

In this landmark case, a shareholder sued the company directors on the basis that they had defrauded the company by selling land to the company at an inflated price. It was held that the company was the only proper plaintiff to bring an action to protect its rights or property and that the company in general meeting should decide whether to bring such legal proceedings. The court would not interfere in the properly conducted internal affairs of the company.

Exceptions to the general rule

Without exceptions, the rule in *Foss v Harbottle* could result in grossly unjust situations which is why, both in the courts and by statute, a number of categories have been developed where the rule will not be applied. Thus the minority will be protected where it can be said that fraud is somehow being perpetuated by the majority against a minority in the company.

Fraud

Thus if a majority decision is taken to pass what belonged to the company to those against whom the claim is being made and the appropriators are in control of the company, then this constitutes a fraud on the company and the company cannot protect itself: *Cook v Deeks*.

In this case brought by a minority shareholder, it was held that the majority could not use their votes to ratify what amounted to a fraud on the minority. The contract belonged to the

company in equity and the directors were ordered to account to the company for the profits they made on it.

Similarly, where the minority shareholders (rather than the company) are defrauded, the general principle of majority rule will not be applied: *Clemens v Clemens Bros Ltd 1976*. Even without fraud, it might be possible for a minority shareholder to sue directors and controlling shareholders where their negligence is coupled with their deriving a benefit from it: *Daniels v Daniels*.

Ultra vires/illegal decisions

If a decision is taken in general meeting which is illegal or ultra vires, it **cannot bind the company** (s 35 CA 1985 now provides a statutory framework for any individual member to seek an injunction to stop the directors from entering into an ultra vires transaction unless ratified by special resolution).

Where a majority decision is taken which fails to comply with a **special procedure** contained in the company's articles and is more than a 'mere irregularity of internal procedure' which could be regulated by a majority approved it, the minority shareholders may be able to enforce compliance: *Edwards v Halliwell*.

An aggrieved minority is more likely to bring an action under **s 459 Companies Act 1985** than at common law (which can be difficult procedurally as well as in substance). This section provides relief for a minority where he can show that a company's affairs are being or have been conducted in a manner which is **unfairly prejudicial** to the interests of the members generally or some part of the members.

The court has extensive powers available to it in giving relief as it sees fit. S 123 Insolvency Act 1986 enables a minority to petition the court for a winding up of the company on the grounds that it is **just and equitable** to do so although such an order will only be given where no other remedy is available.

The **DTI** also has **statutory powers** to investigate the affairs of a company where malpractice is alleged against those persons who manage or control the company: ss 431-432.

A number of other specific statutory rights may afford protection to a minority:

- Holders of at last 15% of the issued shares can apply for cancellation of an alteration of the objects: s 5

- Holders of at least 15% of the shares in a class where rights have been varied can apply for cancellation of the variation: s 127

- Holders of at least one tenth of the paid-up capital carrying voting rights can requisition a meeting (s 368) and individual members can insist on full notice for an AGM: s 369.

Marking Guide	
	Marks
Detailed explanation of rule in Foss v Harbottle	2
Exceptions: Fraud	3
Ultra vires	3
Powers of the court/DTI	2
	10

64   EWAN, FRANK AND GENE

> **Tutor's hint**. This question asks you to consider two aspects of company law, the statutory rules governing insider dealing, and consequences of such activities, contained in the Company Directors' Disqualification Act 1986.
>
> As with all 20 mark 'problem' questions, the best approach is to:
>
> * identify the issues (insider dealing)
>
> * state the law (who is liable; what sort of transaction)
>
> * apply the law (has insider dealing occurred here?)
>
> * conclude by advising Ewan and Frank

(a) Insider dealing covers situations where someone buys or sells securities when he, but not the other party to the transaction, **possesses confidential information** which affects the value of those securities. Usually he is in possession of that confidential information because of some connection he has with the company whose securities are to be dealt in, perhaps as an employee, director or professional adviser to the company.

Clearly **with such information,** someone can **profit from buying shares** at a time when he knows of an anticipated increase in their market value and from selling shares when he has foreknowledge of a decrease in the shares' market value. The announcement of better than expected profits (as in the case of Dome plc) is almost certain to result in an increase in the share value.

The Criminal Justice Act 1993 (which repealed the Company Securities (Insider Dealing) Act 1985) makes it an offence to deal in securities while in possession of inside information as an insider, the securities being price-affected by the information (s 52).

It is also an offence to **encourage another to deal** in them knowing, or having reasonable cause to believe, that dealing would take place. It is irrelevant whether the person encouraged realises that the securities are price-affected and whether any dealing actually takes place. It is also an offence to disclose the information to another person other than in the proper performance of his employment, office or profession.

'Dealing' is defined (s 55) as acquiring or disposing of or agreeing to acquire or dispose of relevant securities whether directly or through an agent or nominee or a person acting according to direction.

'**Inside information**' is defined (s 56) as 'price-sensitive information' relating to a particular issuer of securities that are price-affected and not to securities generally. They are 'price-affected' if the information, being made public, would be likely to have a significant effect on price.

'**Insider**' means (s 57) a person who has information which is (and he knows it to be) inside information where he has that information, knowingly, from an inside source either

(i)   Through being a director, employee , shareholder or issuer of securities, or
(ii) Through access because of employment, office or profession, or
(iii) If the direct or indirect source falls within category (i) or (ii).

Breach of the Act is a criminal offence but it will not in itself invalidate contracts which have been entered into in contravention of its provisions. On indictment, the offence carries an unlimited fine and/or imprisonment for up to seven years.

The Act lays down a number of general and special defences. It is a **general defence** if the offender can show that he did not expect there to be a profit or avoidance of loss, or

that he had reasonable grounds to believe that the information had been widely disclosed or that he would have done what he did even if he had not had the information (s 53).

Application to Ewan

On the present facts, **Ewan is guilty of insider dealing** as an employee of the company who receives what is clearly inside information. He is guilty of two charges:

(i)   Dealing

(ii)   Disclosing the information to Frank (it may be that he is also found to have encouraged Frank).

Frank is also an insider within s 57 as he receives the information from a source who is an employee of the company. He is therefore guilty of insider dealing when he buys shares on the basis of that information. **There is no suggestion that either Ewan or Frank would avoid liability by any of the defences in the Act being applicable.**

(b)   Gene is an insider under s 57 as a director of the company and he, like Ewan, is guilty of insider dealing when he purchases shares on the basis of the information before that information is released to the public. In addition, **he is liable to disqualification under the Company Directors Disqualification Act 1986** (CDDA).

This Act provides that a court **may disqualify** a person from being a director, shadow director, liquidator, administrator, receiver or manager of a company's property or in any way being directly or indirectly concerned or taking part in the promotion, formation or management of a company (s 1).

The court has a discretion to make such an order where a person is convicted of an indictable offence in connection with the promotion, formation, management or liquidation of a company or with the receivership of management of a company's property.

The **maximum period of disqualification** is **15 years** if the indictable offence was tried on indictment, or 5 years if it was dealt with summarily.

Thus if Gene is convicted of an offence of insider dealing, he may be disqualified for up to 15 years. A director was disqualified for insider dealing in R v Goodman 1993.

Even if there is no conviction, the **court may issue a disqualification order on the application of the Secretary of State** (acting on a report made by the inspectors or on documents or information obtained under the Companies Acts) where he believes it to be expedient in the public interest. If the court is satisfied that the person's conduct in relation to the company makes him unfit to be concerned in the company's management, it may disqualify him for up to 15 years (s 8).

65   JEFFREY

Tutorial note. As the examiner notes below, insider dealing is an area of current interest and may well be examined again in the future. Don't forget recent developments such as the Finance and Markets Act 2000. The situation in this question is quite complex, so it is important to make sure that you identify the issue, state the law, apply the law and then conclude by advising all the parties.

Examiner's comments. This was a problem type question, which asked the candidates to consider the parties' potential liabilities for insider dealing. All it required was a straightforward application of the law to the facts, so it was surprising that few candidates chose to answer it.

(a) **Insider dealing**

Insider Dealing is the name given to the offence where someone buys or sells securities as a result of having received **confidential information which affects the value of those securities**. Usually he is in possession of that confidential information because of some connection he has with the company whose securities are to be dealt in, perhaps as an employee, director or professional adviser to the company.

Clearly with such information, someone can profit from buying shares at a time when he knows of an anticipated increase in their market value and from selling shares when he has foreknowledge of a decrease in the shares' market value. The likelihood of a takeover of Large TV by Megacorps TV plc is almost certain to result in an increase in the share value.

The Criminal Justice Act 1993 makes it an offence to **deal in securities while in possession of inside information as an insider, the securities being price-affected by the information** (s52). It is also an offence to encourage another to deal in them knowing, or having reasonable cause to believe, that dealing would take place. It is irrelevant whether the person encouraged realises that the securities are price-affected and whether any dealing actually takes place. It is also an offence to disclose the information to another person other than in the proper performance of his employment, office or profession.

'**Dealing**' is defined (s55) as acquiring or disposing of or agreeing to acquire or dispose of relevant securities whether directly or through an agent or nominee or a person acting according to direction. '**Securities**' include shares and debentures (s54). '**Inside information**' is defined (s56) as '**price-sensitive information**' relating to a particular issuer of securities that are price-affected and not to securities generally. They are 'price-affected' if the information, being made public, would be likely to have a **significant effect on price**. '**Insider**' means (s57) a person who has information which is (and he knows it to be) inside information where he has that information, knowingly, from an inside source either (i) through being a director, employee, shareholder or issuer of securities or (ii) through access because of employment, office or profession or (iii) if the direct or indirect source falls within category (i) or (ii).

Breach of the Act is a criminal offence but it will not in itself invalidate contracts which have been entered into in contravention of its provisions. On indictment, the offence carries an unlimited fine and/or imprisonment for up to seven years.

The Act lays down a number of **general and special defences**. It is a general defence if the offender can show that he did not expect there to be a profit or avoidance of loss, or that he had reasonable grounds to believe that the information had been widely disclosed, or that he would have done what he did even if he had not had the information (s53). In an offence of disclosing the information, it is a defence to show that the offender did not expect any person to deal or, if dealing was expected, that no profit or avoidance of loss was expected.

Application in this case

On the present facts, the following would appear to be the legal position:

(a) **Jeffrey is an insider** by virtue of having received price-sensitive information from the MD of Large TV. The specific and precise information has clearly not been made public and would have a significant effect on the shares' market price if it were. He subsequently deals by buying shares in Large TV. Jeffrey is guilty of an offence of insider dealing under s52 and none of the defences apply.

Jeffrey could also have committed the civil offence of '**market abuse**' under the Finance and Markets Act 2000, because he has behaved in a way that is likely to be regarded by a regular user of the market as a failure to observe a reasonable standard of behaviour.

(b) By passing the **price-sensitive information** to Nat, Jeffrey is also guilty of the offence of disclosing the information and, again, none of the defences apply. Nat is also an insider since he receives the information indirectly (via Jeffrey) from an insider source, the MD. He also deals by purchasing shares in Large TV and is guilty of an offence under s52.

(c) Nat becomes guilty of the offence of disclosing information when he passes the confidential information to Owen. Owen is guilty of dealing when he also buys shares in Large TV, being an insider on the same basis as Nat.

(d) Jeffrey here commits the offence of **encouraging another to deal** under s52, knowing or having reasonable cause to believe that dealing would take place. It is irrelevant that he does not also disclose the full information or that Pete does not realise that the shares in Large TV are price-affected securities. The offence takes place at the time of the encouraging, not the subsequent dealing by Pete. Pete is not guilty of any offence since he has not received any specific price-sensitive information.

Marking Guide	
	Marks
Definition of insider dealing	2
Provisions of Criminal Justice Act 1993:	
• Offences	2
• Dealing	1
• Inside information	1
• Price-affected	1
• Insider	2
• Effect of breach of Act	2
• Defences	2
Finance and Markets Act 2000	1
Impact on Jeffrey	2
Impact on Nat	2
Impact on Owen	1
Impact on Pete	1
Total	20

66   FRANK

> **Tutor's hint**. This is a wide ranging question covering the capacity of a company, director's duties and insider dealing. Do not be misled into thinking that there is a need to write about fraud on the minority, because the question refers to Henry, a shareholder. Remember the rule in *Foss v Harbottle* that the company may take action on its own behalf.
>
> • identify the issues (objects clause, duties of directors, insider dealing)
>
> • state the law (on those three areas, supported by statute and cases)
>
> • apply the law (is the company in breach of its objects clause, is Frank in breach of his duties and has he dealt as an insider?)
>
> • conclude (advise Henry)

Ultra vires acts

The doctrine of ultra vires stipulates that a company must act within its capacity as set out in the objects clause of its memorandum of association. At common law, the law provided

simply that any act which went beyond a company's contractual capacity would be void and unenforceable. Ultra vires acts could not be ratified by the company and third parties would be treated as having constructive notice of the memorandum of association which was a public document.

However, the Companies Act 1989 has changed that position and provides that 'the validity of an act done by a company shall not be called into question on the ground of lack of capacity by reason of anything in the company's memorandum'. Consequently, the contract between Good plc and the supplier of alcoholic drinks is valid and enforceable and neither Good plc nor the other party can plead ultra vires to escape their obligations.

Frank's duties as director

The directors owe a duty to the company to ensure that the company's assets are not used for ultra vires purposes. Where this is breached, the act can only be ratified by special resolution (s 35(3)) and a separate special resolution will be needed to relieve the directors from liability for this breach. An action to make Frank liable to account for losses is not relevant since the contract proved to be profitable.

Internally, the ultra vires rule continues to operate between the company and its members. Shareholders have the right to restrain an ultra vires act (s 35(2)). However, this is of no use where the act has already occurred

The shareholders of Good plc might consider **altering the memorandum of association** to broaden its objects and business operation, either by specific additions or alternations or by adopting the commonly used 'general commercial company' provision as permitted by s.3A. It should bear in mind that retaining an objects clause which is more detailed may be preferable with regard to securing investment in the company. The clause can be altered by the shareholders in general meeting passing a special resolution.

With regard to the articles of association, s 35A(1) provides that in favour of a person dealing with a company in good faith, any limitation on the power of the directors to bind the company (or authorise others to do so) shall be disregarded, thus preventing a company from pleading ultra vires and unenforceability of a transaction because of some restriction on the directors' authority.

Thus, as managing director, **Frank can exercise all the directors' powers** (Art 84) but he is also subject to limitations on those powers contained in the company's constitution. He is in breach of his authority in this case, but the contract cannot be challenged on this ground any more than on the ultra vires ground.

Ultimately, the shareholders of a company have the power to remove a director by passing an ordinary resolution to that effect (s 303 CA 1985). Henry would need to command a simple majority or have sufficient support from other shareholders to achieve this.

Insider Dealing

Section 52 of the Criminal Justice Act 1993 provides that it shall be a **criminal offence to deal in securities while in possession of inside information as an insider,** the securities being price-affected by the information. It is necessary to show that the person with inside information either dealt in price-affected securities or encouraged another to deal in them, or disclosed the information.

'Dealing in securities' is widely defined and there is no doubt that Frank's purchase of shares would be covered by these provisions. 'Inside information' is defined as 'price-sensitive information' relating to a particular issuer of securities that are price-affected. The information must be specific or precise and, if made public, be likely to have a significant

151

effect on price. Again it appears that Frank, an insider by virtue of his position as a director, has inside information and has made use of that information in his purchase of shares.

The Act does contain some special and general defences. The latter are that the individual did not expect there to be a profit or avoidance of loss, or that he had reasonable grounds to believe that the information had been disclosed widely or that he would have done what he did even if he had not had the information.

None of these defences appear to apply in Frank's favour which means that he is liable to be convicted for the offence of insider dealing, the maximum penalties for which are 7 years' imprisonment and/or an unlimited fine (s 61). Insider dealing has constituted a ground for disqualification from acting as a director under the CDDA 1986 (*R v Goodman*).

At civil law, action could be taken against Frank for breach of the fiduciary duties owed by him as a director. A claim would be made for him to account to the company for the profits made on the purchase of shares.

67 PREPARATION QUESTION: BALANCE OF POWER

> **Tutor's hint.** The most important points to bring out in (a) were that the directors have a general power of management which the shareholders cannot usurp, but certain decisions are reserved for the members in general meeting, and that the members have a general right under s 303 to remove directors by an ordinary resolution.
>
> In (b) your answer should have covered the range of solutions rather than concentrating too much on one aspect. The most important remedy for minorities these days though is s 459, and your answer should have discussed this option in some depth.

(a) **Powers of directors**

The board of directors of a company is charged with **managing** the **business** of the company with a view to **maximising** the company's profits. Powers are conferred on the directors **collectively**. These **powers** are **defined** by:

- The company's **articles**
- **Statutory provisions**
- The directors' **contract of employment**

Restrictions on powers

There are certain restrictions placed on the exercise of the directors' powers.

(i) They must **report back** to the **shareholders** on the company's business at the **annual general meeting**.

(ii) In many instances, a **meeting** of the **shareholders** must be called and an appropriate resolution passed (discussed further below).

(iii) Sometimes the **articles** will place **limits** on the directors' powers, such as in the case of maximum borrowing limits.

Challenging directors' decisions

Directors' decisions can also be **challenged** if they exercise their powers for **improper purposes** or not in what they honestly believe to be the **best interests** of the company (*Bamford v Bamford* and *Re Lee Behrens & Co*).

Responsibilities of directors

Directors have a number of responsibilities that they owe to the general body of shareholders.

(i)   They should perform their functions **honestly** and with **reasonable competence**.

(ii) They should exercise their powers **bona fide** in what they honestly consider to be the interests of the company and for a **proper purpose**: *Howard Smith Ltd v Ampol Petroleum Ltd*.

(iii) They must not agree to act **according** to **another person's direction**: *SCWS v Meyer*.

(iv) They must avoid a **conflict of duty** and **personal interest**: *Aberdeen Railway Co v Blaikie Bros*.

(v)   They are only permitted to obtain any **personal advantage** from their position as directors with the **consent** of the **shareholders**: *Regal (Hastings) Ltd v Gulliver*.

Shareholders

The shareholders are the members and owners of the company. The powers and responsibilities of the shareholders are defined by **statute** and the company's **articles**. They exercise their powers in the following ways.

(i)   Shareholders take the **major policy decisions** of the company at general meetings by **passing ordinary resolutions** and **special resolutions**.

(ii) Shareholders can, by **altering the articles**, re-allocate powers between the board and the members as they determine by special resolutions.

(iii) Shareholders have the right to **appoint directors** and can remove them under s 303 by using an **ordinary resolution**.

Limitation on shareholders' powers

The general body of shareholders, however, cannot assume the powers of the directors, which are given to the latter by the articles. Exceptionally the company in general meeting may have a '**residual authority**' to use the company's powers in the event of a deadlock on the board or lack of directors.

(b) **Rule of majority**

Majority shareholders have the **ultimate control** in a company. In the event of a wrong being alleged to have been done by the directors (who may hold a majority of the voting rights), the **company** itself should take legal action and not a minority shareholder.

Significance of Foss v Harbottle

In *Foss v Harbottle*, a shareholder sued the company directors on the basis that they had defrauded the company by selling land to the company at an inflated price. It was held that the **company** was the **only proper plaintiff** to bring an action to protect its rights or property. The company, acting by a majority vote in general meeting, should decide whether to bring such legal proceedings.

Without exceptions, the rule in *Foss v Harbottle* could result in situations grossly unjust to the minority of shareholders. Consequently, a number of situations have been developed, where the minority's voice can be effective.

S 459 action

Under s 459, any member may now apply to the court for relief on the grounds that the company's affairs are being or have been conducted in a manner which is **unfairly prejudicial** to the interests of the members generally or some part of the members.

Applications are commonly made in cases of **discrimination** against a minority or **exclusion** of a partner in a **quasi-partnership** company. Other examples have included improper allotment of shares (*Re DR Chemicals Ltd*) and making an inaccurate statement to shareholders (*Re A Company 1986*).

The prejudice complained of must affect the plaintiff-member in his **capacity** as **member** and not as an employee or unpaid creditor. The member need not show bad faith or even an intention to discriminate.

The court will take into account the **surrounding circumstances** including the parties' conduct and may make such **order** as it **deems fit**. Examples include:

(i)   **Regulating** the company's **future affairs** in some way

(ii)   **Ordering** the **purchase** of the **minority's shares** by the majority or by the company itself

(iii)   **Authorising some person** to bring **proceedings** on the company's behalf

(iv)   **Ordering** the **company** to **refrain** from **doing** the **act** complained of

(v)   **Including** in the **company's constitution provisions** which could then only be altered by the court

Common law exceptions

(i)   If a decision is taken in general meeting which is **illegal** or **ultra vires**, any individual member can seek an injunction.

(ii)   Where a majority decision is taken which **fails to comply** with a **special procedure** contained in the company's articles and is more than a '**mere irregularity of internal procedure**', the minority shareholders may be able to enforce compliance: *Edwards v Halliwell*.

(iii)   If a majority decision is taken which constitutes a **fraud** on the **company** and the company cannot protect itself then the minority shareholders will be protected: *Cook v Deeks*.

(iv)   A minority shareholder may sue directors and controlling shareholders where their **negligence** is coupled with their deriving a **benefit** from it: *Daniels v Daniels*.

(v)   Similarly, where the **minority shareholders** (rather than the company) are **defrauded**, the general principle of majority rule will not be applied: *Clemens v Clemens Bros Ltd*.

(vi)   A minority may sue the company to enforce **personal rights** of **membership**, such as the right to vote: *Pender v Lushington*.

Winding up

In more extreme cases, a member may choose to petition the court for **winding up** of the company on the ground that it is **just and equitable** to do so: s 122 IA 1986.

Other statutory rights of members

In addition a minority of members is given a number of specific statutory rights including the following.

(i)   **Variation of class rights.** Where the rights of any class of share are altered, with the consent of the majority, the holders of **not less than 15%** of that class may apply to the court to have the variation cancelled: s 127.

(ii)   Dissentient holders of **not less than 15%** of the issued shares can apply for **cancellation of an alteration of objects**: s 5.

(iii)   Holders of **not less than one tenth** of a company's paid up capital carrying voting rights can **requisition a meeting:** s 368.

(iv)   Members representing not **less than one twentieth** of the total voting rights of all members or 100 or more members holding shares in the company on which an average sum of not less than £100 per member has been paid up can requisition the company to give **notice of members' resolutions to an AGM:** s 376.

68   JACK AND KEN

> **Tutor's hint.** A comprehensive question on minority protection, indicating the level of detail that you do need to know. As always, identify the issues, state the law, apply the law and then conclude.

(a)   **Foss v Harbottle rule**

Ken is now a minority shareholder holding 75 shares, Jack and Liam together holding 125 shares. Whilst he can block a special or extraordinary resolution, he cannot prevent any ordinary resolution in general meeting or majority decision at board meetings.

The basic rule is that the **majority shareholders** have the **ultimate control** in a company. In the event of a wrong being alleged to have been done by the directors (who may hold a majority of the voting rights or represent a majority shareholder), the **proper plaintiff** is the **company** itself and not a minority shareholder.

In *Foss v Harbottle,* a shareholder sued the company directors on the basis that they had defrauded the company by selling land to the company at an inflated price. It was held that the company was the only proper plaintiff to bring an action to protect its rights or property and that the company in general meeting should decide whether to bring such legal proceedings. The court would not interfere in the properly conducted internal affairs of the company.

Common law exceptions

Without exceptions, the rule in *Foss v Harbottle* could result in grossly unjust situations which is why a number of exceptions have been developed where the rule will not be applied.

Thus, if a decision is taken in general meeting which is **illegal** or **ultra vires**, it cannot bind the company. S 35 now provides a statutory framework for any individual member to seek an injunction to stop the directors from entering into an ultra vires transaction unless ratified by special resolution.

Where a majority decision is taken which **fails to comply** with a **special procedure** contained in the company's articles and is more than a 'mere irregularity of internal procedure', the minority shareholders may be able to enforce compliance: *Edwards v Halliwell*. Further, a minority will be protected where a **general meeting** is **convened** or **held** in an **irregular fashion** by a majority in the company: *Kaye v Croydon Tramways Co.*

If a majority decision is taken where what was taken belonged to the company, and was passed to those against whom the claim is being made and the appropriators are in control of the company, then this constitutes a **fraud** on the company and the company cannot protect itself: *Cook v Deeks*.

Similarly, where the **minority shareholders** (rather than the company) are **defrauded**, the general principle of majority rule will not be applied: *Clemens v Clemens Bros Ltd*. Even without fraud, it might be possible for a minority shareholder to sue directors and controlling shareholders where their **negligence** is coupled with their **deriving a benefit** from it: *Daniels v Daniels*.

Application

In this case, it appears that Jack and Liam have perpetrated a fraud on the company and the minority by selling carpets to a company owned by themselves and then passing a resolution to ratify the sale. The rule in *Foss v Harbottle* would not apply in these circumstances.

Ken could take action in the company's name against Jack and Liam to force them to account to the company for profits and to recover any loss sustained by the company.

If fraud could not be shown, *Daniels v Daniels* could be applied on the basis of negligence coupled with their having taken a profit from the transaction.

(b) (i) Pursuing an action under the appropriate exceptions to the rule in *Foss v Harbottle* addresses the contract made to the detriment of the company, but cannot serve to reinstate Ken as director or compensate him for his removal. The relations between the directors have clearly broken down and so Ken needs to consider further causes of action.

Under s 122 IA 1986, any shareholder who is dissatisfied with the directors or controlling shareholders regarding the management of the company is entitled to petition the court for an order **winding up** the company on the ground that it is **just and equitable** to do so. He must satisfy the court that no other remedy is available and appropriate since winding up what might otherwise be a healthy company is a remedy of last resort: *Re A Company 1983*.

The courts have ordered winding-up under s 122 where there is a **complete deadlock** in the management of the company's affairs (*Re Yenidje Tobacco Co Ltd*), or where the trust and **confidence** between both directors and shareholders in a small, **quasi-partnership**, company has **broken down**: *Ebrahimi v Westbourne Galleries Ltd*.

Here, as in the *Ebrahimi* case, relations have broken down. An action under s 122 might be successful. However, this is a drastic course of action since it involves the whole company being wound up and it may be to Ken's advantage to consider alternative action under s 459.

(ii) **Application to the court**

Under s 459, any member may apply to the court for relief on the grounds that the company's affairs are being or have been conducted in a manner which is **unfairly prejudicial** to the **interests** of the **members generally** or **some part** of the **members** or in respect of a particular act or omission which has been or will be prejudicial.

Applications are commonly made in cases of discrimination against a minority or exclusion of a partner in a quasi-partnership company. The prejudice complained of must affect the **plaintiff-member** in his capacity as **member** and **not** as an **employee** or **unpaid creditor**. The member need not show bad faith or even an intention to discriminate.

The court will take into account the surrounding circumstances including the parties' conduct and may make **such order** as it **deems fit**. It might regulate the company's future affairs in some way, or order the purchase of the minority's shares by the majority or by the company itself: *SCWS v Meyer*. Other possible courses are to authorise some person to **bring proceedings** on the company's behalf, **order** the **company** to **refrain** from doing the act complained of or

include in the company's constitution **provisions** which could then only be altered by the court.

Examples of unfairly prejudicial conduct

The following types of conduct have been held to be unfairly prejudicial:

- **Exclusion** and **removal** from the **board**: *Re Bird Precision Bellows Ltd*

- Where a managing director uses **assets** for his own **personal benefit** and the personal benefit of his family and friends: *Re Elgindata Ltd*

- Where a majority shareholder **transfers sources of profit into another company** owned by the majority shareholder: *Re London School of Electronics Ltd*

- The **diversion** of a company's **business** to a **director-controlled company** or the making of a rights issue which minority shareholders were not permitted to take up: *Re Cumana*

- The **improper allotment** of **shares**: *Re D R Chemicals Ltd*

- The **failure** to **call a meeting** as **requisitioned** by the petitioner-minority: *Re McGuinness and Another*

Ken would almost certainly succeed in an action under s 459. It is likely that the court would order the purchase of his interest by the majority at a fair value (after making good the loss suffered by the company in the sale of carpets to the other company owned by that majority).

69   HARVEY

> **Tutor's hint**. Detailed knowledge is required in (a) on the mechanics of an offer to shareholders and disapplying s 89. Note also the point about directors' powers. Greenhalgh is the most important case in (b). When planning your answer, **identify the issues**, **state** the law, **apply** the law and then **conclude**.

(a) **Offer to members under s 89**

A company's director may only issue shares if there is **authority** to do so contained in the **articles of association**: s 80. If directors allot shares in breach of s 80 they are liable to a fine, but the allotment is still valid. In addition, s 89 provides that before any shares can be allotted to a new member, they must first be offered to **existing holders** of similar shares in proportion to their holdings.

Such an offer to existing shareholders must be made **in writing** in the same way as notice of a general meeting. It must specify a period of at **least 21 days** during which the offer may be accepted and if no acceptance is forthcoming within that period, the offer will be deemed to be **declined** (s 90) and the allotment may then proceed on the same or less favourable terms to non-members. Any particular pre-emption provisions contained in the articles must also be adhered to and they will take precedence over these statutory provisions.

Exclusion of s 89 provisions

The requirements contained in s 89 can be **excluded** by provision in a company's memorandum or **articles** (s 91) or **disapplied** (s 95) but only **by special resolution** requiring a majority of 75% of votes cast in general meeting, either altering the articles or authorising an allotment of shares not in accordance with s 89. If members of a company are invited to authorise by special resolution an offer of shares to a non-

member (without first offering them to existing members) for cash on a particular occasion, the directors must first issue a **circular** setting out their reasons, and justification of the price at which the shares are to be issued.

Failure to observe the pre-emption rights set out in s 89 CA85 means that the company and the officers who knowingly authorised or permitted the contravention (ie Alexander) are jointly and severally liable to compensate the 'victim', in this case Suzanne and Tina, for any loss, damage, costs or expenses incurred. The allotment itself, however, will remain valid.

Under s 92 the company and every officer who authorised the allotment will be liable to a fine. Additionally the allotment will not achieve its purpose. If directors of a company have used their powers irregularly to allot shares, the new shares may not be counted in reaching a decision in general meeting to sanction it. This was seen in *Howard Smith Ltd v Ampol Petroleum Ltd*, where it was held that 'it must be unconstitutional for directors to use their fiduciary powers over the shares in the company purely for the purpose of destroying an existing majority or creating a new majority which did not previously exist'.

Abuse of director's powers

Additionally, even if there has been no breach of articles or the statutory provisions detailed above, the purpose behind the issue of shares to Margaret may be challenged on the basis that it was predominantly concerned with altering the **balance of voting power** rather than raising capital. If this were considered to be the case, Alexander might be held liable for abusing his director's powers on the basis that he used them for an improper purpose. This could render the issue to Margaret voidable at the instance of the other shareholders: *Clemens v Clemens Bros Ltd & Others*.

(b) **Threat of legal action by Suzanne and Tina**

S 459 provides that any member of a company may apply to the court for relief on the grounds that the company's affairs are being or have been conducted in a manner which is **unfairly prejudicial** to the interests of the members generally or some part of the members. Suzanne and Tina would appear to have the necessary grounds to make an application under this section.

It would not be necessary for them to show bad faith but they would need to show prejudice to themselves as members. The court would take into account **all relevant circumstances** including the conduct of the parties: *R A Noble & Sons (Clothing) Ltd*. They will consider the wording of the alteration to the articles and the reasons behind it, in determining whether it was made in good faith and in the interests of the company.

The facts in this case are similar to those in *Greenhalgh v Arderne Cinemas Ltd* where the majority shareholders passed a special resolution altering the articles to remove pre-emption provisions which were preventing them from transferring their shareholdings to a non-member. A minority shareholder claimed that the alteration was prejudicial to the minority's interests.

The court held that the alteration was valid since it entitled majority and minority shareholders alike to transfer their shares to an outsider provided an ordinary resolution was first passed to that effect (as required by the altered article). The fact that the minority shareholder was unable to block the ordinary resolution was held not to render the alteration invalid.

Greenhalgh's case was decided before statutory remedies were available for the aggrieved minority shareholder. On balance it seems likely that an action by Suzanne and Tina

under s 459 would not succeed and that the alteration could more easily be challenged on the grounds of incorrect procedure and abuse of directors' powers as outlined in (a) above. There may be grounds for a s 459 claim but it seems more doubtful whether such a claim would succeed.

If the claim did succeed under s 461 the court may make whatever order it sees fit. Most likely in this case the court may provide that Tina and Suzanne's shares be purchased at a fair price. (This price would not generally be reduced because Suzanne and Tina hold a minority of the shares.)

70   QUENTIN

> **Tutorial note.** Hopefully before you got to this stage of your studies you have worked through the question on minority protection in the Study Text which had an 'approaching the answer' section which you might have found useful in approaching this question. If you did not, go back to your Text and work through that question in the Exam Question Bank. The examiner notes below that this area seems unpopular with students, but it is examined regularly so should be an area you revise thoroughly . Use this answer in your final revision. As always in a question like this with a complex scenario, identify the **issues, state** the law, **apply** the law and then **conclude** on Raj and Sam's position and advise them of their remedies.
>
> **Examiner's comments.** Minority protection features quite frequently in exams but candidates often choose to avoid it, as in this paper.
>
> The main problem was that candidates failed to apply the relevant law, restricting themselves to identifying the relevant issues. Some weaker answers merely repeated the facts of the question, thereby seriously limiting the marks that could be earned.

Although Raj and Sam comprise a majority of directors and, therefore, should be able to influence board meetings, they are clearly unable to exercise this influence because of Quentin's carrying on the business without the board and his ability to convene an EGM at any time and procure the passing of any ordinary resolution (including one to remove them as directors under s303) or special resolution.

The basic rule of law is that the **majority shareholders have the ultimate control in a company** and that in the event of a wrong being alleged to have been done by the directors (who may hold a majority of the voting rights or represent a majority shareholder), the 'proper plaintiff' (or claimant) is the company itself and not a minority shareholder (*Foss v Harbottle*). The courts will not readily interfere in the properly conducted internal affairs of a company.

In certain cases, however, the **courts will protect a minority interest in a company**, for example where a majority decision is taken which fails to comply with a special procedure contained in the company's articles and is more than a 'mere irregularity of internal procedure' (*Edwards v Halliwell*). or where the minority shareholders (rather than the company) are defrauded (*Clemens v Clemens Bros Ltd*). Even without fraud, it might be possible for a minority shareholder to sue directors and controlling shareholders where their negligence is coupled with their deriving a benefit from it (*Daniels v Daniels*). Neither fraud nor personal benefit is alleged in this case however.

Not being a public listed company, Raj and Sam cannot easily sell their shares and leave the company. They should consider two statutory courses of action:

(a)   Under s122 Insolvency Act 1986, any shareholder who is dissatisfied with the directors or controlling shareholders regarding the management of the company is entitled to petition the court for an **order winding up the company** on the ground that it is **just and equitable** to do so. He must satisfy the court that no other remedy is available and appropriate since winding up what might otherwise be a healthy company is a remedy of last resort (*Re A Company 1983*).

The courts have ordered winding-ups under s 122 where the substratum (the only main objects) of the company no longer exists (*Re German Date Coffee Co*), where the company was formed for an illegal or fraudulent purpose, where there is a complete deadlock in the management of the company's affairs (*Re Yenidje Tobacco Co Ltd*) and where the trust and confidence between both directors and shareholders in a small company have broken down (*Ebrahimi v Westbourne Galleries Ltd*).

Here, as in the Ebrahimi case, relations have broken down and so an action under s 122 might be successful. However, this is a drastic course of action since it involves the whole company being wound up and that is likely to involve losses for all concerned.

(b) Under s 459 CA 1985, any member may apply to the court for relief on the grounds that the company's affairs are being or have been conducted in a manner which is **unfairly prejudicial to the interests of the members generally** or some part of the members or in respect of a particular act or omission which has been or will be prejudicial. Applications are commonly made in cases of discrimination against a minority or exclusion of a partner in a quasi-partnership company. The prejudice complained of must affect the claimant-member in his capacity as member and not as an employee or unpaid creditor. The member need not show bad faith or even an intention to discriminate.

The court will take into account the surrounding circumstances including the parties' conduct and may make such order as it deems fit. It might regulate the company's future affairs in some way, order the purchase of the minority's shares by the majority or by the company itself, authorise some person to bring proceedings on the company's behalf, order the company to refrain from doing the act complained of or include in the company's constitution provisions which could then only be altered by the court.

Unfairly prejudicial conduct in successful cases brought under s 459 has included

- The use of company assets for a managing director's personal benefit and the personal benefit of his family and friends (*Re Elgindata Ltd*)

- The transfer of sources of profit into another company owned by the majority shareholder (*Re London School of Electronics Ltd*)

- The diversion of a company's business to a director-controlled company.

More relevant to the present facts, **exclusion and removal from the board** has also been held to constitute unfair prejudice (*Re Bird Precision Bellows Ltd*). Whilst the conduct need not be illegal or even intentional, mere bad management will not necessarily be sufficient (*Re A Company*). There must be an actual act or repeated conduct that is unfairly prejudicial; a mere breakdown of trust or confidence will not suffice (*O'Neill v Phillips*). However, if continued mismanagement causes serious financial damage to the company and the minority's interests, then a claim under s 459 should be successful (*Re Macro (Ipswich) Ltd*).

Quentin's threat of removing Raj and Sam from the board of directors (although legal) and his carrying on the business without consulting them are likely to be seen as excluding their legitimate expectations to participate in the management of the company, since it is clearly a quasi-partnership company. On the basis also of the financial losses of Trio Ltd caused by some of Quentin's recent decisions, his conduct is likely to be regarded as unfairly prejudicial within s 459.

In conclusion, Raj and Sam would almost certainly succeed in an action under s 459 and it is likely that the court would order the purchase of their interests by Quentin at a fair value.

Marking Guide	Marks
Principle of majority rule	3
Examples of exceptions	3
S122 IA 86: just and equitable grounds	2
Examples and cases	3
Application to situation	1
S459 CA 85: unfair prejudice	3
Examples and cases	3
Application to situation	2
Total	20

71   SHARES

Tutor's hint. This is a very straightforward part A question. It would be a good one to choose as it has several parts and many easy marks available.

(a)   **Share capital**

A share is 'the **interest of a shareholder in the company measured by a sum of money**, for the purpose of a liability in the first place, and of interest in the second, but also consisting of a series of mutual covenants entered into by all the shareholders inter se'.

A share must be paid for and it gives a proportionate entitlement to dividends, votes and any return of capital. It also constitutes a form of bargain between the shareholders, underlying such principles as majority control and minority protection.

A share is a form of property carrying rights and obligations, which is transferable in accordance with the company's articles on transferability of shares. Shares in a public company are freely transferable provided the appropriate procedures are followed.

The nominal value of the share usually fixes the amount of the shareholder's liability, ie how much he can be required to contribute to the company's assets. The shareholder's right to share in the company is the right to receive a dividend in the company's profits and not a share of the company's capital assets.

(b)   **Types of share capital**

   (i)   **Authorised share capital**

   This is the total amount of share capital which the company may issue, as authorised by the capital clause of its memorandum of association. This total must be divided into shares of a fixed amount (which is termed the nominal or par value of the shares). A company need not issue shares to the full extent of its authorised share capital.

   (ii)   **Issued share capital**

   This is the nominal value of all shares which have been allotted and issued to members. Where part of its authorised share capital has not been issued, this part is called the unissued share capital. A public company must have at least £50,000 issued share capital.

   The issued share capital (as opposed to the authorised share capital) is the measure of the substance of a company.

(iii) **Paid up capital**

This is the proportion of the nominal value of the issued capital actually paid. An allottee of shares must pay the nominal value of those shares plus any premium due on them.

Once the amount due has been paid, the shares are 'fully paid'. However, it is possible for part of the payment (or all of the payment in the case of private companies only and very rarely) to be deferred to a future date (either fixed or on demand from the directors for example) or to be payable in instalments. In such cases the shares are referred to as 'partly paid'. In the event of the shares being transferred, the unpaid capital passes with the shares as a debt payable by the holder at the time when payment becomes due.

In the case of public companies, at the time of allotment, the company must receive at least one quarter of the nominal value of the shares and the whole of any premium. Thus partly paid shares of a public company (except those issued under an employees' share scheme) must always be at least one quarter paid up (s 101).

72 ISSUE OF SHARES

Tutor's hint. You need to spend a similar amount of time on all the different parts of this question as they are all for similar marks. Remember the golden rule when it comes to issuing shares (never at a discount to nominal value) and state it clearly.

(a) Pre-emption rights are **the rights of existing company shareholders to be offered new equity shares** issued by the company before they are offered to outsiders, on no less favourable terms than they will be offered to outsiders.

The purpose of the law here is the **protection of the existing shareholders** so that their shareholding cannot be diluted without their consent. They are offered the new shares on a pro rata basis with their existing shareholding, so that their proportionate shareholding within the company remains the same.

Pre-emption rights only apply to the issue of equity shares for cash, ie ordinary shares. They do not apply on the issue of any other type of share, such as preference shares, nor do they apply if the shares are being issued for a non-cash consideration.

The company must offer the new shares in writing to the existing shareholders, and must allow them a period of at least 21 days to accept the offer. If a shareholder does not accept within that period, he is deemed to have declined, and the shares can then be allotted to non-members.

There are various provisions that enable private companies to exclude pre-emption rights and any company to disapply them for a specific allotment or for a specified period.

(b) A company may issue shares for a price **in excess of the nominal value** of those shares. The excess is called the **'share premium'** and must be credited to a share premium account (s130 CA 1985).

It is not necessary for the articles of association to include a **power** to issue shares at a premium since it is **implied**. Where the shares are issued for a non-cash consideration in excess of the shares' nominal value, the excess should still be credited to the share premium account, since the statutory rule applies to issues of shares 'at a premium whether for cash or otherwise': *Henry Head & Co Ltd v Ropner Holdings*.

The **general rule** is that reduction of the share premium account is **subject to the same restrictions as reduction of share capital.**

- No part of the account can be distributed as dividend (s 130).

- The account can be used to pay up fully paid shares under a bonus issue since this operation simply converts one form of fixed capital into another.

- It can also be used to pay capital expenses such as the preliminary expenses of forming the company, a discount on the issue of debentures, a premium on the redemption of debentures and the purchase of its own shares out of capital.

There are also detailed provisions in the case of the amalgamation of companies under the accepted '**merger accounting**' procedure (following the case of *Shearer v Bercain*) which exclude the basic rule in s 130.

Furthermore, the share premium account is included in the '**undistributable reserves**' when determining whether a **dividend** can lawfully be declared by a public company (which can only make a distribution if its net assets are not less than the aggregate of its called up share capital and undistributable reserves (s 264).

(c) **Every share has a nominal value and cannot be allotted at a discount to that value.** A company must obtain in money or money's worth consideration of a value at least equal to the nominal value of the shares allotted (s 100). If shares are allotted at a discount, the allottee is liable to pay the full nominal value together with interest at the appropriate rate (s 107, currently 5%).

The issue of shares at a price which is less than the market value (but equal to or more than the nominal value) of existing shares does not contravene the provision.

In the case of **private companies only**, shares may be allotted for inadequate consideration by the acceptance of **goods or services** at an over value. A blatant and unjustified overvaluation will not, however, be upheld (*Re Wragg*). **Non-cash consideration must be valued in the case of public companies.**

It is not a contravention of s.100 to issue shares at par but to pay an **underwriting or other commission** which reduces the net amount received below par value (s 97 CA 1985).

Marking Guide		Marks	
(a)	Definition	1	
	Purpose is protection of creditors	½	
	Equity shares for cash only	½	
	Offer in writing, allow 21 days	1	
	Can be excluded or disapplied	1	
			4
(b)	Definition of share premium	½	
	Must be credited to share premium account	½	
	Share premium is an undistributable reserve	1	
	Examples of its uses	1	
			3
(c)	No issue at discount	1	
	Consequence of contravention	1	
	Some exceptions for private companies	1	
			3
			10

73 DEBENTURES AND CHARGES

> **Tutor's hint.** These topics have always been very popular in exams. As long as you are familiar with the basic definitions and you can draw out similarities and differences you should be able to score well on a question like this.

(a) There is no statutory definition of 'debenture' (though s 744 states that a debenture includes debenture stock, bonds and any other securities of a company, whether constituting a charge on the assets of the company or not).

In essence, a **debenture** is a document which states the terms on which a company has borrowed money (creating or acknowledging the debt).

A debenture is often **secured** (by also creating a fixed or floating charge over some or all of the company's assets) but may be unsecured, in which case it is likely to be called an unsecured loan note to distinguish it from a secured debenture. A debenture might be **redeemable** or **irredeemable**.

A debenture usually takes the form of a printed legal document, setting out the **terms** of the loan and providing for the payment of **interest** to the debenture holder (regardless of profits). It might be a single debenture or one of a series ranking **pari passu** (for example, where the directors or members provide different loan amounts at different times but all loans are intended to rank equally). It might be one which governs the issue of debenture stock subscribed to by a large number of lenders (typically the public at large).

(b) A **fixed charge** attaches to a specific asset as soon as the charge is created. If the company fails to honour its commitment to pay interest or repay the amount borrowed or goes into liquidation, the asset will be sold to realise the debt, and the proceeds of the sale will go to the fixed chargeholder in preference to preferential creditors and floating charges. The company cannot dispose of the asset without the consent of the chargeholder.

The fact that a document is called a fixed charge will not be conclusive where in fact the company is still permitted to deal with the charge without reference to the chargee. It is important to look at the terms of a charge in order to ascertain precisely which type it is.

Examples of fixed charges are legal mortgages of shares or land, or equitable charges over other property.

(c) A **floating charge** is:

(i) A charge on a **class of assets** of a company, present and future

(ii) The class of assets changes (in the ordinary course of the company's business) from time to time, eg stocks

(iii) Until the holders enforce the charge the company may **carry on business** and **deal** with the asset charged: *Re Yorkshire Woolcombers Association Ltd*.

A floating charge can apply to fixed assets and current assets. It does not attach to any assets until crystallisation (when it becomes a fixed equitable charge).

Marking Guide

		Marks
(a)	Definition of debenture	1
	Secured/unsecured	
	Redeemable/irredeemable	1
	Entitlement to interest	1
		3
(b)	Definition of fixed charge	1
	Examples	1
	Name not conclusive	1
		3
(c)	Definition of floating charge	1
	Example	1
	Assets tradable in course of business	1
	Crystallisation	1
		4
		10

74   REGISTRATION OF CHARGES

> **Tutor's hint**. Candidates could waste time in this question talking generally about fixed and floating charges. Concentrate on the precise requirements of the question, ie what are the rules on registration and what happens if a charge is not registered?

If a company creates or acquires property subject to a fixed or floating charge over its assets and the type of charge falls within the categories listed in s 396, the charge must be registered.

Particulars should be sent to the Registrar of Companies within 21 days after the creation of the charge: s 395. Particulars can be delivered by any person interested in the charge although to do so is primarily the duty of the company: s 399.

Register of charges

In addition to registration with the Registrar of Companies, a company is also required to keep a register of charges at its registered office and to enter details of all (relevant) charges: s 407. Wilful or knowing failure to comply with this requirement renders an officer in default liable to a fine.

Additionally ss 406 and 408 require a company to keep **copies** of **every instrument creating a charge** at its registered office and to make them, and the register of charges, open for inspection by any creditor or member without fee. Again, failure to comply with this requirement renders any officer in default liable to a fine.

Effects of non-registration

The effects of non-registration, where registration is required, are twofold.

(a) The **charge** will be **void** against a liquidator or administrator and any creditor of the company: s 395 CA 1985, and any person acquiring an interest in the charged property. The charge will be void even if insolvency proceedings or the acquisition of an interest in the property occur within the 21 days period where no particulars are delivered; creditors who subsequently take security over property and properly register their charge within 21 days will take precedence over a previous unregistered charge.

As a result, the whole of the sum secured by the charge is **payable immediately** upon **demand,** even if the sum so secured is also the subject of other security.

PROFESSIONAL EDUCATION

(b) If particulars are not delivered within 21 days the company and every officer of it who is in default is liable to a fine (and, for continued contravention, to a daily default fine).

75 INHERITANCE

> **Tutor's hint.** This question requires you to explain various types of investment in a company. It tests across the spectrum of types of capital you have studied and also looks at charges as well. It is therefore good practice for any Section A question on capital as well as being a tough Section B question in itself.

(a)/(b) Ordinary shares

A share is 'the interest of a shareholder in the company measured by a sum of money, for the purpose of a liability in the first place, and of interest in the second, but also consisting of a series of mutual covenants entered into by all the shareholders inter se' (*Borland's Trustee v Steel Bros & Co*).

A share must be paid for and it gives a proportionate entitlement to **dividends, votes** and any **return of capital**.

An allottee of shares must pay the nominal value of those shares plus any premium due on them. Once the amount due has been paid, the shares are 'fully paid'.

However, it is possible for **part of the payment** (or all of the payment in the case of private companies only and very rarely) to be **deferred to a future date** - either fixed or on demand from the directors for example - or to be payable in instalments. In such cases the shares are referred to as '**partly paid**'.

In the event of the shares being transferred, the unpaid capital passes with the shares as a **debt payable by the holder at the time when payment becomes due**.

Clare's first inheritance is shares in A Ltd **partly paid** up. There is therefore an outstanding liability on the shares of 25%, or **£2,500**, which may be demanded of her at any time by the directors calling up further capital or in the event of an insolvent liquidation.

Clare has also inherited ordinary shares in B Ltd worth £10,000. As these are **fully paid-up,** Clare has no liability to make any further payments in respect of them.

(c) Preference shares

These carry a prior **right to receive an annual dividend of a fixed amount** and (often) a **priority right to return of capital,** but otherwise are the same as ordinary shares unless differences are expressly stated.

They **do not usually carry voting rights** save in specified circumstances, for example where their dividends are in arrears.

The preference share's right to receive a dividend before any other dividend is paid or declared is not also a right to compel a company to pay the dividend (*Bond v Barrow Haematite Steel Co*), nor does it entitle the shareholder to participate in any dividend over and above the specified rate of dividend attached to the shares.

It is, however, **deemed to be cumulative** unless the contrary is stated. If the company goes into liquidation, **preference shareholders cease to be entitled to arrears of unpaid cumulative preference dividends unless those dividends were declared when liquidation commenced** (but not paid) or where the articles expressly provide that arrears should be paid in priority to a return of capital to members.

Generally, preference shares offer greater security of income and (if they carry priority rights on repayment of capital) greater security of capital. However, there are disadvantages, such as the lack of voting rights and the risk of losing unpaid arrears.

(d) **Debenture – fixed charge**

A debenture is a **document which acknowledges a company's debt** and states the terms on which the company has borrowed money. It may also create a charge over the **company's assets as security for the loan.**

A fixed or specific charge attaches to the relevant asset as soon as the charge is created, for example a charge over named property given as security for a loan to the owner of the property. If the company does need to dispose of the charged asset, it will either repay the secured debt out of the sale proceeds so that the charge is discharged or dispose of the asset subject to the charge.

A **fixed charge** may be legal or equitable and over land or other company assets, from buildings and chattels to book debts. It is not appropriate to give a fixed charge against stock in trade as the company would be prevented from dealing with it without approval.

On a fixed charge, in the event of default, the chargee can appoint a receiver who may sell the asset charged in order to recover the debt. If the proceeds of sale exceed the debt, the excess goes towards paying off other debts. If they are less, then the debentureholder becomes an unsecured creditor in respect of the amount of debt outstanding.

The main advantage enjoyed by a holder of a fixed charge as opposed to a floating charge is that **a fixed charge confers immediate rights over identified assets.** It is therefore more certain as to which of the chargor's assets are subject to the charge and gives an immediate right of sale over them. **A fixed charge will rank in priority to a floating charge even if it was created after the floating charge since it attaches to the property at the time of creation rather than at the time of crystallisation.**

Clare's fourth inheritance means that she is owed £5,000 by D plc and she has a fixed charge over the company's assets. She is therefore a creditor (not a member) of D plc and is entitled to receive interest on the loan, even if the interest has to be paid from the company's capital.

(e) **Debenture – floating charge**

Where a charge is created over **certain assets** but the **company retains the right to deal** with those assets during the ordinary course of business until the charge crystallises, then that charge is a '**floating charge**'.

On **crystallisation**, a floating charge is **converted into a fixed equitable charge** on the assets owned by the company at the time of crystallisation: *Re Griffin Hotel Co Ltd.*

Crystallisation will occur on the happening of any of the events specified in the charge, such as the liquidation of the company or the cessation of its business: *Re Woodroffes (Musical Instruments) Ltd.*

The nature of a floating charge was summarised in *Re Yorkshire Woolcombers Association Ltd* as a charge on a class of assets of a company, present and future, which class is, in the ordinary course of the company's business, changing from time to time and until the holder enforces the charge the company may carry on business and deal with the assets charged. A floating charge over 'the undertaking and assets' of a company applies to fixed as well as to current assets.

Clare is, therefore, also a creditor of E plc and is owed £5,000 which is secured by a floating charge over the company's business assets. Again she is entitled to interest on the loan and in the event of the company's default, will be entitled to enforce her security and recover the debt.

76 DIVIDENDS

> **Tutor's hint.** Beware the mark allocation in this question: do not describe dividends in too much length in part (a) and proceed to run out of time in part (b), for which the majority of the marks are available.

(a) **Dividends**

Dividends are payments made to shareholders out of company profits (to the extent that shares are fully paid up) as a return on their investment in the company. Dividends can only be paid from **profits available for the purpose**: s 263.

Every company has the implied power to declare a dividend although an express power is normally contained in the articles of association.

(b) **Rules governing dividends**

(i) **Private companies**

The general rule is set out in s 263 CA 1985 which provides that 'dividends may only be paid by a company out of profits available for the purpose'. A company's power to declare dividends is given in its **articles**. Table A provides that the company in general meeting may declare dividends by ordinary resolution subject to a maximum amount which is recommended by the directors.

Dividends are usually declared payable on the paid up amount of share capital and can be paid in cash or by other means. Directors may declare interim dividends as they consider such action to be justified.

The **directors** will be **liable** to **make good an unlawful distribution** where they recommend or declare a dividend which they know is to be made from capital or if they make a recommendation or declaration without preparing any accounts and the dividend is in fact paid from capital.

They will also be liable if they make some mistake of law or misrepresentation of the company's constitution which leased them to recommend or declare an unlawful dividend although relief may be available to directors under s 727 where they acted honestly and reasonably. Under s 277 the shareholders may also be liable to repay unlawful dividends where they knew or had reasonable grounds to believe that it was made unlawfully.

'**Distributable profits**' are defined (s 263(3)) as 'accumulated realised profits, so far as not previously utilised by distribution or capitalisation, less accumulated realised losses, so far as not previously written off in a reduction or reorganisation of capital duly made'.

Only profits **realised** at the balance sheet date shall be included in the profit and loss account and losses which have arisen in respect of the current accounting period or between the balance sheet date and the date that the accounts are signed or which are likely to arise should also be taken into account: Sch 4.

'**Accumulated**' means that any losses of previous years must be included in reckoning the current distributable surplus. In order to be treated as 'realised' a profit or loss must be deemed to be realised in accordance with generally

accepted accounting principles prevailing when the accounts are prepared. Depreciation must be treated as a realised loss and debited against profit in determining the amount of distributable profit remaining. However, any increased depreciation provision due to a revaluation of an asset may be treated as profit: s 275. If, on a general revaluation of all fixed assets there is a diminution in value, then any related provision need not be treated as a realised loss.

(ii) **Public companies**

In addition to the principles mentioned above, in the case of public companies, the following rule applies (which can only decrease and not increase the company's distributable profits):

A public company can only make a distribution if its net assets, at the time, are equal to or greater than the aggregate of its called up share capital and undistributed reserves and the amount of any dividend cannot exceed such amount as would leave its net assets at not less than that aggregate amount. Undistributed reserves comprise the share premium account, the capital redemption reserve, the revaluation reserve and any reserve which the company is prohibited from distributing by statute or its own constitution. This means that a public company can only make a distribution from its profits after depreciating fixed assets.

The above mentioned rules apply to all distributions of assets to a company's members except (s 263) the issue of bonus shares, the redemption or purchase of the company's shares out of capital or profits, a reduction of share capital by cancelling liability for unpaid capital or by repaying share capital to members and any distribution of assets on a winding up.

Marking Guide		*Marks*
Dividends clearly defined		2
Private co:	– Authority in articles	1
	– Role of directors	2
	– Distributable profits	1
	– Accumulated profits	1
Public co:	– Net assets rule	2
	– Exceptions	1
		$\overline{10}$

77   **ISSUE AND PREMIUM**

> **Tutorial note.** Notice that the requirement in this question falls into two parts. It asks you to explain both 'the meaning' and 'the effect' of the two issues. This should help you build up marks in your answer by making sure that you address both of these requirements. For example, in part (a), to explain the **meaning** of the concept, you really have to answer the question 'discount to what?' In other words, you have to explain that shares have a **nominal value** attached and that they cannot be issued at a discount to that. The basic **effect** of the concept is that if shares are issued at a discount to nominal value, this is illegal. This means that any money due to make the payment up to nominal value could be called in event of liquidation. This is similar to the effect of having partly paid shares.
>
> **Examiner's comments.** In the first part of the question many candidates were not able to cite s100 CA 1985 as the authority for the prohibition on the issue of shares at a discount, nor could they quote any case law. Few candidates tried to explain why issuing shares at a discount is unlawful, nor could they discuss any of the exceptions to the rule. In part (b) most candidates could explain the purpose of a share premium account, but many answers did not contain sufficient detail of s130 CA 85. Most candidates were aware of how a share premium account is created and that it is a capital account with limited uses.

(a) **Issuing shares at a discount**

A company may issue shares within its authorised share capital (which it may increase at any time by ordinary resolution). Every share has a nominal value and cannot be allotted at a discount to that value. In order to protect the company's creditors, a company must obtain in money or money's worth consideration of a value at least equal to the nominal value of the shares allotted (s 100). The uncalled capital passes as a debt on a transfer of the shares so that it is payable by the holder at the time payment is demanded.

If shares are allotted at a discount, the allottee is still liable to pay the full nominal value together with interest at the appropriate rate (s107, currently 5%).

The issue of shares at a price which is less than the market value (but equal to or more than the nominal value) of existing shares does not contravene the provision.

In the case of private companies, shares may be allotted for inadequate consideration by the acceptance of goods or services at an over value. A blatant and unjustified overvaluation will not, however, be upheld (*Re Wragg*). Any non-cash consideration must be valued in the case of public companies.

It is not a contravention of s100 to issue shares at par but to pay an underwriting fee or other commission which reduces the net amount received below par value (s97 CA 1985) provided the company is permitted to do so by its articles.

(b) **The share premium account**

A company may issue shares for a price in excess of the nominal value of those shares. The excess is called the 'share premium' and must be credited to a share premium account (s130 CA 1985). Where the shares are issued for a non-cash consideration in excess of the shares' nominal value, the excess should still be credited to the share premium account, since the statutory rule applies to issues of shares 'at a premium whether for cash or otherwise' (*Henry Head & Co Ltd v Ropner Holdings*).

The general rule is that reduction of the share premium account is subject to the same restrictions as reduction of share capital. No part of the account can be distributed as dividend (s 130).

The account can be used to pay up fully paid shares under a bonus issue since this operation simply converts one form of fixed capital into another. It can also be used to pay capital expenses such as the preliminary expenses of forming the company, a

discount on the issue of debentures, a premium on the redemption of debentures and the purchase of its own shares out of capital.

There are also detailed provisions in the case of the amalgamation of companies under the accepted 'merger accounting' procedure (following the case of *Shearer v Bercain*) which exclude the basic rule in s 130. Furthermore, the share premium account is included in the 'undistributable reserves' when determining whether a dividend can lawfully be declared by a public company.

Marking Guide

		Marks	
(a)	Explanation of nominal value	2	
	Protection of creditors needed	1	
	Explanation of issue at discount	1	
	Valuation of non cash consideration by plcs	1	
	Other exceptions	1	
			6
(b)	Explanation of share premium	2	
	Examples of uses	2	
			4
			10

---

78 PURCHASE OF OWN SHARES

Tutor's hint. You must know the circumstances in which a company can purchase its own shares. In part (b) your answer should describe what happens when an own share purchase is made out of capital.

Common mistakes are to state that a company cannot purchase its own shares and to confuse a company purchasing its own shares with it giving financial assistance for someone else to purchase its shares.

(a) Any company may purchase its own shares by **market** or **off-market purchase** out of profits or the proceeds of an issue of new shares.

In addition **private companies** may **purchase** their **shares out of capital** (off market).

A company **cannot purchase** its **ordinary shares** if as a result **only redeemable shares** are left.

(b) The **capital redemption reserve** acts as a means of replacing the share capital purchased, thus **maintaining** the **creditors' buffer**. The **reserve** is treated as if it were **share capital**.

If a purchase of own shares is funded wholly out of profits, the **amount** by which issued **share capital** is **diminished** should be **transferred** to the **capital redemption reserve**: s 170(1).

If the **purchase** is wholly or partly out of the proceeds of a **fresh issue**, and the **total proceeds** are less than the **nominal value** of the shares redeemed, the **difference** should be **transferred** to the **capital redemption reserve**: s 170(2).

The above rules do not however apply to **private companies purchasing** their **own shares** out of **capital**. When paying for shares out of capital, a company may make a **permissible capital payment**, which is the difference between:

(i) The purchase price, and

(ii) Any available profits plus the proceeds of any fresh issue made for the purchase of the company's own shares.

In these circumstances a **transfer** must be **made** to the capital redemption reserve when the **permissible capital payment** is **less** than the **nominal amount** of the **shares redeemed**; the transfer must equal the difference between the two.

(c) The uses to which the balance on the share premium account may be put are very limited. It may be used:

(i) To **return share premium** under an authorised reduction of capital

(ii) To pay a **fully paid bonus issue,** since this operation merely converts one form of fixed capital into another

(iii) To pay **capital expenses** such as the preliminary expenses of forming the company

(iv) To pay a **discount** on the **issue** of **debentures**

(v) To pay a **premium** (if required) on the **redemption** of **debentures**: s 130(2)

	Marking Guide		Marks
(a)	Any company by market or off-market purchase		1
	Private companies out of capital		1
	Not if only redeemable shares left		<u>1</u>
			3
(b)	If purchase funded from profits: rules		½
	If purchase funded from a fresh issue: rules		½
	If purchased from capital: rules		<u>2</u>
			3
(c)	1 mark for each; max. 4		<u>4</u>
			<u><u>10</u></u>

79   PREPARATION QUESTION: CAPITAL MAINTENANCE

(a) A limited company is permitted without restriction to cancel unissued shares and in that way to reduce its authorised share capital. That change does not alter its financial position.

If a limited company with a share capital wishes to reduce its issued share capital (and incidentally its authorised capital of which the issued capital is part) it may do so provided that:

- It has **power** to do so in its articles, and
- It passes a **special resolution**, and
- It obtains **confirmation** of the reduction **from the court**: s 135.

The first requirement is simply a matter of procedure. Articles (Table A Art 34) usually contain the necessary power. If not, the company in general meeting would first pass a special resolution to alter the articles appropriately and then proceed, as the second item on the agenda of the meeting, to pass a special resolution to reduce the capital.

There are three basic methods of reducing share capital specified in s 135(2):

- **Extinguish** or **reduce liability** on partly-paid shares.

- **Cancel paid up share capital** which has been lost or which is no longer represented by available assets.

- **Pay off part of the paid up share capital** out of surplus assets.

Although these are the methods specified in s 135, they are not the only possibilities.

If the first or third methods are is used (or is part of a more complex scheme to reduce capital) creditors must be invited to object, and their consent must be granted. An alternative is that they are paid off, which will allow the court to approve the reduction. These requirements, along with other court procedures, are contained in s 136.

Public companies are subject to a minimum capital requirement, currently of £50,000: s 11. This means that any public company wishing to reduce its capital below this figure will only be allowed to do so by the court if it **re-registers as a private company**, which is not subject to the minimum capital requirement. This situation is, of course, relatively rare.

(b) **General rule**

S 151 lays down a general **prohibition** on companies providing financial assistance to purchase their own shares. S 151 is concerned with the general principle of the maintenance of capital. However, there are a number of definitions and exceptions which accompany this rule (ss 151-158).

Definition

Financial assistance is widely defined to include a gift, loan, guarantee, indemnity, security, purchase of such rights from a third party or 'any other financial assistance given by a company which reduces to a material extent its net assets'. The prohibition extends to such assistance **directly** or **indirectly given**. Financial assistance for the purpose of acquiring shares either of the company or its holding company or to discharge liabilities include in making the acquisition is prohibited.

Exceptions

Furthermore, certain types of transaction are specifically excluded from the prohibition contained in s 151.

- **Payments of dividends** out of profits.
- **Distribution of assets** in a winding-up.
- **Allotment of bonus shares.**
- **Reduction of capital** approved by the court.
- Certain **transactions incidental to reconstruction** or **amalgamation** or liquidation under relevant Companies Acts provisions.
- **Making a loan,** if lending is part of the company's ordinary business and the loan is made in the ordinary course of its business, is excluded.
- Providing money, in good faith and in the best interests of the company, for the purpose of an **employees' share scheme.**
- **Making loans to persons** (not directors) **employed by the company** in good faith with a view to those persons **acquiring fully paid shares** in the company to be held by them as beneficial owners is excluded from the prohibition.

Purpose other than financial assistance

In the case of private and public companies, the financial assistance may not be prohibited. This applies if the **principal purpose** of the transaction was **not** to give **financial assistance** for the purchase of its shares or was an **incidental part** of some **larger purpose** and it can be said that the directors acted in **good faith** in what they deemed to be the interests of the company and not of a third party. However case law suggests this exemption may be interpreted narrowly by the courts, who have drawn a distinction between the reason for financial assistance and its purpose: *Brady v Brady*.

Private company

The provisions of the Companies Act do enable a private (but not public) company to give financial assistance for the purchase of its (or its holding company's) own shares subject to certain conditions.

(i)   The financial assistance must **not reduce the net assets** of the company or, if it does, must be provided out of distributable profits.

(ii)   The directors must issue a **statutory declaration** of solvency with a verifying auditors' report.

(iii)   A **special resolution** must be passed approving the transaction.

(iv)   **Members** (not creditors) **holding at least 10% of the issued shares** (or class of shares) have the right to **apply to the court** objecting to the transaction, for which purpose a 28 day period must elapse before the resolution can be implemented.

80   CLASS RIGHTS

> **Tutor's hint**. Think carefully before choosing a question like this. Part (a) is relatively straightforward but part (b) requires very detailed knowledge, and you may find it difficult to do yourself justice here.
>
> **Examiner's comments**. Most candidates had a reasonable attempt at part (a), although many only discussed voting rights and did not mention rights for return of capital. Part (b) was poorly answered as candidates did not know enough about the statutory provisions for variation of class rights. Candidates did well when explaining minority objection rights.

(a)   There are no statutory definitions of what particular rights are enjoyed by particular classes of shares. Rather, **class rights are those provided by the company's articles of association** and on the issue of the relevant shares. If no differences between shares are expressly provided then it is assumed that they all carry the same rights. A company may choose to specify particular rights and attach them to particular classes of shares. Such rights will deal with matters concerning dividends, return of capital, voting and the right to appoint directors.

All shares carrying identical rights are grouped together into a class of shares. The most common instances of different classes are **ordinary shares** and **preference shares** but a company may also have ordinary shares with voting rights and ordinary shares without voting rights, for example. The main difference between ordinary shares and preference shares is the implied right attaching to preference shares to receive an annual dividend of a fixed amount.

The right to receive a dividend is merely one to receive the dividend at a specified rate before any other dividend may be declared or paid, but it does not entitle the preference shareholder to compel the company to pay the dividend rather than transfer the available profits to reserves (*Bond v Barrow Haematite Steel Co.*). The **right to receive a preference dividend is deemed to be cumulative unless the contrary is stated**. The preference shareholders cease to be entitled to arrears however, where the company goes into liquidation unless the dividend was declared at the time liquidation commenced or unless there is express provision in the articles or other terms of issue. Preference shareholders are not entitled to participate in any additional dividend over and above their specified rate. In other respects, preference shareholders carry the same rights as ordinary shareholders unless otherwise stated.

The **holders of ordinary shares will be entitled to the surplus profits** once other commitments have been met whereas preference shares carry no such right beyond payment of the fixed dividend. Similarly holders of ordinary shares will be entitled to a share of the **surplus assets on a winding up** whereas other types of shareholder will normally only be entitled to a return of their capital. Preference shares will normally be expressed not to carry voting rights or only limited voting rights, unlike ordinary shares. Shareholders may have some class rights which attach to them as members even though those rights are not attached to particular classes of shares (see *Cumbrian Newspaper Group v Cumberland and Westmorland Herald Newspapers and Printing Co Ltd*).

(b) A variation of class rights is an alteration in the position of shareholders with regard to those benefits or duties which they have by virtue of their shares. The rights vested in the holders of a class of shares can only be varied by the company with the consent of all the holders or with such consent of a majority as is prescribed (usually) by the articles. Normally the procedure is that an extraordinary resolution be passed giving approval for a proposed variation by a three-quarters majority cast either at a separate meeting of a class or by written consent (s 125(2)).

If the rights are set by the memorandum or otherwise and there is a variation procedure laid down by either the memorandum or articles then that procedure must be followed (s 125(4)). If class rights are defined other than by the memorandum and there is no variation procedure in the articles, then a 75% majority of the class in question is necessary although a minority has a right to appeal to the court (s 125(2)). If rights are attached by the memorandum and there is no variation procedure prescribed, the consent of all the company members is necessary to vary those rights (s 125(5)).

Whenever class rights are varied in pursuance of a procedure laid down by the company's constitution, holders of at least 15% of the issued shares of the relevant class who have not themselves consented to or voted in favour of the variation may apply to the court within 21 days of the class consent being given for an order cancelling the variation (s 127). They must satisfy the court that the variation is 'unfairly prejudicial' to the class, usually by showing that the majority who voted in favour were seeking some advantage to themselves as members of a different class instead of considering the interests of the class in which they were then voting (*Re Holders Investment Trust*). The court can either approve or cancel the variation but cannot modify its terms or give conditional approval.

It might be noted that the subdivision of shares in one class with the effect of increasing that class's voting strength is not strictly a variation of class rights (*Greenhalgh v Arderne Cinemas Ltd*), even though the effect is prejudicial to members of another class by reducing the value of their rights. Similarly, issuing shares of the same class to allottees who are not already members of the class, is not a variation of class rights (*White v Bristol Aeroplane Co Ltd*).

81   IMPROVE LTD AND JUDDER LTD

Tutor's hint. Only attempt this sort of question if you are absolutely confident about the topic examined. It is a very short sharp question based entirely on statute, and you will only score well on it if you have a detailed knowledge of the provisions.

Examiner's comments. This question was generally not done very well. Candidates tended to be vague in their answers and seldom referred to the statute. It seemed that a lot of candidates only did this question because they did not have a better alternative available in Section B.

(a) A company limited by shares is entitled to issue shares up to the level of its **authorised share capital,** that is the amount of share capital with which it is registered, in accordance with the stated division of that capital into shares of a fixed amount.

Once shares up to the authorised share capital have been allotted, the company may **increase the company's share capital** by passing a resolution in general meeting (or by written resolution) provided the company's articles authorise them to do so (s 121 CA 1985). Article 32 of Table A requires only that an **ordinary resolution** be passed which requires a simple majority of votes cast. Improve Ltd should, therefore, call an extraordinary general meeting and propose the necessary resolution. Once the resolution has been passed, a copy of it and the amended memorandum and particulars of the new shares must be delivered to the Registrar of Companies within 15 days of the resolution.

If Improve Ltd has articles of association other than Table A that do not contain the necessary power, then it must first pass a special resolution (requiring 75% of votes cast) amending the articles accordingly, before passing the resolution to increase the share capital.

(b) There is an established principle of company law that the subscribed capital of a company limited by shares must be held for the payment of debts and may not be returned to members except under clearly defined procedures which safeguard creditors' interests. This is the '**maintenance of capital principle**' which might be described as the price members pay for limited liability. Broadly speaking, there are three exceptions to the rule, one of which gives a company the opportunity to reduce its issued share capital.

A limited company with a share capital may, without restriction, **cancel unissued shares,** thereby reducing its authorised share capital. Where shares have already been issued, the company may reduce its issued share capital (and therefore also its authorised capital) provided that it has the power to do so in its articles. Article 34 of Table A contains such a power. The company must pass a **special resolution** authorising a reduction, which resolution need not state the reason for the reduction being made but must set out the method of reduction. The company must also apply for and obtain prior approval for the reduction from the court (s 135 CA 1985).

The share capital might then be reduced in a number of ways, the most common of which are:

(i) extinguishing or **reducing liability on partly paid shares** by reducing their nominal value;

(ii) **cancelling paid up share capital** which has been lost or which is no longer represented by available assets by reducing the nominal value of fully paid shares and applying the amount of the reduction to write off the debit balance on reserves; or

(iii) **paying off part of the paid up share capital** out of surplus assets by reducing the nominal value of fully paid shares and repaying the amount of the reduction to shareholders.

In considering whether to make an order approving the reduction, the court's main concern will be any consequences of the reduction on the company's ability to pay its debts. If the method of reduction is (i) or (iii) above, the court must usually invite **creditors** to state their objections (and may do so in the case of (ii)). It need not do so where the company pays off the creditors before applying to the court or produces a bank (or similar) guarantee that existing creditors' debts will be paid in full. The court will also have regard to any effect on different classes of shareholder and whether the reduction might cause confusion or mislead people who may have dealings with the company.

Judder Ltd should therefore begin by preparing a resolution setting out the method of reduction and apply to the court for approval.

Marking Guide		*Marks*	
(a)	Can issue shares up to authorised limit	1	
	Authorisation to increase in Articles	1	
	Ordinary or written resolution	2	
	Probably at an EGM	1	
	File with Registrar	1	
	May need to change Articles to allow	<u>2</u>	
			8
(b)	Principles of capital maintenance	2	
	Reduction needs authority in Articles	1	
	Special resolution	1	
	Prior approval of the Court	2	
	Court considers ability to pay debts	1	
	3 ways of reducing	3	
	Creditors' rights	<u>2</u>	
			<u>12</u>
			<u><u>20</u></u>

82 PREPARATION QUESTION: DTI INVESTIGATIONS

(a) **Application for investigation**

S 431 provides that the Department may appoint inspectors to investigate the affairs of a company on the application of not less than **two hundred members** or of members holding not less than **one-tenth of the issued shares**. If there is no share capital then application must be made by 20% of the members. The company itself may apply to the

DTI, following an ordinary resolution to that effect. In both cases the Secretary of State requires evidence to show that there is a good reason for appointing an investigator.

Court order

S 432(1) requires the appointment of inspectors if the court by order declares that the company's affairs should be investigated.

Appointment on fraud or prejudice against minority

S 432(2)(b) empowers the Department to appoint inspectors on the application of any person if there appears to be conduct **unfairly prejudicial** to some members of the company, or **fraud**, misfeasance or misconduct, or if members are not receiving all reasonable information. Such an appointment will also be made where there is evidence that the company has been conducted to defraud creditors or prejudice a minority, or if the company has a fraudulent or unlawful purpose. Following a preliminary investigation of a company's affairs under s 447 inspectors will be appointed under the provisions contained in s 432(2). This power is the one most frequently used for the appointment of inspectors.

Inspectors are empowered by s 433 to investigate the affairs of companies related to the company which is the subject of the investigation.

(b) The DTI has the power to appoint an inspector to investigate the ownership of a company and to find out who is or has been interested financially in its shares: s 442.

(c) A director is **prohibited** from **dealing in options** in listed shares or debentures of his company (in practice this would be a public company): s 323. Directors of all companies are also required to give notice to the company of the interests of himself and of persons connected with him (spouse and children) in shares or debentures of the company: ss 324 and 328.

If it is suspected that there has been an infringement of these rules the Department of Trade may appoint inspectors to investigate with a view to civil or criminal proceedings: s 446.

Inspectors have extensive **statutory powers** to call for books and documents from past and present directors and agents, and to require them to attend before them, assist them and answer questions on oath. Refusal to comply is contempt of court. This power extends to any other persons whom they believe to have relevant information. If necessary their investigation may be extended to related companies.

Inspectors may submit interim reports to the Secretary of State, and must do so if called upon, relating to their suspicions that criminal offences have been committed.

83 COMPULSORY WINDING UP

> **Tutor's hint**. Note that the question relates to **compulsory** winding up: do not get side tracked into other types of liquidation.

The statutory provisions on compulsory winding up are in the Insolvency Act 1986.

The two **general effects** of compulsory liquidation are:

- That the management of the company passes to a liquidator and the directors' powers cease, and

- Dispositions of the company's property or shares, and actions against the company are restrained.

There is no automatic cancellation of company contracts, but many commercial contracts provide for cancellation at the option of the other party if the company goes into liquidation.

Compulsory winding up is deemed to commence from the date on which the petition was presented, unless the company was then already in voluntary liquidation. In effect the order for compulsory liquidation is retrospective.

The more **specific effects** of compulsory liquidation are as follows.

(a)   The Official Receiver becomes liquidator from the making of the order, and he continues until some other liquidator, who must be an insolvency practitioner, is appointed: s 136 (2).

(b)   The powers of the directors are terminated and they are dismissed.

(c)   Any disposition of the company's property from the commencement of the liquidation is void unless approved by the court.

The court may give approval with retrospective effect but it is safer to apply for it in advance, when the petition has been represented. The court will only give its approval if it considers that it is in the interests of the company and its creditors that the company should continue to carry on its business pending a decision on the petition.

(d)   Any transfer of the company's share is void unless approved by the court: s 127 IA.

(e)   No creditor may commence or continue legal action against the company except with the leave of the court: s 126 IA.

(f)   The employment of the company's staff ceases unless the liquidator retains them to carry on the business.

84   EXPLAIN WINDING UP

> **Tutor's hint**. This is a straightforward factual question, but you need to ensure that you are fully familiar with the distinction between voluntary (both members' and creditors' as the question does not specify which) and compulsory winding up.
>
> **Examiner's comments**. Some candidates regarded winding up as merely being a case of a company ceasing to trade, which is not enough. Few candidates were able to explain the sub-division of voluntary winding up between members' and creditors' voluntary, many candidates wrongly thinking that a members' voluntary liquidation meant that the shareholders initiated proceedings. Very few candidates were able to refer to Insolvency Act 1986.

(a)   'Winding-up' refers to the process of **liquidation leading to dissolution**, where the life of a company is brought to an end, its debts are paid and any surplus assets distributed among its members and/or creditors. A company liquidation may be compulsory or voluntary, solvent or insolvent and will be governed by the provisions of the Insolvency Act.

(b)   (i)   A **voluntary winding-up** is where the **members** in general meeting resolve to wind up the company. Whether it is a members' or creditors' voluntary winding-up will depend on whether the directors believe that the company will or will not be able to pay its debts in full. Only an ordinary resolution is required where the articles provide for liquidation at some point, but more commonly a special resolution is required. Alternatively an extraordinary resolution may be passed where a company cannot continue in business due to its liability in which case the company can go into liquidation on 14 days' notice.

A **members' voluntary winding-up** occurs only where all the directors, or a majority of them, make and deliver to the Registrar a **declaration of solvency**, including a statement of the company's assets and liabilities, (s 89 IA86). Such a declaration must state that, having made full enquiries into the company's affairs, they believe that it will be able to pay its debts together with interest, within a specified period (up to 12 months). It is a criminal offence punishable by fine or imprisonment, for a director to make a declaration of solvency without having reasonable grounds for it.

The liquidator is appointed by the members and his task is to wind up the company's affairs, realise the assets and distribute the proceeds. A voluntary liquidation is generally quicker, simpler and less expensive than a compulsory winding-up.

Where no declaration of solvency is filed, the liquidation proceeds as a **creditors' voluntary winding up**. In this case, the directors convene an EGM for the passing of an extraordinary resolution and also convene a meeting of the creditors (s 98), giving at least 7 days' notice. Although the members will appoint a liquidator at the EGM, the creditors (who normally meet 14 days later) have the final say in selecting and appointing a liquidator. They may also appoint a **liquidation committee** with five representatives from each of the members and the creditors to work in conjunction with the liquidator.

Once the liquidator has wound up the company affairs and performed his duties, he calls a final meeting of members (and creditors if appropriate) and delivers his final account, following which he sends a copy of the accounts to the Registrar who dissolves the company 3 months later, by removing the company name from the register.

(ii) A **compulsory winding-up** is one ordered by the court under s 122 IA 86 on one or more of seven specified grounds. The most important of these grounds are (a) that the company is **unable to pay its debts** and (b) that it is **just and equitable** to wind up the company. Where a creditor is owed more than £750 and makes a written demand for payment and the company fails to pay the debt, or offer reasonable security for it, within three weeks, the company is deemed unable to pay its debts. The creditor may persuade the court of the company's inability to settle its debts in other ways, for example by proving that the company's assets are less than its liabilities.

The just and equitable ground is usually relied on by a member who is dissatisfied with the directors' or controlling shareholders' management of the company, provided he can show that no other remedy is available and satisfactory.

The **DTI may petition for a compulsory winding up** if it considers it just and equitable and in the public interest to do so or if the company has not obtained a s 177 certificate within one year of incorporation. Once a court orders a compulsory winding up, the Official Receiver becomes the liquidator, the employees are automatically dismissed, any floating charge crystallises and any legal proceedings against the company are halted unless the court gives leave for their continuation. Once the liquidation is complete, the liquidator reports to the DTI and applies to the court for an order dissolving the company.

Marking Guide

			Marks	
(a)		Liquidation leading to dissolution	1	
		Outline of application of assets	1	
				2
(b)	(i)	Members' voluntary description	1	
		Procedure	1	
		Creditors voluntary description	1	
		Procedure	1	
				4
	(ii)	Supervised by the Court	1	
		Definition of solvency	1	
		Just and equitable explanation	1	
		DTI involvement	1	
				4
				10

85   KEN AND DORIS

Tutor's hint. In part (a) do not confuse a members' and creditors' winding up on the one hand, and a voluntary and compulsory winding up on the other. In part (b) you must respond to the large hint given in the question, that Doris must legalise her position in the company.

(a)   The winding up is instigated by an extraordinary resolution of the company in general meeting, by which the company states that it cannot continue to trade because of its liabilities.

The company must call a meeting of creditors for a day not later than the 14th day after the day on which the extraordinary resolution was passed: s 98(1). The creditors must receive at least 7 days notice of the meeting.

The notice must state either:

(i)   The name and address of an insolvency practitioner who will furnish creditors free of charge with such information as they reasonably require, or

(ii)   A place in the locality where on the two days before the meeting of creditors is held, a list of the names and addresses of the company's creditors will be available for inspection free of charge.

Notice of the creditors' meeting must be **advertised** in the *London Gazette* and in at least two newspapers circulating in the locality in which the company's principal place of business was situated.

During the period before the creditors' meeting but after the resolution for winding-up the **members' nominee** will act as **provisional liquidator**. He will have restricted powers to act during this period, subject to application to the court. This restriction is necessitated by the practice of 'centrebinding', whereby the assets are fraudulently disposed of before the creditors' meeting.

At the creditors' meeting the **creditors may appoint their own nominee** to act as liquidator. The **creditors' choice will prevail** over the members' choice if there is a conflict; usually there is not.

The directors of the company must **prepare** and lay before the creditors' meeting a **statement of affairs** of the company but, importantly, they do not have to make a statutory declaration of insolvency.

(b) The company will be put into liquidation as a **members' voluntary winding up**, since it is apparently still solvent. The procedure for this is outlined below, but before it can be adopted there are **two specific issues** which must be dealt with.

Doris' position in the company

Doris is currently the sole shareholder of the company. The company has become a single member private company. The company does not need to re-register as a result of this, but the register of members should be amended to state that it is now a single member company.

Ss 282 and 283 provide that any private company must have at least one director, and further that the company secretary cannot also be a sole director. This is the position in which Doris finds herself after the death of her husband. The solution, however, is relatively straightforward.

Doris must resign her post as secretary and appoint another person to that position. She would thus become a sole director who is not secretary, which is permissible.

Procedure for winding up

After these problems have been rectified, the procedure is as follows.

The company must hold a **general meting** at which a **special resolution** is passed resolving that it should be wound up voluntarily.

Once the resolution to wind up has been passed the company must, within 14 days, give **notice** of the resolution by advertising in the *London Gazette*: s 85 IA. The winding up is by s 86 IA deemed to commencement at the time of the passing of the resolution for voluntary winding up.

In the five weeks before the passing of the resolution mentioned the directors, or a majority of them, must make a **statutory declaration of solvency** at a meeting of the directors: s 89 IA.

The declaration is to the effect that they have made full inquiry into the company's affairs and have formed the opinion that the company will be able to pay its debts in full (together with interest) within a period of 12 months from the commencement of winding up.

The declaration must be **delivered to the registrar of companies** within 15 days of the passing of the resolution. If the declaration is not delivered within 15 days, the company and every officer in default are liable to a fine: s 89(6).

If a director makes a declaration under s 89 without having reasonable grounds for his opinion that the company will be able to pay its debts, he will be liable to imprisonment or a fine or both: s 89(4). If the company does not in fact pay its debts within the period specified in the declaration it will be presumed that the declaration was made without reasonable grounds.

In a members' voluntary winding up, the **company** in general meeting **can appoint one or more liquidators**: s 91 IA.

182

86   FABULOUS FOODS

> **Tutor's hint.** This question examines a fairly complex area of law. It is important that you read it carefully a couple of times, in order to establish who is involved and the relevant dates. When you are dealing with issues like preferences and the registration of charges it can be helpful to draw up a timeline on a sheet of rough paper, so that you can see exactly how long there has been between transactions. As usual, identify the **issues** (here they are registration of charges, preferences, transactions at undervalue and wrongful trading), **state** the law, **apply** the law in each of these situations and then **conclude** by advising the liquidator.

Charge in favour of Borset Bank

Although the charge was created on 2 August 20X3, it was not actually registered until 31 March 20X4. This part of the problem therefore deals with the issue of the **late registration of charges**.

A fixed charge such as this one must be registered within 21 days of its creation (S395 CA 85). The company is responsible for registering the charge, although the Bank could also register it, as they have an interest in the charge. Clearly the charge has not been registered within this timescale.

A charge can only be **registered late** if it is registered 'without prejudice to the rights of parties acquired prior to the time when the charge was actually registered'. It has been established that if a fixed charge is created but not presented for registration until nine months after it should have been, a fixed charge that was created and properly registered during that period would then take priority (*Re Monolithic Building Co*). On this basis it can be argued that since the fixed charge was only registered the day before the onset of liquidation, the rights of the other creditors of the company will have intervened.

It is not clear whether the necessary court consent was obtained when the charge was registered. If it wasn't the registration will not be valid and the **charge will therefore be void against the liquidator**. This would mean that the Bank will rank as an unsecured creditor, equally with the other unsecured creditors. The Bank will therefore receive less than the full amount due to it.

Another factor to consider is whether the company has effectively preferred the Bank by taking the action of registering the charge immediately before the commencement of liquidation. A company gives **preference** to a creditor if it does anything by which the creditor's position is advantaged should the company go into insolvent liquidation and the company does the action with the intention of producing this result (s 239 IA 86). The registration of the charge is within the required six months prior to the liquidation. By registering a previously invalid charge immediately before liquidation, it can be argued that the company is intending to prefer the Bank. If this is the case, the liquidator should be able to have the security given by the company set aside, by applying to the Court.

Repayment of loan to Simon

As we have seen, a company gives preference to a creditor if it does anything to put that creditor in an advantageous position in the run-up to an insolvent liquidation.

It seems that all of the necessary criteria for a preference to exist apply:

- Simon is a **connected person**, as he is a director

- The repayment of the loan has taken place within the **two years prior to the liquidation** (the time limit is two years for a connected person)

- Therefore the liquidator should be able to apply to court for an order requiring Simon to **return the money to the company**. Simon would then rank as an unsecured creditor.

> **Tutor's hint.** The fact that the company is insolvent at the time of repaying the loan is irrelevant here as Simon is a connected person. Where a preference is alleged in favour of an unconnected person the company must have been insolvent at the time of the transaction or become insolvent as a result of it.

Sale of the company car

A **transaction at an undervalue** is a gift or a transaction in the two years prior to the liquidation of a company by which the company gives consideration of greater value than it receives in the transaction. The company must have been insolvent at the time of the transaction or become insolvent as a result. Fabulous Foods plc had been insolvent since the end of December.

Since the company has sold the car to James for substantially less than the market price, this seems to be a transaction at an undervalue. The liquidator can apply to the court for an order to restore the position to what it would have been if the transaction had not taken place.

In some situations a transaction at undervalue does not become void:

- If it was made in good faith
- If it was made for the purpose of the company carrying on its business
- If there was a belief on reasonable grounds that the transaction would benefit the company.

None of these criteria seems to apply in this situation, as the sale of the car is unlikely to have been for the purpose of the company carrying on its business, nor would it have been for the benefit of the company. James could argue that the transaction was done in good faith and was a bona fide part of his leaving package, but since he was a director the court is more likely to take the view that the transaction was intended for his personal advantage.

Wrongful trading

S214 IA 86 says that the directors of a company can be liable to contribute to the company's debts if the liquidator can prove that:

- The directors of the insolvent company knew or ought to have known that there was no reasonable prospect that the company could have avoided going into insolvent liquidation
- The directors did not take sufficient steps to minimise the potential loss to the creditors.

Directors of a company can be deemed to have known that the company could not avoid insolvent liquidation if that would have been the conclusion of a reasonably diligent person with the general knowledge, skill and experience that might reasonably be expected of a person carrying out that director's duties.

The liquidator of Fabulous Foods Plc can therefore go to court and argue that Simon, James and Emily should have been aware of the fact that the company was unlikely to avoid insolvent liquidation. Even though James has left the company he will probably still be liable, as he was a director at the time the company was trading while insolvent.

The standard of knowledge expected of a director of a listed company is higher than that of a director of a small private company. Fabulous Foods Plc is obviously a public company

but it is not clear if it is a listed company, in which case the duty of care of the directors would be higher. In any event it is highly likely that the three directors will be liable for wrongful trading, and they will probably be ordered to contribute to the assets of the company, thereby reducing the deficit of the creditors.

Fraudulent trading

The liquidator may also be able to apply to the Court on the grounds that the directors of the company have engaged in **fraudulent trading**. This is the carrying on of business with intent to defraud the creditors or for any fraudulent purpose. It is not clear from the facts of the question whether this has happened, but if it is the case the Court will be able to order Simon, James and Emily to contribute to the assets of the company.

Marking Guide	Marks
Charge	
Registration of charges: 21 days	1
Late registration: court consent	1
Case or illustration	1
Possible preference to the Bank	1
Repayment to Simon	
Explanation of preference	2
Connected person	1
Simon will have to repay money	1
Sale of car	
Explanation of transaction at undervalue	2
Company must be insolvent at the time	1
Situations where not void	1
Court will probably set transaction aside	1
Wrongful trading	
Explanation of wrongful trading	1
Criteria that apply	2
Differing standards of knowledge	1
Directors probably liable to contribute to company assets	1
James liable even though he has left	1
Fraudulent trading	1
	20

87   CONSTRUCTIVE DISMISSAL AND DISABILITY DISCRIMINATION

Tutorial note. The question was specifically focused on constructive dismissal and justification within the area of disability discrimination and was therefore quite hard, unless you had worked through and revised the employment law part of your syllabus in detail. However, neither of the questions was intrinsically difficult, and if you were prepared, you should have been able to score well. It is essential that you are prepared to answer questions in every subject area for this exam. If you 'topic spot' and then a very specific question like this comes up, unless you have studied every facet of your chosen topic, you will not gain marks. It is inadvisable to limit your performance in this way.

Examiner's comments. About half of the candidates attempted this question, although in general their performance was very poor, with very few high marks awarded. Many candidates seemed confused between 'constructive dismissal' as required by the question, and 'unfair dismissal', often just writing all they could about the latter. Some candidates also included all they knew about redundancy. In part (b) few candidates had much knowledge of the Disability Discrimination Act 1995, and could not write about it in any depth.

The examiner felt that candidates were ill-prepared for this question, possibly highlighting the fact that some candidates do not revise employment law fully, as it is such a wide-ranging subject. Hopefully performance on such questions will improve.

185

(a) **Constructive dismissal**

Constructive dismissal takes place where the employer repudiates some vital term of the employment contract and, despite his willingness to continue the employment, the employee resigns because of it.

In such circumstances, the employer is liable for breach of contract. No notice of termination is served on either party. Provided the breach is sufficiently serious, the employer will be liable for breach of contract and the employee may still make a claim for unfair dismissal notwithstanding the resignation. If the employee waits for too long before resigning, he may be taken to have accepted the breach and waived his rights in respect of them. However, delaying for a reasonable period while he finds alternative employment may be acceptable.

The employee must show that the employer has committed a serious breach of contract, that he left because of it and that he has not waived the breach, thereby affirming the contract.

The breach must be serious and amount to a repudiatory breach (*Western Excavating (ECC) Ltd v Sharp*).

Unilaterally imposing a complete change in the employee's duties or reducing the employee's pay have been held to be sufficiently serious to entitle the employee to claim breach of contract and constructive dismissal (*Ford v Milthorn Toleman Ltd* and *Industrial Rubber Products v Gillon*). Similarly, a failure to provide a suitable working environment (*Waltons and Morse v Dorrington*) and a failure to follow the prescribed disciplinary procedure (*Post Office v Strange*) have also been held to be sufficient grounds for a constructive dismissal.

(b) **Justification**

The **Disability Discrimination** Act 1995 gives disabled people similar rights to those enjoyed in relation to sex and race.

Employers are prohibited from discriminating against disabled applicants when recruiting and selecting, when offering terms, in providing opportunities for advancement and training and in dismissal. A disabled person is one with a 'physical or mental impairment which has a substantial and long-term adverse effect on the ability to carry out normal day-to-day activities'.

There is discrimination where the employer treats a disabled person less favourably for a reason related to his disability or where he fails to make 'reasonable adjustments' without justification.

Justification can be claimed on the basis that the cost of making the necessary adjustments is unreasonable or that it is impracticable to make them. It may also be claimed on the grounds of disruption to the organisation or working environment which would be caused by facilitating the disabled employee to operate. Under s.5 the employer may show grounds that are both substantial and material to the circumstances of the particular case in order to justify less favourable treatment of the disabled person.

Marking Guide

		Marks	
(a)	Explanation	2	
	Employer liable for breach of contract	1	
	Prompt resignation of employee	1	
	Can find alternative employment	1	
	Cases or examples	2	
			7
(b)	Basic provision of DDA	1	
	Explanation of justification	1	
	Example of justification	1	
			3
Total			10

88   PREPARATION QUESTION: THE EMPLOYMENT CONTRACT

Tutor's hint. This question asks about the implied duties of an employee. Remember that, if they are implied, they will be found somewhere other than her contract of employment. Part (b) is an application question.

If you drew a different conclusion from ours, well done for drawing a conclusion. Employment law is a complex area and there may not always be an obvious right answer. Always try to draw a conclusion, giving reasons why you have done so, linked to the scenario. In the meantime, see if you follow the reasoning we have used in our answer and compare it to your own. Is yours fair, or would you rethink some of it now?

(a)   The law of employment was developed under common law principles arising from contract law. One of the key questions in employment law is that of what terms exist in a contract of employment.

Since it is not practicable to include all the terms of employment in a written agreement, the law **implies** a number of terms. These relate to **duties** of the employer, the employee or both parties.

Faithful service

The employee's fundamental duty is one of **faithful service** to his employer. In *Hivac Ltd v Park Royal Scientific Instruments Ltd* the Court of Appeal held that employees who worked in their spare time for a company in competition with their employer were in breach of this implied duty of fidelity, even though no confidential information had been disclosed.

A number of cases illustrate particular aspects of the general duty of faithful service.

Duty to account

An employee has a duty to account for all money and property received during the course of his employment. He has a duty **not to take bribes** or **accept commissions** on his own account in respect of contracts negotiated on behalf of his employer: *Boston Deep Sea Fishing and Ice Co v Ansell*.

Reasonable skill and care

An employee must carry out his job with **reasonable care and skill**: *Lister v Romford Ice and Cold Storage Co Ltd*. The definition of reasonable depends on the degree of skill and experience which the employee professes to have.

Obedience

An employee has a duty to obey those orders of his employer which are **lawful and reasonable**. The employer cannot expect the employee to carry out an unlawful act or to expose himself to personal danger (*Ottoman Bank v Chakarian*).

Personal service

The contract of employment is a personal one. The employee may not delegate his duties without the consent of the employer, either express or implied.

Importance of employee implied duties

These implied duties of the employee are important, as any breach may entitle the employer to treat the contract as discharged and claim damages for **breach of contract.**

(b) **Carol**

Contract of employment

In assessing whether or not Carol will be breaking her contract of employment by accepting George's offer, it will first be necessary to examine the express terms included in the contract of employment.

If her written contract of employment expressly states that she is not permitted to take on any such work outside the boundaries of the work she does for her employers, then she would be breaching her contract by doing so.

Assuming that the written contract of employment addresses only the matters required as a minimum by statute, Carol should consider the implied terms of her employment.

Implied duties to the employer

She has an overriding duty of faithful service to her employer. The work she has been invited to perform appears to be similar in nature to that undertaken by her employer, and to this extent she may be depriving her employer of work.

George's business is clearly not in competition with Carol's employers, and so she is not providing assistance to a competitor: *Hivac Ltd v Park Royal Scientific Instruments Ltd*.

Carol is not a senior employee and is not likely to manipulate confidential information belonging to her employer in doing this work.

Conclusion

The key question is likely to be whether the part-time work affects her performance in working for her full-time employers.

If it doing the work for George does not affect the work carried out for her employers (which it shouldn't if she does do it in her spare time as George suggests), it does not appear that she would be breaking her contract of employment by undertaking this work.

However, if carrying out the work for George means that she is less effective in her work for her employers and is not doing her job to the best capacity then she would be in breach of her contract of employment.

89   COMMON LAW DUTIES

> **Tutor's hint**. Notice in this question that it is asking for the common law duties of the employer, not the employer's duties in general. Make sure that you don't waste your time by listing all of the duties you can think of from whatever source: focus your answer on what the question requires.
>
> **Examiner's comments**. Answers to this question were disappointing. Many candidates could only produce two common law duties at most, and many fell into the trap of describing statutory duties instead. In general, part (a) was better answered than part (b) as many candidates had little knowledge of constructive dismissal and confused it with redundancy.

(a)   The duties owed by an employer to his employee will be as set out **expressly in the contract of employment** and, in the absence of relevant express terms, **as implied by common law and statute**. The overriding duty of the employer at common law is a duty of mutual trust and confidence. Neither the employer nor the employee should act in a manner which could damage such mutual respect. In addition, the common law implies several other terms into the contract of employment, all of which are fundamental to the relationship.

First, the employer has a duty to take **reasonable care for the safety** of the worker. Thus, he must provide competent staff, safe premises and equipment and a 'safe system of work'. The employer could be liable in negligence if this is not done.

In the unlikely circumstances of there being no agreement as to remuneration, the rate of **remuneration** must be reasonable. However, statute largely governs the method and rate of payment (including the Equal Pay Act 1970 and the National Minimum Wage Act 1998).

In certain circumstances, the common law will imply **a duty to provide work**. Employees protected include those paid on a piecework or commission basis and those whose earning power and reputation is founded on active occupation, for example actors and journalists. If there is in fact no work available, the duty will not be breached as long as the employee continues to receive remuneration, unless the employee is skilled and needs relevant work in order to prevent the skills falling into disuse. If an employee properly incurs expenses or losses in the performance of his duties, the employer has a common law duty to reimburse him.

Breach of such common law duty may entitle the employee to treat the contract as discharged and/or to claim damages for breach of contract.

(b)   **Constructive dismissal** takes place where the employer repudiates some vital term of the employment contract and, despite his willingness to continue the employment, the employee resigns because of it. No notice of termination is served on either party. In such cases, the employer is liable for breach of contract. Provided the breach is sufficiently serious, the employee may still make a claim for unfair dismissal (s.136 ERA).

The employee must show that the employer has committed a serious breach of contract, that he left because of it and that he has not waived the breach, thereby affirming the contract. If the employee waits for too long before resigning, for example, he may be taken to have accepted the breach and waived his rights in respect of them. However, delaying for a reasonable period while he finds alternative employment may be acceptable.

The breach must be serious and amount to a repudiatory breach (*Western Excavating (ECC) Ltd v Sharp*). Unilaterally imposing a complete change in the employee's duties or reducing the employee's pay have been held to be sufficiently serious to entitle the

employee to claim breach of contract and claim for constructive dismissal (*Ford v Milthorn Toleman Ltd and Industrial Rubber Products v Gillon*). Similarly, a failure to provide a suitable working environment (*Waltons and Morse v Dorrington*) and a failure to follow the prescribed disciplinary procedure (*Post Office v Strange*) have also been held to be sufficient grounds for a constructive dismissal.

Marking Guide			*Marks*	
(a)	Overriding duty is mutual trust and confidence		1	
	Reasonable care for safety		1	
	Reasonable rate of remuneration if not agreed		1	
	Duty to provide work (discuss)		2	
	Breach enables employee to treat contract as discharged		<u>1</u>	
				6
(b)	Repudiation of a vital term		1	
	Employer liable for breach; maybe unfair dismissal		1	
	Three conditions for employee to show		1	
	Examples of type of breach		<u>1</u>	
				<u>4</u>
				<u>10</u>

90 CAROL

> **Tutor's hint**. This question is nicely structured for you to state the rules of law and then apply them in part (c). Remember that the application is likely to be brief, relying on the points you have made in parts (a) and (b), so direct your time on this question accordingly.

An **employee** is an individual who has entered into or works under a contract of employment (s 230 ERA 1996) (which is defined as a contract of service). An **independent contractor,** on the other hand, is an individual who works under a contract for services.

(a) **Importance of the distinction**

The following distinctions illustrate why it is important to distinguish between employees and independent contractors.

(i) **Employment protection legislation** offers protection to employees under a contract of service but not to the self-employed, in relation to minimum periods of notice, remedies for unfair dismissal and for redundancy payments

(ii) The contribution rates payable under **social security legislation** differ as between the employed and the self-employed, and there are also differences in entitlement to benefits and statutory sick pay

(iii) Deductions must be made by an employer for **income tax** under Schedule E from salaries paid to employees under contracts of service, whereas the self-employed are taxed under Schedule D and are directly responsible to the Inland Revenue for all due deductions

(iv) The employer may be **vicariously liable for tortious acts** committed by his employees during the course of their employment, but such liability is severely restricted in the case of independent contractors

(v) Should the employer go into **liquidation** or become bankrupt, the employee under a contract of service has preferential rights as a creditor for payment of outstanding salary and redundancy payments, up to certain limits

(vi) The **implied rights and duties** which apply in the employer/employee relationship under a contract of service would not apply to the same degree to a contract for services

(vii) An independent sub-contractor may have to register his business for VAT purposes and charge VAT on services supplied

(b) **How the courts make the distinction**

In some cases, the distinction between employees and independent contractors is very obvious but often it will not be straightforward. The **expressed intentions** of the parties will not necessarily be conclusive (*Ferguson v John Dawson & Partners*) and the courts will look at the **reality of the situation** rather than at the labels attached to the contract or working arrangement between the parties.

The courts have generally applied one or more of three **tests**.

Tests of distinction

The **control test** asks whether the employer has **control over the way in which the employee performs his duties**.

In *Mersey Docks & Harbour Board v Coggins & Griffiths (Liverpool) Ltd*, a driver of a crane could be instructed by the employer what to do but not how to do his work and it was held that he was an independent contractor since (inter alia) the 'employer' lacked sufficient control properly to be called an employer.

The control test is less definitive now, at a time where many employees have a degree of skill which makes apportioning such great significance to the question of control inappropriate.

The **integration test** was developed to overcome this difficulty and applies where the employee has such a **degree of skill** that he cannot be 'controlled' in the performance of his duties.

Applying this test, the court asks whether he was appointed and assigned to his duties by the employer, that is, did he become an integral part of the employer's business organisation or did his work remain outside of and merely accessory to it?

Thus in *Cassidy v Ministry of Health*, it was held that a skilled surgeon was the employee of the Ministry of Health since, although the Ministry could not possibly control the doctor in his medical work, it (and not the patient) had selected him and integrated him into the organisation.

The **economic reality** or **'multiple' test** is a further development and asks, basically, whether the employee is working on his own account.

In answering this, the court will consider all relevant factors including

- The employer's right to appoint and dismiss
- The basis on which payment is made
- Whether tax and NI is deducted
- Who provides the tools and equipment
- The number of 'employers'

The **mutuality of obligations** between the employer (to provide work) and the employee (to perform that work) is an important factor. The courts will also consider whether the employee is entitled to **delegate all his obligations** (in which case there is no contract of employment), whether he is restricted in his place of work, whether he is obliged to work and whether holidays and hours of work are agreed: *O'Kelly v Trusthouse Forte plc*.

191

(c) **Application to Dan and Eve**

Dan

In this case Dan does not appear to work on his own account save that he pays his own tax as a self-employed person. The fact that he is labelled self-employed is not conclusive. Adding up the other factors, namely that his equipment is supplied by Carol and he is subject to her control over the hours and place of work, it appears that he is in fact an employee of Carol.

Eve

Eve, on the other hand, is an independent contractor. Although Carol provides here equipment, she is free from Carol's control in that she can work for other employers, she can work at home at times determined by her, she manages her own tax payments and, significantly, she is free to delegate her work commitments to others.

Marking Guide		Marks
Definitions		2
Importance of the distinction – 7 factors		7
Courts making the distinction	– Express intention not conclusive	1
	– Control test	2
	– Integration test	2
	– Multiple test	2
Application	– Dan (employee/why)	2
	– Eve (IC/why)	2
		20

91 REDUNDANCY AND CONSTRUCTIVE DISMISSAL

Tutor's hint. This question should be reasonably straightforward if you have revised the topic. Ensure that you define both the different areas carefully, they are complicated areas of law.

(a) **Redundancy**

The law relating to redundancy is now found in the Employment Rights Act 1996 (ERA).

An employee is made redundant where:

- The **only or main reason for dismissal** is that the **employer** intends to, or has, **ceased carrying on the business in which the employee has been employed**/where he has been employed.

- The **employer's requirements** for employees to carry out the **work done have ceased** or **diminished**.

If the employer requires the employee to move to a different place of work and that is within the terms of the contract of employment, then there is no redundancy. The place or work for these purposes is, therefore, any place where the employee can properly be required to work within the terms of his or her contract of employment.

In *High Table Ltd v Horst and Others*, the Court of Appeal stated that the proper test for determining whether or not an employee is redundant is to see whether there has been a reduction of the employer's requirements for employees to work at the place where the person concerned is employed.

192

Alternative employment

The employer may choose to offer a redundant employee alternative employment (s 141 ERA), which offer must be made before the old employment comes to an end and must take effect within 4 weeks thereafter. If the employee unreasonably refuses the offer, he loses his entitlement to a redundancy payment.

The alternative employment should not be seen as being lower in status. It must be in the same capacity, at the same place and on the same terms and conditions as the old employment or, if it differs in any of those respects, must constitute suitable employment in relation to the employee. What constitutes suitable alternative employment will be a question of fact taking into account all relevant circumstances.

Redundancy payment

Where an employee has been dismissed because of redundancy, he will be **entitled to a redundancy payment** if he is **under the normal retirement age** for the business (or 65 where no age is specified) and has been **continually employed for 2 years** or more.

Redundancy pay is calculated as follows:

- 1.5 weeks pay for each complete year of employment during which the employee was aged 41 or more

- 1 week's pay for each year where he was aged between 22 and 40

- 0.5 week's pay for each year where he was aged between 18 and 21

The above payments are subject to a maximum of £260 gross per week.

The **entitlement to a redundancy payment is lost if the employee does not claim a payment within 6 months of the relevant date** (such as the expiry of the dismissal notice). If the employer disputes his claim, the employee should refer it to an Industrial Tribunal.

(b) **Constructive dismissal**

Constructive dismissal occurs where the **employer repudiates some essential term of the contract**, thereby committing a **serious breach of contract** (a repudiatory breach) which causes the employee to resign.

The **employee must not have waived the breach and affirmed the contract**, for example by delaying his resignation too long. However, he is entitled to wait until he has found another job before he resigns and claims against the employer.

Acts which have been accepted as giving rise to constructive dismissal include:

- A reduction in pay
- A complete change in the nature of the job
- Failure to comply with the prescribed disciplinary procedure
- Failure to provide a suitable working environment

Suspension without pay for misconduct was not held to be sufficient. The employer's behaviour must amount to a serious breach of the employment contract.

92   EMPLOYEES AND RESTRAINT OF TRADE

Tutor's hint. This question shows the key link between the employment law and contract law on your syllabus. Be prepared for the examiner to set questions which cover more than the area of your syllabus. The question involves quite a complex problem, so make sure that you identify the **issues, state** the law, **apply** the law and then **conclude**, by advising all the parties involved.

PROFESSIONAL EDUCATION

Written contract

Since there are no specific terms in the written contract, there is no express restraint clause to which Mr Cox may have recourse. The courts will not imply a restraint of trade clause except to the extent that an employer may be protected where an employee has used **trade secrets** or otherwise **breached his employer's confidence**.

The basic principle is that any restriction on a person's normal freedom to carry on a trade, business or profession in such a way and with such persons as he chooses is a restraint of trade which is contrary to public policy and therefore void unless it can be justified under certain legal principles which have been developed by the courts.

Breach of confidence

An action for breach of confidence is available where a person has **entrusted information** to another in circumstances which impose an obligation on that other not to use or not to disclose the information without the permission of the person who has imparted it.

The right of action (for which an injunction or damages or account of profits would be the appropriate remedy) may be against the person entrusted with the information or, in an appropriate situation, against a third party acquiring it from that person.

If it can be shown that an employee has access to **trade secrets** such as a manufacturing processes or sensitive commercial information, then a restraint may be upheld: *Forster & Sons v Suggett*.

However, where specific information is part of a package of information which the employee possesses, **of which much is his own skill**, it will be difficult to establish that the information is a trade secret and an employee cannot be restrained from simply exercising a personal skill acquired in the employer's business: *Morris v Saxelby*.

Application

It would seem unlikely that the information used by Mr Bean and his colleagues could be regarded as trade secrets or its use considered to be a breach of confidence. Mr Cox, therefore, seems unlikely to be able to prevent Mr Bean and the other former employees from going ahead with the new business.

Restrictive terms

Mr Cox should note for future reference the potential use of restrictive terms in contracts of employment. A restriction in a contract must be reasonable in itself. This means that a wide range of matters will be considered including the duration of the restriction.

In *Fitch v Dewes* a lifelong restriction was held valid, but modern practice would probably feel this to be too harsh; usually a restriction will be allowed to operate for a year or two only. The restriction must relate to the area of the employer's business and must not extend beyond that. The prohibition may be applied to existing customers for one product but not for all products: *Home Counties Dairies v Skilton*.

Blue pencil test

Usually the entire restriction is void if the restraint is too wide, and not merely the excess. Although the court will not rewrite an excessive restraint by **limiting it to the reasonable part**, in some cases it has concluded that the parties did not intend such a wide restraint and have modified the offending words by using the 'blue pencil' rule of simple deletion: Skilton's case.

The courts may strike out the offending words and allow the remaining terms to stand. Any attempt by an employer to enforce its terms indirectly by making agreements with other

firms or drawing up new 'codes of practice' will be judged on the same principles as are applied directly to the contract of employment.

Conclusion

In conclusion, Mr Cox should note that a restraint clause may be justified and enforceable if:

- He has a legitimate interest to protect
- The restraint is reasonable between the parties as a restriction of that interest in terms of duration, scope of business and geographical area, and
- It is reasonable from the standpoint of the community.

93   RIGHTS AT WORK

> **Tutor's hint.** Look at the law from the point of view of the employer, and what he can rely on when justifying dismissal. The question even told you how many you should come up with – a helpful hint.

(a)   **Fair dismissal**

The five reasons which an employer can rely on in order to justify dismissing an employee fairly are as follows (s98 ERA1996).

(i)   The **capability** or **qualifications** of the employee were insufficient for performing the work of the kind that he was employed to do. The statute provides that 'capability' is to be assessed by reference to skills, aptitude, health or any other physical or mental quality. 'Qualification' means any academic or technical qualifications relevant to the employee's position.

(ii)   The **employee's conduct was such as to justify dismissal**. Gross misconduct which under the common law would justify summary dismissal on the first occasion will satisfy s 98. Ordinary misconduct may be sufficient where it is persistent, continues despite warnings or is aggravated by other circumstances.

Examples of misconduct which has been held to satisfy s98 include unpleasant behaviour towards the employer's customers, persistent and intermittent absences from work, assault on a fellow employee and conduct exposing others to danger.

(iii)   Dismissal was for reason of **redundancy**. This will not be fair however, if the employee can show that either there were one or more employees in similar positions who might have been made redundant, and that he was selected for redundancy in breach of a customary arrangement or agreed procedure, or he was selected for a reason connected with trade union membership.

(iv)   The **existence of a legal prohibition or restriction**, by which the employee could not lawfully continue to work in the position he held, led to dismissal.

Examples include where a solicitor or doctor is struck off the relevant professional register, or where an employee who needs to drive in the course of his work loses his driving licence.

(v)   Some **other substantial reason** which justifies dismissal.

This reason has been held to apply where the employee was married to one of his employer's competitors and where the employee refused to accept a change in the shifts worked, such reorganisation having been agreed by the large majority of employees and made in the interests of the business.

(b) **Discrimination**

It may be lawful for discrimination to occur where a job is to be taken abroad in a country whose **laws or customs** would make it difficult for a woman to perform her duties.

Similarly, **standards of decency** may require, for example, that only a male attendant works in male lavatories or sports facilities. **Some occupations are excluded altogether** from the legislation such as ministers of religion and police and prison officers, although these categories are not exempt from the new Race Regulations implemented in July 2003.

It is essential to preserve **authenticity** in some areas, such as modelling or the performing arts. Until recently this need for authenticity was also one of the few grounds for racial discrimination. A black man would be needed by a production to play *Othello*, for instance. However in the new Race Regulations, the old genuine occupational requirement provision of the 1976 Act has been amended. Employers now will only be able to recruit staff on the basis of a genuine occupational requirement if it can be shown that it is a genuine and determining requirement of the job to be of a particular race or of a particular ethnic or national origin.

Some jobs are advertised that require a married couple to fill two posts. These are typically live-in arrangements such as wardens or caretakers.

An employer owes a duty to take reasonable steps to avoid relying on 'genuine occupational qualification' exceptions. If there are enough employees of the other sex who could be called upon to perform certain duties of the job then discrimination will be unlawful. On the other hand, discrimination against one sex may be lawful where there are not enough employees of the other sex to carry out certain functions.

94   GRACE AND HILDA

> **Tutor's hint.** The rules relating to unfair dismissal are an important part of your syllabus. You should be able to apply various stages to a question on unfair dismissal to gain goods marks. The requirement in this question states the basic things that you should be considering when facing any question on unfair dismissal. There are a few others that you should bear in mind. Have a checklist like the following in your head:
>
> * Does the employee qualify? (continuous service/automatically unfair/dismissed)
> * Is the dismissal fair? (per the qualifying reasons given in statute)
> * Has the employer acted reasonably? (show that you have considered this)
> * Am I required to discuss possible remedies?
>
> You may find that some parts of this checklist are unnecessary to a given question (for example, a question might state that an employee qualifies to the right not to be unfairly dismissed, or that a person has been dismissed) so you can discount an element of the checklist. In such cases, you should not write down matters in your answer that will not gain marks, just so that you are following your checklist. However, using this checklist wisely should ensure that you consider all the relevant factors and gain enough marks to pass a question like this.

(a) **Fair dismissal**

Statute gives qualifying employees a right not to be unfairly dismissed. Unfair dismissal is a statutory concept, and is determined by employment tribunals. Statute sets out a number of fair reasons for dismissal.

The five potentially fair reasons are:

(i) **Lack of capability or qualification of the employee**

The employee's competence will be judged with reference to **the requirement of the contract**, the **work standards achieved by employees generally** and by the standard achieved by the employee in question.

The Act states that 'capability is to be assessed by reference to **skills, aptitude, health or any other physical or mental quality**'. Qualification means 'any academic or technical qualifications relevant to the position that the employee holds'.

The **employer** must have been reasonable consulting with the employee, **allowing time for improvement, providing training** if necessary and **considering alternatives to dismissal**. If the employer relies on ill health as the grounds for incapability, there must be proper medical evidence.

(ii) **Misconduct**

Misconduct must either be very **grave** (for example a physical attack on a colleague) or **persistent**, despite warnings. A distinction is sometimes made between 'gross misconduct', which may justify dismissal on the first occasion (such as theft) and 'ordinary misconduct', which is usually not sufficient grounds unless it is persistent (such as rudeness to customers or persistent absence from work).

(iii) **Redundancy**

Redundancy is a fair reason for dismissal as long as the **employer** has implemented a redundancy **procedure in accordance with good industrial relations practice**. This requires consultation and objective criteria of selection.

(iv) **Legal restriction**

Dismissal may be fair where continued employment would be illegal (for example if an in-house solicitor is barred by the Law Society or an employee who is employed as a driver is banned from driving).

(v) **Other substantial reason**

A reason other than those stated above may suffice if is it substantial, for example **refusal to accept changed working practices agreed by a majority of the workforce**, personality conflicts, refusal to disclose material facts and legitimate commercial reasons.

In order to have the tribunal find dismissal fair, the employer must show that the principal reason that the employee was fired was one of these reasons. The reasons given above are general, and it will be up to the tribunal to determine whether the reason qualifies as such a fair reason.

In this instance, it does not appear that Hilda would have a fair reason for dismissing Grace, as it appears that the only reason that she would take such a course of action is that they have fallen out on a non-work related issue.

(b) **Automatically unfair dismissal**

There are some instances given in statute where dismissal is automatically unfair. In such a situation, unless the employer can disprove that the principal reason for dismissal was the automatically unfair reason, dismissal is unfair.

Such reasons include:

- Pregnancy
- A spent conviction

- Trade union membership or activities
- On transfer of undertakings (there are some permitted exceptions to this)
- On taking steps to avert a danger to health and safety at work
- For enforcing a statutory right

Again, in this situation, it does not appear that were Grace to be fired, it would qualify as an automatically unfair reason, so she would have to apply to the employment tribunal, and Hilda would be given the opportunity to show that the reason for dismissal was actually a qualifying fair reason (in (a) above).

(c) **Remedies for unfair dismissal**

There are several remedies for unfair dismissal, although in practice, the most common form of remedy is compensation.

Reinstatement

Where an employee is reinstated, they return to the job from which they were dismissed, and it is treated for the purposes of continuous employment as if they had never been dismissed, even if they have been away from work for a period during the tribunal process.

Re-engagement

Where an employee is re-engaged, the employer must give the former employee new employment on comparable terms to the previous employment, according to terms specified in the order from the employment tribunal.

Compensation

Clearly, if an employee has been dismissed unfairly and has taken the matter to an employment tribunal, relations between the employee and the employer are likely to have broken down.

It is therefore often inappropriate for the tribunal to order the two remedies above. The most common form of remedy is therefore compensation. It is paid under formulae set out in legislation.

A basic award is calculated in relation to years of service and basic pay. An additional compensation award can also be made. This is limited by statute to £53,500.

An award of compensation can be reduced by the employment tribunal if they feel that the employee has contributed to his own dismissal, has unreasonably refused to be reinstated, or if it is just and equitable to do so.

		Marks	
Marking Guide			
(a)	Five instances of fair dismissal (1 mark each)	5	
	What the employer must demonstrate	1	
	Application to Grace's situation	2	
			8
(b)	Examples of automatically unfair dismissal (max. 4 marks)	4	
	Application to Grace's situation	2	
			6
(c)	Reinstatement	1½	
	Re-engagement	1½	
	Compensation	1	
	More suitable than other alternatives	1	
	Formula for calculation	1	
			6
			20

Corporate and Business Law
BPP Mock Exam 1

Question Paper:	
Time allowed	**3 hours**
This paper is divided into two sections	
Section A	**SIX questions ONLY to be answered**
Section B	**TWO questions ONLY to be answered**

paper 2.2

SECTION A: SIX questions ONLY to be attempted

1   Explain the nature and significance of arbitration and tribunals as means of settling legal disputes.

What are the advantages of using this means of settling disputes over the ordinary courts?

(10 marks)

2   Outline the main provisions of the Unfair Contract Terms Act 1977 and the Unfair Terms in Consumer Contracts Regulations 1999.

(10 marks)

3   Explain the presumptions relating to intention to create legal relations with respect to:

(a) Domestic and social agreements   (5 marks)
(b) Business agreements   (5 marks)

(10 marks)

4   What are the advantages of incorporating as a private limited company rather than trading as a sole trader or a partnership? Are there any disadvantages of incorporation?

(10 marks)

5   What are the duties owed by an agent to his principal? What rights does the agent have in return?

(10 marks)

6   Explain, in relation to private companies, what is meant by and the procedure involved in passing:

(a) a written resolution;   (5 marks)
(b) an elective resolution.   (5 marks)

(10 marks)

7   Explain:

(a) The rule governing the provision of financial assistance by a company for the purchase of shares   (2 marks)

(b) The exceptions to the rule, enabling a private company to provide such assistance   (8 marks)

(10 marks)

8   Explain what is involved in insider dealing and describe how the law deals with it.   **(10 marks)**

SECTION B: TWO questions ONLY to be attempted

9   Aerial Ltd is a small independent television production company which specialises in making television programmes which it then sells to television broadcasting companies in the United Kingdom. In January 20X1 it signed a contract with an actor called Bob for him to play a leading role in one of its productions to start filming in August 20X2. In the course of 20X1 Bob became extremely famous and in great demand and Aerial Ltd launched a large advertising campaign publicising his appearance in their forthcoming production. The campaign was expensive, costing £300,000, but it was successful in generating great interest. As a result Aerial Ltd got a contract to sell their production to one of their usual UK clients in a deal that would enhance their usual profit of £500,000 by a further £250,000. More importantly, however, it allowed them to sell their production to an American television company at a profit of £1 million. Unfortunately in May 20X2, Bob informed Aerial Ltd that he had no intentions of making a film with them. Aerial Ltd have been told that if they replace Bob with a lesser known actor, who is available and willing to do the work, their profit from the UK deal will be reduced to its usual level and they will lose the American deal completely.

Required:

Analyse the scenario from the perspective of contract law and advise Aerial Ltd as to any action it may take.

(20 marks)

10   Fawn Ltd manufactures clothes and used to sell them through its own retail shop. Grace, who is 33 years old, was employed by Fawn Ltd for three years as manager of the shop. Grace has been told that her services are no longer required as Fawn Ltd has decided to close its store and concentrate solely on manufacturing. Grace has also been told that she will not receive any recompense for her job loss.

Required:

Advise Grace as to the likelihood of her successfully claming for unfair dismissal or redundancy.

(20 marks)

11   Hilary is the managing director of Artworks Ltd, a company which distributes and sells the work of modern artists. Chris and Martin are the other directors. Hilary owns 60% of the issued shares in the company and Chris owns 25%. Hilary is also a shareholder in Oilprojects Ltd, a company which mass produces original oil paintings.

In her capacity as managing director of Artworks Ltd Hilary ordered 10,000 paintings from Oilprojects Ltd. Oilprojects Ltd paid Hilary personal commission for the order; the shares in Oilprojects Ltd also doubled in price because of the order. Hilary sold her shares in Oilprojects Ltd and made a considerable profit.

Artworks Ltd operates from a large Victorian mansion. Hilary and Chris, without the benefit of any professional advice, agreed to sell the mansion to Lance for £200,000. The mansion was in fact worth £300,000 and although there has been no fraud by Hilary and Chris, Eleanor, the minority shareholder in Artworks Ltd, holding 5% of the shares is angry at the agreement which has been made.

Required:

(a) Advise Chris and Martin as to whether Artworks Ltd has any claim against Hilary in relation to the commission paid by Oilprojects Ltd and to the profit made by Hilary on her share in Oilprojects Ltd.   **(12 marks)**

(b) Advise Eleanor as to whether she can bring an action against the directors of Artworks Ltd, and the company itself, in relation to the sale of the property to Lance.   **(8 marks)**

(20 marks)

12   Exe plc has a fully paid-up issued share capital of £450,000 divided into 360,000 ordinary £1 shares and 90,000 £1 preference shares. The company's Articles of Association provide as follows.

Article 20. The preference shareholders shall be entitled to a non-cumulative preference dividend of 7% of nominal capital and in all other respects shall be entitled to the same rights as the ordinary shareholders.

Article 21. Class rights may only be varied with the consent of three-quarters of the class affected.

The recession has caused Exe plc to trade at a loss for a number of years, and the board has now decided to cancel 60% of the nominal value of each issued share, thereby changing the nominal value of both the preference and ordinary shares to 40 pence.

Required:

As the company's finance director, provide the following advice to the board in the form of an internal memorandum.

(a) Whether the preference shareholders will be able to utilise Article 21 to block the proposed changes.   (5 marks)

(b) Whether the company's creditors have any right to object to the scheme.   (5 marks)

(c) The procedure to be followed to effect the proposed changes.   (10 marks)

(20 marks)

ANSWERS

WARNING! APPLYING THE BPP MARKING SCHEME

If you decide to mark your paper using the BPP marking scheme, you should bear in mind the following points.

1   The BPP solutions are not definitive: you will see that we have applied the marking scheme to our solutions to show how good answers should gain marks, but there may be more than one way to answer the question. You must try to judge fairly whether different points made in your answers are correct and relevant and therefore worth marks according to our marking scheme.

2   If you have a friend or colleague who is studying or has studied this paper, you might ask him or her to mark your paper for you, thus gaining a more objective assessment. Remember you and your friend are not trained or objective markers, so try to avoid complacency or pessimism if you appear to have done very well or very badly.

3   You should be aware that BPP's answers are longer than you would be expected to write. Sometimes, therefore, you would gain the same number of marks for making the basic point as we have shown as being available for a slightly more detailed or extensive solution.

It is most important that you analyse your solutions in detail and that you attempt to be as objective as possible.

Professional Examination - Paper 2.2   **Marking Scheme**

Corporate and Business Law

This marking scheme is given as a guide to markers in the context of the suggested answer. Scope is given to markers to award marks for alternative approaches to a question, including relevant comment, and where well-reasoned conclusions are provided. This is particularly so in the case scenario questions where there may be more than one definitive solution.

A PLAN OF ATTACK

If this were the real Corporate and Business Law exam and you had been told to turn over and begin, what would be going through your mind?

Perhaps you're having a panic. Stop that now! What you should do is spend a good five minutes looking through the paper in detail, working out which questions to do and the order in which to attempt them. So turn back to the paper and let's sort out a plan of attack.

Looking through the paper

You have choices in both halves of the paper, so read all the questions carefully to decide which you are going to attempt. It is vital that you understand what each question is asking, so that you do not reject a question you can answer, and attempt a question that you are not so strong on. The questions in this paper are as follows:

Part A (you must answer 6)

- Question 1 requires you to talk about arbitration and tribunals, an area currently of interest to the examiner.

- Question 2 asks for an explanation of the provisions of the Unfair Contract Terms Act and the Regulations of 1999.

- Question 3 asks for an explanation of the law relating to intention to create legal relations.

- Question 4 asks for the advantages and disadvantages of incorporation.

- Question 5 asks for the duties owed by an agent to his principal.

- Question 6 is on the procedures for written and elective resolutions.

- Question 7 examines an aspect of share capital: financial assistance for the purchase of a company's shares.

- Question 8 asks about insider dealing and how the law deals with it.

Part B (you must answer 2)

- Question 9 is quite a complex and detailed question on anticipatory breach of contract and the remoteness and measure of damages.

- Question 10 is a short scenario based question on unfair dismissal and redundancy in employment law.

- Question 11 discusses the fiduciary duties that a director has to a company, and the courses of action available where a director is in breach of those duties.

- Question 12 is a difficult question on the variation of class rights and the procedure for the reduction of capital.

Part A

You can answer the questions in any order, but we would advise you to **undertake Part A first**. This is because the questions are more straightforward than the questions in Part B and you can build up marks quickly, by ensuring that you get the simple marks in each of the question you undertake in this section. Also, if you do miscalculate your time apportionment and you have done Part B first, you run the risk of missing a complete question out, and consequently losing the straightforward marks in that question, in favour of marks which are harder to get in other questions.

Additionally you can sometimes find that the fact that you will consider six areas of law in part A will often act as a trigger to **enable you to recall relevant areas of the law** when you move on to part B, as there can sometimes be an overlap between the two sections.

When choosing which questions you are likely to answer, you may do one of the following two things:

- Choose the six that you can answer best
- Eliminate the two that you cannot do

Here are some points to note:

- It is not wise to ignore a syllabus area when revising because you have a choice of questions, in case the questions that come up on your revised areas are more difficult to get marks in.

- If you think that there are more than two questions that you cannot do, look through them all carefully. Do any of the questions have parts that you think you can attempt? **You should always attempt six questions in Part A.**

- If you have a choice between two questions, ensure that you can answer **all the parts of the questions**. If you can't answer all the parts of one of them, do the other one, even if the first was related to your favourite topic area.

If you have revised the syllabus fully, in this Part A, we would advise that you do questions 3, 4, 5 and 6, as these are the most straightforward. Question 7 is also a straightforward question, although there is the temptation to over-run on time as the question examines quite a wide topic. Questions 1 and 2 are more difficult in our opinion. We would particularly avoid question 8, which asks you to detail complicated legal rules on insider dealing, although obviously if you are fully familiar with this area this question is a gift.

Part B

The questions in Part B are longer than Part A and usually require you to apply legal principles to situations. We suggest that you tackle it second therefore, when you have 'warmed up' by answering the questions in Part A.

A key skill in Part B is to be able to break down the larger questions into the components within them, to see where you will build up your marks. It is often easier to tackle questions where the examiner has broken them down with a mark allocation than ones which are just for 20 marks straight.

In this Part B, Question 9 should enable you to score a reasonable mark if you have revised anticipatory breach and damages. You would have to spend quite some time on remoteness of damage and the measure of damages.

Question 10 is a straightforward question on redundancy and unfair dismissal, and would be worth attempting if you are familiar with this area. Although the scenario given is quite short, try to apply the points in your answer to the scenario as much as possible, to **demonstrate your skills in applying the law.**

If you are confident on the subject of directors' duties, then you will want to attempt question 11, but the rules on directors' duties are complicated, and you might find them difficult to remember under pressure.

Question 12 has an easy third part on the procedure for the reduction of capital, but parts (a) and (b) are quite hard and this may be a question to avoid.

Allocating your time

BPP's advice is always allocate your time according to the marks for the question in total and for the parts of the question. That means for paper 2.2 that you should spend 1 hour and 48 minutes on Part A (18 minutes per question) and 1 hour 12 minutes on Part B (36 minutes per question). However, use your common sense. If you are doing a question but know you can't answer part (c), allocate those minutes to another question, where you may be able to pick up more marks.

Forget about it!

And don't worry if you found the paper difficult. More than likely other candidates will too. If this were the real thing you would need to forget the exam the minute you left the exam hall and think about the next one. Or, if it is the last one, celebrate!

BPP
PROFESSIONAL EDUCATION

1

> **Tutor's hint**. Another opportunity to ensure that you are familiar with a subject which has been a popular examination topic in recent years. Make sure that you are aware of the disadvantages of these two alternatives as well.

Arbitration

Arbitration is settlement of a dispute by an independent person usually chosen by the parties themselves. A dispute may be referred to arbitration by the agreement of the parties, by statute or by court order. They are usually governed by the rules set out in the **Arbitration Act 1996**.

The arbitrator is usually an expert in the field of dispute, appointed by the parties or by some agreed third person (or in some cases by the court). The procedure is less formal than in the courts, but the parties are bound by the ordinary rules of evidence (subject to agreement to the contrary), including discovery of documents and evidence on oath.

The arbitrator's decision on the dispute is final. Furthermore the 1996 Act restricts the right of appeal to preliminary points of law, but only where either the court gives leave or the parties agree. The right may be excluded by agreement. The arbitrator is usually not required to give reasons for his decision.

If either party, in breach of an agreement, seeks to institute proceedings in court in respect of the dispute, the court will usually grant an application to stay those proceedings pending the arbitration. The arbitration decision may be enforced in the same manner as a court decision.

Tribunals

Administrative tribunals are specialist courts established by statute to deal with disputes between individuals or between individuals and government agencies. They are specialised in jurisdiction. For example disputes regarding a refusal of social security benefits are settled in the Social Security appeals tribunal; this consists of a chairman (usually a lawyer) and two other persons drawn from a panel of employer and employee representatives. There are other tribunals to deal with issues of:

- Property valuation - **the Lands tribunal**
- Setting of rents - **the Rent tribunal**
- Mental health review - **the mental health review tribunal**
- Employment - **employment tribunals**
- Town and country planning - **administrative tribunals**

As well as these administrative tribunals there are also domestic tribunals established by various professional organisations designed to deal with breach of membership rules, for example the Solicitors' Disciplinary Tribunal.

The working of tribunals is subject to the supervision of the Council on Tribunals. There is also usually a right of appeal from the decision of the tribunal to the court on a point of law. The High Court may also review the workings of the tribunals to prevent abuses of natural justice or procedure.

Advantages

There are many advantages of **arbitration** over court procedure:

- Commercial disputes are often **commercially sensitive**; arbitration is relatively **private** as the press and public do not have a right to attend the proceedings.

- The **parties may choose the arbitrator**; they can ensure the decision is made by an expert in the field.

- It is possible to modify the rules of procedure and evidence which may assist in making the proceedings **quicker and cheaper** than a court action.

For these reasons arbitration clauses are popular in business contracts. However the use of arbitration clauses in consumer contracts is restricted by the Consumer Arbitration Agreements Act 1988, as the Small Claims Court may prove an even speedier and cheaper forum for smaller claims.

The advantages of **tribunals** lie largely in their **informality**.

- They are not subject to the strict rules of evidence and procedure, and are thus usually quicker and cheaper than a court action.

- They also develop specialist knowledge as a consequence of their specialised jurisdictions.

However this specialisation and informality may lead to the impression of bias or injustice, something which the court's supervisory jurisdiction attempts to prevent.

Marking Guide		
		Marks
(a)	Definition of arbitration	1
	Covered by Arbitration Act 1996	1
	Qualification of arbitrator	1
	Decision is final	1
	Definition and examples of tribunals	2
	Advantages of arbitration (1 mark each; max. 2)	2
	Advantages of tribunals (1 mark each; max. 2)	2
		10

2

> **Tutor's hint.** This question purely requires a statement of the law. Before you start writing it is worth spending a couple of minutes making a plan and formulating the order in which you will cover the topic.

The **Unfair Contract Terms Act 1977** seeks to clarify the law and supplement case law on the validity of exclusion clauses by making it clear that in some situations an exclusion clause will not be enforceable, notwithstanding the wording of the clause itself.

The Act seeks to strike a balance between:

- The principle that parties should have complete freedom to contract on whatever terms they wish, and

- The need to protect the public from unfair exclusion clauses.

However it does not seek primarily to limit the use of exclusion clauses between businesses trading together who have equal bargaining power, rather it seeks to protect the consumer who is dealing with a company.

There is a clear distinction between business contracts and consumer contracts. A **business contract** arises when two businesses are entering a contract together, for example buying goods for use in a business. The law assumes that they can look after themselves in the making of a contract, and they have equal bargaining power. In some cases, exclusion clauses in business contracts are valid if they are reasonable. A **consumer contract** arises when a **private buyer deals with a person in business**. A consumer contract does not include the situation when a private buyer and a private seller contract together, so the legislation does not cover, for example, an individual buying from someone else at a car boot sale.

Death and personal injury

A person acting in the course of business cannot exclude or restrict liability for death or personal injury resulting from negligence. For example if a supermarket has a sign on its premises stating that it accepts no responsibility for any injury to customers however caused, that clause will be totally ineffective. A company injured on the premises due to the negligence of a member of the supermarket's staff will still be able to sue the supermarket for damages.

Sale and supply of goods

No contract, whether consumer or non consumer, for the sale or hire purchase of goods can exclude the implied condition that the seller has a right to sell the goods.

A consumer contract for the sale or hire purchase of goods cannot exclude or restrict liability for breach of the conditions relating to:

- description
- satisfactory quality
- fitness for purpose and
- sale by sample

that are implied by the Sale of Goods Act 1979. In the case of a non-consumer contract, such exclusions are subject to a **reasonableness test**.

Reasonableness test

The term must be fair and reasonable having regard to all the circumstances which were, or which ought to have been, known to the parties when the contract was made. The burden of proof lies with the person who is seeking to rely on the clause. In judging what is reasonable the courts will consider factors such as:

- The relative bargaining strengths of the parties

- Whether any inducement such as a reduced price was offered to the customer to persuade him to accept the existence of the exclusion clause

- Whether the customer knew or ought to have known of the existence and extent of the exclusion clause

- Whether the goods were made to a special order of the customer.

The **Unfair Terms in Consumer Contracts Regulations 1999** implemented an EC directive on unfair contract terms, but UCTA 1977 still applies.

There are now three 'layers' of law:

- The common law, which applies to all contracts regardless of whether or not one party is a consumer

- UCTA 1977, which applies to all contracts (business or consumer) but which has specific provisions for consumer contracts

- The Unfair Terms in Consumer Contracts Regulations, which apply only to consumer contracts and to terms that have not been individually negotiated.

According to the Regulations, an unfair term is any term that causes a significant imbalance in the parties' rights and obligations under the contract, to the detriment of the consumer.

Certain terms in consumer contracts are rendered unfair by the Regulations:

- Excluding or limiting liability of the seller when the consumer is injured or dies resulting from an act or omission of the seller

- Excluding or limiting liability where there is partial or incomplete performance of a contract by the seller

- Making a contract binding on the consumer where the seller can still avoid performance

Where a consumer is bound by a contract containing an unfair term, he can go to court to ask the court to ask that the unfair term should be declared not to be binding, or he can complain to the Director General of Fair Trading. Additionally, under the terms of the Regulations it is possible for the offending clause to be removed from the contract altogether.

Marking Guide	Marks
Purpose of the UCTA	1
Private individuals have the right to restrict liability	1
Exclusion of liability for negligence causing physical harm	1
Exclusion in sale of goods	2
What is reasonable	1
UTCCR 99: effect	1
Definition of an unfair term	1
Certain consumer contracts unfair	1
Redress available to consumers	1
	10

3

> **Tutor's hint.** State any points that are relevant to both parts of the answer in a general introduction so that you do not waste time by repeating yourself. Remember that the two parts have equal marks so try to make as many points in part (b) as you do in part (a).
>
> In a question like this, you must ensure that you address both parts of the question, as even if you produce an excellent answer for one part but ignore the other you can still only earn 5 marks.
>
> In a very straightforward question like this, it is vital that you state the presumptions and also back them up with cases. Additionally, try to think of any exceptions to the basic presumption, for example as seen in *Simpkin v Pays*.

(a) **Domestic and social agreements**

Domestic agreements are **generally presumed to be informal** rather than contractual, unless the facts indicate otherwise. At one time, it was firmly considered that in an agreement made in a domestic context there was no implied intention to create legal relations if none had been expressed. Thus an agreement by a husband to pay an allowance to his wife during his absence abroad was not legally binding (*Balfour v Balfour*).

The presumption that no legal relations are intended is, however, rebuttable and the **courts may decide that there was an intention to create legal relations in an**

213

agreement between husband and wife. This is particularly the case if they are no longer living together and/or if there is other **evidence that legal relations were intended**, such as the agreement being formally drawn up and signed (*Merritt v Merritt*).

Where the agreement relates to **property matters**, it is perhaps more likely that the courts will infer an intention to create legal relations.

In *Jones v Padavatton*, a mother promised her daughter a monthly allowance if the daughter would return to England to read for the Bar. The daughter did so and the mother refused to pay the allowance. It was held that there was no intention to create legal relations and that the agreement was not therefore legally binding.

In other relationships, for example those involving relatives or friends, the courts appear to be more readily disposed to assume that the parties did in fact intend that a financial agreement should be binding.

This may apply if there is a '**mutuality in the arrangements**' amounting to a joint enterprise, for example where persons jointly enter a competition (*Simpkins v Pays*). In this case, a woman, her granddaughter and a paying lodger took part in a weekly competition in a newspaper, which they entered in the grandmother's name. One week they won £750 and the lodger was denied a third share. It was held that there was a mutuality of agreement and that this was not a 'friendly adventure' but a contract.

(b) **Business agreements**

In commercial agreements, the **courts will normally infer that there is an intention to create legal relations** unless there is evidence to the contrary (*Rose and Frank v Crompton*). In *Edwards v Skyways* an agreement entered into to make an 'ex-gratia' payment as part of a larger negotiation was held to be legally binding.

The issue of whether legal relations were intended may sometimes arise when a **supplier of goods has published an advertisement** which may be an offer to sell the goods or to give some guarantee in respect of them. This was the case in *Carlill v Carbolic Smoke Ball Co*. In this case the manufacturer argued (unsuccessfully) that his offer to pay a sum of money to any user of his medicine whom the medicine did not cure was a mere 'puff' not intended to create a legally binding agreement.

The court decided against him because his advertisement stated that as proof of the seriousness of his assurance he had deposited money in a bank account to meet claims. This fact **implied** that his advert was **intended to be legally binding** and it overrode any deduction about the general effect of an advertisement.

Some commercial agreements may be described by the parties as '**binding in honour only**'. This amounts to an express denial of intention to create legal relations and is effective to rebut the presumption (*Jones v Vernon Pools*). '**Letters of comfort**' given to creditors of subsidiary companies are presumed to be statements of present intentions only and not legally binding (*Kleinwort Benson Ltd v Malaysia Mining Corpn Bhd*).

A lock-out agreement which is unsupported by consideration will be presumed not to carry the necessary intention to create legal relations. As mentioned above, in *Rose and Frank v Crompton*, a statement that the arrangement was not subject to legal jurisdiction was held to be effective.

```
Marking Guide
                                                              Marks
(a)  General presumption for domestic agreements               1
     Case illustration or example                              1
     Presumption is rebuttable                                 1
     Case or illustration                                      1
     Exceptions eg Simpkins v Pays                             1
                                                                      5
(b)  Normally an intention                                     1
     Case illustration or example                              1
     Effect of an advert (eg Carlill)                          2
     Effect of 'binding in honour only' clause                 1
                                                                      5
                                                                     10
```

4

> **Tutor's hint**. This a very straightforward question and since it is worth ten marks you should be thinking in terms of making ten points, if not more, as some points may only score half a mark. Don't overlook the requirement to discuss the drawbacks of incorporation as well. Make sure that some of your points are disadvantages so that you have a balanced answer. The question does not indicate the mark allocation for that part, but you can probably earn three or four marks from it. Notice that the question asks for a discussion of private companies, so do not waste your time by covering public companies too.

The main advantages of incorporation as a private limited company are these:

(a) The **separate legal personality** of the company. This means that the company is a separate entity in the eyes of the law from its members. The company owns its own assets and is responsible for its own liabilities, and it provides a degree of separation between ownership and management that is not available to the partners in a partnership.

(b) The **limited liability of the members**. The shareholders of a company are only liable for the company's debts to the extent of the amount that remains unpaid on their shares. A sole trader or the partners in a partnership, in contrast, are liable for all of the business's debts, potentially to the point of bankruptcy. Indeed partners may incur personal liability in this way not only for the contracts that they have entered into on behalf of the firm, but also for the contracts entered into by other partners, or those who are apparently partners.

(c) **Perpetual succession.** A change in the ownership of a company does not affect its continued existence. As long as one shareholder is left, the company will continue. In contrast, when a partner retires from or otherwise leaves a partnership, the firm will be dissolved (unless the partnership deed provides otherwise).

(d) **Transferability of interests.** Shareholders in a company can sell their shares either to other shareholders or to outsiders, subject to the provisions of the company's Articles and the Companies Act. It is not possible for partners to assign or transfer their interest in a partnership (unless the other partners consent). They would have to retire from the partnership, hence causing its dissolution.

(e) **Security for loans**. A company has the ability to offer creditors a floating charge over the assets (as well as fixed charges) to secure a debt, which in the event of the debt not being repaid would allow the creditor to apply for the appointment of an administrator. Partnerships and individual traders do not have the ability to create floating charges, thus restricting their funding opportunities.

However, although there are many advantages to incorporation, anyone making such a decision should also consider some of the drawbacks of incorporation. These include:

(a) **Participation in management**. A sole trader and the partners in a firm can all participate in the day-to-day management of the entity: it is effectively 'their' business. The shareholders of a company, however, do not have such a right, and their input really is limited to what can be achieved by the passing of resolutions.

(b) **Ownership of assets**. Due to the concept of separate legal personality, a company owns its own assets and a shareholder does not have any right to take a share in them. A sole trader owns his own business's assets, and the partners in a firm own the assets jointly, so that when a partner leaves he or she is entitled to the value of their share of the assets

(c) **Accounting records and returns**. Sole traders and partnerships do not have to keep their accounting records in any format prescribed by the Companies Act, and they do not have to undergo an audit. Companies, both private and public, are subject to stringent rules governing the keeping of accounting records, the filing of accounts and the annual return with the Registrar and in the case of larger companies, the requirement to have an audit. This degree of bureaucracy can deter people from incorporation.

(d) **Publicity**. Due to the need to file accounts, discussed above, it is possible for third parties, such as competitors and creditors, to obtain information about the company's financial position and such sensitive issues as the remuneration of directors. Partnerships and sole traders do not need to make any of this information publicly available.

(e) **Regulations and expense**. CA 85 sets out very stringent rules that all companies must follow, on areas as diverse as the maintenance of capital, the contents of the Memorandum and Articles and the amount that can be lent to directors. This adds to the bureaucracy encountered by companies, and can be expensive.

Marking Guide	
	Marks
For identification and explanation of each advantage, 1 mark	6
(max 6; ½ mark only for mere identification)	
For identification and explanation of each disadvantage, 1 mark	<u>4</u>
(max 4; ½ mark only for mere identification)	
	<u><u>10</u></u>

5

> **Tutor's hint**. Don't overlook the fact that as well as the main part of the question, on the duties of agents, there is also a small section requiring you to discuss their rights.

When an agent undertakes to act on behalf of a principal, there is often a formal contract between them, the terms of which must be observed by both of them. However over and above those terms there are certain basic implied duties that any agent owes to the principal.

Performance

Where the agent is acting for a reward (ie there is consideration) he has an obligation to **carry out the agreed task**.

Obedience

The agent has a duty to **follow the principal's instructions,** as long as they are lawful and reasonable. He cannot disobey the principal's instructions, even if he believes that to do so would be in the principal's interests (for example to carry out a purchase at a later date when prices may have reduced). An agent may refuse to carry out an illegal act.

Skill

A paid agent has a duty to **maintain the standard of skill and care** expected of a person in his particular profession. An unpaid agent should show the skill and care which people ordinarily use in managing their affairs.

No delegation

It is assumed that a principal selects an agent because of the latter's ability to do the task and personal qualities. The agent therefore has a duty to carry out the tasks himself and **not to delegate.** In limited situations, however, delegation is necessary, for example if a solicitor has to delegate to an accountant, and it is then permissible.

Accountability

The agent has a duty to provide full information to the principal and to account for all money arising from transactions carried out.

No conflict of interest

The agent must not put himself in a position where **his own interests conflict with those of the principal.** For example he should not engage in purchases and sales of property directly with the principal, unless he discloses the conflict and any profit and has the principal's consent to proceed.

Confidentiality

The agent must **maintain confidentiality** as regards the principal's affairs, even after the agency relationship has ceased.

Benefits

Any **benefits** arising as a result of the agency relationship must be handed over to the principal, unless the latter agrees that the agent can keep it. For example an agent may earn a commission or a discount, or even accept a bribe, as a result of the transactions he enters into on the principal's behalf. The agent must disclose such benefits and account to the principal for them. An example is seen in *Boston Deep Sea Fishing & Ice Co. v Ansell*. In such a situation the principal has the right to dismiss the agent and recover the amount from him.

Rights of the agent

The two main rights that an agent has are:

- A right of **indemnity,** whereby the agent is entitled to be repaid his expenses and to recoup any losses and liabilities (as long as the agent has acted properly and within his authority as agent)

- The right to receive the agreed **remuneration** from the principal. The amount may have been agreed in advance, or it may be established by trade or professional practice. If not fixed in some way, the agent is entitled to a reasonable amount.

Marking Guide	
	Marks
Duties:	
Terms of any contract	½
Performance	½
Obedience	1
Skill	1
No delegation	1
Accountability	½
No conflict of interest	1
Confidentiality	½
Benefits	2
Rights:	
Indemnity	1
Remuneration	1
	10

6

Tutor's hint. Try to give as much detail as you can in questions like this. It is not enough just to define written and elective resolutions and set out the required majorities. You also need to discuss the required procedures to maximise your marks.

Examiner's comments. The question was generally answered well. In part (b) candidates tended to score better marks when they explained the reason for the introduction of elective resolutions, ie to reduce bureaucracy. The weakest answers to the question were just vague descriptions about resolutions generally.

(a)   A **written resolution** is a resolution signed **by all members entitled to attend and vote** and can be any resolution which could ordinarily be passed in general meeting or in a class meeting. It is a procedure available to **private companies only**. The Act provides that the written resolutions shall be 'equivalent' to resolutions passed in general meeting. Essentially, they enable the company to carry on business without the need to call meetings. A written resolution need not be contained in a single document so long as all documents signed set out the resolution. The date of a written resolution is the date of the last member's signature and the company is required to keep a record of all written resolutions.

A written resolution can be used notwithstanding any provision in the company's articles. However, **a written resolution cannot be used to remove a director or auditor from office** under s 303 or s 391 respectively, since both have a right to attend and speak at a meeting where any proposal for removal is to be discussed. A copy of any proposed written resolution or details thereof must be sent in advance to the company's auditors at or before the time notice is sent to shareholders, in order to keep the auditors fully informed about what is happening in the company. Failure to comply with this requirement renders the directors and/or the secretary liable to a fine but the validity of the resolution is not affected.

(b)   An **elective resolution** is an additional means by which **private companies** can avoid some of the greater degree of regulation and control applicable to public companies. It may be passed for any one or more of the following purposes:

(i)   the conferring of **authority to issue shares** indefinitely or for a fixed period which may exceed 5 years (s 80A);

(ii)   the **dispensing with the laying of accounts** before a general meeting, unless required by a member or the auditors (s 252);

(iii)   the dispensing with the **annual appointment of auditors** (s 386);

(iv)   the dispensing with the **need to hold an AGM** unless required by a member (s 366A); and

(v)   the reduction to 90% or more of the majority required to **consent to short notice** under s 369(4) or s 378(3).

All members who are entitled to attend meetings and vote must agree to the passing of an elective resolution, in person or by proxy. 21 days notice must be given or less where all members entitled to attend and vote agree to shorter notice (s 379A). The resolution must be registered within 15 days (s 379).

An elective resolution can be revoked by ordinary resolution, which must also be registered (s 379,380).

Marking Guide

		Marks	
(a)	Explanation of written resolution	2	
	Exceptions (removal of directors and auditors)	1	
	Procedure	2	
			5
(b)	All members to consent	1	
	21 days notice	1	
	Reasons (½ each)	2½	
	Revocation	½	
			5
			10

7

Tutor's hint. Sort out the rules on this issue in your own mind before starting to write your answer. If you jot down a brief plan of the rule, the main exceptions and the private company exceptions, you will have virtually all the points you need to make.

(a)   CA85 S151 states that **no company may provide financial assistance for the purpose of the acquisition of the shares** of the company or its holding company, either directly or indirectly. This is illustrated by cases such as *Belmont Finance Corporation Ltd v Williams Furniture Ltd (No 2)*, where an artificial transaction was undertaken to enable an individual to obtain the funds to buy shares in the company.

For these purposes 'financial assistance' constitutes:

- A loan (direct financial assistance)
- A guarantee, indemnity or security of a loan (indirect financial assistance)
- The purchase of such rights from a third party (indirect financial assistance)

The general rules apply to all public companies and to private companies where they cannot follow the procedure set out in part (b).

(b)   There are some basic exceptions applicable to all companies, both public and private (s 153 CA85). Companies can enter into these transactions:

- A transaction whose principal purpose of the transaction is not financial assistance

- Making **a loan** if lending is part of the company's ordinary course of business, the company is a money-lending company and the transaction is in the normal course of its business

- Providing funds for an **employee share scheme** or for other share transactions by genuine employees or their connected persons

- Making **loans to employees** (other than directors) for the recipient to buy **fully paid shares in the company** or its holding company

- However, these transactions must not reduce the net assets of the company

Under ss 155-158 CA85, it is possible for a **private company** to provide financial assistance for the acquisition of its shares or the shares of its holding company provided it adheres to certain conditions and follows a specific procedure.

- The financial assistance given must **not reduce the net assets** of the company, or, if it does, the assistance must be provided out of distributable profits

- The directors must make a **declaration of solvency,** to the effect that after the financial assistance is made the company will still be in a position to pay its debts and to carry on business for at least the next year. A report by the company's auditors in support of the declaration of solvency must accompany it

- The members must pass a **special resolution,** ie a 75% majority.

- A dissenting minority (holding at least 10% of the issued shares or a class of them) then have a four week period in which to object to the scheme.

If these conditions are followed, then a private company can provide financial assistance for the acquisition of its shares, even if it does not fall into one of the three basic exceptions to the s 151 rule described above.

		Marks	
Marking Guide			
(a)	Basic rule under S151	1	
	Types of financial assistance covered	1	
			2
(b)	3 exceptions for all companies (1 mark each)	3	
	Private co. procedure		
	No reduction in net assets	1	
	Declaration of solvency	1	
	Auditors report	1	
	Special resolution	1	
	Minority rights	1	
			8
			10

8

> **Tutor's hint**. Points that would have gained you high marks would be identification of insiders and knowledge of special defences. Reference to the Finance and Markets Act 2000 would also be useful.

The laws against insider dealing are designed to prevent people from dealing when they have access though their position to confidential information which other parties dealing do not have, and can use it to gain a price advantage. Such dealing undermines the Stock Exchange as a mechanism for trading shares fairly.

The **Criminal Justice Act 1993** sets out the rules on insider dealing.

Definition

S 52 of the 1993 Act provides that an individual who has inside information as an insider is guilty of insider dealing if he deals in securities that are price-affected in relation to this

information in circumstances where the acquisition or disposal of shares occurs on a regulated market, or he relies on a professional intermediary or himself acting as a professional intermediary.

An **insider** is someone who has information which must be, and he must know it to be, inside information. Furthermore he must have it, and know he has it, from an inside source.

The Act defines **inside information** as price-sensitive information which:

- Must relate to a **particular issuer** of securities which are price-affected and not securities generally.

- Must, if made public, be likely to have a **significant effect on price**.

- Must be **specific or precise**: s 56. An insider is defined by s 57 as someone who has insider information and has it (and knows he has it) from an inside source:

    ° Through being a director, employee or shareholder of an issuer of securities
    ° Through access because of employment, office or profession, or
    ° If the direct or indirect source is a person within these two previous categories.

Thus **insiders** can include people with no connection with the company who have nevertheless received inside information from a source with a connection with the company.

Such a person also commits an offence if:

- He **encourages another** person to **deal** in these securities in the above circumstances, or

- He **discloses** the information otherwise than in the proper performance of the functions of his employment, office or profession, to another person.

Section 53 contains general defences to the above offences and Schedule 1 to the Act also provides special defences.

(a) **General defences**

   S 53 gives a general defence where the individual concerned can show that:

   - He **did not expect** there to be a **profit** or avoidance of loss

   - He had reasonable grounds to believe that the **information** had been **disclosed widely,** or

   - He would have **done what he did even if he had not had the information**, for example, where securities are sold to pay a pressing debt.

   Defences to disclosure of information by an individual are that:

      ° He did not expect any person to deal
      ° Although dealing was expected, profit or avoidance of loss was not

(b) **Special defences**

   These are given in Schedule 1 and are available to:

   - Market makers and their employees in the course of business

   - Those in possession of 'market information', for example, information provided by a market such as the Stock Exchange under its rules

   - Those engaged in a price stabilisation exercise provided they act within the relevant rules.

Penalties

The maximum penalties given by s 61 are **seven years' imprisonment** and/or an **unlimited fine**. The person convicted may also be disqualified as a director under the Company Directors' Disqualification Act. Contracts remain valid and enforceable at civil law.

Finance and Markets Act 2000

The provisions contained in the Criminal Justice Act 1993 have often been criticised as ineffective. The Finance and Markets Act 2000 introduced a new offence called 'market abuse'.

Market abuse is defined as behaviour by a person or a group of people in connection with qualifying investments on a designated market that is **likely to be regarded by a regular user of that market as a failure to observe the standard of behaviour reasonably expected of a person in that position in relation to the market.**

In order to be classed as market abuse the behaviour of the person concerned must be:

- Based on information not generally available to those using the market

- Regarded as relevant for decision-making if available to a regular user of the market

- Likely to give a regular user of the market a false or misleading impression as to the supply or demand for or price or value of the investments concerned

- Likely to distort the market in the opinion of a regular user.

The published code on market abuse suggests that it covers not only insider dealing itself, but also artificial transactions, price manipulation and the dissemination of misleading information.

Under the Act the authorities can impose a penalty of whatever amount they consider appropriate on people found to have engaged in market abuse.

Marking Guide	Marks
Purpose of the law	1
Definition from the CJA 93	1
Definition of insider	1
Definition of price-sensitive information	1
Nature of the offence (dealing, encouraging to deal)	1
General defences	1
Special defences	1
Penalties	1
Market abuse definition	1
Penalties under FMA 2000	1
	10

9

A party is said to be in breach of contract where he fails to perform his contractual obligations fully and precisely without lawful excuse (which applies, for example, where performance is impossible or where the contract has been discharged by frustration). Breach of contract always gives rise to a secondary obligation to compensate the other party for losses sustained. The primary obligation under the contract will remain unless the contract is repudiated by the other party or the party committed a fundamental breach of the contract, in which case the innocent party may treat the contract as discharged and be released from his own contractual obligations.

An **anticipatory breach** is a breach of contract which occurs before the due date for performance of the contract. An **express** anticipatory breach occurs where one party declares that he has no intention of complying with the terms of the agreement (*Hochster v De la Tour*). Alternatively, anticipatory breach may be **implied** from the circumstances, for example where one party does something which makes subsequent performance of the contract impossible (*Omnium D'Enterprises v Sutherland*).

When an anticipatory breach occurs, **the innocent party may treat the contract as discharged immediately** and sue for damages or he can **elect to affirm the contract** but must then wait until the due date for performance before he can sue for breach. In these circumstances, he is entitled to continue to prepare for performance and recover the agreed price for his services (contrary to the normal duty to mitigate losses). It was made clear in *White & Carter (Councils) v McGregor* that repudiation does not of itself bring the contract to an end but it merely gives the innocent party the option of affirming or rejecting it.

However, by allowing the contract to continue, the innocent party runs the risk of the contract being **frustrated** (or discharged for some other reason) and thus of losing his rights to sue in respect of the anticipatory breach (*Avery v Bowden*).

In this case, there is clearly an anticipatory breach of the contract between Aerial Ltd and Bob which occurs in May 20X2 when Bob declares that he has no intention of performing his obligations under the contract. Aerial Ltd therefore has the option of affirming the contract and continuing to prepare for production (which it may consider to be a futile exercise) or it may sue Bob at this stage for damages, regarding the contract as repudiated.

An order of **specific performance** is an equitable remedy and is an order to the party in breach to perform his part of the contract. It is in the discretion of the court and will only be awarded where **damages would not be an adequate remedy**. It will not be awarded where performance would be required over a period of time and the court could not properly supervise the performance, for example in a contract for personal services (as is the

case here). Aerial Ltd must therefore sue for damages. It is assumed that there is no provision for liquidated damages in the contract.

Damages are a common law remedy primarily intended to restore the person who has suffered loss to the same position he would have been in had the contract been performed. Where there is no contractual provision for liquidated damages, the courts will determine the damages payable with reference to the following factors: the remoteness of damage and the measure of damages.

Remoteness of damage. With regard to remoteness, the courts consider how far down the chain of cause and effect the consequences of breach should be traced before they become so remote that no compensation should be awarded in respect of them. First, damages may be awarded only in respect of (i) losses which arise naturally, according to the usual course of things, from the breach or (ii) losses which arise in a manner which the parties may reasonably be deemed to have contemplated as the probable result of breach of contract. Secondly, if the resulting loss is of an unusual type, that is, outside the natural course of events, it may be claimed only if the defendant was aware of the unusual circumstances which might give rise to that abnormal loss. This two-part ruling was established in the case of *Hadley v Baxendale*.

The application of the rule is illustrated by the case of *Victoria Laundry v Newman Industries* where the claimant was allowed to recover damages for loss of normal profits due to the defendant's delay but not for loss of the profits which would have resulted from an unusually lucrative contract unknown to the defendant.

Measure of damages. As mentioned, **damages are intended to restore the wronged party to the position he would have been in if the contract had been performed but not to put him in a better or more profitable position**. This is sometimes referred to as protecting the expectation interest of the claimant. The claimant's expectation loss may be defined as the loss of what the claimant would have received had the contract been properly performed. A claimant may alternatively seek to have his reliance interest protected; this refers to the position he would have been in had he not relied on the contract. Because they compensate for wasted expenditure, damages for reliance loss cannot be awarded if they would put the claimant in a better position than he would attain under protection of his expectation interest.

The amount of damages payable is usually quantified as a financial loss, based on the actual loss suffered, although some types of non financial loss are recoverable, for example personal injuries or distress caused by a holiday failing to match the brochure's promises (*Jarvis v Swan Tours*). The claimant must take reasonable steps to mitigate his loss or he may not receive his full losses (*Payzu v Saunders 1919*). This means that he must take reasonable steps to put himself in as good a position as if the contract had been performed.

It is assumed that as a result of Bob's anticipatory breach, Aerial would claim for its losses of £300,000 in wasted advertising, £250,000 in its contract with the UK client and £1m from its American contract. The costs of advertising his appearance would appear to flow naturally from the contract. However, they will only be recoverable from Bob to the extent that they are normal and to the extent that the advertising was based on Bob's part in it, given that the film could still go ahead, albeit with a less famous actor.

The £500,000 profit has not been lost, given that Aerial originally planned a film with an actor not especially famous and so presumably this profit would still be attainable. The additional £250,000 attributable to Bob's new fame would not appear to be recoverable unless Aerial could persuade the court that both parties may reasonably be supposed to have contemplated Bob's increased fame. This would be a question of fact.

The American deal falls under the second limb of *Hadley v Baxendale* and will not be recoverable unless Bob had actual knowledge of its likelihood. There is nothing to suggest that this would be the case.

Marking Guide	Marks
Definition of anticipatory breach	2
Cases	1
Options open to injured party	2
Delay: runs risk of losing right to act	1
Bob is in anticipatory breach	1
Options open to Aerial	2
Specific performance not possible	1
Purpose of damages	1
Consideration of remoteness of damage	2
Cases	1
Consideration of measure of damages	2
Cases	1
Application of rules to Aerial's situation	3
	20

10

Tutor's hint. Try to distinguish clearly in your answer between unfair dismissal and redundancy as these are the two topics asked for. Even in relatively short Section B questions like this, follow our suggested approach: **identify** the issue, **state** the law, **apply** the law and **conclude**.

Examiner's comments. Some candidates seemed to think that unfair dismissal and redundancy are the same thing and were not sufficiently familiar with the statutory provisions governing either. The application of the law to the situation in the question tended to be poor.

Redundancy

The law relating to redundancy is now found in the Employment Rights Act 1996.

A **qualifying employee** has a right to a redundancy payment (as compensation) in the event that he is dismissed because of redundancy, that is (s 139) 'where the only or main reason for the dismissal is that:

(a) the employer has ceased or intends to cease carrying on the business in which the employee has been employed or at the local establishment where the employee has been employed or

(b) his requirements of that business for employees to carry on the work done by the employee have ceased or diminished'.

If the employer requires the employee to move to a different place of work and that is within the terms of the contract of employment, then there is no redundancy (*Rank Xerox Ltd v Churchill*).

The onus is on the employee to show that he was dismissed and then on the employer to show that the dismissal was for some reason other than redundancy. The employee must show that he or she was dismissed in one of the following ways:

(a) dismissal by the employer bringing the contract to an end, with or without notice;

(b) dismissal where a fixed term contract ends and is not renewed (although protection may be lost if the contract is for more than one year's duration); and

(c) when the conduct of the employer is sufficiently serious that it amounts to a repudiation of the employment contract and the employee resigns as a result, lawfully

terminating the contract without notice by reason of the employer's conduct. If the employee is dismissed for misconduct, he will not be entitled to a redundancy payment (*Sanders v Neale*). Similarly if he resigns voluntarily there is no entitlement.

The employer may choose to offer a redundant employee **alternative employment** (s 141). If the employee unreasonably refuses the offer, he loses his entitlement to a redundancy payment. Broadly speaking, the alternative employment must be in the same capacity, at the same place and on the same terms and conditions as the old employment. It should not be perceived as being lower in status (*Cambridge District Co-operative Society v Ruse 1993*).

An employee qualifies for redundancy pay if (s 109) he is under the normal retirement age for the business (or 65 where no age is specified) and has been continually employed for 2 years or more.

Redundancy pay is calculated as follows (s 162):-1.5 weeks pay for each complete year of employment during which the employee was aged 41 or more, 1 week's pay for each year where he was aged between 22 and 40 and 0.5 week's pay for each year where he was aged between 18 and 21.

The entitlement to a redundancy payment is lost if the employee does not claim a payment within 6 months of the relevant date (such as the expiry of the dismissal notice). If the employer disputes his claim, the employee should refer it to an Industrial Tribunal. A right of appeal lies to the Employment Appeals Tribunal.

The employer should have a **redundancy selection procedure** which conforms to good industrial relations practice (*Williams v Compare Maxam Ltd*). Thus he should give as much warning as possible of impending redundancies, consult with the relevant trade union, make the selection fairly and consider whether offers of alternative employment can be made. Protective awards may be made against an employer who fails to consult trade unions or to give notice of impending redundancies to the Department of Employment.

Unfair dismissal

An employee who has been dismissed may have a claim for **unfair dismissal** if he is below the normal retirement age for that job (or under 65 if there is no normal retirement age), has been continuously employed for one year or more and the dismissal has been made for an unfair reason. It is for the employer to show that the dismissal was fair and he must be seen to have acted reasonably.

To defeat a claim for unfair dismissal the employer must show his main or sole reason for the dismissal was one of those listed in s 57 of the 1978 Act or **some other substantial reason which justifies dismissal**. The **listed reasons** are a lack of capabilities or qualifications of the employee, misconduct of the employee, redundancy, legal restrictions or 'some other substantial reason' of a kind which justifies dismissal.

Clearly in this case Fawn Ltd would point to redundancy as the reason for dismissal. This is a fair reason for dismissal as long as the employer has implemented a redundancy procedure in accordance with good industrial relations practice. This requires consultation and objective criteria of selection.

The grounds for dismissal that are **automatically unfair** are not relevant to this case (including dismissal on grounds related to the employee's pregnancy or trade union activity or a spent conviction).

Even if the employer proves an acceptable reason for dismissal, the employment tribunal may still decide that the dismissal was unfair if it considers on the basis of equity and the substantial merits of the case, that the employer acted unreasonably in dismissing the employee (s 98 ERA). There is no burden of proof on either employer or employee, it is

simply the case that a dismissal, even if for a satisfactory reason, is unfair unless the tribunal also finds that the employer acted reasonably. The employer must firstly have applied the correct disciplinary procedure (for example by giving warnings in the case of all but the most serious misconduct or consulting the appropriate employee representatives when considering redundancies). Secondly, he must have taken account of all the relevant circumstances. This means that he must take previous conduct into account before dismissing for misconduct, or must offer help to an employee who has difficulties with his work before dismissing on grounds of incapacity. The tribunal will have regard to the guidance laid down by the ACAS Code of Practice in considering whether the employer acted reasonably.

An employee must apply to the employment tribunal with a claim for unfair dismissal within three months of the dismissal. Where unfair dismissal is shown, three remedies are available:

(a) **reinstatement** to the same job without any break in the continuity of employment (s 114 ERA);

(b) **re-engagement** in a different but comparable and suitable job with the same employer or his successor or associate;

(c) **compensation**.

Compensation is the most usual award. This consists of a **basic award**, calculated in the same way as redundancy pay. There may also be a **compensatory award** for additional losses of earnings, expenses and benefits, calculated on ordinary common law principles of damages for breach of contract.

Grace is clearly a qualifying employee in respect of redundancy and unfair dismissal and has been dismissed by Fawn Ltd terminating her contract. **She is entitled to a redundancy payment of three weeks' pay.** If the tribunal considers that Fawn Ltd failed to act reasonably in making her redundant rather than, for example, retraining her in connection with the manufacturing business, then she may also be entitled to additional compensation for unfair dismissal. This will be a question of fact.

Marking Guide	Marks
Redundancy	
Criteria for redundancy	2
Qualification for redundancy pay	2
Calculation of redundancy pay	2
Redundancy selection procedure	2
Grace qualifies for redundancy	1
Unfair dismissal	
Criteria for unfair dismissal	3
Employer to show it was fair	1
Reasons for fair dismissal	3
Redundancy a fair reason	1
Procedure for bringing action	1
Possible remedies	1
Grace may be able to claim unfair dismissal	1
	20

11

> **Tutor's hint**. In tackling a question like this:
>
> - identify the **issues** (directors' duties)
>
> - **state** the law (what their duties are)
>
> - **apply** the law (to this situation)
>
> - **conclude** (advise the parties)

(a) Two of the main duties owed by a director to a company are to avoid conflicts of duty and personal interest and to account to the company for any profits or personal advantage obtained from his position as director without the company's consent.

Concern for company's interests

A director must show undivided concern for the company's interests, regardless of whether or not the company is prejudiced by a conflict of interests. Conflicts are inevitable where a director has an interest in a contract with his company, for example a contract between the company and one of its directors employing that director in the management of the business. A statutory and common law framework exists enabling directors to be interested in contracts with the company but only subject to certain safeguards (declaration to the board under s 317).

Directors' personal advantage

The principal common law condition is that a director **cannot obtain personal advantage** from his position as director unless permitted by the company.

In *Regal Hastings v Gulliver*, the directors of one company, which owned one cinema, subscribed for shares in a new company which purchased two further cinemas since the first company had insufficient funds for the acquisition. The directors made substantial profits from the later sale of their shareholdings in the new company.

The House of Lords held that the directors were accountable to the company for their profits since they had obtained it from an **opportunity** which **came** to them as **directors**. The fact that the company had lost nothing since it was unable to make the acquisition itself was irrelevant. Had the company agreed by resolution passed in general meeting, the directors could have retained their profits and, in the absence of fraud, their controlling shareholdings could have been used to pass such a resolution.

Defrauding the company

This should be compared with *Cook v Deeks* where the directors could not have ratified their own actions as members in general meeting because they had **defrauded** the **company** by appropriating the company's property. In this case, the directors, who were also controlling shareholders, negotiated a contract in the name of the company. They then took the contract for themselves and passed a resolution in general meeting declaring that the company had no interest in the contract. It was held that the contract belonged in equity to the company and the directors' purported resolution was invalid.

Hilary's position

In the present case, Hilary, a director and majority shareholder received a commission from Oilprojects Ltd and makes a profit from the sale of her shares in that company. Both sums have come to her as a result of her directorships and **conflicts of interest** in the two companies. Consequently any profit can only be retained with the **consent** of the **company** in general meeting and may be not even then, if the courts hold that

approval would be a **fraud** on the **minority**. In any event there is no suggestion that any such approving resolution has been passed. Hilary will be required to account to the company for the commission and profits she has received.

(b)   **Foss v Harbottle**

Directors Hilary and Chris have entered into an agreement to sell property owned by the company at an undervalue negligently rather than fraudulently. The basic rule of law is that the majority shareholders have the ultimate control in a company. In the event of a wrong being alleged to have been done by the directors (who may hold a majority of the voting rights or represent a majority shareholder), the proper plaintiff is the company itself and not a minority shareholder.

In *Foss v Harbottle*, a shareholder sued the company directors on the basis that they had defrauded the company by selling land to the company at an inflated price. It was held that the company was the only proper plaintiff to bring an action to protect its rights or property and that the company in general meeting should decide whether to bring such legal proceedings.

Exceptions to Foss v Harbottle

Without exceptions, the rule in *Foss v Harbottle* could result in grossly unjust situations which is why, both in the courts and by statute, a number of categories have been developed where the rule will not be applied. One of the exceptions if where the act complained of is a **fraud** by **the majority** who are in control of the company. In such cases, a minority member is entitled to bring a derivative action essentially suing on behalf of the company naming the directors as the defendants.

Even without fraud, it might be possible for a minority shareholder to sue directors and controlling shareholders where their **negligence** is coupled with their **deriving** a **benefit** from it: *Daniels v Daniels*. However, in *Pavlides v Jensen*, property passed to third parties rather than to controlling shareholders and it was held that this did not allow the company to take proceedings against a director - there was no appropriation of assets by the majority and no fraud involved.

S 459

Alternatively Eleanor could take action under s 459 on the grounds that the directors' actions have been **unfairly prejudicial** to the position of the members. However the courts have tended to be reluctant to treat management, even 'bad management' as detrimental to the minority. Thus in *Re Five Minute Car Wash Service Ltd* the complaint was of incompetent management causing loss but tolerated by the controlling shareholder. The petition failed.

Given the absence of fraud (or the directors deriving personal benefit) on the part of the controlling directors in this case, it seems unlikely that an action by Eleanor would be allowed by way of exception to the general principle of majority rule.

Marking Guide		Marks
(a)	Directors must avoid conflicts of interest	2
	Directors cannot obtain personal advantage	2
	Case or illustration	2
	Defrauding the company	1
	Case or illustration	1
	Hilary can only retain profit with shareholder consent	2
	Maybe a fraud on the minority	1
	Hilary must account to company	1
		12
(b)	Basic rule is majority rule	1
	Foss v Harbottle	1
	Exception: fraud by majority	1
	Derivative action	1
	Negligence causing benefit actionable	1
	Cases or illustrations	1
	S 459 action for unfairly prejudicial conduct	2
		8
		20

12 EXE

Tutor's hint. You should appreciate the point that the creditors can have no objection to the capital reduction because it will not affect the 'creditors' buffer'. You should also remember that there are a number of situations where the court has held a variation of class rights has not taken place.

There was no need to start every part of the question with a memo heading; you can use this format for the answer as a whole.

MEMORANDUM

To: Board of Directors
        Exe plc
From: Finance Director   Date: 23 November 20X4
Subject: Proposed capital reduction

(a) **The preference shareholders and Article 21**

Class rights

Any company may choose to attach special rights to different shares relating to, for example, dividends, voting, the right to appoint directors or return of capital. If therefore some shares have different rights from others, each grouping of shares with identical rights is referred to as a '**class of shares**' and those rights as '**class rights**'. If, as here, the company's articles (or memorandum or resolution or terms of issue) provide that a class's rights may only be varied by adopting a special procedure, that might in itself be a class right: s 125.

Variation of class rights

To decide whether the preference shareholders can use Article 21 to block the reduction, it is necessary to determine whether it in fact constitutes a **variation** of **class rights**.

A relevant case on this subject is *Greenhalgh v Arderne Cinemas Ltd*. In this case, the company had two classes of ordinary shares, 50p shares and 10p shares, each carrying one vote. The company passed an ordinary resolution to subdivide each 50p share into five 10p shares, thus multiplying the number of shares in that class by 5 (as here). The

230

claimant argued that the subdivision of shares had reduced his voting power and thus varied his class rights. The claimant also argued that as the variation had been effected by an ordinary resolution and not a special resolution (as required by the company's articles for a variation of class rights), it was unlawful. The court held that the rights attached to the original 10p shares had **not** been **varied** since they **still** had **one vote** per share as before.

The courts maintain a distinction between the **nature** of the class rights and the **value** derived from those rights. A **variation** of the **nature** of rights would require that **Article 21** be **applied** but a **variation** of the **value** would **not**. This distinction was also upheld in *White v Bristol Aeroplane Co Ltd.*

Thus the preference shareholders would not be able to block the cancellation.

(b) **Objections by the creditors**

The capital which a limited company obtains from its members is sometimes called the **creditors' buffer**. No one can prevent an unsuccessful company from losing all or part of its capital by trading at a loss. However whatever subscribed capital remains in the hands of the company must be held for the payment of the company's debts.

In this case the amount of capital held to pay the company's creditors is in no way affected by the capital reduction. Its purpose is as specified in s 135 (2), namely 'to cancel paid up share capital which has been lost or which is no longer represented by available assets'. The **resources** of the company are **not reduced** by the part cancellation of the nominal value of the shares.

It follows, therefore, that the creditors will not be able to challenge the capital reduction in the courts.

(c) **Procedure for capital reduction**

The procedure is as follows.

(i)   The company's **articles** must **permit** the **reduction** to take place. In a company regulated by Table A this authority is conferred by Article 34.

(ii) S 135 requires that a **special resolution** effecting the reduction is passed. This will usually be at an extraordinary general meeting called for the purpose, though there is no objection to passing the resolution at an annual general meeting if it is due.

(iii) The **court** must **confirm** the **reduction** by issuing an order to this effect: s 136.

The registration requirements are as follows.

(i)   The **court order** confirming the reduction must be **sent** to the **registrar**.

(ii) Along with the order, a minute must be sent which gives details of the **new amount** of **share capital**, the **number of shares**, the **amount** of each share and the amount **paid up** on each share.

(iii) The registrar then issues a **certificate of registration** (in relation to both the order and the accompanying minute). This certificate can be relied on as conclusive evidence that the share capital is as stated in the minute and that the requirements of the law in relation to their reduction have been properly complied with.

231

Marking Guide

		Marks
(a)	Class rights	1
	Variation of class rights	1
	Greenhalgh v Arderne Cinemas (or similar)	1
	Application to situation	2
		5
(b)	Protection of creditors' buffer	2
	Not affected here	1
	Creditors have no right of challenge	2
		5
(c)	Authority in articles	2
	Special resolution	1
	Court confirmation	2
	File court order with registrar	2
	File minute detailing scheme	2
	Certification of registration	1
		10
		20

Corporate and Business Law
BPP Mock Exam 2

Question Paper:	
Time allowed	**3 hours**
This paper is divided into two sections	
Section A	**SIX questions ONLY to be answered**
Section B	**TWO questions ONLY to be answered**

paper 2.2

DO NOT OPEN THIS PAPER UNTIL YOU ARE READY TO START
UNDER EXAMINATION CONDITIONS

Section A – SIX questions ONLY to be attempted

1   (a) What are the main provisions of the European Convention on Human Rights, now enshrined in the Human Rights Act 1998? Who is bound to observe these rights and who is protected by them?   (7 marks)

    (b) In what ways has the Human Rights Act 1998 had an impact on UK law?
                                                                              (3 marks)

                                                                          (10 marks)

2   (a) Briefly explain in the law of contract what is meant by the doctrine of privity.   (3 marks)

    (b) Examine the exceptions, both common law and statutory, to the doctrine.
                                                                              (7 marks)

                                                                          (10 marks)

3   Explain the ways in which a contractual offer can come to an end.   **(10 marks)**

4   State and explain the remedies available for breach of contract.   **(10 marks)**

5   In relation to employment law:

    (a) Describe how the courts distinguish between contracts of service and contracts for services.   (7 marks)

    (b) Explain the importance of the distinction.   (3 marks)

                                                                          (10 marks)

6   Explain in relation to the formation of a company what is meant by the terms:

    (a) promoter;   (5 marks)
    (b) pre-incorporation contract.   (5 marks)

                                                                          (10 marks)

7   Distinguish between:

    (a) unlimited companies;   (3 marks)
    (b) companies limited by guarantee;   (3 marks)
    (c) companies limited by shares.   (4 marks)

                                                                          (10 marks)

8   (a) Explain the rules governing the payment of dividends in relation to:

         (i)   private companies;   (4 marks)
         (ii) public companies.   (3 marks)

    (b) State the consequences of any dividends being paid in contravention of those rules.   (3 marks)

                                                                          (10 marks)

Section B – TWO questions ONLY to be attempted

9   In January 20X2 Alex, a business consultant, won a lucrative contract with Ball Ltd to provide them with a highly specialised computer system. The terms of the contract required the system to be fully operational by 30 May subject to a penalty of £1,000 for every day's delay. Alex entered into three subcontracts. One was with Chris to provide the software for the new system, a second was with Dick to provide the necessary computer hardware and a third was with Eric to write a manual explaining the operation of the new system. All of these tasks were to be carried out by 23 May. Chris, Dick and Eric were each to receive £5,000 for their work.

At the end of March, Chris told Alex that he would not complete the software in time unless Alex agreed to increase his payment by a further £1,000. Alex agreed to pay the increased sum in order to ensure that the job was done on time. However, he thought it was only fair that he should increase the money promised to the others, so he promised them a bonus of £1,000 if the job was done on time. At the same time he asked Eric if he could produce his manual by 16 May so that he could demonstrate it in advance to the managers of Ball Ltd.

In the event, all three completed their tasks by 16 May and the system was successfully installed before Alex's contractual deadline with Ball Ltd. However, Alex has now refused to make any additional payments beyond the original contractual price to Chris, Dick or Eric.

Required:

Advise Chris, Dick and Eric whether they have any rights in law to enforce Alex's promise to pay them an extra £1,000.   **(20 marks)**

10   Rob, Sam and Tom formed a partnership to run a petrol station. Each of them put £75,000 into the business. As Rob had no prospect of raising any more money, it was agreed between them that his maximum liability for any partnership debts would be fixed at his original contribution of £75,000. The partnership agreement expressly stated that the partnership business was to be limited exclusively to the sale of petrol.

In January 20X0 Sam received £10,000 from the partnership's bank drawn on its overdraft facility. He told the bank that the money was to finance a short-term partnership debt but in fact he used the money to pay for a round the world cruise. In February Tom entered into a £15,000 contract on behalf of the partnership to buy some used cars which he hoped to sell from the garage forecourt. In March the partnership's bank refused to honour its cheque for the payment of its monthly petrol account on the basis that there were no funds in its account and it had reached the limit of its overdraft facility.

Required:

Advise Rob, Sam and Tom as to their various rights and liabilities.   (20 marks)

11   Ian, John and Ken are the three directors of Driver Ltd, which had recently been the subject of approaches from another company, Road plc. Road plc launched a take-over bid for Driver Ltd, which was supported by Alex, a minority shareholder of the company, who holds 15% of the shares. In order to thwart the take-over bid, the directors of Driver Ltd allotted 100,000 unissued shares to Ben.

A month after the allotment, an EGM of Driver Ltd was held and an ordinary resolution was passed ratifying the allotment to Ben, who did not vote on the resolution. Alex is now proposing to bring an action against the directors for breach of fiduciary duty, on the grounds that the allotment has not been made for the proper purpose.

Required:

(a) **Discuss the issues involved and advise Alex as to whether she is likely to be successful in her claim. You should also consider whether the directors have breached any other requirements of company law.**

(16 marks)

(b) **What difference would it make to your answer if Ben had been allotted the 100,000 new shares in return for his agreement to act as a consultant to the company for the next two years?** (4 marks)

(20 marks)

12   Frank has had a number of dealings with a variety of companies.

(a) First of all he entered into an agreement to sell some goods to George. However, the contractual document actually stated that the contract was made with George's company George Ltd. Although they have been delivered, the goods have not been paid for. George is claiming that his company rather than he personally is responsible for any debts owed to Frank. Unfortunately George Ltd has just gone into insolvent liquidation.

(b) Next Frank has discovered that a former employee, Hal, who has just stopped working for him, has set up a company to compete directly with Frank's business. Due to the sensitive nature of the business, Frank had insisted that Hal enter into a legally binding agreement not to compete with him for a period of 5 years.

(c) Frank had entered into a contract to buy land from Ian in order to expand his business. He has learned, however, that Ian has transferred the title in the land to a private company controlled by Ian, who is refusing to complete the original contract.

(d) Finally, Frank entered into a contract with Jug Ltd which was controlled by Ken. Jug Ltd went into insolvent liquidation and Frank was unable to recover any of the money he had lost on the contract. He has subsequently learned that before the liquidation Jug Ltd transferred its assets to a separate company, Keg Ltd, also controlled by Ken.

Required:

Advise Frank as to the legality and likely outcome of the above situations.

(20 marks)

238

ANSWERS

DO NOT TURN THIS PAGE UNTIL YOU HAVE COMPLETED MOCK EXAM 2

WARNING! APPLYING THE BPP MARKING SCHEME

If you decide to mark your paper using the BPP marking scheme, you should bear in mind the following points.

1   The BPP solutions are not definitive: you will see that we have applied the marking scheme to our solutions to show how good answers should gain marks, but there may be more than one way to answer the question. You must try to judge fairly whether different points made in your answers are correct and relevant and therefore worth marks according to our marking scheme.

2   If you have a friend or colleague who is studying or has studied this paper, you might ask him or her to mark your paper for you, thus gaining a more objective assessment. Remember you and your friend are not trained or objective markers, so try to avoid complacency or pessimism if you appear to have done very well or very badly.

3   You should be aware that BPP's answers are longer than you would be expected to write. Sometimes, therefore, you would gain the same number of marks for making the basic point as we have shown as being available for a slightly more detailed or extensive solution.

It is most important that you analyse your solutions in detail and that you attempt to be as objective as possible.

Professional Examination - Paper 2.2   **Marking Scheme**

Corporate and Business Law

This marking scheme is given as a guide to markers in the context of the suggested answer. Scope is given to markers to award marks for alternative approaches to a question, including relevant comment, and where well-reasoned conclusions are provided. This is particularly so in the case scenario questions where there may be more than one definitive solution.

A PLAN OF ATTACK

If this were the real Corporate and Business Law exam and you had been told to turn over and begin, what would be going through your mind?

Perhaps you're having a panic. Stop that now! What you should do is spend a good five minutes looking through the paper in detail, working out which questions to do and the order in which to attempt them. So turn back to the paper and let's sort out a plan of attack.

Looking through the paper

You have choices in both halves of the paper, so read all the questions carefully to decide which you are going to attempt. It is vital that you understand what each question is asking, so that you do not reject a question you can answer, and attempt a question that you are not so strong on. The questions in this paper are as follows:

Part A (you must answer 6)

- Question 1 requires you to talk about the impact of the Human Rights Act, a topical area of recent development in the law.

- Question 2 asks for an explanation of the law relating to privity of contract and the common law and statutory exceptions to the rule.

- Question 3 asks for an explanation of the ways in which an offer can come to an end.

- Question 4 asks for an explanation of the remedies available in the event of breach of contract.

- Question 5 is a two part question on the distinction between contracts of service and contracts for services and the importance of the distinction.

- Question 6 asks for an explanation of the terms promoter and pre-incorporation contract.

- Question 7 examines three different types of company.

- Question 8 asks about the rules governing the payment of dividends.

Part B (you must answer 2)

- Question 9 is a scenario based question examining aspects of consideration in contract law, especially when a party to a contract can demand more consideration.

- Question 10 is a scenario based question on the liability of partners for each other's actions.

- Question 11 examines the topic of directors' duties and the issue of shares.

- Question 12 is very wide-ranging, covering separate legal personality contracts in restraint of trade and fraudulent and wrongful trading.

Part A

You can answer the questions in any order, but we would advise you to **undertake Part A first**. This is because the questions are more straightforward than the question in Part B and you can build up marks quickly, by ensuring that you get the simple marks in each of the question you undertake in this section. Also, if you do miscalculate your time apportionment and you have done Part B first, you run the risk of missing a complete Part A question out, and consequently losing the straightforward marks in that question, in favour of marks which are harder to get in other questions.

Additionally you can sometimes find that the fact that you will consider six areas of law in part A will often act as a trigger to **enable you to recall relevant areas of the law** when you move on to part B, as there can sometimes be an overlap between the two sections.

When choosing which questions you are likely to answer, you may do one of the following two things:

- Choose the six that you can answer best
- Eliminate the two that you cannot do

Here are some points to note:

- It is not wise to ignore a syllabus area when revising because you have a choice of questions, in case the questions that come up on your revised areas are more difficult to get marks in

- If you think that there are more than two questions that you cannot do, look through them all carefully. Do any of the questions have parts that you think you can attempt? **You should always attempt six questions in Part A.**

- If you have a choice between two questions, ensure that you can answer **all the parts of the questions**. If you can't answer all the parts of one of them, do the other one, even if the first was related to your favourite topic area.

If you have revised the syllabus fully, in this Part A, we would advise that you do questions 2, 3, 4, 5, 6 and 7, as these are the most straightforward. Questions 1 and 8 are more difficult in our opinion, but obviously if they are on areas about which you feel completely confident there is no reason why you should not try them.

Part B

The questions in Part B are longer than Part A and usually require you to apply legal principles to situations. We suggest that you tackle it second therefore, when you have 'warmed up' by answering the questions in Part A.

A key skill in Part B is to be able to break down the larger questions into the components within them, to see where you will build up your marks. It is often easier to tackle questions where the examiner has broken them down with a mark allocation than ones which are just for 20 marks straight.

In this Part B, question 9 should be an easy question to score well on, if you have thoroughly revised consideration and variation of contract terms. However the scenario is quite complex and you will need to be able to analyse it in detail and cite many cases if you are to maximise your marks.

The partnership question, question 10, is quite straightforward, and you may want to have a go at this one. Make sure that you clearly distinguish between the parties involved in the question and you bring out the respective points of law.

The two company law questions on this paper are quite tough and question 12 also wanders back into contract law. You need to be able to think fast across areas of the syllabus to tackle this.

If you are confident on the subject of directors' duties with regard to the issue of shares, then you will want to attempt question 11. This is not a particularly difficult question, but make sure that you read the scenario carefully to make sure that you fully understand what is going on.

Allocating your time

BPP's advice is always allocate your time according to the marks for the question in total and for the parts of the question. That means for paper 2.2 that you should spend 1 hour and 48 minutes on Part A (18 minutes per question) and 1 hour 12 minutes on Part B (36 minutes per question). However, use your common sense. If you are doing a question but know you can't answer part (c), allocate those minutes to another question, where you may be able to pick up more marks.

Forget about it!

And don't worry if you found the paper difficult. More than likely other candidates will too. If this were the real thing you would need to forget the exam the minute you left the exam hall and think about the next one. Or, if it is the last one, celebrate!

1

> **Tutor's hint.** You should note that there are three requirements for part (a). Not only are you asked about the main provisions of the Human Rights Act, but also who is bound by the Act and who it is intended to protect. Don't fall into the trap of omitting one of the parts and thereby denying yourself the credit available. If you are stumped for an answer to the second part, try to think of some of the more topical issues that have appeared in the news recently, such as the fact that courts are to set minimum sentences for convicted murderers.
>
> On the assumption that there is a mark available for each of who is bound and who is protected in part (a) there are then five marks for the provisions of the Human Rights Act. You should aim to produce at least five, for a mark each, and there may be extra credit for elaborating on them.

(a) The Articles of the European Convention on Human Rights have now been enshrined into UK law as the Human Rights Act 1998, enacted in 2000. The main provisions are:

- The right to life

- The prohibition of torture and inhuman or degrading treatment or punishment

- The prohibition of slavery and forced labour

- The right to liberty and security of person (although the Article sets out the situations when a person can be deprived of his liberty, such as when sentenced by a court after committing a criminal act)

- The right to a fair trial, within a reasonable time by an independent and impartial tribunal established by law. Additionally anyone charged with a criminal offence is to be presumed innocent until proven guilty according to law

- No punishment to occur without law, meaning that no one can be found guilty of an offence that was not an offence at the time that it was committed, or given a greater penalty than was in force at the time the act was committed

- The right to respect for private and family life

- Freedom of thought, conscience and religion

- Freedom of expression

- Freedom of assembly and association, including the right to form and join trade unions

- The right to marry

- Prohibition of discrimination

The Act binds **public authorities**, which can be defined as bodies undertaking functions of a public nature, including government departments, local authorities, courts and schools. Any person, whether individual or corporate, group of individuals or non-governmental organisation can rely upon the terms of the Human Rights Act. Government departments or organisations such as local authorities cannot rely upon it.

(b) The main impact of the Human Rights Act on UK law is that UK courts are now required to interpret UK law in a way that is compatible with the Convention.

Existing legislation must be interpreted in a way that is compatible with convention rights, meaning that the courts must take into account the previous decisions of the European Court of Human Rights. If a court feels that a provision of primary legislation (ie an Act of Parliament) is incompatible with the Convention it can make a declaration of incompatibility. It is then up to the Government to take action to remedy the incompatibility.

Areas in which the human rights legislation has already affected UK law include the following:

- Courts are now to decide the minimum sentence for convicted murderers sentenced to life imprisonment, rather than the Home Secretary

- The limitation on defendants in rape cases to question the victims have been removed following *R v A (2001)*.

		Marks
Marking Guide		
(a)	Examples of the provisions (1 marks each, max 5)	5
	Public authorities bound	1
	Examples of persons who can rely	1
		7
(b)	Interpretation must be compatible	1
	Courts to make declaration of incompatibility	1
	Examples of effects	1
		3
Total		10

2

> **Tutorial note.** This is another question in which basic preparation in this area could have stood you in good stead. Privity may seem like a complex area, but just learning the Key Term given in the Study Text would have gained you some marks in part (a). Giving a reference to the *Dunlop v Selfridge* case to illustrate the rule would have been excellent. In part (b) you should have been able to list sufficient exceptions to gain a pass mark, particularly the important Contract (Rights of Third Parties) Act 1999. Again, if you struggled when answering this question, use the suggested answer below in your revision.
>
> **Examiner's comment.** Although this topic has been examined in the past, it was not widely chosen, and candidates who did attempt it did not seem well prepared. Marks awarded were therefore disappointing. In part (a) the better candidates could cite cases to support their explanations of the rules of privity of contract. Part (b) was generally poorly done and very few candidates could provide both statutory and common law exceptions to the general rule. Not many candidates mentioned the Contracts (Rights of Third Parties) Act 1999.

(a) **The doctrine of privity of contract**

The doctrine of privity of contract provides that **only a party to the contract** has **enforceable rights and obligations under it** and a person who is not party to the contract cannot enforce it, even if the promises are given for his benefit.

In the leading case in this area, *Dunlop v Selfridge*, D supplied tyres to X, a distributor, for resale, and X sold them to S. The contract between S and X provided for payments to D if S sold the tyres at less than a fixed price. Although S failed to observe this clause and sold the tyres at a lower price, D was unable to enforce the promise. It was held that this was part of the contract between S and X, to which D was not a party.

(b) **Exceptions to the rule**

There are some exceptions to the general rule of privity of contract, both at common law and under statute, where a third party may be allowed to enforce a contract:

(i) *Common law*

(1) **Where the beneficiary may sue in some other capacity**: In *Beswick v Beswick* a widow sued for specific performance in her capacity as her husband's administrator (rather than simply as his widow) to enforce a

contract between her husband and the successor to his business. The contract provided for payment of an annuity to the widow. In her capacity as administrator, she was able to enforce the contract for her own benefit as third party to the contract. In her personal capacity as recipient, she had no right of action.

(2) **Where there is a collateral contract**: In *Shanklin Pier v Detel Products Ltd*, the claimant entered into a contract to have his pier repainted. The painters used a particular paint produced by the defendant as required by the claimant. The paint was unsatisfactory. The defendant fought an action by the claimant on the basis that it had only entered into a contract of supply with the painters and since the claimant was not a party to that contract he could not enforce it. The court held that there was a collateral contract between the claimant and the defendant by which the defendant guaranteed the suitability of the paint in return for the claimant requiring the painters to use it.

(3) **Where a party validly assigns the rights contained in a contract** (other than rights of action for unliquidated damages or rights so personal that they are unassignable) to a third party: A party may not assign the burden of his contractual obligations without the other party's consent.

(4) **Where equity provides that an implied trust has been created**: Thus in *Gregory and Parker v Williams*, P owed money to G and W and agreed to transfer his property to W if W paid P's debt to G. When the property was transferred, W refused to pay G who was clearly not a party to the contract between P and W. Nonetheless, the court held that P could be regarded as a trustee for G under an implied trust and so G could bring an action jointly with P.

(5) **Where there is an agency relationship**: If an agent enters into a contract with a third party apparently on his own behalf but in fact on behalf of an undisclosed principal, the agent may sue the third party (since he is treated as the other party to the contract) until such time as the principal intervenes and enforces the contract on his own behalf. Where the principal is disclosed, the contract is treated as one between the principal (and thus enforceable by the principal) and third party even though made by the agent.

(6) **Where there is a restrictive covenant that attaches to the land** so that successors in title are bound by covenants to which they were not originally covenanters.

(ii) *Statutory exceptions*

Some statutory exceptions to the doctrine exist, for example a road accident victim can claim from the other party's insurers (Road Traffic Act 1972) and the Married Woman's Property Act 1882 allows a husband or wife to enforce life insurance taken out by the other for his or her benefit.

Contracts (Rights of Third Parties) Act 1999

The principal statutory exception is contained in the Contracts (Rights of Third Parties) Act 1999 which sets out the circumstances in which a third party can enforce a contract in the event of breach, or have it varied or rescinded.

These are either

• Where the contract expressly so provides, or

- Where the term confers a benefit on the third party (unless it appears that the contracting parties did not intend him to have the right to enforce it).

The third party must be identified in the contract by name, class or description but need not be in existence when the contract is made. The Act does not confer third party rights in relation to employment contracts nor does it affect the operation of s14 CA 1985.

Marking Guide		
		Marks
(a) Explanation		2
Case or illustration		1
		3
(b) Common law exceptions (1 mark each: max 4)		4
Contracts (Rights of Third Parties) Act 1999		2
Other statutory exceptions		1
		7
		10

3

> **Tutor's hint**. This is a straightforward section A question. Any introductory material must be kept brief. Remember, as is often the case with section A questions, to write about all the different aspects of end of offer instead of putting too much detail about one area. Refer to the marking guide: only a limited number of marks are available for each reason for termination.

An **offer may be accepted** so as to form a binding contract **only for so long as it remains open**. It is therefore important to be able to identify the point at which an offer is terminated. The most **common reasons** for the termination of an offer are **lapse of the offer**, **rejection** of the offer by the offeree or **revocation** of the offer by the offeror.

Lapse

An offer may be **expressed to remain open** (or the parties may agree that it shall remain open) for a **specified length of time**, in which case it will **terminate upon expiry of that time**. It cannot be accepted thereafter.

If no express time limit is set, it will be deemed to **expire after a reasonable time**. What is reasonable depends upon the circumstances of each individual case (*Ramsgate Hotel v Montefiore*).

Rejection

A **clear rejection** of an offer **will terminate the offer**. A request for further information is not a clear rejection of the offer, as in *Stevenson v McLean*, where one of the parties asked if the other would accept payment by instalments.

However, an offer is terminated where a **response introduces a new term**. This is known as **counter-offer** (for example, if one party is asking for £1,000, the other saying 'I'll give you £950). **Counter offer always terminates the original offer** (*Hyde v Wrench*).

Revocation

The general rule regarding revocation or cancellation is that the **offeror may revoke** the offer **at any time up to acceptance** (*Payne v Cave*). However, this is not true if he has granted a separate option agreement to keep the offer open for a period of time, for which consideration has been given (*Routledge v Grant*). **Once accepted, an offer cannot be revoked.**

Revocation may be an **express statement** to that effect. It may also be an **act of the offeror** indicating that the offer is no longer in force (for example sale of the goods to a third party). Whatever form it takes, it is **essential that the revocation is communicated** to the offeree in order to be effective. Revocation of an offer may be communicated **by the offeror or by any third party who is a sufficiently reliable informant** (*Dickinson v Dodds*).

While a postal acceptance of an offer is usually effective from the time of posting, a **postal revocation of an offer does not take effect until received by the offeree** (that is, it has actually been communicated to the offeree). Thus, where a letter of revocation of offer crosses in the post with a letter of acceptance, a legally binding contract will have been formed from the time the letter of acceptance was posted (*Byrne v van Tienhoven*).

Where an **offer is intended to be accepted by conduct** (a unilateral contract), is has been held that the **offer cannot be revoked once the offeree has begun to perform the necessary act** required to accept the contract.

Death

An offer will terminate in the event of death of the offeree. Death of the offeror normally has the same effect, although if the offeree accepts the offer in ignorance of the offeror's death and the offer is not of a personal nature, a valid contract may still result (*Bradbury v Morgan*).

Failure of condition

In the case of a **conditional offer, if the stated condition fails or is not satisfied**, then the offer cannot be accepted (*Financings Ltd v Stimson*).

Marking Guide	Marks
Lapse within a fixed or reasonable time	½
Case or example	1
Rejection	½
Request for further information	1
Counter-offer	1
Case or example	½
Revocation at any time up to acceptance	1
Unless an option granted	1
Express revocation	½
Or via a reliable third party	1
Revocation by post	½
Death	1
Failure of condition	½
	$\underline{\underline{10}}$

4

Tutor's hint. Notice that this question effectively has two requirements: to state what the remedies are and also to explain them. It may not be entirely clear what is meant by 'explain' the remedies. Most likely it is a requirement to:

- Explain when they apply or when they are not applicable
- Explain any significant features
- Set out any drawbacks that might restrict their use.

This a very broad question, and you could be tempted to spend far more than the allotted 18 minutes on it. Don't give in to that temptation: spend a couple of minutes at the beginning planning what you are going to say about each area and jotting down a few case names, try to cover the main issues, and then stop after 18 minutes.

There are two broad categories of remedy for breach of contract:

- Common law remedies, most notably damages, which are available as of right when a breach of contract is established

- Equitable remedies, such as specific performance and injunctions, which are available only at the discretion of the court, usually when damages are not a suitable remedy.

Damages

The main purpose of damages is to restore the injured party who has suffered loss as a result of a breach of contract to the same position that he would have been in had the contract been performed.

There are two issues to be considered when a court is assessing an award for damages:

- Remoteness of damage
- The measure of damages

Under the rule in *Hadley v Baxendale*, the loss suffered must arise naturally from the breach and the loss must have arisen in a manner which was reasonably within the contemplation of the parties, at the time of making the contract, as being a probable result of a breach.

A defendant will also be liable for damages if there are special circumstances from which abnormal consequences of breach (for example large lost profits) could arise, as in *Victoria Laundry (Windsor) v Newman Industries* and *The Heron II*.

The general principle with the measure of damages is to compensate the injured party for the actual financial loss he has incurred, *Thompson Ltd v Robinson (Gunmakers) Ltd*. If the defendant has not actually suffered a loss, as in *Charters v Sullivan*, nominal damages only would be payable.

It is sometimes possible for damages to be recovered for a non-financial loss arising from a breach of contract. Damages can be awarded for mental distress if that has been the main result of the breach, as in *Jarvis v Swan Tours*.

The claimant, however, does have a duty to take any reasonable steps to mitigate his loss. The burden of proof is on the defendant to show that the claimant failed to mitigate when it was reasonable to do so, as in *Payzu Ltd v Saunders*.

Other common law remedies

These include:

- Action for the price, where property in goods has passed to the buyer

- Quantum meruit, as an alternative to damages, whereby the claimant is awarded the value of the contractual work that has been carried out

Equitable remedies

The most important of these in contract law are specific performance, injunctions and rescission.

Specific performance

The court can sometimes order a defendant to carry out his part of the contract, for example in a contract for the sale of land, or some other unique property for which damages would not be an adequate remedy.

There are many restrictions on the use of specific performance: it will not be applied in a contract for personal services or of employment, nor if it would require supervision by the court over a period of time.

Injunction

An injunction is an order of the court requiring a defendant to observe a negative restriction of a contract. For example in *Warner Bros. Pictures v Nelson*, an actress was ordered by the court to observe a contractual term that forbade her from working for another film company for a period of time.

Rescission

Rescinding a contract means that it is cancelled, as if it had never been, and the parties are restored to their original conditions. Rescission is only available as a remedy if certain conditions are met:

- It must be possible for each party to be returned to their original position, for example the goods must not have been sold on to an innocent third party from whom they cannot be recovered

- The right to rescind must happen within a reasonable time

- If the claimant has affirmed the contract by word or action, he cannot then rescind.

Marking Guide	Marks
Distinction between common law and equitable remedies	1
Damages as a common law remedy	1
Remoteness	1
Case or example	1
Measure of damages	1
Case or example	1
Other examples of common law remedies	1
Specific performance	1
Injunctions	1
Rescission	1
	10

5

> **Tutor's hint.** Be careful to follow the breakdown of the available marks and focus on part (a) when structuring your answer. Reference to each of the three tests should be supported by a case example.

(a) **Distinction between the two**

An **employee** is someone employed by an employer under the terms of a formal contract of employment (a '**contract of service**'). An **independent contractor** is a self-employed person who contracts to provide services for another party (a '**contract for services**') but who does not enter into a contract of employment. Sometimes the distinction between the two is very obvious - such as where the employer deducts PAYE and NI from the worker's gross pay - but often it is not. The expressed intentions of the parties will not necessarily be conclusive (*Ferguson v John Dawson & Partners*).

The courts will look at the **reality of the situation** rather than at the expressed intentions of the parties. The courts have generally applied one or more of three tests - of **control, integration** and **economic reality**.

The **control test** asks whether the employer has control over the way in which the employee performs his duties. In the past, this has been quite a good indication of the existence of an employee relationship, but working practices are changing. The control

test is less definitive now, at a time where many employees have a degree of skill which makes the relationship difficult to define.

The **integration test** was developed to overcome this difficulty, and applies where the employee has such a degree of skill that he cannot be 'controlled' in the performance of his duties. Applying this test, the court asks whether he became an **integral part of the employer's business organisation**, or did his work remain outside of and merely accessory to it? Thus in *Cassidy v Ministry of Health*, it was held that a skilled surgeon was the employee of the Ministry of Health since, although the Ministry could not possibly control the doctor in his medical work, it (not the patient) had selected him and integrated him into the organisation.

The **economic reality** or 'multiple' test is a further development and asks whether the employee is **working on his own account**. Here the court will consider all relevant factors including the employer's right to appoint and dismiss, the basis on which payment is made, whether tax and NI is deducted, who provides the tools and equipment, the number of 'employers' (*Ready Mixed Concrete (South East) v Ministry of Pensions and NI*). The courts will also consider whether the employee is entitled to delegate all his obligations (in which case there is no contract of employment), whether he is restricted in his place of work, whether he is obliged to work and whether holidays and hours of work are agreed (*O'Kelly v Trusthouse Forte plc*).

(b) **Reasons for the distinction**

There are several reasons why the distinction between a contract of service and a contract for services is important:-

(i)   Legislation may offer **employment protection** to employees under a contract of service but not to the self-employed. This provides for minimum periods of notice, remedies for unfair dismissal and for redundancy payments;

(ii) The **contribution rates** payable under social security legislation differ as between the employed and the self-employed, and there are also differences in entitlement to benefits and statutory sick pay;

(iii) Deductions must be made by an employer for **income tax** under Schedule E from the salary paid to employees under a contract of service, whereas the self-employed are taxed under Schedule D and are directly responsible to the Inland Revenue for all due deductions;

(iv) The employer may be **vicariously liable for tortious acts** committed by his employees during the course of their employment, but such liability is severely restricted in the case of a contract for services;

(v)   Should the employer go into liquidation or become bankrupt, the employee under a contract of service has **preferential rights as a creditor** for payment of outstanding salary and redundancy payments, up to certain limits;

(vi) The **implied rights and duties** which apply in the employer/employee relationship under a contract of service would not apply to the same degree to a contract for services; and

(vii) An independent sub-contractor may have to **register his business for VAT** purposes and charge VAT on services supplied.

Marking Guide		Marks
(a)	Brief definition of employee	½
	Brief definition of independent contractor	½
	Control test	1
	Example or case	1
	Integration test	1
	Example or case	1
	Economic reality test	1
	Example or case	1
		7
(b)	Reasons for distinction (1 mark each; max. 3)	3
		10

6

> **Tutor's hint**. Take a minute or two to plan how you are going to tackle a question like this. The risk otherwise is that you will confuse the two parts and waste time by repeating points in both.
>
> **Examiner's comments**. Some candidates did not use the guidance of the structure of the question and included points in part (a) which should really have been in part (b). They did not lose marks because of this, but it probably meant that they wasted time.

(a) A promoter is 'one who undertakes to form a company with reference to a given project and to set it going and who takes the necessary steps to accomplish that purpose' (*Twycross v Grant*). The term promoter also includes anyone who makes any **business preparations** for the company. He will normally require the company to agree to reimburse his expenses incurred in the promotion and formation once the company has been incorporated.

A solicitor, accountant or other professional who acts in his or her professional capacity in connection with the formation of a company is not a promoter on that basis. Whether someone is a promoter is a question of fact.

A promoter owes a **general duty of reasonable skill and care**. Where some or all of the shares are to be allotted to persons other than the promoter, he also owes the customary fiduciary duties of an **agent**. It follows that a promoter must not put himself in a position where his own interests conflict with those of the company and he must account for any benefits he receives through acting as promoter. He must make a full and proper disclosure (usually in any listing particulars or prospectus) of any personal advantage to existing and prospective shareholders or to an independent board of directors (*Erlanger v New Sombrero Phosphates Co*). The promoter will be in breach of his fiduciary duty if he profits personally from a contract as promoter but not where he acquires property and then sells it to the promoted company at a profit (which he has disclosed) (*The Lady Forrest (Murchison) Gold Mine Ltd*). In the event of a breach of his fiduciary duty, the company may rescind the contract and recover its money. If rescission is not possible, the promoter must account for his wrongful profit and may also be sued for damages.

The general rule is that a promoter is personally liable on any completed pre-incorporation contract (see (b)) entered into with a third party.

(b) A **pre-incorporation contract** is a contract purported to be made by a company or its agent at a time before the company has received its certificate of incorporation. Since the company does not exist at the time the contract is made, it cannot be held liable in respect of its terms, nor can it ratify it. It may however enter into a new contract (a

'novation') on similar terms after incorporation. Mere recognition of the pre-incorporation contract by performing it or accepting benefits under it is not sufficient to constitute a new contract.

The promoter is liable for damages for **breach of warranty of authority** in any pre-incorporation contract where the promoter can be said to have warranted to the other party that the company (his principal) existed when in fact it did not (*Kelner v Baxter*). Section 36C(1) CA 1985 provides that **the person purporting to act for the company shall be personally liable on the contract subject to any agreement to the contrary.** It was held in *Phonogram Ltd v Lane* that any agreement to the contrary must be an express agreement and cannot be implied. It is irrelevant whether the other party knew that the company did not exist or whether the contract is made in the company's name or in the agent's name.

The promoter might seek to avoid liability by postponing completion of the contract until after incorporation of the company or by providing that his liability shall cease as and when the newly incorporated company enters a new contract on identical terms.

Marking Guide			
		Marks	
(a)	Definition, eg *Twycross v Grant*	2	
	Not solicitors/accountants	1	
	Duty of skill and care	1	
	Duty not to benefit secretly	1	
			5
(b)	Definition/explanation	2	
	Co. not bound	1	
	Promoter personally liable	1	
	Novation possible	1	
			5
			10

7

> **Tutor's hint**. At first sight this looks like a gift of a question, but do make sure that you can write sufficient worthwhile points about each type of company to maximise your mark. If you can only write about two of them well, think carefully about whether to attempt this question, as you will not be able to score a very high mark.
>
> **Examiner's comment**. Generally answers to this question were satisfactory. Some students wasted time by discussing the subject of company formation, not the subject of this question at all. The issue of unlimited liability caused difficulties to some candidates, and there was confusion with the unlimited liability of the partnership or the sole trader. Some candidates were also confused by companies limited by guarantee, relating them to commercial guarantees.

The Companies Act provides that an incorporated company may have either (a) no limit to the members' liability ('an unlimited company') (s 1), (b) the liability of its members limited to the amount unpaid on the shares respectively held by them ('a company limited by shares'), or (c) the members' liability limited to such amount as the members undertake to contribute to the assets in the event of a winding up ('a company limited by guarantee'). The matter of limited liability relates to the liability of the company members and not the company itself. In all cases, the company is a separate legal person with ownership of its assets, debts and other liabilities.

(a)   An **unlimited company** cannot be a public company but must be a **private company**. Such a company's memorandum of association makes no reference to members' liability as there is **no limit to their liability**. In the event of a liquidation, all members can be required to contribute as much as necessary in order to pay the company's debts in full. An unlimited company has the advantages of not being required to file copies of its annual accounts and reports (save in certain cases) and it may purchase its shares from its own members without following any formal processes.

(b) In a **company limited by guarantee,** each shareholder is liable to contribute to the company the amount specified in the **company's memorandum** (which cannot be varied) in the event of the company going into liquidation but not before. Creditors have no direct claim on members since the guarantee is between the member and the company only.

A company limited by guarantee would be particularly appropriate to **non-commercial activities,** such as a trade association or a charity where the aim is to balance annual income and expenditure rather than to generate surpluses to be distributed to shareholders. The members' guarantee is really a form of reserve capital.

(c) In a **company limited by shares,** the fixed amount of each share will be specified in the company's memorandum and that amount fixes the maximum liability of each shareholder which, on being allotted the shares, the shareholder agrees to pay in money or money's worth either in one sum or by instalments. In the event of a winding up, the **members can be required to contribute any part of their stated liability which remains unpaid at that date** but not more. As above, creditors are owed debts by the company and have no claim against the members save in the event of liquidation.

Marking Guide		Marks
(a)	Unlimited company	
	Can only be private	½
	No reference to liability in the Memo	½
	Extent of members' liability	1
	Advantages	<u>1</u>
		3
(b)	Limited by guarantee	
	Extent of members' liability	1
	Guarantee between company and members	1
	Examples	<u>1</u>
		3
(c)	Limited by shares	
	Liability established in Memo	2
	Position on winding up	1
	Creditors have no direct claim against members	<u>1</u>
		<u>4</u>
		<u><u>10</u></u>

8

> **Tutor's hint.** The law relating to dividends is traditionally quite a tricky area, so make sure that you are confident about all aspects of it before choosing a question like this. Note that it is not just asking for the rules relating to payment, but also the effects of contravention of the rules, worth three marks.
>
> **Examiner's comments.** Relatively few candidates attempted this question, and those who did tended not to have a sufficiently precise knowledge. Some candidates did not explain how the profits available for distribution should be determined, while others thought that shareholders had an automatic right to a dividend. Very few candidates could answer part (b).

(a) (i) Dividends are payments made to shareholders out of company profits or other distributable reserves as a return on their investment in the company. The general rule is set out in s 263 CA 1985 which provides that '**dividends may only be paid by a company out of profits available for the purpose**'. Every company has the **implied power** to declare a dividend although an express power is normally contained in the articles of association.

Table A provides that the company in general meeting may declare dividends by **ordinary resolution subject to a maximum amount which is recommended by the directors**. Dividends are usually declared payable on the paid up amount of share capital and can be paid in cash or by other means. Directors may declare such **interim dividends** as they consider justified.

'**Distributable profits**' are defined (s 263(3)) as 'accumulated realised profits, so far as not previously utilised by distribution or capitalisation, less accumulated realised losses, so far as not previously written off in a reduction or reorganisation of capital duly made'. Only profits realised at the balance sheet date shall be included in the profit and loss account and losses which have arisen in respect of the current accounting period or between the balance sheet date and the date that the accounts are signed or which are likely to arise should also be taken into account (Sch 4). '**Accumulated**' means that any losses of previous years must be included in reckoning the current distributable surplus. In order to be treated as '**realised**' a profit or loss must be deemed to be realised in accordance with **generally accepted accounting principles** prevailing when the accounts are prepared. Depreciation must be treated as a realised loss and debited against profit in determining the amount of distributable profit remaining. However, any increased depreciation provision due to a revaluation of an asset may be treated as profit (s 275). If, on a general revaluation of all fixed assets there is a diminution in value, then any related provision need not be treated as a realised loss.

The above mentioned rules apply to all distributions of assets to a company's members except (s 263) the issue of bonus shares, the redemption or purchase of the company's shares out of capital or profits, a reduction of share capital by cancelling liability for unpaid capital or by repaying share capital to members and any distribution of assets on a winding up.

(ii) In addition to the principles mentioned above, in the case of **public companies**, s 264 applies and may decrease (but not increase) the company's distributable profits. Under this section, **a public company can only make a distribution if its net assets, at the time, are equal to or greater than the aggregate of its called up share capital and undistributed reserves** and the amount of any dividend cannot exceed such amount as would leave its net assets at not less than that aggregate amount. Undistributed reserves comprise the share premium account, the capital redemption reserve, the revaluation reserve and any reserve which the company is prohibited from distributing by statute or its own constitution. This means that a public company can only make a distribution from its profits after depreciating fixed assets.

(b) If a dividend is paid in contravention of the rules concerning distribution of profits, the **directors may be liable to make good to the company** the amount unlawfully distributed as a dividend, for example if they knowingly recommend or declare a dividend to be paid out of capital (*Re Exchange Banking Co*, otherwise known as *Flitcroft's case*) or if they make a recommendation or declaration without preparing any accounts and the dividend is in fact paid from capital (*Re Oxford Benefit Building and*

Investment Society 1886). They will also be liable if they make some mistake of law or misinterpretation of the company's constitution which leads them to recommend or declare an unlawful dividend, although relief may be available to directors under s 727 CA where they acted honestly and reasonably. If the directors rely on proper accounts which reveal an apparent distributable profit in declaring a dividend and it later transpires that the accounts were based on unsound assumptions or estimates, the directors will not, in the absence of fraud, be liable (*Re Mercantile Trading Co*).

A member may obtain an injunction to prevent a company paying an unlawful dividend but **members cannot authorise the payment of an unlawful dividend** nor release the directors from their liability to repay an unlawful dividend. Members who receive a dividend knowing or having reasonable grounds to believe that it was unlawfully paid will be liable to repay that dividend (or the unlawful portion of it) to the company (s 277).

Marking Guide

			Marks	
(a)	(i)	Basic rule in s 263	1	
		Ordinary resolution; directors state maximum	1	
		Definition of distributable profits	2	
				4
	(ii)	Plc's net assets position	2	
		Definition of undistributable reserves	1	
				3
(b)		Directors' liability	1	
		Relief available for directors	1	
		Rights of members	1	
				3 / 10

9

Tutor's hint. Read through this kind of question very carefully, at least twice. Notice that you are required to advised three different people, so try to pick out the points of law relating to each of them. Remember to:

- **identify** the issue

- **state** the law

- **apply** the law

- **conclude** in this situation

Examiner's comments. The best answers analysed the situation in detail, set out the legal principles and applied them (as outlined in the Tutor's hint above). However, many candidates started this way but then ran out of steam. As is often the case some candidates treated the question as a general exposition of consideration or contract law generally. Candidates should try to plan their answers sufficiently to avoid making the same point in their answers to different parts of the question.

This question concerns the extent to which performance of existing contractual obligations can constitute valid consideration.

Where there is already a contract between A and B, and B promises an additional reward to A if he (A) will perform his existing duties, there is no consideration from A to make that promise binding. **A assumes no extra obligation and B obtains no extra rights or benefits.** This was the general principle established by *Stilk v Myrick*. In this case, two members of a crew deserted and the master of the ship promised the remaining crew-members a share of the deserters' wages if they completed the voyage. It was held that the

remaining crew-members had in fact provided no additional consideration but had only performed what they were already contractually bound to perform and so the promise was not binding.

However, if a claimant does more than perform an existing contractual duty, this may amount to consideration (*Hartley v Ponsonby*). In this case, in contrast to *Stilk v Myrick*, the large number of desertions made the voyage exceptionally hazardous, and this had the effect of discharging the original contract. The claimant had therefore been left free to enter into a new contract, under which his promise to complete the voyage formed consideration for the promise to pay an additional £40.

More recently, however, in *Williams v Roffey Bros & Nicholls (Contractors) Ltd*, the court took a different approach. In this case, the claimants agreed to do carpentry work for the defendants, who were engaged as contractors to refurbish a block of flats, at a fixed price of £20,000. The work ran late and so the defendants, concerned that the job might not be finished on time and that they would in that event have to pay money under a penalty clause in the main contract, agreed to pay the claimants an extra £10,300 to ensure the work was completed on time. They later refused to pay the extra amount. It was held that the fact that there was no apparent consideration for the promise to pay the extra was not held to be important, since, in the court's view, **both parties derived benefit from the promise.** The defendant avoided the onerous position of having to engage extra workers and also avoided liability under the penalty clause in the main contract. It was considered material that the defendants' promise had not been extracted by duress or fraud. The promise of extra payment was therefore binding.

Applying the law to the present facts, it would appear that Chris has exerted undue pressure on Alex by refusing to perform his part of the contract under the agreed terms save in return for an increased payment. This will be a question of fact, but if, as appears likely, there is found to have been duress, *Williams v Roffey Bros* would be distinguished (where there was no undue influence or duress) and the rule in *Stilk v Myrick* would be applied. The fact that Alex avoided the penalty clause and benefited from Chris's renewed performance would, therefore, not be relevant. Since Chris provided no additional consideration, but simply performed his original obligations, he is not entitled to the extra money. The fact that he finishes early is not relevant since it was not requested by Alex and he cannot legally charge more for early performance.

Dick too is unable to enforce the promise of additional money since he provided no additional consideration (*Stilk v Myrick*). Again, the fact that he performed before the deadline, not at the request of Alex, is irrelevant.

Following *Hartley v Ponsonby*, however, Eric will be able to enforce the promise of the additional payment, since he provided additional consideration by agreeing to Alex's request to bring forward the date for performance to 16 May, which obligation he duly performed.

	Marks
Marking Guide	
Basic rule of performance of existing or extra obligations	2
Cases or examples	3
Recent developments eg *Williams v Roffey Bros.*	3
Chris	
Unable to sue for extra	1
No additional consideration	1
Applied duress	2
Irrelevant that A avoided penalty	2
Dick	
No additional consideration	1
Unable to sue for extra	1
Eric	
Has provided additional consideration	1
At Alex's request	1
Can sue for additional money	2
	20

10

> **Tutor's hint**. You need to look at the rights and duties of partners. Remember to conclude on the position of all three partners in this situation.
>
> * identify the **issues** (liability in partnership law)
> * **state** the law (partners' duties to each other and liability for each other's acts)
> * **apply** the law (to the transactions described)
> * **conclude** (advise Rob, Sam and Tom)

Rob, Sam and Tom have set up in partnership together. They have a partnership agreement and debts in the name of the partnership amounting to over £25,000.

Partners' relationships with each other

A partner has several rights in connection with his partnership.

* To be involved in **decisions** which affect the business
* To **examine the accounts**
* To insist on **openness and honesty** from fellow partners
* To **veto the introduction** of a new partner

He also has a number of duties or responsibilities.

* Utmost **good faith** to fellow partners
* **Divulge** relevant facts to fellow partners
* **Share profits** made by the partnership
* **Share losses** made by the partnership

These rights and responsibilities can be varied by the partnership agreement. Rob, Sam and Tom have a partnership agreement. It states that Rob's liability will be limited to £75,000. It also states that the purpose of the partnership is to sell petrol.

In the given scenario then, Sam and Rob appear to have failed in their duties to each other and to Rob.

Sam has taken a loan from the partnership's bank account and used it to go on a cruise. This would appear to breach his duty of utmost good faith to Rob and Tom. They may choose as a result of this action, to expel him from the partnership, if the agreement gives them the

right to do so. They may feel that trust has degenerated to the degree that they wish to dissolve the partnership.

Tom has entered into a contract which is outside of the partnership agreement. This would also appear to breach his duty of good faith and also the right of Sam and Rob to be involved in partnership decisions.

Partners' relationships with third parties

Each partner is the agent of the firm and when a third party contracts with a partner, he contracts with all the partners.

There is are exceptions to this third party principle. One is that the partners are bound to an act which a partner has carried out in the normal course of business, unless

- The partner acting had no authority to do so, **and**
- The third party was aware that the partner did not have authority to do so.

Another exception is that if where one partner pledges the credit of the firm for a purpose apparently not connected with the firm's business, the firm is not bound unless the partner is specifically authorised to undertake that transaction.

However, as a general rule, the firm (that is, all the individual partners) is liable to third parties for actions of a partner where he has apparent or actual authority.

The bank loan

Sam has taken money from the firm's bank account to use for a personal holiday. However, as a partner, and in the absence of any specific mention to the contrary in the agreement, he has authority to withdraw money from the bank account.

His action has therefore incurred a debt to a third party that is owed by all three partners, not just himself, and if he cannot repay the money to the bank, the bank is entitled to sue the other partners for the balance.

The debt for the cars

Tom has entered into a contract to buy cars in the name of the partnership. The partnership act specifies that the partnership should only sell petrol, so he does not have authority to undertake this contract.

However, the third party is not privy to the partnership so **is not aware that the contract is beyond the scope of the partnership**. As a partner, Tom has apparent authority to undertake the contract on behalf of the other partners.

However, as the trade of the partners is to sell petrol, it is possible that this contract might fall into the other exception to the authority rule, because the sale of cars is not connected to their business. It is a moot point whether selling cars is connected to selling petrol and a court might well rule that the two were connected, in which case, all three partners would be liable for this debt.

The debt for the petrol

Purchasing petrol is obviously a normal part of business for this partnership. Whoever made the contract would have had authority to do so and their act has bound the other partners to the contract. They are all liable for the petrol bill.

The scenario does not state the level of the petrol bill. However, if the debt mounts to higher than £75,000 each, Rob would still be liable for the petrol above that figure, because the partnership agreement does not bind third parties.

Rob

Rob's right to expect the utmost good faith and disclosure from his fellow partners has been breached. However, their actions have bound him and his is likely to be liable for all three debts.

His agreement with Sam and Tom that he will only be liable for debts up to £75,000 might form a contract under which he could sue them for any sums over £75,000 he is liable to third parties for.

He has the right to **dissolve the partnership** or seek the **expulsion** of one of the partners and given the actions of Sam in particular, may want to consider those rights carefully.

Sam

Sam has breached his duty of good faith to Tom and Rob. He is also liable for the debt and will continue to be even if they expel him from the partnership as he will be liable for debts incurred while he was a partner. He may also be liable to Rob for any debts Rob personally incurs on behalf of the partnership over £75,000.

Tom

Tom has overreached his actual authority per the partnership agreement and probably bound the firm to the contract. He should consider his duty to involve his fellow partners in decision making which goes beyond the partnership agreement in the future. He too may be liable to Rob for any debts Rob personally incurs on behalf of the partnership over £75,000.

Marking guide. The issues to be dealt with, for which specific marks are available are the:

• Relations of partners with each other	4
• Relations of parties with outsiders	4
• Bank loan	4
• Debt for the used cars	4
• Debt for the petrol	4
	20

Advice must be given to:

- Rob
- Sam
- Tom

11

Tutor's hint. There is more to this question than meets the eye. At first sight part (a) concerns the improper use of directors' powers, which is certainly the main issue, but do not forget the issues of authority to allot and pre-emption rights, as these will attract a fair number of marks too. Don't overlook part (b). It is a relatively easy four marks.

(a)   The main issue here is the impact of the irregular use of directors' powers, specifically in relation to the allotment of shares. There are also the issues of authority to allot and pre-emption rights.

Use of directors' powers

It was established in *Howard Smith v Ampol Petroleum Ltd* that where the directors of a company irregularly use their powers to allot shares, **the votes attached to the new shares may not be used in reaching a decision in general meeting to sanction the allotment**. It was held that 'It must be unconstitutional for directors to use their fiduciary powers over the shares in the company purely for the purpose of destroying

an existing majority or creating a new majority which did not previously exist'. In such a situation, any shareholder may apply to the court to declare the transaction void, but the court will normally remit the issue to the members in general meeting.

However, in the case of Driver Ltd, the facts are slightly different. Ben, the holder of the newly-allotted shares, has not voted on the resolution to ratify the allotment. The facts are similar to *Bamford v Bamford*, where an ordinary resolution was passed to ratify an allotment that was done to thwart a take-over bid. In that case it was held that the ratification was valid and the allotment was good. Although there had been a breach of fiduciary duty by the directors, their act had been validated by the ordinary resolution passed in general meeting.

The *Bamford* case can be distinguished from the *Howard Smith* case (in which the allotment was void) because in the latter the original majority before the issue of the new shares would not have approved the allotment, whereas in Bamford the decision was sanctioned by a vote excluding the new shareholders.

The same principle would be followed in the case of Driver Ltd. Since Ben has not voted on the ratification resolution, the ordinary resolution ratifying the allotment has been validly passed. Alex will be unsuccessful in her claim alleging breach of fiduciary duty.

Authority to allot

With regard to the issue of authority to allot, we are not told by the question what arrangements are in place at Driver Ltd for the giving of authority to the directors to allot shares.

CA 85 s 80 says that private companies may grant authority to allot either by ordinary resolution or by the provisions of the articles. Authority to allot can be given:

- indefinitely; or
- for fixed periods greater than five years.

The company must specify the maximum number of shares that may be allotted. It is likely that these provisions have been satisfied, and we can assume that the directors have the authority to allot.

However if they do not the allotment will still be valid although the directors are liable to a fine. Alex cannot be successful in her claim merely because the directors did not have the authority to allot.

Pre-emption rights

S 89 CA85 says that where a company intends to allot equity securities wholly for cash, the **new shares must be offered to the existing shareholders** in proportion to their existing shareholdings.

The offer must be made in writing and allow the existing shareholders a period of at least 21 days to accept.

Private companies are able by the terms of their Memorandum or Articles to exclude pre-emption rights, and any company may pass a special resolution to disapply pre-emption rights. It is not clear whether either of these has happened in the case of Driver Ltd.

If the shares have been issued in breach of these rules, the members to whom the shares should have been offered may claim compensation within two years from those who are in default, ie the directors. The allotment however will still be valid, especially, as in the case of Driver Ltd, when it has been ratified by the members in general meeting, excluding the votes attached to the new shares. The fact that the pre-

emption rights may not have been observed will not enable Alex to be successful in her claim.

(b) Had Ben been allotted the shares in return for a promise to supply a service, the issue of **consideration for shares** would become relevant. The basic rule for the allotment of shares is that they **cannot be issued at a discount**. The law is concerned to ensure that issue at a discount does not occur indirectly, for example with non-cash consideration.

Such consideration would have been valid, as it is possible for private companies such as Driver Ltd to receive payment for shares either in money or 'money's worth'. It is not a problem if Ben's consideration appears inadequate in comparison to the value of the shares, as the courts tend not to overrule directors in their valuation of an asset or service (*Re Wragg*) unless the over-valuation is blatant and unjustified.

Had the issue been made for a consideration of a promise to perform a service, the issue of pre-emption rights would become less relevant. This is because s 89 CA85 setting out the law relating to pre-emption rights says that they only apply for the issue of equity securities for cash. If the consideration is not cash, then pre-emption rights can be ignored. The members would not then be in a position to claim compensation.

	Marking Guide	Marks
(a)	Cannot use new votes to approve issue	1
	Howard Smith case or example	1
	Bamford v Bamford or similar example	2
	Distinguish *Howard Smith* and *Bamford*	1
	Application to Driver Ltd	1
	Alex will not succeed	1
	Authority to allot: how given	2
	If not given, allotment still valid	1
	Will not affect Alex's case	1
	Pre-emption rights: rule in S89 CA85	1
	Can be excluded or disapplied	1
	If breached, members claim compensation	1
	Allotment still valid	1
	Alex's claim not affected	1
		16
(b)	Issue of consideration becomes relevant	1
	Private co: consideration can be money's worth	1
	Non cash consid. affects pre-emption rights	2
		4
		20

12

> **Tutor's hint**. It is fair to assume that the marks are spread evenly on this question and split your time accordingly. However, you may want to make some points which are relevant to each part of the question in a general introduction, as we have done. Remember for each of the situations the best approach is to identify the issue, state the law, apply the law and then conclude by advising Frank.

The fact that a company has limited legal liability means that the shareholders of the company cannot be required to contribute more than the amount outstanding (if any) on their shares.

A company is distinct as a separate legal person from its owners or members and hence a 'veil of incorporation' exists between them. The distinction between a company and its members was clearly set out in *Salomon v Salomon and Co Ltd*.

In this landmark case, the court held that Salomon, although he owned 20,001 out of 20,007 shares in Salomon & Co Ltd, was under no personal liability to the failed company or to its creditors and that debentures issued to him by the company created a valid security over the company's assets which ranked before the claims of unsecured creditors of the company.

Since then the distinction has been developed in both case law and statute. In limited circumstances the metaphorical veil will be lifted by statute or common law in order to avoid the inequitable consequences of adhering strictly to the rule of law in Salomon's case.

(a) **George Ltd**

Frank has entered into a contract with George Ltd and not George as he thought. As a separate legal entity, George Ltd can sue and be used on contracts entered into by it and so it is the company that is liable not the individual shareholders. On the face of it, therefore, **Frank has no right against George and stands as an unsecured creditor in the insolvent liquidation of George Ltd** (which makes it unlikely that he will recover any payment for the goods delivered).

However, if it appears on the winding up of George Ltd that the business was conducted with intent to **defraud creditors**, the court may decide that the directors or others who were knowingly party to the fraud should be personally responsible for the debts and other liabilities of the company: s 213 IA 1986.

Alternatively, if the court considers for other reasons that George used the company in order to rely on its separate legal liability to evade payment to Frank for the goods under the contract, the court may hold him **personally liable** on the contract. Much will depend on the circumstances, George's conduct, the timing of events and the reasons for the insolvent liquidation.

(b) **Hal**

Hal would argue that it is his company and not him personally who is in competition with Frank and, following Salomon, that Hal therefore has no liability to Frank since he, personally, is not in breach of the contract between them.

In *Gilford Motor Co Ltd v Horne*, the defendant was contractually bound not to solicit his employer's customers after leaving his service. He formed and managed a new company which did so in an attempt to evade the covenant. It was held that the company had been formed as a 'mere cloak or sham' and an injunction was granted ordering the defendant to observe the covenant.

The facts are so similar here that it appears likely that Frank would obtain an injunction requiring Hal and Hal's company to observe the restraint on his trade.

(c) **Ian**

In this case, Ian has deliberately transferred the land to his own company in order to avoid his contractual obligations under the contract of sale with Frank.

In *Jones v Lipman* a vendor of land purchased a company into which he transferred land that he was due to sell, in order to avoid an order for specific performance. The court held the acquisition of the company and the transfer of land to it to be a sham for the evasion of the contract and specific performance was ordered against the company.

The facts are similar here. Ian has transferred the land to his company which is not a party to the original contract for sale in an attempt to avoid liability for an order for specific performance against him. Again the corporate veil would be lifted and an order for specific performance would be given against Ian and his company in Frank's favour.

(d) **Ken**

Ken owns both Jug Ltd and Keg Ltd and has transferred assets from Jug Ltd to Keg Ltd before the liquidation of Jug Ltd. Applying the rule in Salomon's case, Ken cannot be held liable for the debts of either company save to the extent of any unpaid amounts on his shares.

However, the transfer was almost certainly an abuse of the corporate form and an attempt to evade liability and so it is likely that the veil would be lifted and Frank would be able to recover against the assets of Keg Ltd. The courts will uphold transactions between group companies where they are in the ordinary course of business but not in cases of asset stripping or other fraudulent, illegal or improper purpose as appears to be the case here.

Additionally, where Ken can be shown to be guilty of **fraudulent or wrongful trading**, he can be held personally liable to the creditors of Jug Ltd on its insolvent liquidation. Fraudulent trading is where a person has carried on a business with the intent to defraud creditors or for any fraudulent purpose (and this looks likely to apply in this case). Wrongful trading is where a director knows or should have known that there was no reasonable prospect of the company avoiding insolvent liquidation.

In either case, a director may be **disqualified** from acting as a director (or other person concerned with the promotion, formation or management of a company) for 10 years (in the case of wrongful trading) or 15 years (in the case of fraudulent trading). A court must disqualify a person where it considers that his conduct as a director of a company which has become insolvent makes him unfit to be concerned in the management of a company under s 6 CDDA 1986.

Marking Guide	
	Marks
General discussion of separate personality	4
George Ltd – Summary of situation	2
– Defrauding creditors	1
– Personal liability	1
Hal – Summary of situation	2
– Evasion of responsibilities/sham	1
– Injunction likely	1
Ian – Summary of situation	2
– Jones v Lipman	1
– Specific performance	1
Ken – Summary	1
– Evasion of liability	1
– Possibility of wrongful/fraudulent trading	1
– Disqualification	1
	20

Scottish variant appendix

This index gives you some important guidance on which questions in the body of this kit are relevant for the Scottish stream and any minor points of difference which you should note. Questions where no comment has been added can be answered without amendment in the Scottish stream.

		Marks	Time allocation Mins	Page number Question	Answer
PART A: ENGLISH LEGAL SYSTEM					
1	County court (6/98)	10	18	3	35
This question is not suitable for Scottish candidates. You should not attempt this question.					
2	Civil courts and tracks (12/02)	10	18	3	36
This question is not suitable for Scottish candidates. You should not attempt this question.					
3	Arbitration	10	18	3	38
4	*Preparation question: Sources of law*	-	-	3	39
In your answer to this question you should also consider the source of 'institutional writings'.					
5	Binding precedent (6/00)	10	18	3	41
In part (a) of this question, your answer should consider the hierarchy of the Scottish courts, not the English ones. Refer back to Chapter 2 in your supplement to be sure of these.					
6	Interpretation and human rights (12/01)	10	18	3	43
7	Delegated legislation (Pilot paper)	10	18	3	45
8	EC law (6/02)	10	18	4	47
9	EU institutions	10	18	4	49
PART B: LAW OF CONTRACT					
10	Offers and invitations to treat (6/02)	10	18	5	50
11	Adam (Pilot paper)	20	36	5	51
In part (d) remember that in Scottish law a simple promise to keep an offer open would be binding.					
12	Ann's Art (12/01)	20	36	5	53
13	Adam and Ben (12/00)	20	36	6	55
You should ignore the references to consideration (not a Scottish concept) made in the answer to this question.					
14	*Preparation question: Consideration*	-	-	6	57
This question is not suitable for Scottish candidates. You should not attempt this question.					
15	Forms of consideration (12/02)	10	18	6	59
This question is not suitable for Scottish candidates. You should not attempt this question.					
16	Axel (6/99)	20	36	6	60
This question is not suitable for Scottish candidates. You should not attempt this question.					
17	Contract issues (12/99)	20	36	7	62
This question is not suitable for Scottish candidates. You should not attempt this question.					
18	Express and implied (12/02)	10	18	7	64

BPP
PROFESSIONAL EDUCATION

Scottish variant appendix

		Marks	Time allocation Mins	Page number Question	Answer
19	Terms of a contract (Pilot paper)	10	18	7	66
	This question is not suitable for Scottish candidates. You should not attempt this question.				
20	Exclusion clauses (6/02)	10	18	8	67
21	Seller Ltd and Transport Ltd	20	36	8	69
	Bear in mind that the section numbers quoted in this answer are the English section numbers and the relevant sections in Scotland are different although the law is very similar.				
22	*Preparation question: Laptop Ltd*	-	-	8	71
	Bear in mind that the section numbers quoted in this answer are the English section numbers and the relevant sections in Scotland are different although the law is very similar.				
23	Mina	20	36	9	74
24	Express and implied terms	20	36	9	76
25	Performance	20	36	10	79
26	Termination of contracts (12/01)	10	18	10	80
27	Breach (12/99)	10	18	10	82
28	Damages (Pilot paper)	10	18	10	83
29	Emma and Sidney	20	36	10	84
	Remember that some Scottish terminology is different from the English terminology for remedies. So for 'specific performance' in this answer, read 'specific implement'.				

PART C: AGENCY AND BUSINESS ASSOCIATIONS

		Marks	Mins	Question	Answer
30	Rights of an agent	10	18	12	86
31	Types of authority (12/01)	10	18	12	86
32	Frederick and George	20	36	12	88
33	*Preparation question: Personality and partnerships*	-	-	12	91
34	Fran, Gail, Hannah and Ian (12/01)	20	36	12	94
35	Unlimited and limited partnerships	10	18	13	96
36	Clare, Dan and Eve (6/02)	20	36	13	98
37	Termination of partnerships (12/02)	10	18	13	100

PART D: COMPANY FORMATION AND CONSTITUTION

		Marks	Mins	Question	Answer
38	Company formation (Pilot paper)	10	18	14	101
39	Tom's company	20	36	14	102
40	Imran and Jane (6/02)	20	36	14	105
41	Ike, Jan and Kit (12/99)	20	36	14	107
42	Business terms (12/01)	10	18	15	110
43	*Preparation question: Incorporation and promoters*	-	-	15	111

		Marks	Time allocation Mins	Page number Question	Answer
83	Compulsory winding up	10	18	27	178
	This answer refers to the Official Receiver. In Scotland this position is known as the interim liquidator				
84	Explain winding up (6/02)	10	18	27	179
	This answer refers to the Official Receiver. In Scotland this position is known as the interim liquidator				
85	Ken and Doris	20	36	27	181
86	Fabulous Foods	20	36	28	183

PART G: LAW OF EMPLOYMENT

87	Constructive dismissal and disability discrimination (12/01)	10	18	29	185
88	*Preparation question: The employment contract*	-	-	29	187
89	Common law duties (6/02)	10	18	29	189
90	Carol	20	36	29	190
91	Redundancy and constructive dismissal (12/99)	10	18	30	192
92	Employees and restraint of trade	20	36	30	193
93	Rights at work	20	36	30	195
94	Grace and Hilda	20	36	30	196

MOCK EXAM 1

1	Arbitration and tribunals	10	18	201	210
2	Unfair contract terms	10	18	201	211
3	Intention to create legal relations (Pilot paper)	10	18	201	213
4	Incorporation	10	18	201	215
5	Agents' duties	10	18	201	216
6	Written and elective resolutions (12/02)	10	18	201	218
7	Financial assistance	10	18	201	219
8	Insider dealing	10	18	201	220
9	Aerial Ltd (6/02)	20	36	202	223
10	Fawn Ltd (12/02)	20	36	202	225
11	Artworks Ltd	20	36	202	228
12	Exe plc	20	36	203	230

Bear in mind that the section numbers in the answer to question 2 would not be relevant in Scotland.

		Marks	Time allocation Mins	Page number Question	Answer

MOCK EXAM 2

		Marks	Mins	Question	Answer
1	Human Rights Act 1998	10	18	235	244
2	Privity of contract (12/01)	10	18	235	245
3	End of offer	10	18	235	247
4	Remedies for breach (12/02)	10	18	235	248
5	Contract and contracts for services (Pilot paper)	10	18	235	250
6	Promoters and pre-incorporation contracts (12/02)	10	18	235	252
7	Types of company (6/02)	10	18	235	253
8	Dividend payments (6/02)	10	18	235	254
9	Alex and Ball Ltd (12/02)	20	36	236	256
10	Rob, Sam and Tom (Pilot paper)	20	36	236	258
11	Driver Ltd	20	36	236	260
12	Frank's transactions	20	36	237	262

You should disregard question 9 in this exam, which would not be examinable in the Scottish variant.

You should note in answer 4 that some of the terminology used is not relevant in Scots law. For example for 'specific performance' in this answer read 'specific implement'.

MOCK EXAM 3 – JUNE 2004

Download from the ACCA's website: www.accaglobal.com/students

MOCK EXAM 4 – DECEMBER 2004

Download from the ACCA's website: www.accaglobal.com/students

The rest of this appendix contains five past exam questions from the Scottish variant for you to practise on areas of the syllabus that diverge from English law to a greater extent.

SCOTTISH VARIANT QUESTIONS

		Marks	Mins	Question	Answer
1	Scottish courts (6/01)	10	18	273	274
2	Terms of a contract (6/01)	10	18	273	275
3	Gratuitous promises (12/02)	10	18	273	276
4	Civil jurisdiction (12/02)	10	18	273	277
5	Angus (12/02)	20	36	273	279

Please review all the Scottish variant exams at www.accaglobal.com/students.

BPP
PROFESSIONAL EDUCATION

QUESTIONS

1 SCOTTISH COURTS (6/01)   *18 mins*

Explain the importance of the hierarchical structure of the courts in the Scottish legal system in relation to the operation of the doctrine of binding precedent.   **(10 marks)**

2 TERMS OF A CONTRACT (6/01)   *18 mins*

Distinguish between material and non-material terms of a contract, explaining their relative significance in a breach of contract.   **(10 marks)**

3 GRATUITOUS PROMISES (12/02)   *18 mins*

Explain the extent to which gratuitous promises are legally enforceable in Scottish law.

(10 marks)

4 CIVIL JURISDICTION (12/02)   *18 mins*

Describe the main civil courts in the Scottish legal system, outlining the jurisdiction of each.   **(10 marks)**

5 ANGUS (12/02)   *36 mins*

Angus runs a business selling potatoes. He sent a telex to a Dutch company, offering to sell them a quantity of potatoes for a fixed price, on condition that the offer was accepted by 6pm the following day. The next morning the Dutch company sent a telex accepting the offer, but seeking to introduce certain conditions. Angus telephoned immediately, rejecting these conditions. The Dutch company sent another telex in the afternoon, still within the original time limit, purporting to accept the original offer. Angus has changed his mind and does not wish to sell the potatoes.

Angus wrote to Bob, the owner of a local fish and chip shop, offering to sell him a quantity of potatoes at a fixed price. This letter was written three months ago, but Bob is now claiming that he accepts the offer. Angus is reluctant to sell, claiming that his costs have risen.

Angus has also sent a list of his prices to various wholesalers, one of whom, Charles, has ordered a vast quantity of potatoes. Angus has supply problems which make it difficult for him to meet his order, and has told Charles he will not deliver the potatoes.

Angus is now being sued by the Dutch company, by Bob, and by Charles for breach of contract.

Required

Advise him of the likely outcome of these three cases.   **(20 marks)**

ANSWERS

1   SCOTTISH COURTS

> **Tutor's hint**. The article written by the inspector on the difference between Scottish and English law in January 2003 also heavily covered the area of the courts in Scotland, which are different in structure from the English courts. Again, had you read the article, you probably would have found this question quite straightforward, as an important element of the operation of the doctrine of precedent is the status of courts within the system. Remember to provide a full answer to the question by defining the terms within the question, as well as explaining the court structure and its importance. This topic was also examined in the Scots variant in June 2004.

Doctrine of binding precedent

A **precedent** is a previous court decision which another court is bound to follow by deciding a subsequent case in the same way. The doctrine of binding precedent states that in any later case to which that principle is relevant the same principle should (subject to certain exceptions) be applied. This doctrine of consistency, following precedent, is expressed in the maxim **stare decisis** which means 'to stand by a decision'.

There are certain conditions to be met in order for a precedent to be binding on a judge, including the fact that the precedent has to be a point of law (known as *ratio decidendi*, as opposed to *obiter dicta* (literally, 'other words'), not of fact and the facts of the case must be materially the same.

Another important element is that only precedents made in particular courts are binding and only then on certain other courts.

Lower courts

Lower courts **do not create precedents** themselves, although they **are bound** by the precedents of most of the higher courts.

In the Scottish system, the lower courts consist of:

- The Sheriff Court (in both civil and criminal cases), and

- The District Court (in criminal cases)

Precedent tends not to be applied as much in the criminal courts as in civil cases.

Higher courts

Decisions of most of the higher courts bind the lower courts (listed above). In addition, there is an order of superiority within the higher courts, so that courts lower in the order are bound by courts above them.

In the Scottish system, the higher courts, in order of superiority (beginning with the most inferior) are:

- The Court of Session (divided into two houses, the Inner House and the Outer House)

- The House of Lords

- The European Court of Justice

Decisions of the **Outer House of the Court of Session do not create binding precedents**. However, the **Outer House** is **bound** by **decisions of the Inner House** and the superior courts. The Inner House is bound by its own decisions, unless 7 judges in the Inner House sit together to overturn a previous decision.

Decisions of the House of Lords are not all binding precedents on Scottish courts. Decisions of the House of Lords in criminal matters are not binding in Scotland. Precedents are restricted to civil matters. However, even then, only decisions of the House of Lords on matters appealed from the Court of Session will apply in Scotland. Decisions of the House of Lords in English cases will not be binding precedents in Scotland, unless they concern statutes that are applicable in both England and Scotland.

On questions of European law, decisions of the European Court of Justice are binding in Scotland, as they are binding throughout the UK.

2 TERMS OF A CONTRACT

> **Tutor's hint**. This question was also examined in December 2003. It is an important area in the syllabus and you should expect questions on this topic regularly. It is also a fairly straightforward area of your syllabus, so you should not find it too difficult to obtain marks. Remember to define the terms used in the question and also not to forget to carry out the second part of the question 'explain... their relative significance in a breach of contract.'

Terms of a contract

When persons are contracting with each other, they may make a number of representations to each other about their intentions and the particular details of the contract. Terms are statements that become incorporated and therefore form part of the contract.

Parties to a contract are required to give full and complete performance according to the particulars of the contract, so it is important to be clear as to what constitutes the terms of a contract, as if they are not precisely fulfilled, the contract may be in breach and the offender be required to pay damages.

The precise nature of the remedy for breach of contract will depend on the nature of the promise broken, and whether it is central or incidental to the contract. Thus terms of a contract are classified as being material or non-material to that contract. This will not usually be set out in the contract, and, while it is sometimes clear, this can often be a matter for the courts to determine when an action for breach is taken.

Material terms

A material term is one which goes to the heart of the contract, that is, it is central to the contract, whereupon breach renders the contract completely unmet. For example, delivery of apples instead of oranges would be material. It relates to the seriousness or importance of the contractual item in question.

If a material term is breached, the injured party will have more options in terms of remedies available to him. He may rescind the contract entirely, and therefore not perform his own obligations under it and claim for damages.

Non-material terms

Non-material terms are terms of less significance or importance to the contract, which could be considered to be incidental. Continuing the example of the contract for oranges above, it might be incidental to a contract for oranges that they come from Florida rather than Spain.

Breaches of terms with less significance to the contract do not entitle the injured party to rescind the contract, but instead, only claim damages.

As can be seen from the examples given, the determination of whether a term is material to a contract or not is a matter of judgement, often undertaken by the courts. A purchaser of

oranges might consider where they come from a material term, particularly say, if there had been a blight or a drought in a particular orange growing region.

A Scottish case shows this issue of the courts determining whether a term is material or not. It is *Wade v Waldon 1909*, where a comedian was in breach of a clause in his contract with the theatre in which he was to perform stating that he was to provide publicity materials to the theatre. The theatre rescinded the contract, claiming that the breach was material. However, the courts disagreed and awarded damages to the comedian.

In this situation, the part of the contract where the comedian was given opportunity to perform at the theatre was considered to be a material term, so the theatre committed a serious breach of contract by not performing this element of the contract, whereas the comedian's breach was not so serious and the contract should have continued.

3 GRATUITOUS PROMISES

> **Tutor's hint**. The Scottish variant inspector wrote an article on the difference between the English and Scottish variants for this paper in January 2003 which you should make sure you have read. The article concentrated heavily on this area of Scottish law, so if you have read it, you should find it fairly straightforward to produce a good answer to this question. This question was also asked in December 2001, and is very similar in wording to a question asked in December 2004.

Gratuitous promise

A gratuitous promise, sometimes known as a unilateral obligation, is where one party undertakes to another that it will perform a service or provide something to that other party receiving nothing in return from the other party.

An example of such an arrangement is where a person promises to donate to a charity. They give money to the charity, but they receive no direct benefit from the charity in return. Other examples include gifts, or a promise to keep an offer to contract open for a period of time. In all these cases, a person is giving a benefit to another party that it is not reciprocated.

Legally binding?

In some legal systems, notably across the border in England, such promises are rarely binding. English law has a complex doctrine of consideration (the exchange of value to support a contract), which renders unilateral promises not legally binding.

However, in contrast, Scottish law recognises circumstances in which such gratuitous promises are legally binding. Precedent is found in *A & G Paterson v Highland Railway Co 1927* where it was decided that a promise to keep an offer to sell property at a certain price open for a certain time was binding, even though nothing was offered in return for the offer being kept open.

This has some implications for people making such promises. Firstly, such a promise, once made, is binding on the person making the promise, regardless of whether the person to whom the promise is made accepts the offer.

In writing

However, the Requirements of Writing (Scotland) Act 1995 does provide that in order to so be binding, such a gratuitous promise is required to be in writing and signed by the promisor in order to be validly constituted.

Exceptions

There are two key exceptions to the rule that gratuitous promises have to be in writing.

(i) **Course of business**. A gratuitous promise made in the course of business does not have to be written down and signed.

(ii) **Significant actings**. An unwritten gratuitous promise may become binding if the promisee has acted on the strength of the promise and 'significant actings' follow. This covers a situation where a person (promisor) makes a promise, and the recipient of the promise (promisee) acts upon it, with the acquiescence of the promisor, and the acts were so material to the promisee that he would be prejudiced if the promisor withdrew the promise.

4   CIVIL JURISDICTION

The diagram below sets out the Scottish civil law system.

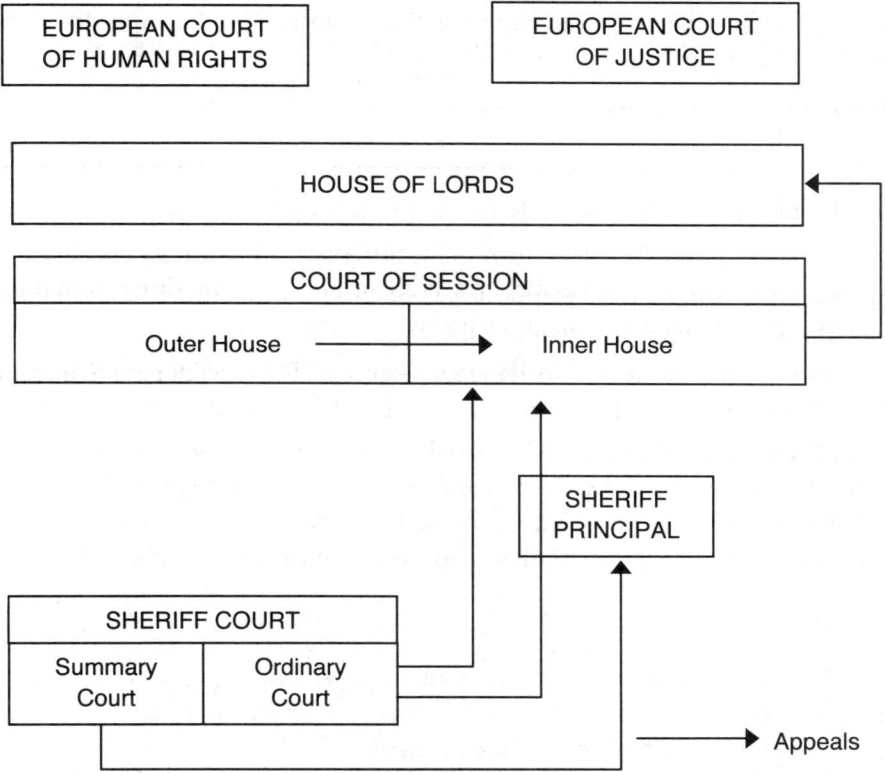

Sheriff Court

The majority of civil cases in Scotland commence in the Sheriff Court. Scotland is divided into six sheriffdoms. Each sheriffdom is divided into Sheriff Court Districts, each of which has a Sheriff Court. Each Sheriff Court will have one or more sheriffs attached to it who act as judges in the Sheriff Court. The senior judge in the Sheriffdom is known as the Sheriff Principal.

Jurisdiction

The jurisdiction of the Sheriff Court is determined by **subject matter** and **geography** relating to the **defender** in the case.

In civil matters, the Sheriff Court will have jurisdiction over the defender where:

- The defender is **resident** within the geographical jurisdiction of the court
- The action is against the defender's business, which has a **place of business** within the geographical jurisdiction of the court
- The action is concerned with a **contract to be performed** within the geographical jurisdiction of the court

The Sheriff Court has a **wide jurisdiction over subject matter**. This includes actions relating to debt, family life, **contract** and property.

Certain matters **can only be brought in a Sheriff Court**. These are matters where the case does not exceed **£1,500 in value**. Some matters may not be dealt with in the Sheriff Court, for example, petitions for the winding up of a company with a share capital of more than £120,000.

There are two main types of procedure for civil matters in the Sheriff Court:

- **Summary cause** procedure, dealing with claims up to £1,500 (a sub-division of which is the small claim for amounts less than £750)
- **Ordinary cause** procedure

Appeals

For **small claims**, appeal may be made to the **Sheriff Principal only**. There is no further appeal.

Under the **summary procedure**, an appeal may be made to the **Sheriff Principal** on a point of law. The Sheriff Principal will require that the Sheriff prepares a Stated Case setting out his findings in fact and law. It is possible to make a **further appeal** to the **Inner House of the Court of Session**.

Under the **ordinary procedure**, an appeal can be made to the **Sheriff Principal** and then on to the Inner House of the Court of Session as in a summary case. However, it is **also possible** under the ordinary procedure to **appeal directly** to the **Inner House of the Court of Session**. There is a further appeal on a point of law to the **House of Lords**.

Court of Session

The Court of Session is divided into the Outer House and the Inner House. The Outer House is a court of first instance for civil claims not initiated in the Sheriff Court. The Inner House is a court of appeal, as has been seen above.

Jurisdiction

The jurisdiction of the Court of Session is similar to the Sheriff Court, except that the Court of Session has jurisdiction over the whole of Scotland.

Outer House

There are two types of case which may be brought in the Outer House of the Court of Session. These are actions (such as those brought at Sheriff Courts) and petitions.

Inner House

The Inner House has two divisions which are equal in authority. Generally an appeal may be heard by either division. In some difficult cases, the divisions may sit together.

Personnel

Judges attached to the Court of Session are known as **Senators of the College of Justice**. There are eight judges attached to the Inner House, split equally between the two divisions. The quorum for each division is three. All the other judges are allocated to the Outer House, except for one who chairs the Scottish Law Commission.

Appeals

Appeals may be made from the Outer House to the Inner House. Appeals on decisions in the Inner House may be made to the House of Lords.

House of Lords

The House of Lords is staffed by Lords of Appeal in Ordinary (also called Law Lords). It has two separate roles which should not be confused.

- **Legislative** role as one of the two Houses of the UK Parliament (see Chapter 2)
- **Judicial** role, as the highest appeal court in the civil system

Appeal from the Inner House of the Court of Session is made by way of a petition. Appeals from Scottish Courts will usually be heard by Scottish Law Lords, but this is not necessarily the case.

5   ANGUS

There are three separate problems to be considered here, all relating to the issue of **offer and acceptance** in contract law.

Offer to Dutch company

Angus has clearly made an offer to the Dutch company, which the latter purports to accept by means of its second telex. However, the fact that the company sent the first telex to Angus gives rise to a debate as to whether Angus' offer remains open.

The Dutch company's first telex seeks to apply certain conditions to Angus' offer to sell. Following cases such as *Hyde v Wrench*, this constitutes a **counter-offer**. The effect is that Angus' original offer is rejected and the Dutch company makes a new offer to buy the potatoes on its stated terms, which Angus is then free to accept or reject.

It could be argued that the Dutch company's first telex to Angus constitutes a **request for further information**, as in cases such as *Stevenson v MacLean*, in which case it is not a rejection of the offer. However that seems to be unlikely in this case, as the question clearly states that the Dutch company has tried to apply certain conditions.

The facts are similar to the Scottish case *Wolf and Wolf v Forfar Potato Company*, where a counter offer was held to have terminated the original offer in a similar situation.

The Dutch company will not therefore be successful in suing Angus, as there is no contract.

Offer to Bob

The question here is whether the offer made by Angus to Bob has **lapsed**. This is particularly important in situations where an offer has been made at a fixed price, which may then need to change over time.

An offer lapses either after a fixed time specified in the contract, or after a reasonable time (*Ramsgate Victoria Hotel Co. v Montefiore*). The concept of what is 'reasonable' will vary from case to case, but it is possible to argue that three months would be too long a time for an offer for the sale of a perishable commodity such as potatoes to remain open.

This principle has been seen in Scottish law in *Wylie and Lochead v McElroy and Sons*, where there was a delay of five weeks in accepting an offer to carry out iron works, at a time when the price of iron was fluctuating. This was held to be an unreasonable delay and the offer was held to have lapsed. The principle was also followed in *Glasgow Steam Shipping Co. v Watson*, when an offer was held to have lapsed when the offeree attempted to accept it after two months.

Therefore Angus' offer has lapsed through passage of time and Bob will be unable to sue him.

Charles

This problem concerns the difference between an offer and an **invitation to treat**. When an offer is accepted, a contract ensues, but an invitation to treat is merely an expression of willingness to negotiate, on the basis of which an offer may or may not be made.

A list of prices would be regarded as an invitation to treat, following the precedent of cases such as *Partridge v Crittenden* and *Boots v Pharmaceutical Society of Great Britain*. Therefore Angus has not made an offer to Charles, so it cannot be accepted. There is no contract between Angus and Charles. On receipt of the pricelist, Charles can make an offer to Angus to buy the potatoes, which it is then open to Angus to accept or reject.

In conclusion, Angus should win all three of the cases against him.

REVIEW FORM & FREE PRIZE DRAW

All original review forms from the entire BPP range, completed with genuine comments, will be entered into one of two draws 31 July 2005 and 31 January 2006. The names on the first four forms picked out on each occasion will be sent a cheque for £50.

Name: _____   **Address**: _____
_____
_____

How have you used this Kit?
(Tick one box only)

☐ Self study (book only)

☐ On a course: college (please state)_____
_____

☐ With 'correspondence' package

☐ Other _____

Why did you decide to purchase this Kit? *(Tick one box only)*

☐ Have used the complementary Study Text

☐ Have used other BPP products in the past

☐ Recommendation by friend/colleague

☐ Recommendation by a lecturer at college

☐ Saw advertising in journals

☐ Saw website

☐ Other _____

During the past six months do you recall seeing/receiving any of the following?
(Tick as many boxes as are relevant)

☐ Our advertisement in *Student Accountant*

☐ Our advertisement in *Pass*

☐ Our advertisement in PQ

☐ Our brochure with a letter through the post

☐ Our website

Which (if any) aspects of our advertising do you find useful?
(Tick as many boxes as are relevant)

☐ Prices and publication dates of new editions

☐ Information on product content

☐ Facility to order books off-the-page

☐ None of the above

When did you sit the exam? _____

Which BPP products have you used?

Text	☐	Tape	☐	i-Learn	☐
Kit	☑	Success CD	☐	i-Pass	☐
Passcard	☐			Virtual Campus	☐

Your ratings, comments and suggestions would be appreciated on the following areas of this Kit.

	Very useful	Useful	Not useful
Effective revision and revision plan	☐	☐	☐
Exam guidance	☐	☐	☐
Websites and mindmap	☐	☐	☐
Preparation questions	☐	☐	☐
Exam standard questions	☐	☐	☐
'Tutor's hints' section in answers	☐	☐	☐
Content and structure of answers	☐	☐	☐
'Plan of attack'	☐	☐	☐
Mock exam answers	☐	☐	☐

	Excellent	Good	Adequate	Poor
Overall opinion of this Kit	☐	☐	☐	☐

Do you intend to continue using BPP products?   ☐ Yes   ☐ No

Please note any further comments and suggestions/errors on the reverse of this page. The BPP author of this edition can be e-mailed at: pippariley@bpp.com

Please return this form to: Catherine Watton, ACCA range manager, BPP Professional Education, FREEPOST, London, W12 8BR

REVIEW FORM & FREE PRIZE DRAW (continued)

Please note any further comments and suggestions/errors below.

FREE PRIZE DRAW RULES

1   Closing date for 31 July 2005 draw is 30 June 2005. Closing date for 31 January 2006 draw is 31 December 2005.

2   Restricted to entries with UK and Eire addresses only. BPP employees, their families and business associates are excluded.

3   No purchase necessary. Entry forms are available upon request from BPP Professional Education. No more than one entry per title, per person. Draw restricted to persons aged 16 and over.

4   Winners will be notified by post and receive their cheques not later than 6 weeks after the relevant draw date.

5   The decision of the promoter in all matters is final and binding. No correspondence will be entered into.

See overleaf for information on other
BPP products and how to order

To BPP Professional Education, Aldine Place, London W12 8AW

Tel: 020 8740 2211   Fax: 020 8740 1184

email: publishing@bpp.com

Order online www.bpp.com   website: www.bpp.com

Mr/Mrs/Ms (Full name)

Daytime delivery address

Postcode

Date of exam (month/year)   Scots law variant   Y / N

Daytime Tel

Occasionally we may wish to email you relevant offers and information about courses and products. Please tick to opt into this service. ☐

	6/04 Texts	1/05 Kits	1/05 Passcards	***Success CDs	8/04 i-Learn	8/04 i-Pass	Virtual Campus
PART 1							
1.1 Preparing Financial Statements UK	£24.95 ☐	£12.95 ☐	£9.95 ☐	£14.95 ☐	£34.95 ☐	£24.95 ☐	£90 ☐
1.2 Financial Information for Management	£24.95 ☐	£12.95 ☐	£9.95 ☐	£14.95 ☐	£34.95 ☐	£24.95 ☐	£90 ☐
1.3 Managing People	£24.95 ☐	£12.95 ☐	£9.95 ☐	£14.95 ☐	£34.95 ☐	£24.95 ☐	£90 ☐
PART 2							
2.1 Information Systems	£24.95 ☐	£12.95 ☐	£9.95 ☐	£14.95 ☐	£34.95 ☐	£24.95 ☐	£90 ☐
2.2 Corporate and Business Law UK **	£24.95 ☐	£12.95 ☐	£9.95 ☐	£14.95 ☐	£34.95 ☐	£24.95 ☐	£90 ☐
2.3 Business Taxation FA2004 (8/04 for 6/05 & 12/05 exams)†	£24.95 ☐			£14.95 ☐	£34.95 ☐	£24.95 ☐	£90 ☐
2.4 Financial Management and Control	£24.95 ☐	£12.95 ☐	£9.95 ☐	£14.95 ☐	£34.95 ☐	£24.95 ☐	£90 ☐
2.5 Financial Reporting UK (7/04)	£24.95 ☐	£12.95 ☐	£9.95 ☐	£14.95 ☐	£34.95 ☐	£24.95 ☐	£90 ☐
2.6 Audit and Internal Review UK	£24.95 ☐			£14.95 ☐	£34.95 ☐	£24.95 ☐	£90 ☐
PART 3							
3.1 Audit and Assurance Services UK	£24.95 ☐	£12.95 ☐	£9.95 ☐	£14.95 ☐		£24.95 ☐	
3.2 Advanced Taxation FA2004 (9/04 for 6/05 & 12/05 exams)†	£24.95 ☐			£14.95 ☐		£24.95 ☐	
3.3 Performance Management	£24.95 ☐	£12.95 ☐	£9.95 ☐	£14.95 ☐		£24.95 ☐	
3.4 Business Information Management	£24.95 ☐	£12.95 ☐	£9.95 ☐	£14.95 ☐		£24.95 ☐	
3.5 Strategic Business Planning and Development	£24.95 ☐	£12.95 ☐	£9.95 ☐	£14.95 ☐		£24.95 ☐	
3.6 Advanced Corporate Reporting UK (7/04)	£24.95 ☐	£12.95 ☐	£9.95 ☐	£14.95 ☐		£24.95 ☐	
3.7 Strategic Financial Management	£24.95 ☐	£12.95 ☐	£9.95 ☐	£14.95 ☐		£24.95 ☐	
INTERNATIONAL STREAM							
1.1 Preparing Financial Statements (Int'l)	£24.95 ☐	£12.95 ☐	£9.95 ☐			£24.95 ☐	
2.2 Corporate and Business Law (Global)	£24.95 ☐	£12.95 ☐	£9.95 ☐				
2.5 Financial Reporting (Int'l)	£24.95 ☐	£12.95 ☐	£9.95 ☐		£34.95 ☐	£24.95 ☐	
2.6 Audit and Internal Review (Int'l)	£24.95 ☐	£12.95 ☐	£9.95 ☐		£34.95 ☐	£24.95 ☐	
3.1 Audit and Assurance Services (Int'l)	£24.95 ☐	£12.95 ☐	£9.95 ☐				
3.6 Advanced Corporate Reporting (Int'l)	£24.95 ☐	£12.95 ☐	£9.95 ☐				
Success in Your Research and Analysis							
Project - Tutorial Text (10/04)	£24.95 ☐						
Learning to Learn (7/02)	£9.95 ☐						

SUBTOTAL £ ☐

POSTAGE & PACKING

Study Texts

	First	Each extra	Online
UK	£5.00	£2.00	£2.00 ☐ £
Europe*	£6.00	£4.00	£4.00 ☐ £
Rest of world	£20.00	£10.00	£10.00 ☐ £

Kits

	First	Each extra	Online
UK	£5.00	£2.00	£2.00 ☐ £
Europe*	£6.00	£4.00	£4.00 ☐ £
Rest of world	£20.00	£10.00	£10.00 ☐ £

Passcards/Success Tapes/CDs

	First	Each extra	Online
UK	£2.00	£1.00	£1.00 ☐ £
Europe*	£3.00	£2.00	£2.00 ☐ £
Rest of world	£8.00	£8.00	£8.00 ☐ £

Grand Total (incl. Postage)   £ ☐

I enclose a cheque for
(Cheques to *BPP Professional Education*)

Or charge to Visa/Mastercard/Switch

Card Number ☐☐☐☐☐☐☐☐☐☐☐☐☐☐☐☐

Expiry date ☐☐☐☐   Start Date ☐☐☐☐

Issue Number (Switch Only) ☐☐

Signature